23rd Deloitte-University of Kansas Auditing Symposium 2016

Increasing Audit Quality

Lawrence, Kansas, USA
19 - 21 May 2016

ISBN: 978-1-5108-4009-6

Printed from e-media with permission by:

Curran Associates, Inc.
57 Morehouse Lane
Red Hook, NY 12571

Some format issues inherent in the e-media version may also appear in this print version.

Printed by Curran Associates, Inc. (2017)

University of Kansas School of Business
1654 Naismith Drive
Lawrence, KS 66045
USA

Phone: 785-864-7500

bschoolinfo@ku.edu

Additional copies of this publication are available from:

Curran Associates, Inc.
57 Morehouse Lane
Red Hook, NY 12571 USA
Phone: 845-758-0400
Fax: 845-758-2633
Email: curran@proceedings.com
Web: www.proceedings.com

TABLE OF CONTENTS

Joe Ucuzoglu[i]

Opening Remarks

Well, thank you, Howard – appreciate the kind introduction. We really are proud of our sponsorship of the symposium since its inception in 1972, and, Howard, you said it well – this is a unique platform to bring together the regulatory community, the auditing profession, the academic community, and have a transparent dialogue around current topics. I know I always leave smarter from the insights that I received from all of you.

I do have to begin with sincere congratulations to everyone associated with the university on this beautiful new facility, and we had a nice ribbon-cutting ceremony last night. This is truly exceptional, and I know from experience – we went through a process to put up our own structure, Deloitte University, several years back – and it really does become a sense of pride for everyone involved with the institution. It is a cultural unifier. It gives the students a leg up having a facility where they have access to the latest in technological innovation and collaborative facilities. And I'm blown away – I said to somebody walking in this room that a screen like this is what you expect to find when you walk into an NFL football stadium. And to have it here and accessible to students in the academic community is truly phenomenal. And so – congratulations!

If I had my way, I would probably jump right into Q&A and dialogue because, like I said, I actually always gain a lot from your insights. But, they made me pick a few topics and deliver some introductory remarks before we get into dialogue, and so, I will oblige. I'll tell you at the outset what those three topics are that I selected to talk about. First, innovation. The pace of technological change in the business community is rapid and it is having a profound effect on the auditing profession. And, this is an area where it's going to be really important for us as a profession to work in collaboration with the academic community to ensure that curricula are evolving, and that students are prepared for success, because the opportunities are absolutely endless.

Second, the evolution that's taking place in the needs of the capital markets. And, I really do think it only adds to the vibrancy around our profession and the opportunities going forward – and it allows us to increase our position on the value curve in the broader economy. And so, I'll just share a few thoughts about some of those macro trends. And finally, I do want to spend a few minutes on the regulatory environment. It's been very, very active the last five or six years, and I know that it leads to chatter on campus and the students asking questions about what will it be like to enter the profession. And so, I just want to offer up some thoughts, and also have a task for you in terms of how you introduce the topic and the lens through which the students view the environment as they come into the profession – because it really does have an opportunity to be a net positive.

So, let me start with innovation and transformation. I believe that the profession will change more over the next five or six years than it has over the last fifty. I mean, the proliferation of advanced technologies have the ability to fundamentally alter how we go about conducting an audit and obtaining reasonable assurance. And, I know there's a lot of talk out there, there are a lot of fancy terms, everybody's discussing this at a high-level – big data, data analytics, artificial intelligence – but it's rare that you actually have an opportunity to get past the headlines and talk about what does it actually mean. How does it fit into the auditing standards? And so, I thought what I'd do is to offer up a few thoughts – a little more granular level and high-level concepts.

I'll start with what it's not. So, what it's not is a mechanism to automate the whole audit. I cannot foresee pushing a button and having the answers come out – no matter how advanced the technology has evolved to, at least in the span of my career – I won't make predictions as to what technology will evolve to in a hundred years – but in the foreseeable future. The professional judgment and expertise of an auditor is still essential to the process, but what this does do is it enables us to digest much larger volumes of information, and to get smarter, and have better data at our disposal to make those professional judgments. It enhances the quality of our work, because we're able to become much more sophisticated as to the populations we're looking at, and hone in on the areas of interest – and so quality goes up. It really enhances the talent and experience.

One of the unintended side effects – now we didn't undertake this effort and invest several hundred million dollars with the primary objective of making the workplace more enjoyable, but the reality is that's actually been one of the greatest benefits that we have seen to date – is excitement in our young people. I was just with one of our teams in Chicago working on a large multi-national retailer a couple days ago – and even at the level of the first year professional – and they are talking about these innovative technologies, and using them to transform the way in which we do our work – and much of the actual thought layer and evolution and procedures. It's not all being dictated from the top – that's a 1960s mindset that there's an R&D facility that pushes out one piece of know-how, and everybody does it the exact same way – feels like a checklist. That's not very exciting for our younger professionals. That they want to be using their skills and expertise, and have the opportunity to really be part of this transformation.

And so we put out the technology, we put out underlying objectives and methodologies – but then we've asked them to use their professional creativity and to experiment with it – and not just to follow what was done in last year's work papers, and for filling them out the same way this year – but to look at whether there is a better way to accomplish the objective at an equal or higher level of quality, but leverages these advanced capabilities. And they're really excited about it. Our turnover this past year is way down. I don't know whether I can contribute it to any one factor in particular, because we made a lot of investments into our people, but I have no doubt in my mind that the vision of the future, and their excitement over the transformation of how an audit is delivered, and their personal role in bringing audit into the future is a big part of that.

And, lastly, there's a real value play here that with these advanced technologies we're able to deliver greater levels of insights today – primarily to the board of directors and company's management. And I actually think, tomorrow, there's an element that can ultimately be communicated to the markets – I will talk a little bit about that in a couple of minutes – but, again, elevating the profession on the value curve. Now, I'm often asked – okay, that all sounds great, but which auditing standard does this impact, or how does it fit into the assurance framework? And, I obviously don't have the time to go do an in-depth into every aspect of the audit process, though what I thought I'd do is just pick one element of the audit process and to talk a little bit about that - and that's the risk assessment base.

Risk assessment has been foundational to the way in which an audit is executed for decades. That the idea that, up-front, you assess the levels of risks in various accounts and classes of transactions, and you vary the nature, timing, and extent of auditing procedures performed to be responsive to that risk assessment. That's not a new concept, but the tools at an auditors' disposal to accomplish that has been relatively limited. We had our knowledge of the industry. We had our general knowledge of the client. But, if that's all you've had, that in and of itself doesn't give you a tremendous amount of assurance. And so, you primarily relied on your tests of controls and your substantive tests to gain the necessary level of assurance that you've reduced the risk of material misstatement, and ultimately obtain reasonable assurance on the accuracy of the financial statements.

With the proliferation of these technologies, and the ability to run advanced analytics up-front in the audit cycle, you now have a much more sophisticated mechanism with which to conduct that risk assessment process, and so it enables us to move work up in the audit cycle – which is a real positive on multiple fronts – and you're actually going to achieve more of your assurance from the risk assessment process than you ever have before. And that then gives you a much better basis to differentiate where you want to focus your time in terms of designing truly tailored customized procedures for those areas of greatest risk – those things that popped out as anomalies or areas of interest and, in turn, spend less of your time and effort and focus and gain more of your assurance from having done that initial risk assessment. Very, very powerful - all encompassed within the current auditing standards.

If you read the PCAOB's risk assessment standards – AS 8 through 15 - this notion is already embedded in the standards. It doesn't take some drastic change in standards, but the technologies are now allowing us to really bring this to life. And so, my message would be this is a really exciting time for the students entering the profession, and I hope that they had that same sense of vision in terms of where the profession is ultimately headed. It really does offer them greater opportunities, and greater potential to truly make a difference at the outset of their careers - and that's one of the phenomenon that we found with respect to the Millennials – is they have different career aspirations. They want to make an impact on society, and they want to make an impact immediately – and this really does allow for a platform, and Scott, my counterpart at KPMG, will be talking a little bit later about the evolution of the talent model – and there's a lot of excitement around the direction of the profession.

Second topic I thought I'd touch on is the evolution of the needs of the capital markets. You know, the needs of investors are growing, and there are demands on the profession both to become more transparent with respect to the core service we perform today, and ultimately to expand what it is that we're able to offer assurance on. So I'll start with the first - become more transparent about what we do today. For decades, the auditor's report is essentially a pass/fail model – three boilerplate paragraphs unless something's really gone off the rails – and investors have understandably asked the question if they're the real beneficiary of this effort. If we're the consumer of this information, aren't we entitled to a little greater insight into what it is that you did, how you went about your work for what kept you up at night, and how you then addressed those issues to ultimately form your opinion that you obtained reasonable assurance? And, globally, the profession is headed in this direction. In the UK, the FRC put out a requirement for an expanded auditor's report a few years back. The international auditing standards board – the IAASB – has similarly put out new requirements, and I commend the PCAOB for taking this up.

It's a complicated topic, particularly in the U.S. environment which tends to get litigious and concerns get raised over liability risk, but when I think about risk - for it is how we formulated our view and ultimately became very, very supportive here - there's two different types of risks. There's the risk of liability with respect to the work you do, and then there's the risk of becoming irrelevant if you don't evolve to meet the needs of your core customer – the capital markets. And I'm far more worried about the second risk than the first one. I want to make sure we have an underlying service that's valued within the capital markets, and we have an obligation as a profession to evolve and become more transparent. And I think the direction that this reporting model project is headed is very, very positive.

Second area of evolution relates to – just what it is we provide assurance on. I mean, today, our effort is almost entirely focused on auditing the core financial statements – and for public companies above a certain size – the internal controls. And, that is an incredibly important function. That assurance, you know, forms the basis upon which investors trade trillions of dollars of securities. But, the population of information that investors are relying upon – and that moves markets – is expanding exponentially. And often times, what's moving markets is monthly metrics that companies are putting out – key performance indicators and non-GAAP measures and press releases – a whole series of information that today falls outside the scope of the auditors' responsibility. And this is a hot topic – it's out there in the press – there's an increasing level of concern around the use of non-GAAP measures, and, as is usually the case with issues like this, the pendulum tends to swing, and it swings too far in each direction.

So, if you went back to the late 1990s where a lot of these dot-com enterprises were going public with little or no profitability, and there were a whole host of alternative metrics that were being used, and ultimately the dot-com bubble burst, and there were a few financial reporting scandals, and the regulators crack-down, and one element of Sarbanes-Oxley instructed the SEC to issue some rules clamping down on the use of non-GAAP measures. At the time there were articles sort of criticizing the metrics certain companies were using – characterizing them as earnings before bad stuff – and it was – we saw a huge decline in the usage of these metrics and a tightening up. Over a number of years, I'd say sort of plateauing with 2010, 2011, you started to see a more liberal attitude in terms of the usage of these metrics. And my own view is that – part of the view was taken that as long as there's transparency, as long as there is clear disclosure of what the metric represents, how it was computed, how it reconciles back to the GAAP measure, then what's the harm in investors having more information? You think about it for a minute – efficient market perspective, they have the GAAP numbers at their disposal, they have the alternative metrics at their disposal, let them pick and choose what it is that they want.

Well, over the past year or so the concerns have been increasing that once again the pendulum has swung back too far. And there's quite a bit of research out there that the gap – no pun intended – between the GAAP numbers and these alternative metrics has grown drastically, and, of course, the direction – as you'd expect – is that generally the non-GAAP metric would suggest a higher level of performance, profitability, liquidity – you pick your metric. That delta between the two has grown significantly. And, in many cases, when you look at the metrics that are being used, reported by the media – turn on CNBC – often times the scrolling at the bottom of the screen will say – XYZ company reports adjusted EBITDA up twenty-seven percent. That's essentially being reported out to the markets as the primary metric. And even in analyst reports, in many cases, the analysts are taking this information that's been provided by companies and using that as a primary measure of performance – that, we're high on XYZ company. We expect adjusted funds from operations to grow by thirty-six percent.

The issue that comes into play is whether there is an expectation gap as to the rigor of the process around producing these numbers, and whether there's an understanding of how different it is from what goes into the regulated GAAP numbers. And I actually think there is a lack of understanding and, in many cases, the general public, the media, and investors don't fully appreciate the fact that there's a whole regulatory infrastructure that drives the production of the GAAP numbers. And, that ultimately have to be produced in conformity with rigorous standards that went through due process, that are reviewed and regulated by the SEC – that are audited by us, the firms, and our work is then inspected by the PCAOB, and that whole regulatory infrastructure isn't applicable. Companies have a lot of latitude in terms of how they produce these metrics. They're not subject to audit as long as they plainly disclosed what's in there. There has been very little constraint on how these numbers are, in fact, produced. And, you know, some high-profile issues have hit the press, where, perhaps, liberties were taken. And so the question is – what's the long-term answer here?

I really do believe there is a role for assurance with respect to these broader measures of performance, broader key industry indicators, some of these adjusted metrics – and we can have a long debate around how do you go about doing that. Do you have a standard set of metrics by industries? Do you have standards that dictate the underlying computations so you know you get consistency from company to company? Do you eventually have an independent audit requirement? That's the conversation that we need to be having from this, the academic community, the profession, the investor community, the regulators, and the corporate community. And I actually see, given the level of interest right now in this topic, that there really is an environment that's conducive to having that conversation. And, ultimately, again, this creates more opportunities for the students coming into the profession that potentially have the opportunity to be associated with a much broader range of information and metrics, and the credibility that comes with us as an auditing profession passing assurance, and giving investors that confidence and credibility with which to make their investment decisions.

Last topic I was going to touch on before getting into the dialogue is the regulatory environment. And, that there is no secret that the regulatory environment with respect to the auditing profession has become, you know, very, very rigorous over the past number of years. And sometimes I will even hear stories about how people are talking on campus about the attractiveness of the profession – I will tell you what I always share with our professionals. I tell them that they ought to be thrilled with the level of scrutiny. Because the fact that the regulators across the globe are so interested in what we do, the fact that politicians across the globe are so interested in what we do ought to reinforce just how important our role is in the capital markets. If what we did wasn't important, nobody would be paying much attention to it. People are paying attention to it and demanding a high standard of performance because of the integral role that we play in the capital markets. And that ought to give our people a lot of pride in the role that we play in the broader economy.

Now, is it rigorous in terms of having our work looked at? Absolutely, but we've transformed our culture over the past number of years to look at this as a learning opportunity. We're all professionals. We hold ourselves to very high standards. We want to get better at what we do, and to have an interested third party to come in and look at our work, and provide us with feedback – it gives us an opportunity to continue to hone our craft and enhance our level of professionalism – and that's a net positive. And so, I would ask that as your students ask questions, and as you introduce the dynamic in the profession, that sort of a balanced perspective be part of the dialogue, and that they really do understand the important role that this plays in continuing to make the profession valued and relevant and attractive.

There's a lot of other areas that you could cover with respect to the regulatory environment. I sort of put down a list of them - audit quality indicators, naming the audit partner, the inspection process, scrutiny over the business model of the firms and the fact that we are multidisciplinary and making big investments across broad cross-sections of our practice. Happy to talk about any and all of those, but rather than continue on, as I said up-front, I really like to do some Q&A and have some dialogue with you. No topic is off-limits – feel free to ask about anything at all that is an interest, and let's just have a good healthy dialogue.

Questions and Answers

When you are talking about data analytics and the audit, we hear a lot of good things, you know, transformative, evolving, better risk assessment – what are the pitfalls or concerns or risks that you see with that?

Great question. Of all the pitfalls, concerns, risks around the use of big data. The most complicated element of this is actually not using the tools and technologies to run the analysis. It's building the tools and technologies to get the data in a state where you're confident that it's complete and accurate. So, if every company out there had the IT infrastructure of the future – one instance of an ERP system around the globe that seamlessly processed the inventory, the purchasing, the sales – they are all linked up neatly into a central data warehouse. This would be a slam dunk. That's not the state of play in the current corporate IT environment.

There's a lot of legacy systems – many of which go back to the '50s and '60s. There are manual interfaces in many cases. There are significant manual processes to reconcile, to account for discrepancies, to take an adjustment that comes out of the system because the system was programmed under the old APB opinion for leases – that it never got updated for FAS 13 – and it still hasn't been updated for the new standard. So, you pick your area of accounting, and the system doesn't produce it the way it's supposed to come out for GAAP purposes – and it gets adjusted. And that series of interfaces and manual processes does give rise to challenges in getting the dataset in a state that's credible so that, because of the old adage of garbage in, garbage out. And so, we've actually been investing just as much in what we call data wrangling technologies which enable you to take data off of different platforms and smash it together in a way that's apples to apples, and then have some credibility around ensuring that it's complete and that it ties into the underlying accounting records.

That, in my mind, is the biggest challenge. There's a whole host of subsidiary challenges. Tell me, there are certainly evolving needs in terms of the capabilities that our professionals have. I know that Scott will spend some time talking about that. There are questions around data protection and cyber, and, you can imagine, with companies so concerned about protecting their data and insuring against a cyber breach. When I walk in as the auditor and I say I've got a great proposition here – I'm going to, sort of, put a little code in your computer. It's going to automatically download all your stuff, real-time, you know, 24/7 – naturally they have some questions. Well, what kind of data security do you have? What kind of risk do I have of a breach? And so, all of those things are to your question of what are the challenges. But, none of them are insurmountable, and none of them ought to stand in the way of the significant value that we can derive from getting this right.

You've suggested a number of intrusions into the market for information. Why don't we - we are going to give all this information to the capital markets including the expanded auditor's report, you know? Why don't we go on down the road and intrude on into the analyst role, and actually provide some direct information relative to the future of the stock?

I think it's a great question. I mean, you can go back and for decades there is the debate and the questions as to where does the role of the auditor end, and where does the role of the analysts begin? And there is no clean-cut dividing line, and, in my own personal opinion, there is an opportunity for the auditor to continue to offer more and more insight and perspective.

Now, historically – again, historically – the role of the auditor is not to produce original content. The role of the auditor has been to take what the company reports out under the securities laws, and attach our assurance to it. And so, whenever questions have come up in the past as to what should the auditor in free-form talk about – what the company's risks are, what the company's opportunities are – we've generally shifted conversation to – well, that's the company management's role. That company should produce that stuff, and then if there's interest in investors understanding somebody independent has looked at it, we can expand our report to potentially provide assurance over those core characteristics. And – in trying to stay true to that model – has probably been the biggest challenge in progressing with respect to this auditors' reporting model project. Because, questions were raised as to whether this is taking the auditor out of their attestation role, and becoming an original source of information. And I think that the changes that the PCAOB has made in their latest re-proposal are trying to be responsive to that underlying concern, and that the information we will be providing isn't so much new and unique information on the company. It's more information about the audit process, and what we did in our role as auditors.

Now, as we continue to progress the role of the auditor, the one constraint that we always need to keep in mind is that the auditor needs to come across to the public as independent in fact and appearance. And that's a constraint that the analyst community doesn't have. And so, many have said – if not for the understanding of the public that the auditor is independent and objective, then what value is there from having an independent attestation process? And if you had an auditor out there that appeared to be a cheerleader that said – we've been there, and, boy, this company looks great, their prospects for growth are tremendous. I do have some concerns as to whether that would impede the credibility from an independence and objectivity standpoint of the profession in the public's mind.

But, we're obviously taking some of that market space that the analysts - the financial analysts - have provided in the past.

Yep, absolutely.

And that's going to place us somewhere further up the value chain, you said.

Absolutely, and it will be a difficult balance to deal with the competing tensions.

I'd like to follow-up on Jack's point. So, to me, practicing assurance involves GAAP measures, and non-GAAP measures are more about focus and analysis, and valuation, and to the extent that auditors might be involved in that latter part, as you were just saying, what are the risks that we also do not have the skills and competencies to contribute meaningfully, and actually fully erode trust in the profession (that we do a less than optimal job)?

That's a great question. If we get into analysis and valuation, do we have the skills necessary, and if we don't and we attach our name to it, does it further erode the credibility of the profession? Whether we like it or not, we're already there. And so even though there's a perception of the financial statements or the historical measures, and then predictions about the future are really to be left to the analyst community, the move to fair value in the accounting model has essentially already put the auditor in the position of having to look at the future business prospects.

And having to audit the reasonableness of projections - take goodwill as an example. Goodwill is a historical cost accounting metric. It derives from the purchase price that was paid over the fair value of the net assets acquired. So, the initial measure is a historical cost metric, but the ongoing accounting test is a fair value measure. In order to do that accounting test, the company has to project out future sales and profitability, discounted back, and ultimately look if it's better than sufficient to recover the carrying value. That then puts us in the position - in order to appropriately audit it - of having to look at future business prospects, of having to evaluate forecasts, of having to look at analysts' reports, and come to our own conclusion as to whether the numbers have been prepared with reasonableness. And so, that dividing line that historically existed, I actually think has been obliterated by the infusion of fair value into the accounting model.

You brought up the point about your first-year staff having – being innovative with the technology that you rolled out to them. So, my question is what are the new skills that you would expect out of these first year staff? That, in other presentations of data analytics, for example – and not from Deloitte – it sounds more like they're trying to sell it to me than they are trying to tell me what it is that students, that might go to work for them, need in terms of new skills. And I think speaking to that would be very helpful to, at least to me.

So, it's a great question, and it's one that I have a lot of passion around. I ask that we just hold it in conveyance, because there will be a robust presentation from my counterpart, the leader of KPMG's audit practice, Scott Marcello, a little later this morning that will go into that in a lot of depth.

I've got a question about fraud. You talked a little bit about regulation had strengthened, but what's your thoughts on the trend of fraudulently prepared financial statements, and especially given that fraudsters are resourceful, can you talk about the cost if that hits you guys and the capital markets?

There's a number of dimensions to that question, and so let me start with, just the very definition of the word fraud. Clearly, if somebody's making-up entries – the numbers roll up, and then at the end of the process management books a top-side journal entry to add to sales, and, with a corresponding increase to receivables, and it is just complete fiction. That's one kind of fraud. There is a more subtle kind of fraud that deals with formulating subjective estimates and whether it, when there's a range of potential outcomes – particularly as more and more of the accounting requires predictions of the future – and whether the company's personnel are truly using their best estimate for the future without regard to what they would like the answer to be – and whether it's being biased to achieve a particular earnings number. That's another, but equally important, type of fraud.

So, on the first one – the making up stuff – there is so much less of that, and I attribute that to – when you look at the underlying provisions of Sarbanes-Oxley, they were truly effective. Having CEOs and CFOs of public companies having to personally certify financial statements at risk of criminal liability – it tends to sharpen pencils. But then, I think the rigor of the audit process, the regulatory regime, and the extent to which our work is ultimately inspected – that kind of stuff, the Worldcoms, the Sunbeams. I mean, it's incredibly rare. It's very, very positive for the capital markets that the incidents have been cut down so much. Obviously, we still have to be alert to red flags – it's a professional responsibility of ours to conduct the audit with diligence, but we've seen much, much less of that.

What you've seen in the past couple of years is a renewed regulatory focus, and Mary Jo White, this is a centerpiece of her platform at the SEC, of really renewing a regulatory vigor and enforcement mechanism around looking up at that ladder that I described. Looking at the way in which companies are making subjective estimates. Looking at whether they were prepared and performed in good faith. Because when you have a bunch of data points, when you're putting together an accounting estimate, you're trying to estimate how many loans are going to go bad three years from now, or, you know, what is the sales going to be five years from now that feeds into my goodwill impairment projection?

There's a wide latitude of estimates that somebody might come up with, and then as auditors, it puts us in the position of having to look at all those data points and ensure that we're not suffering from confirmation bias. That we're not simply looking for the three pieces of data that support the company's estimate, but disregarding the other six pieces of evidence that might refute the company's estimate. But we're actually looking at it in a balanced way and taking all the evidence into account as we conduct our audit – it's the biggest fundamental challenge in the audit environment today.

It's the reason why, when you look at the regulatory inspection reports, that management's estimates tend to be right up at the top in terms of the level of findings, that the internal controls related to the production of those estimates tend to be right up at the top in terms of the number of those findings. And you have a regulator, and yes, you see, that's very focused from an enforcement standpoint – on investigating tips, or maybe a computation was biased – and what they'll then do is that they'll come in and they'll subpoena the email traffic. We don't have subpoena power. We do our very best under the auditing standards to execute with the level of diligence, but the SEC will come in and they'll look at the behind-the-scenes communication. What was being communicated between the CEO, the CFO, the accounting personnel? Does it look like there was undue pressure being placed? Does it look like there was evidence that the company didn't want to take a charge this quarter versus next quarter? And that's a very healthy part of the regulatory process to ensure that, ultimately, the statements are being prepared in a neutral and credible way, and not with the objective in mind of trying to reach a certain EPS number and manage earnings.

Now, you were saying that risk assessment is foundational to audit, and this base in audits can be effective to find errors in fair value accounting or other risky areas like that. Do you believe one of the drawbacks is that there could be fraud in other accounts like what happened in Satyam? There were six bank accounts and they had more than a billion dollars going through them, okay? Can you talk about the drawbacks of excessively focusing on just the risky accounts?

Absolutely - the question is as we move toward a much more sophisticated risk assessment, we devote our time to the assessed levels of risk that are highest, what then happens to the lower risk areas, and would that create an environment in which a fraud could occur in the lower risk areas? And that's what this is – all a matter of balance. It's not swimming at a hundred percent and suggesting you do nothing in certain areas and spend all your time in other areas. What it is asking is that given for scarcity of hours – there are only so many hours in the day, there's only so many corporate resources that you can devote to the audit function – how do you best deploy them based on assessed levels of risk?

And you obviously want to put your highest level of effort in the highest risk areas, and that auditing standards ask you to do that, but you still put a level of effort to assist in the lower risk areas. Including through the writing of these very advanced data analytics that are designed with the algorithms programmed into them to spot anomalies – to spot trends that might be indicative of something sinister having taken place – and to continue to perform your age-old tests of details to ensure that there's robust support and back-up to support the underlying accounting. And so, this is all a matter of balance. It's not swinging the pendulum one hundred percent in one direction.

So, I'm curious about your opinion on the interaction of two of your talking points. And, you began by talking about innovation and the audit process, and really a defined model of experimentation to get a better audit – and then you ended talking about regulation. And I'm curious about how those two things work together. Is the regulatory environment that you're working under now – is it encouraging innovation? Or is it discouraging it? Or is a neutral?

From my perspective, it's been heavily encouraging. The prospect of driving higher levels of quality through these advanced technologies – that's a win-win. Now there are questions around risks that are being asked of us, and we have to ensure that in our audit methodology – that we're accounting for those risks – ultimately produces a higher quality result, and not put quality at risk.

But, let me take the example you mentioned around our first-year professionals experimenting with tools and technologies. The end decision isn't to be left to the first-year professionals. If they come up with a method of ultimately gaining assurance in a particular area that they are assigned to, that's then filtered up and reviewed by more senior levels of the team, and that's then filtered up nationally. So we have cohorts across industries who are sharing what are the new methodologies that are being developed, and how can we ensure that we're getting consistency across our teams, and then we have our national attestation experts looking at the methodologies to bless them, and then to roll them back out into the field.

So, it's essentially filtering the innovative ideas up, but not leaving it to the initial individual who designed it to make the ultimate call. Someone more senior in the organization - a senior partner - is looking at it across the industry, taking the best ideas, and then putting that into methodologies and playbooks that we roll out to all of our people. So, you do gain assurance that we are in full compliance with the auditing standards, and you do get assurance that there's consistency across our issuer base in terms of how we're going about doing our general audit work.

You mentioned, and maybe I misunderstood, but, when you're talking about non-GAAP measures that there might be a role for the auditor in providing assurance. Was that, okay?

Yes.

Why don't the capital markets demand that? Why isn't there an issuer who says my non-GAAP measures are better because they've been audited by Deloitte. So, it seems like if there was a demand for that we would already be seeing it.

It's a fascinating question, and the history of capital markets regulation suggest that, generally, the investor community hasn't effectively demanded things until regulation requires companies to produce it. And, we can debate endlessly why that is. The SEC ended up – was ultimately created, by virtue of the '33 and '34 acts requiring and independent audit – between then and 2002, it was almost unheard of for investors to demand the report on effectiveness of internal controls. Even though, when Congress enacted the Foreign Corrupt Practices Act in 1977, which required companies to have an effective system of internal controls – until a big corporate blow-up and Congress stepped in and enacted a requirement – now I think there's relatively universal improvement. There's a little bit of businesses in the system we can certainly talk about around the depths of their compliance, but there's general agreement in the value of having auditors attest to the effectiveness of internal controls. And I think there's been a number of academic studies that demonstrated the impact on cost of capital as a result of going through the exercise. Why did it not happen naturally before legislation – regulation stepped in to mandate it?

Now we face a similar phenomenon. I mentioned that I do believe there's an expectations gap. I'm not sure that the investment community universally understands what falls within the scope of the GAAS audit, and what doesn't, and that troubles me. And, in fact, I even asked some investors about how they get comfortable with these alternative metrics – given that we're not auditing them? That's the answer that I've gotten back is – well, you guys are out there, and you're looking at the core numbers that come out of the system, and these metrics are being produced, you know, derived from those core metrics, and we figured if there was something way off, then you would find it. I mean, literally, that's the response I get. It's not very satisfactory.

But history suggests that, in part because the investing community is relatively dispersed, that it's harder for them, being individual, to band together. Companies generally perceive this to be a cost unless they can truly prove to themselves there will be a reduction to their cost of capital that's greater than the fees that they have to pay. They haven't generally agreed with this. So, I'd like to hope that in a utopian world that you might see the market forces work here – I'm not overly optimistic.

It just seems like, you know, there's a difference between an audit of internal control versus auditing a couple of non-GAAP measures.

Tangible.

Yeah, well, and to some extent you have already audited – I mean it's different than with your example of an internal control audit which is a massive undertaking, so?

But let me ask you, so, let's say a company produces a metric and they call it adjusted EBITDA, and it's what they believe they used to measure performance internally. And they strip out seven different costs from it – they strip out stock-based compensation, they strip out restructuring charges – so we come into audit it. Audit it against what? There's really no standard out there that says how these things should be produced or some recognizable criteria against which we can attest to – which adds to the challenge.

I'm just wondering if you could do something like, okay, they strip out these seven costs, how much of those costs are actually cash? I mean, that would be something that you could do.

But even though, take the line – I'll use this as an example – stock-based compensation in many cases is getting stripped out. It is non-cash, and company describes it as having stripped out non-cash – that's absolutely accurate and transparent. And then we could get into a debate – I guess, Warren Buffet always says – well, if equity awards aren't compensation, I'm not sure what is. And if compensation doesn't belong in the P&L, I'm not sure where it does belong.

What are you seeing in terms of Deloitte's global operations with respect to what's happening here in the US? Any trends that are noteworthy?

Absolutely, a couple key trends. Regulation is undergoing a lot of changes across the globe. First, with respect to quality. A rising high tends to lift all votes. And the audit regulators around the globe are now collaborating through a combined forum, an independent forum, called Independent Audit Regulators. And I actually think that a couple of leaders around the globe in audit regulation – the PCAOB, the AFAM in the Netherlands, the FRC in the UK – the high standards that they have engendered are filtering through to capital markets broadly, and audit regulators are demanding increased levels of performance, and that's a really good thing.

The other big trend out there right now is the EU going through the adoption of the legislation that was passed in 2014 – most significantly which requires rotation of audit firms on, generally a 10-20 year basis. It's a massive period of disruption, and I have my own personal views that I think it's actually detrimental to quality when you've turned everybody's attention toward – you lose all your current clients, and now, you, for your very survival, you have to put a ton of energy in ensuring that you go out and win new ones. And I know this is another area where there is a lot of academic research on the subject, and differences of view as to the efficacy of that type of regime.

But, whether we like it or not, it's reality, and it's being implemented in Europe. And I actually think it's a real-life laboratory for all of you to go out and study. So, people have debated conceptually for years. You can go back and trace to some of the congressional hearings of the profession in the 1970s where this topic was raised, and it's always been cast aside – I think legitimately so here in the U.S. Now, we have – in a major capital market – a real-life experiment where this is being implemented, and it ought to be fertile grounds for academic research.

Ally Zimmerman from Northern Illinois University – thank you so much for coming today.

Is that the Salukis?

Huskies.

The Huskies.

Sort of a two-part question - so there's an increasing number of specialists that are being used in audits. How is that changing the future of auditing? It seems to me that auditors are more project managers then – they're doing more project management of all the specialists than auditing themselves, so if you could speak to that.

Absolutely, the question is, given the proliferation of specialists, how is that changing the auditor? Are auditors simply project managers? There is no doubt that, given the complexity of this, that you need a broad set of disciplines to do a high quality audit. If you're going into one of these major multi-national institutions, they have a complex systems environment. You need people that are skilled in ERP and cyber. They have very, very complicated valuation measurements – you need valuation professionals involved. They have pensions that require actuarial estimates. They have environmental liabilities that require environmental specialists.

And I can keep going down the list. But what we continuously preach to our people is that you will get a poor quality result if you simply outsource the work to those specialists.

If you say, here's the reported income taxes, or give it to the income tax specialists, and they send you a memo back saying here's the result – you don't get a very good quality. Because there's too much interconnectedness across the financial statements, and there's too much context that is lost if you simply send in one number to a professional who is not integrally involved in the overall audit. The auditor has to be sufficiently skilled to direct the work that's being performed by the specialist. So, understand enough as to what are the risks, and what are the objectives that you have assigned to the specialist, and then sufficiently skilled to digest the results. Not just to see that it says pass or acceptable, but to look at the work that was done, to look at the findings, and make sure that it makes sense in the context of the overall audit that's being conducted.

And that's asking a lot of an auditor, and I've, at times, asked myself, have we sufficiently prepared those coming into the profession for what's being asked of them? You want to go to the legal profession, you have to go to law school for three years. Okay, we have a model where – the hundred-fifty hour rule is great. Some people have expressed concern to me that we haven't really specified what has to be taken in terms of classes within part of that hundred and fifty hours, and that that might not be optimal. And you get a lot of benefit from going into a Master's of Accounting program, but not so much from the other course work that might fill up the hundred and fifty hours. That's an interesting issue to debate.

But whatever isn't captured through the academic curriculum then falls on us obviously. We have an obligation to appropriately train our individuals to accomplish that very high standard. There's a plus side to this. I mean, think about it as an opportunity from a diversity of experience standpoint. And yet, as an auditor, being in the middle of all this, seeing it all come together, directing it, analyzing it. And ultimately, as important as any of those steps, communicating it. I firmly believe the most important differentiator of a successful auditor is all auditors are technically proficient – they're all coming through your programs with a level of technical know-how – but who can distill the complex into the understandable, and you can have a conversation at the c-suite level, at the board level to deliver insights to ultimately drive the company for higher levels of conduct in the way that resonates. It isn't simply viewed as a compliance exercise. It really is demanding a lot of an auditor to have the know-how to do all of that and communicate it effectively.

You mentioned that investors are now seeing the value of a 404(b) internal control audit. Why do you think we don't see more voluntary compliers with non-accelerated filers if it is a valuable service?

I think it goes right back to the initial debate around or whether the markets are sufficiently positioned to demand of issuers certain incremental levels of attestation which we've never really had success in driving. Some of the early stage companies to make the argument that, with limited capital, that given they're not as systemically important to the market as a whole – it's not a fifty billion dollar market cap company that's pervasively held throughout a multitude of mutual funds – that their scarce resources are better spent on R&D and hiring employees versus work which they might refer to as compliance. Investors to this point haven't demanded it, but it’s a fascinating question – and one that I know that’s been subject to a lot of research.

I want to be respectful of the agenda here.

Thanks Joe.

Is that the last question?

Perfect – yeah, that’s perfect timing.

Okay, great dialogue, great questions. Thank you.

---

[i] Transcription Note: The original transcript has been edited for flow and ease of reading. Any changes to content were not intended to change the overall message associated with the applicable discussion.

Scott Marcello[i]

Opening Remarks

Good morning. I think it's still morning, right, or close? Yep, still morning. Good morning. I have to start by saying I am not drunk, but I did spend the first half of this week in London and just did get back Wednesday night – so I am sleep deprived. So, if some of the things don't make sense – that I say – that's why. Like Joe did, first of all, let me thank every one of you for allowing me to be here. It's a privilege and an honor. Let me also thank Deloitte for putting on this symposium – for sponsoring it – it's a fantastic event. Joe and Howard, just a fantastic job, and it's just a privilege to be part of it.

I also wanted to – similar to Joe – leave a significant amount of our time for dialogue – for Q&A, conversation – because, in fact, the topic I'm speaking on is one that I think is a little bit important and emotional among some of the members of this group, right? Because, if we're honest, one of the things – I speak to a lot of deans, and chairs of audit departments, and professors in my role – and one of the things I hear time and time again: look, I get you want students that know D&A, you want students that can do this and that – that can have great judgment and do all these things – but we need more than that. That's fifty thousand foot – we know that. We're smart enough to understand what's going on around us – we need more discussion around what does it really look like. What's the change that you need to see?

And I'm not going to sit here and tell you that I'm qualified to give you all those answers. What I would like to do, though, is have a good conversation around some of the things that are – I think – are driving that. And also, get your input and questions around it. And I'll offer you my thoughts – but certainly, you know, it's not going to be the perfect answer to any of these. One of the reasons that's the case is because everything is evolving so quickly. So, quite frankly, we're not sure. If we're really honest about what's happening around – and, in fact, what I want to do is to discuss with you three questions that I think help level-set this conversation.

The first one is – how do we as a profession remain relevant? Joe started on that topic, but I do want to dig into it because I think that's one of the things that's going to drive what our students need to look like in the future. The second – and related to that thought – well, let's call it 1A – is how well do we really understand the rate of change – and the velocity of change that is happening to us right now? That affects our relevance, and also affects everything around us. So, I want to take on that – just try to add more. Item two – in light of that, what do we need students, professionals to have in their toolkit? What does good look like? Who's going to carry our legacy forward, and what skills and capabilities do they need to have to address that world? And a third – and I think probably just as important – is what is the education – and, I'll broaden that – was does the learning need to look like in order for those students, those professionals – because it's not a student issue, it's a professional issue – need to have to deal with those things?

Now, none of the things I'm going to cover – you're going to say – wow, I never thought of that. But I want to stimulate your thought – I want you to put them on the table and think about them with me. Because, too often, we jump right to – alright, what skills do they need? Well, let's step back and ask why do they need different skills? What's happening around?

So, first of all, audit quality is absolutely central. You've heard that – it's important because – we just had a panel on it. Yet, I would say it is not enough. If we are the greatest auditors – in fact, I often talk to my partners in this context. I say, imagine a world where we have now mastered audit quality. In fact, we have no comments in our PCAOB reports – zero. Part One, Part Two is perfect. We are there – imagine that world. But, what we produce is viewed as highly irrelevant to our stakeholders. What do you think of that? Now, I'm not the smartest guy in the world, but I would not build a business model that is predicated on the very best at something that is unimportant. And, so, we have to be both high quality and highly relevant in the world we live in – if we want to actually have a viable profession to bring our students into, and to actually make a difference. So, then you say – well, what does that look like? What does it mean to be highly relevant?

Well, Joe got some of the things – absolutely, it's not just financial statement auditing any more. The reality is – whether we like it or not – the marketplace will go on with that information and a whole bunch of other data and information to make a very important decision. In fact, I think one of the mistakes we make as a profession is the same mistake that some of the firms that went before us in totally other industries – and that is that we don't understand what it is that we really do. If we say that we're financial statement auditors, it's very easy to say – well, who else in the world would ever want to do that? Look at the competitive landscape – who else, other than the Big Four and maybe the next ten or fifteen firms would want to become the biggest accounting firms in the world? Certainly, no third party would want to be a financial statement auditor – it's just not, you know, it's not a model we love, etc.

But I'll change that question – ask a different question. What if I said our goal is to provide high levels of assurance on quoted information that people use to make some of the most important decisions in the world – whether it's in capital markets and business or somewhere else. It's about data and the integrity of that information. Well, now, if I change that model, there's a lot of people that want to be in that business. Think about Google. Google is the master of providing information. What if they decided – one day – we're going to spend just ten percent of our resources to actually build a model where we not only give you this infinite amount of data, but we actually take some of it and make sure that it's accurate and right – and you can go on.

Think about Dun & Bradstreet, Thompson Reuters – what if they decided – we're not just in the provision of market reference data, but we're in the business of providing highly certifiable, high quality information that you can rely on. What if blockchain allows Accenture to now become a fierce competitor with the Big Four, because now technology is the alternative? And Joe said – in our lifetime, there won't be an automated audit. I hope that's true, but I do think blockchain and other things are going to radically change the world around us, so other people will be able to reinvent what we do.

If you take that, and then combine it with this other very kind of pesky item called Moore's Law and the infinite amounts of data storage and computational capability that comes along with it, and you see how fast in the last five to seven years technology has advanced with the ability to manage data – to make that data sing, dance, and tell stories that we never envisioned before. You know, Joe talked a bit about data analytics – and think about it – it's incredibly powerful, right? If we can do three-way matching – a very simple concept - without ever touching the document – because we can digitize and bring that data in, use it, and automate the entire process – that's pretty powerful. We can do that today, as long as – as Joe said – we can get the data.

Imagine a world where we go one step further – and satellite imagery can be used to predict sales volume at a major retailer. I can look at the number of cars in the parking lot. I can look at weather patterns and other factors. I can prove regression analysis that shows sales are highly correlated. Could that be the next step? All those things are going to radically change the world we live in. And then, I add one more piece that were thinking about – that, to me, I think makes a really important change – if I combine data analytics with cognitive. What if I can do the same with IBM Watson? It was able to win a Jeopardy episode – and by the way, you may not notice this – but they actually had to slow it down by one-half second. They have put a latency in it so it couldn't answer the question as fast as it could have, because there was no chance a human being was going to be able to respond to the questions – hear it, acknowledge it, and respond – so they wanted at least make it somewhat equitable and fair. And that was several years ago. Watson's platform has gone way beyond that.

And Microsoft and Google are all building platforms around this whole notion of artificial intelligence and cognitive thought. In fact, we just entered into a relationship with IBM Watson to build a platform in audit. Think about how we would we use this cognitive capability in the audit? And think about combining that D&A capability to see patterns – and the ability to actually reason and understand those patterns in a different way. What worlds will open up for us as firms, for the stakeholders that we serve in the capital markets, and think about the change that our people are going to have to go through?

So, I start with this whole notion that – if we're going to stay relevant as a profession, we have to move into these areas. We can't say – well, you know, we like our model better. We can't say – well, it's not good for social fabric because machines will affect the way people work. In fact, it's very clear – City GPs did a study with two Oxford professors that basically predicted that by – in 25 years – forty-four percent of all American jobs will be gone – they'll be replaced by computers and machines. Now, that doesn't mean those people will be unemployed – hopefully – but it does mean there's going to be a massive upheaval about what those jobs look like. And that's not a new phenomenon – it's just accelerating, right?

Today, fifty percent of the jobs people do or are recruited to do, basically, weren't really in vogue or existing twenty-five years ago. And the Department of Labor predicts that twenty years from now, half of the jobs that people take have yet to be invented. So, that cycle is going to continue – with or without our permission, with or without our environment, and I believe – to stay relevant – one of the most important assets we have are the people joining us, and part of our organization. So, to me, that kind-of frames the imperative, right? And I don't think – if anyone disagrees, I'd love to hear your thoughts and comments on it. But I start there – I start with that we have to adapt and respond to that environment if we're going to be successful.

So, then I said – okay, well, with that in mind, what do our people need to look like? And I would encourage us not to think about it as students and professionals – I think one of the most important things that's changing right now is that we should almost think about the career of the people who are attracted to public accounting starting the minute they make that decision, and we should be working very closely together to figure out how we equip those people to live in this world that we're thinking about and talking about.

And think about it – they absolutely will have to know about technology, and data, and analytics – they will. And, they'll have to be really good auditors and accountants. And, they'll have to be professional and skeptical. And, they'll have to have the ability to do critical thinking, and challenge things, and really think differently. And, they're going to have to be agile and be able to reinvent themselves – because the one thing I can guarantee you is that no one will predict the skills they will need five and ten years from now. They're going to have to be able to reinvent themselves. They're going to have to be able to think about what they need to do next to be relevant in the marketplace and the organizations they serve. So, they're going to need this, and strategy – all these skills and capabilities – and I think that's a really, happy challenge for all of us.

How do we help people get to that place where they really can – not just survive – but thrive in an environment that'll be subject to that rate of change with all those different skills that are needed? They also say – no one's going to master them all, so how do we help people understand them well enough? I think there was a question over here – I can't remember who asked it – about what do when – you know – we're facing all these auditors with specialists, and so does the audit simply become a bunch of administrative people project managing? I would say absolutely not, because where the real issues are is in the scenes between the specialist's understanding ability to add value, and the real judgments, and the understanding of the business and capabilities that has to be brought together. And that – all the auditors have to do that.

In fact, I think that is going to make our job so interesting in the future – is the ability to sit between all these different skills and capabilities. Maybe not be a master of all – maybe even a master of one or two – but have that critical ability to really challenge – critically think about what's going on – does it make sense? To really ask the hard questions and to bring all that expertise there. In essence, to be a team leader. Andrew Carnegie once said that teamwork is basically a formula that allows common people to act in uncommon ways – to paraphrase. I don't think I'll nailed it exactly right – but the point was teams are better than individuals, and teamwork does something special. I think one of the things our people are going to have to do is to be exceptional at building, and leading, and driving teams – if they want to be successful in the profession in the future.

So, if you think about some of the traits and characteristics – it's going to be critical thinking, it's going to be actually – I like to think of it this way. I was talking to the dean of a business school about a month ago. I said – if you really think about it, what we're saying is that we want people that are professionally very competent, combined with really strong liberal arts capabilities, and they have a bit of rocket science added together – pretty easy to deliver, right? So, I'll take as many of those students as you can give me as a professional. The reality is that's a hard recipe, and one that no university by themselves can deliver. I think we together have to look at this as a journey that basically helps our – positions – our students to have those core capabilities that will let them keep growing, change, and adapt as we go through time.

I do think there's some salient factors, and so I think the third question is – so what does the education need to look like? What does learning need to look like? The first thing is it has to be continuous. We can't think of this any longer – and I know we've always thought about our profession as having continuing education, right? But if you really think about it, what we were saying is – well, we want to hire people out of school that have all the core capabilities they need, and then we'll continue to keep them current. We'll give them the newest FASB statements. We'll help them understand the auditing standards. We'll work with that raw material, and help them develop the new skills they need as the world around them changes.

I don't think that's the model anymore. I think the model is – the moment we get a high-performing, bright person who we can attract into our profession – we need to do it. And then, we need to help them start to build all the tools that they're going to need, including the ability to actually continuously learn and continuously thrive in the world – for they're going to have to keep learning. That starts to feel a little bit more like a liberal arts education – if you think about it – in a profession. But, they also have to have the building blocks of the profession, right? You can't have people going out doing audits at the same time they don't know the auditing standards – so, together, we've got to give them those skills.

We also have to make sure that they really can be skeptical and ask the hard questions, and really think about that kind of intuitive knowledge of – when you listen to someone, are you hearing the full picture or not? We talk about audit quality – what makes an excellent auditor? Well, one of the things is knowing when they actually got to the fundamental issue, right? Not just asking the first question, but asking then the second, and the third, and the fourth. Well, if that's true, then what about this? And then being able to go out and validate it, and make sure that what they were told makes sense. That's a hard job.

And I also know – because I've heard this loud and clear – that, look, we got a hundred-fifty hours. That's not really that long to train up these people. And then, if we're honest, twenty, thirty, forty of those hours are cut away – because the most of the kids come to us with some level of AP classes or other forms of the ability to have some of those hours pushed away. So, let's say we have a hundred-twenty hours. The university has certain things we have to teach, we have to do – pick your favorite university, no matter where you teach at, right? There's certain core classes, and you might say – I don't think those core classes help me with that end result, but I got to deal with them – they're a reality. And then I'm left with this other step.

And by the way, I need people who have passed the CPA exam, so I got to give them enough credit hours and the right subjects to help them prepare for the exam. They've got to actually get licensed in their state – so they need certain classes to make sure that happens. And now you want to throw on top of that a little data analytics, a little bit of critical thinking skills, a little bit of data analysis. You pick all those other things – I think that drives us to a couple places, personally, and this is where I would love to engage in some conversation with you. One is – we can't think of classes in silence anymore. We can't – I know this is part of the universities because sometimes one school owns data and analytics, and other schools accounting and business – it's not easy to work across some of those silos. It's certainly not easy to change curriculum in some states and some universities, but I think we've got to think about the fact that we've got, in essence, overlay some of these critical things across – so the students are getting the same stuff – hit multiple times, but in different venues.

As an example, speech and communication's critical, but you don't necessarily need a communications class to make sure that people can learn to communicate. Why can't we layer that into core curriculum around accounting and auditing, and make it part of what we actually have to deliver day in and day out – because that's the real world. What about data analytics – but not a data analytics class, but a data class that helps people understand what is the real challenge of extracting it and getting to the right data, and making sure it's accurate – but in a real life example. I'm now doing an audit using a sophisticated analytics tool, and I need to make sure that the data from this company is being brought in – in the right way, in the right sense – that gives them context. It allows us to leverage those capabilities. I know there's all kinds of challenges with that, by the way, and I think that's why I want to hear your thoughts and your reaction.

But I don't think there's any other way to do it, unless we make a doctorate of accounting required to find a professional, and I don't think that will work. I don't think – I think we're really pushing the envelope by challenging kids to get a hundred and fifty hours to be an auditor in our profession versus a hundred and twenty – or whatever it is – to be sitting on Wall Street working for Morgan Stanley. So, I think pushing out the education right now is not a viable option.

I also think that we have to be partners with you. We have to be willing and ready to accept that certain things we can help to do. In fact, I think one of the things that is really important is how do we work together in this area? So, one of the things were planning to do is to create a – we've done things like this before – and what we'd like to do is create a professorship program where we are going to ask professors – if they're accepted into the program and interested – to spend three months with us and basically work right along-side our national office dealing with some of the stuff that's really challenging the accounting and the auditing world right now – to be part of our innovation team – to actually build in.

We have a whole team committed in audit innovation around Watson, cognitive, D&A tools – sit alongside them for a period of that time, work on our Montvale facility and our New York facility – get exposed to some of those things. The idea being – I know this is just isolated to a couple of professors doing it at a time – but the idea being you helping us see things differently. How do we change our training? How do we get the simulation? How do we get to a place where every one of our people are being challenged in a different way once they join us? And, can you take some of that back and put it into the curriculum at your universities and more broadly across the profession? So, that's one thing we want to do that's just a small but quick add. We're going to actually announce the criteria for that very shortly – in the next several weeks. We'd love to have some of you, or your peers, participate in that program. Again, I think we've got to work together if this is really going to work.

So I'm going to stop there – I know I've rambled on, and I apologize for that – but I'd love your thoughts. I'd love your comments – if you disagree, I want to hear it. We want to get this right, quite frankly.

Questions and Answers

So, right here.

So, my perception is – this year we made major upgrades in our masters – I'm from the University of Tennessee – we made major overhauls to our Masters of Accounting program, and they have not been happily accepted by our students. They don't want to learn data analytics or valuation, and we've put partners in front of them to tell them it's important.

What would be more important would be salary differential – if you would pay them differently for graduating from a school where data analytics was part of their program versus where it's not – has that been talked about?

It has. Well, I'll speak for us, because some of these are profession-wide questions. I didn't really don't know – for example, Deloitte has a lot of innovative things they are doing in this area as well. I can tell you what we're doing. So, yes, we are thinking exactly about compensating or rewarding people for taking the right classes. The other thing we're really looking at is providing other incentives or benefits that would help people see how important those curriculums are – and motivate them to want to go do that.

I think part of it is – a lot of kids entered school, and they said my ambition – let's go where they were really motivated, and as freshman, they knew they wanted to be accountants. I'm not sure if that's true for all students, but we'll take that they want that. I think they have a vision in their mind of how quickly they can do that. Their vision is – I want to get into the workforce as quickly as possible. When I start getting paid, I want to stop paying for school. And they're not necessarily stepping back and asking themselves – could I be better off? And so the other thing we're looking at is can we not only create a salary difference, but can we create a half-way difference – where if they come in with certain capabilities and they're are high quality student, we actually put them on a fast track program to be exposed to some things with D&A and other things that gives them a chance to be promoted faster, the opportunity to work on bigger engagements, and to do, what we hope, would be viewed by them as more exciting things. There's just going to have to be a combination of those different things, quite frankly.

Yeah, you talked about skepticism three times in your speech. What are you doing to enhance professional skepticism? For first-year auditors, are you expecting us to turn our students into Sherlock Holmes?

I'm not. What I am, though, expecting is that we would put a premium on those critical thinking skills and problem solving skills that I think are really important to getting the skepticism, right? Skepticism is rooted in the belief or confidence, I think, that it's interesting to go find out the truth, and if possible, to discover it if I really push, and prod, and look at the right stuff. And to answer your question specifically, I'm not expecting you to get them to that level, but you can get them some of the groundwork that helps them be thinking more critically about problems and issues.

For example, showing them that when something looks to be one way, but, in fact, it's really something different. It's funny – we started back about four years ago trying to help change our training around this, and we did one simple thing – you may have seen this. We actually showed a lot of our first year people a video, and we said – we're going to watch a video – they're going to bounce a basketball, and you're going to count how many times it bounces. And in the middle of it, a gorilla comes in, and starts dancing around and jumping around, and then leaves. And, by and large, most of the people who watch the video never saw the gorilla. All they did is count the basketball, because you said count the basketball, right? That is a very telling exercise, and it worked outside in public accounting, inside public – and that's also scary to me that we didn't have a discernible difference for the people working for us.

So, giving people tools and showing them – hey, did you realize you did that? Now, let's figure out how we could avoid that, and we are making into – that's where I think simulation becomes really important. Because the way you teach people, I think, is by learning through experience – often to be more skeptical. And the best way to teach people is to let them fail. You don't want to fail in an audit engagement. If I'm failing in an environment that's safe, and then fix it. Also, on the job is going to be – it's something that's really important.

And so, one of the things were also pressing – it's easy, with technology and other things, for partners to become more removed from our people – and so we're really pressing them to become much more engaged with our people. In fact, we have surveys now for every one of our professionals that asks – very specifically and confidentially – how interactive was the partner on the engagement? Did they provide you with guidance and training and oversight that you needed? Did you feel like they were available? That they helped you learn things on the engagement? Questions that get to – do we need to change partner behaviors so that we're really setting the right tone across the organization.

Sure.

Good morning or afternoon – I don't know what time it is.

It's still morning – it depends on what time zone you're in.

I'm still on the Eastern.

There you go.

Ally Zimmerman from Northern Illinois University. I have a related question to…

And I learned those are the Huskies, right, as well. Thank you.

...a related question to attracting students to the audit profession versus, perhaps, consulting. My understanding is there's a salary difference, even at the beginning, between audit and consulting. And so, I wanted your thoughts on what's been done there.

Yeah, and that is emerging – and some of it is a question of – well, why? And I'll tell you – part of it is there's a lack of resources that wanted to go into advisory, so the only way they could find them is to start paying up for it. The other thing is being an advisor – being an auditor is really hard – but being advisor is harder in different ways, right? So, for example, a lot of our – at least in our structure provided for advisory – it's a national practice – they travel constantly. You do not live at home. You do not audit or work around your market very often. You might – but there's no guarantee. So, part of it is educating people to make sure you're not just jumping in because I get five thousand or seven thousand more dollars over here versus over there.

I think there also is a problem in that students, even more specifically, are starting to say – well, auditing – what is that? Versus – hey, it sounds really cool to advise people, right? You go in, and give them advice on how to do something better as opposed to the way audit has been perceived in the past. And so, I think, one is we do have to look – we continually have to look – at salary structure – and that's something we have to be careful about. One of the hard things about audit is the minute I change my starting salary by a significant amount, I start compression – incredibly – up a chain. I have 9500 professionals, and 1500 or 2000 of them are entering in a given year – which means for every five percent I give them, I now have to worry about another eighty-five percent of my world, and how it affects them – that's a real challenge. And so we have to be careful about just throwing money at people.

But, I also – I do think that's part of it. I think we better be also telling the story about what are you going to get if you become an auditor. What does it really look like? As far as what this is – I do think that if we can help people really get into data analytics, and see cognitive as an ally in helping them get better, then getting more involved with c-level executives younger in their career, asking hard questions, thinking about themselves as protecting the capital markets – as opposed to just doing audits. I think we can get hearts and minds – that's even more important to me. I know this easy said – hard to do. I think it's going to take time and energy to do it, but I think it's got to be a combination of the two.

It's funny – one last thing I'll say here – when we talked to Watson IBM, we were entering into an agreement to help us with audit, and they were willing to give us things to do it – which was unusual for them – and we asked why? And they said – we kind of see this similar to what we've done in medicine and fraud – because it's not about auditing, it's about protecting the capital markets. And the way IBM's thinking about Watson – they want to get into places where it has a social impact, not just a business impact. Their idea is – we want to do things that are enterprise-driven, but really have a social element to them. Because that's how we think we'll get greater acceptance of the Watson platform, because we know people are afraid of it. They're afraid of this notion of machines doing things people do. So, it's got to be socially friendly if that will – it's got to be doing things that matter. And so – they even said – the capital markets really matter, and this is important. And I'm thinking – well, you're right, it is. Maybe we don't tell ourselves that often enough.

So, in the tax area, we've seen - I've seen - introductory training for various areas in tax, but one of the things that I think would be helpful for those of us thinking about teaching data analytics is - are you willing to share what you think your basic, minimum level of skills are?

So that, given that we know what our students lack – not that we want to redo what you're doing – but at least target that in the areas in which they would be beneficial at that level. So, sharing that training with the faculty would help us understand where they need to go, as opposed to – I mean we all do some form of data analysis – analytics – ourselves, but what we would need to actually structure in class to get them to where you want them to be – would be very helpful.

Good observation, and the short answer is – yes, we are. In fact, one of the things we started talking about after a lot of visits with universities this year – is how far can we push the envelope about not only helping them see what we think are the necessary and specific skills, and get as specific as possible? Also, what we can do – what we are willing to do – is to share our technology platform for what we're doing – at least at some level – and let them use it and experiment with it in class. There's a trade-off obviously, right? Some of it's very proprietary. Some of it's what we've been working very hard on to create. On the other side, the idea that we could accelerate the knowledge and the usage of these types of tools in the people we hire – is very, very intra-valuable from my perspective.

And so, we're pushing ourselves to say – let's push the envelope. Let's see how far we could go. And, also, make sure we respect the fact that, again, we don't have all the answers. This group is incredibly important in this discussion. You know – you live this stuff. You know what works. You know what doesn't work. You know what challenges you'll have in your particular universities. So, let's work together. We'll show you what we'd been thinking about – maybe you tell us – will this really help? Nah, this wouldn't, but this would. To me, that's the kind of dialogue we need to have and want to have in doing this.

I really enjoyed the way you've started the presentation, and you reminded me of the Oxford historian Arnold Toynbee – in his book – The Prospects of Western Civilization[ii] *– very beautifully said – it is the perfectly adapted species that is the first to perish when the environment changes. So, I think that's kind of where you were going, so that was great. So my background, Scott, is…*

So, don't seek perfection, right? I got it.

…my background is in psychology. So, one of the things I like to ask you is – what are firms doing in terms of promoting emotional and social intelligence. That is something that, unfortunately, has sort of not been emphasized. And I'll tell you what – it was very, very troubling to me. The media – I've read too many papers now about this. So, recent neuroscience is showing something dramatic of our complete misconception for most of the twentieth century. We are not thinking beings that feel, it is telling us; we are feeling beings that think. Emotions come first. Cognition comes later.

Yep.

And then, what is another, sort-of, revelation is – the reason, it turns out, that rationality can really help you make inferences and reach conclusions. It is emotions that are the gateway to action. You can have all the reason you want, but if you don't have the passion and the emotion behind it, you will just not be able to act. On the other hand, you may be able to – if you're a Martian, it may work.

We haven't hired any Martians, lately, so…

So, I just wanted a conclusion – to find out – what are the firms doing with that?

It's a great, great question. We are – at the very high level – starting to analyze and think about that – and we're doing it in two ways. One is – I'll call it the notion of pressure, because I know that's not specifically the issue. But, one of the things that really affects human performance and behavior is pressure and being put in pressure situations – like working too hard, too long; like being pressed to give an answer that someone really doesn't like or will get angry about – all those things. And so, we've included a very famous psychologist – who specializes in this area – and say – how – help us design training. Create awareness – but even beyond that – design training to help people deal with it. And what we learned were some very practical things. No human being performs well under pressure – notwithstanding the myth – but what some human beings do is cope with pressure better than others – and put themselves in a better place where pressure doesn't affect them. How could we do that? So, that's one of the things.

More broadly on the emotional element of being a human being, we started asking ourselves – so, what are we missing in our training that is changing behaviors? And part of it is coming right back to that question, right? As we looked at the root cause of why the training was limited in effectiveness, we've discovered the same thing, right? That it's usually some emotional element that follows – that has some impact on why people do or don't do what they're supposed to do. So, we're looking at it. I'll be honest with you, we'd love ideas there. Any specific direction, research, etcetera would be very valuable, because it's something we're not necessarily equipped to do other than to see it's an issue, and then start to think about how we would resolve it.

Scott, I'd like to ask – you had a question at the start that I'd like to ask – add to it and ask it back to you.

Sure.

You said something like this – suppose you had zero inspection defects in your practice, but the practice had become irrelevant. So, that – here's your question back to you now is – in my view, most of the changes in auditing standards since 2003 – and especially recently – are changes in what the auditor reports about what he or she has already done, which is largely unchanged from the last century – instead of research about new ways of doing audits better. Of course, with data analytics is where you're doing things better.

Right.

But the question is – do the firms feel there's a need for more research – either behavioral, or model-building, or other kinds of research – to do – to produce – better audits as opposed to reporting more about how the old audits have been done. Is that a concern of the firm?

I would have to say for us – for me – yes, absolutely. I would love research in that regard. I'd also love it in not only how to do it better, but what to do it to. Because one of the questions you get to is what really is value creation – value enhancement – in the market we live in? What is it that stakeholders really want to know? And how could – you know, we get to this dilemma that was brought up before and Joe addressed, right? Which is – why aren't people asking for things if it really would create value? I don't know, but sometimes people don't know what to ask for, right?

I kind of equate it to the first person that flew on an airplane. They probably didn't know that what they wanted was this big metal object with wings – all they know is that I want to get from New York to California faster. That's my goal. Then, we struggle with the same thing. How do we engage with the specific cultures to say what would create more value to them? Some of this is obvious – some of it's not. So, I think research in both of those areas about what to do it to, and how to do it better – is totally valuable – especially when you link – when you look through – the lens of the way technology is going to change both of those things, right? Today, I can report things I never could dream of reporting before, and I can attest to things I never could dream of before – so simply because technology will allow it. So, yeah, it's sure changing.

I think we're close to our time – what is out time here, when do we finish? Okay, I can take one more question – it's 11:45.

First, I want to put in a plug for your professional judgment training materials that you've provided for professors. Someone mentioned something about teaching professional skepticism, and they're really great if you'll look at them.

To kind of build on what Bill was saying, I wonder if we need to step back and see if auditors are efficiently using the tools that they currently have, as opposed to – woohoo, big data. Because there's research that shows that, for instance, using a simple bankruptcy prediction model with publicly available data, we can predict bankruptcies better than going concern opinions. And so – and another thing I've wondered about, too – is why don't auditors read blogs? Why don't they do the things that financial analysts do to perform a better audit? You know, before we start thinking about big data.

Yeah, so, actually that's a great point, and it is balanced because there are a lot of things we could do and we should be doing. I will – your blog example – you're right. Part of the problem gets to touch, right? So we prep people to do a certain amount of work. We're very focused on getting all the things done, and make sure that it's documented properly so that the inspection goes well – all those things. And so, having the available time is difficult. I'll also say – part of this is just comfort and aptitude. One thing that's very noticeable, and Joe alluded to, in the innovation side – it's also in our tool side – our young people do do that sometimes.

They will go and they'll tell us – tell me – things. Did you know blah, blah, blah, blah, blah? And I'm like, well no – because I don't follow that particular blog or whatever. They're very much tech-savvy and social media minded. That mindset shift is very valuable to us. What we've got to do is allow it to flourish in a good way – not in a bad way, but in a good way – to help us. I also agree with you there's plenty of tools out there. In fact, again, that's an area that I love to hear more about if you think – any of you think – there's some things that are being underutilized. We'd love it.

Bankruptcy prediction models – I mean there's lots of papers out there that show, I mean – woohoo, I did a bankruptcy prediction model with this sample of banking firms and going concerns firms, and I did better than the firms did. And as far as blogs go – I mean, I was an auditor a long time ago, so I'm much older than my students. But, I understand how to read a blog.

Well, yeah, absolutely – it's not a question of not – I think it's more of an aptitude to do it, right? My kids like to do it – I have to force myself to do it. That's the main difference…

Yeah.

…but you're right. I do know how to read a blog – I know that's not a problem.

Well, I want to just say thank you again. I really appreciate the opportunity to be here. I appreciate your time, and hope you enjoy the rest of the symposium, and have a great lunch. Thank you.

---

[i] Transcription Note: The original transcript has been edited for flow and ease of reading. Any changes to content were not intended to change the overall message associated with the applicable discussion.

[ii] Here is a reference for this text: Toynbee, A. (1949). *The prospects of western civilization.* New York: Columbia Univ. Press.

Jeanette Franzel[i]

Opening Remarks

I'm very happy to be here. Thank you. I plan to speak for a bit, using some slides, and then I'm happy to do a deep dive on any of these topics during the Q&A. And I'm happy to have my slides be distributed to all the participants, afterwards, so that you can remember what I talked about.

But before I get started, I have to tell you that the views that I express today are mine alone, and do not reflect the views of the board, or the board members, or the PCAOB staff – that's our required PCAOB disclaimer. We copied the SEC when we made this rule, but I like to remind people that I am one-fifth of the board.

So, I want to give you just a brief snapshot of where we are right now at the PCAOB. You know, of course, we were established with four statutory mission areas, and the law says that we must do these things – registration, inspection, enforcement, and standards. And the law even has some parameters around how we inspect, and how often we inspect. But we've got flexibility in how we inspect, and I'll talk about that in a little bit. In terms of staff, we've got eight-hundred and seventy-six budgeted for 2016. PCAOB has been a in a very high growth mode ever since it started in 2003 with the staff of – well, they started with five people on board, and now up to 876 – so that's pretty fast growth, at the same time as building programs and developing programs.

Since I've been at the board, I've been asking the question – when is this organization going to stabilize? We stopped using assumptions of constant, high growth and have slowed our growth considerably. I think we are going to stabilize, with a little encouragement from some SEC commissioners, who have told us we had better start thinking about a "steady state." And I'm very happy for us to try to work in a more disciplined type of environment. It's interesting to see the staff starting to think differently in such an environment. So, stay tuned on this. We'll have to figure out how to rearrange our resources a little bit, and how to do things more efficiently. We'll always face new risks, but we can't keep taking an incremental approach.

I'll talk a little bit about our registered firms. We've got about 2100 right now – 950 of those aren't subject to our oversight because they don't report doing any work that would require registration with the PCAOB. So, we still have this large pool of firms that for whatever reason want to register with us. I'll talk in more detail about our numbers of inspections.

Next, I'll give you an idea of the equity markets around the world. Global equity market cap is estimated to be about $62.8 trillion around the world, and you can see up here[ii] the different regions and the market equity cap traded in each region. You can see Asia-Pacific is catching up to the U.S. It's kind of an interesting phenomenon. If you look at the global equity market cap for U.S. traded companies – and we regulate the auditors of those companies – it's about $32.6 trillion. So, some of this market cap is overseas for the companies – the audits – that we regulate. There's $8.2 trillion of market cap audited by non-US firms, and that's a sizable portion of the $32.6 trillion audited by registered firms that we regulate.

We've had trouble getting access to inspect and investigate auditors in certain markets. We do a lot of non-U.S. inspections – however, about $1.8 trillion of that market cap is audited by firms in blocked jurisdictions. So, if you look at the red, those are the jurisdictions that are blocked. And as you can see, $1.3 trillion of that is in Asia. That's our biggest issue right now-- China and Hong Kong. We are in some heavy negotiations right now. The strategic and economic dialogue is coming up between the United States and China, and we are part of that. Chairman Doty will be joining the Secretary of the Treasury, and others from United States, at this summit. The dialogue includes strategic issues – military and other strategic issues – and economic issues. We're part of the economic discussion.

The other areas where we're blocked include a couple of EU countries – Ireland and Italy are the big ones – although we continue to make some progress in negotiations. So, we're getting to the point where, at some point, we're going to stop negotiating deals and have to think about what we do in those jurisdictions where we are blocked. And, of course, that will take coordination with the SEC, but it's been a long time now negotiating these deals.

Now, some information about firms registered with the PCAOB. I want to show you some trends since 2010, because there's been consolidation among the firms – with mergers and acquisitions among firms. And so, you'll see that the number of firms that audit issuers has decreased from 692 firms registered with the PCAOB in 2010 to 584 in 2015. This reflects consolidation that's happening among firms; and in some cases, firms have decided they don't want to audit issuers if, for instance, they were only doing one, in light of the need to manage regulatory issues for only one audit client.

Also, over the years, we've thrown a few firms out of the system through our enforcement program. We've revoked the registration of over 60 firms, almost 40 of which were permanent revocations. And we've had sanctions against 125 firms total – and some of those may have withdrawn their registration voluntarily. We are still removing some bad actors from the system to protect investors.

Regarding the firms that audit SEC-registered brokers and dealers, but not issuers, we've also seen a lot of consolidation in that space. There has also been consolidation of the broker-dealers themselves, and the number of brokers and dealers that file with the SEC has been shrinking significantly.

The number of PCAOB inspections follows that same trend down a little bit. We conducted 181 domestic triennial inspections in 2010 compared to 142 in 2015. The numbers of inspections are shrinking a little bit because the number of firms that come under our oversight is shrinking. And interestingly, within the 142 firms inspected in 2015 – there's quite a number that we've accelerated because of risk. You can't just take the number of firms that audit 100 or fewer issuers and divide it by three to arrive at the number of inspections in a given year. There's a quite a number of firms, where, due to risk, we've accelerated their inspections. Among broker-dealer auditors – we're inspecting 75 firms again this year as part of our interim program.

So, I hope that gives you a feel for the scope and size of our oversight.

These[iii] are the inspection results for the U.S. Big Four firms – I talked about that a little bit this morning. We expect those inspection findings to come down, and they're going to be grouping a little bit. The firms' results will be getting closer to each other on that chart. And, hopefully, we will get those numbers out soon, and we're also thinking about what these results mean for future inspections.

Areas of frequent findings – I'm not going to go over this. You've all seen this before. There was one blogger that referred to PCAOB inspection reports as Groundhog Day – we've been reporting the same frequent areas of findings for a long time. The good news is the numbers of findings are coming down. I will just mention one thing in there – that audit sampling – that's something that's cropped up in the second-tier firms recently, but they're working on those issues.

So, let's talk about improvements. What have we seen as improvements? We've seen some significant improvements in tone at the top at the big firms. And not just messaging, but tone backed by resources – serious resources – and actions taken. And we're starting to see that take hold through the systems of quality control. We talked about that this morning. First the firms responded to inspection findings with training; then they improved practice aids and checklists; and now they've focused a whole lot on project management skills and approaches, and tracking the audit through the process – which has yielded some good results.

So, what is the state of audit quality today? That's the big question. We've seen the large firms make significant improvements in audit quality. They're continuing to remediate the systemic issues that we found, but I think the really good news is – the firms have gone beyond just remediation. At first, it was a big project to deal with the findings and deal with the issues that we identified, but the firms' root cause analyses are taking them beyond just remediating what we have found. And they're being proactive and somewhat creative in figuring out what is the real root cause of certain problems, and how to address the issues. And we heard this morning that the firms are thinking an awful lot about people, and behavior, and that's really what it comes down to.

We still need to see an increased focus on quality across the global networks and their affiliated firms. And that's something we're pushing with the U.S. Big Four, and the other U.S. global firms. How are they ensuring quality through the network? The primary challenge in the past with the global firms was their inclination to hide behind the legal boundaries and the legal structures of the firms. On the one hand, for marketing purposes, it was all one big firm usually with the same name, and using a common methodology. But when it comes to regulation, and liability, and enforcement, they're completely different legal structures. Well, that's not acceptable for audit quality. So, the firms are starting to get creative about how to work across the networks, and not use legal boundaries as barriers anymore. So, that's a new focus and we should hopefully see some improvements in the global affiliates' quality.

The triennial firms' results are a little bit harder to figure out, because the mix of firms in that group changes so much. We have firms coming in and coming out based on their mix of clients, firm consolidation, and our risk-based inspections, which I described earlier. I've tried to encourage our staff to do something like a same-store sales measure for our triennial firms. So, for the same firms that have been in the mix, how have they done over time? The staff tried to do that a few years ago, and the results weren't meaningful. I think that was because it was still too early and we were changing our inspection focus. I think it'll be important for us to do that in the future.

In 2015, fifty-eight percent of the U.S. triennial firms that we inspected had clean inspection reports – with no audit deficiencies identified. That's really good news in my view. And then, some of the other U.S. triennial firms had really bad reports, unfortunately. So we still have variation among the small firms, but there are some smaller firms out there with sizable practices that have very good inspection results. It's certainly encouraging to see that. And, in fact, every now and then I'll ask how a firm is accomplishing that. They'll have a high number of issuer clients – the number of issuers is still under a hundred – but they've somehow found the magic sauce for high audit equality.

So, what does all this mean for future inspection approaches? I gave a speech in New York a couple weeks ago when I focused on this issue. The two big issues are non-risk-based selections, sometimes referred to as randomization. And you all – with your statistical knowledge – know this is not randomization, but it's basically adding some non-risk-based selections to our inspection mix. That's happening right now, and we'll see what the trends look like. It's interesting because people have different views on this. Some people say that because we're looking at the risky audits and audit areas, we'll find problems, and if we were looking at the lower risk items, we wouldn't find problems. So, therefore, we must be over-reporting problems. And others say just the opposite. They say that the firms aren't paying attention to the low risk items, so we're going to find lots of problems in those areas. So, we'll have to see what the results are.

The really interesting thing about this is the Canadian regulator did this last year. And so, for the Big Four - anybody know what the results were? Anybody want to guess? So, for two of the firms, the results were worse when they looked at the smaller issuers. For the other two firms, the results were the same. So, I don't know what we'll find in the United States. I think it's a valuable and worthwhile exercise, and what we find will also help us figure out where we need to go in the future for inspections.

Another very important area for us going forward is an increased focus on testing the firm's QC system – especially in cases where firms are bringing down the audit deficiency rates. If there's a high level of deficiencies out there that we need to find and point to in order to get the firms to remediate the underlying issues – that's one thing. But, if the firms can become successful in designing their QC systems – so that they're putting out high-quality audits on a fairly consistent basis – well, then, that's a QC system that works, and we want to make sure that the QC system continues to work. It would seem to make sense that we want to focus there. So, stay tuned on our approach to that.

We've got a lot of people thinking about this in our building. We have people with different views, but we need to let some of this play out for the next year or so. And, like I said, we're expecting to see a significant reduction in findings for this next year. The current cycle is going to include some non-risk-based selections. It's time for us to start thinking about the future and where we might put some additional focus. And it's entirely possible that we would use different approaches for different firms, depending on where they are – just like you do when doing an audit – using different approaches depending on risk.

Next, I want to mention audit quality indicators. We touched on that topic this morning, but the big question is – where is the PCAOB on this? But before I get into that, I want to level-set just a little bit – because I think we've almost got an expectation gap out there about what AQIs can do. I thought we had a very balanced discussion this morning, but there seems to be some perception out there that we're trying to come up with magic measures that, if you get the measures right, you're going have a good audit – and that's not the intention at all. The idea originally came out of the U.S. Department of the Treasury ACAP report that recommended we determine the feasibility of even doing this, and there's discussion in the ACAP report about how difficult this is. And then, assuming that the development and disclosure of indicators is feasible, the ACAP report recommends that PCAOB monitor these indicators.

The ACAP report was very clear that we should look into whether and how this could be done. It's interesting how auditing can sometimes become so political – in terms of should we mandate and whether we should require reporting. So I think it's good to go back and level-set to the intent of the original recommendation.

And it is important to go back to our original Concept Release. We were seeking comment on the possible uses of a set of potential audit quality indicators that may provide new insights about how to evaluate the quality of audits. This would be part of a bigger process for talking about audit quality and evaluating audit quality along with qualitative context. I don't think anybody in the PCAOB building has ever thought you could do this only in a quantitative fashion. This has to be used in connection with qualitative context.

That leads to questions about who should be using audit quality indicators. Clearly, audit committees and firms would be a logical group. But, there is also a question about whether in the future there should be some kind of mandate for public reporting.

One of the things I didn't mention this morning – and this came out of the ACAP report and it's in our Concept Release – is the notion of using AQIs so that firms can compete on quality. And, some of the audit committees that I talked to say that if they're going to use a Big Four audit firm, their decision is not going to be based on that type of thinking. They feel like there's an oligopoly out there, and there is not competition on quality – at least right now. And they're not quite sure if we could ever achieve that. They're mainly concerned about getting the right engagement team at the firm they are using. So, we'll see if we can ever shift the discussion toward a competition on quality in addition to getting the right engagement team with the right expertise. And in some cases audit committees may have to go with a particular firm because of industry specialization.

So, what are our next steps? The staff provided us a memo in February recommending the direction that the board should go on this. Basically, the plan is for us to encourage voluntary use and experimentation of audit quality indicators. We'll keep coordinating with the CAQ and others, and monitor the use of AQIs. We do outreach with and receive feedback from audit committees and others on this, and we're learning a lot. For me, the exciting thing is to see what others are learning, and to see them experiment. I'm really encouraged that firms are doing a deep dive on some of these process controls, because I think this will be important going forward. Maybe we'll publish some additional information related to AQIs based on what we're learning. If we do, it might be next year. So, we don't have any hard and fast plans for publishing, and we certainly don't have any plans for rule-making right now. So, our time horizon is pretty long, but our staff is staying on top of it. And if we do publish something, it will probably be in the form of white paper. What are some of the best practices? How are people calculating or considering these measures? Etcetera.

We're also doing some thinking on what qualitative factors, in context, might need to be paired up with these potential audit quality indicators. So, for instance, if we are putting out information for audit committees to consider, we don't want to simply say here are five indicators that audit committees might find helpful. We probably want to add some context around that, including good experiences that we've seen out there with a particular measure that, combined with context, has been helpful in some cases. So, there may be some type of a white paper coming out from the PCAOB in 18 to 24 months.

And then, there are the questions that are way down the road – public reporting versus use by firms and audit committees. And as I said this morning – if somebody told us we had to mandate something, we couldn't do it right now because we don't have a basis or the justification to do so. Firms are starting to voluntarily report firm-wide data, which I think is very interesting. And, actually the data that I find most interesting that they're reporting involves some trends and staffing information. Some of these measures of staffing – over-time, for instance – are actually getting better. We're highly encouraging firm reporting of AQIs, and we'll keep monitoring that.

I want to switch over to our standard-setting. I'm not going to dive into any of this in detail. I'm happy to answer any questions that you have. We did put out our rulemaking on transparency of participants in audits. We approved that in December 2015 and we've got two other proposals out right now on audits involving other auditors and the auditor's reporting model. And we're hoping to get two more proposals out this year – auditing estimates, including fair value measurements; and the auditor's use of the work of specialists. We are finally clearing some items off of the standard-setting agenda that have been there for some time. And we now have the opportunity to take a look at the whole process, and, fundamentally, where do we need to be putting our efforts next?

The quality control standards are going to become a big focus of ours, and we're in the research and outreach phase right now. That project has been delayed, because of everything else. As you know, our standard-setting process has not been very efficient, and we've been working on fixing that, and pushing out some of these older projects. But actually, I think it's good that we're really just starting to focus now on quality control standards – because we have learned so much; and the firms have learned so much through their remediation and their root cause analysis in response to our inspections; and now through some of this AQI work. So, I think we're far better off doing a deep dive on quality control starting now then we would have been two years ago.

And when I think about what needs to happen on quality control standards – if you look at the current standards, they use the term monitoring – but it's not really monitoring. It's mainly a focus on internal inspection after the fact. And so, I think, if we focus on quality monitoring, and if the firms can figure out how to do effective real-time monitoring, and if those quality control systems can be properly built, we should be much better off systemically in the future.

I mentioned that we're trying to improve our standard setting process. We've done a top-to-bottom review. We've got a consultant in – I'm sure some of you have been through that routine – interviewing staff and interviewing board members – and they've actually put together a four-phase process for our standard-setting. The first phase uses environmental scans and an improved research approach – so that before something even gets on the agenda, we have defined a problem and we've done a fair amount of research. I think, in the past, the problem was things would get onto the agenda because a board member would pound his or her fist on the table. And, if a board member pounded long enough on the table, it got onto the agenda. That's not a good way to do policy.

So, we're trying to get a well-reasoned and research-based approach in place – and we're working to integrate economic analysis – which is includes defining the problem that needs to be solved and then evaluating alternatives and costs and benefits. Also, we are now coordinating on a project-by-project basis with the IAASB. This is long overdue. We don't need to reinvent the wheel at the PCAOB, and so, I think that this is going to accelerate our work flow a bit. I've seen tremendous developments in this area on projects where our staff are coordinating with the IAASB staff. I think everybody realized we have more in common than we do differences, and we always reserve the right to write our own standard or to add-on – if we think that the IAASB standard missed the boat. But, we might as well take a look at what they're doing.

So, before I talk about additional focus areas any questions about our statutory areas – inspections, standards, enforcement, registration?

Questions and Answers

So, one of the major causes of deficiencies is with ICFR audits. And I was wondering – two questions – wondering if you can comment on maybe any of the root causes there? And second question, I don't see on the standard setting list under any things that you're working on for helping out the internal control audit standards?

We are not doing anything on the standards side related to ICFR. You know, we put out Practice Alert No. 11, and that changed practice – which was good. We didn't need to change the standard. We're seeing the inspection findings come down – so that's good. I think that the problems there are rooted in the long, sordid history of this issue. When the Sarbanes-Oxley Act was passed – of course, there was 404(a) and (b) – (b) was the audit requirement – many were opposed to the audit requirement. There was lobbying to have that requirement repealed. So, initially, there was some denial, I think, that the audit requirement was really going to stick.

Also, there was no SEC guidance for how management should do its assessment of ICFR. And the PCAOB put out AS 2 – the auditing standard – before the SEC guidance was out. AS2 was an extremely detailed standard. I was at GAO at the time, and wrote the comment letter over to the PCAOB saying – this standard is way too detailed, and we listed all the areas where we thought it was too detailed. The PCAOB realized, soon after it went out, that it was too detailed – started putting out guidance telling auditors to pull back.

Then PCAOB put out AS 5 – which went to a top-down, risk-based approach to auditing ICFR. And then PCAOB inspections focused on looking to see if auditors had properly pulled back in the ICFR area. That was the initial inspection approach. So, overall, that's kind of a rough start to auditing ICFR. Then SEC put out its guidance for management– and I think the guidance is well aligned with the auditing standard, AS 5. When we started inspecting ICFR auditing in 2010, we started seeing a lot of issues. I think we're now seeing a good rationalization of this issue. We've had a lot of dialogue with preparers and audit committees – so I'm hoping we can get to a good point on this. I'm hoping that the 2015 results show that we're getting there and we shouldn't need more standard setting in this area – but stay tuned on that.

Any other questions?

Jeanette – on the auditing accounting estimates – that I think – this is the exposed, respective proposal in fourth quarter of this year?

Correct.

And that has to do, with – I guess – with improving audits of accounting estimates?

Correct, yes.

Fair value estimates – and you said also that you're going to be integrating economic analysis to do cost-benefit on new standards?

Yes.

Will this auditing accounting estimates – which many in the room know and have done a lot of research about the costs and benefits of auditing accounting estimates – will the economic analysis be used on that standard? Or is that too soon?

Economic analysis will definitely be included. It will be in the proposal, and then we tend to bolster it even further for a final rule. So, when the proposal comes out, we will be scanning the academic research on this topic. If you want to – if you have relevant papers that you think we should look at, we'd be happy to look at them. But, we do have staff looking through the relevant research. We will cite research on both sides of the issue – because we often find that the researchers present a full spectrum of results. And so, we will cite academic research.

We'll ask further questions about costs and benefits, and we've found that often when we've got a proposal out, there's some academic interest in it. So if anybody's doing research in this area now, finish up your paper so that we can cite to it. Sometimes we cite to working papers, but we'd rather not. We'd rather cite to something that's published.

If you want to look at an example of how we've been doing this lately, look at the economic analysis in the re-proposal for the auditor's reporting model, and the proposal for other auditors. So, we're not all the way there yet with where we need to be on economic analysis, but we've made a lot of progress. And, to get auditors – especially audit standard-setting people – to talk to economists is really difficult. But, they're getting good at this.

So, last week at the European Accounting Association, we - there was a paper presented where they did a content analysis for positive and negative words in the inspection reports, and then the response from the accounting firms – and they're highly correlated. In other words, if the accounting firms protested the inspection report, the next inspection report was nastier than the prior one.

So, the audit firms are now gaming the system by sending in boilerplate letters that just kind of say – thank you very much in three or four paragraphs. Any comments on being gamed by the Big Four accounting firms?

I'd actually be interested in that study, if you want to send it to me. There are a lot of layers here – that's why I want to read that study. Today, the big firms and some of their affiliates have a standard, nice approach of thanking us for coming in, and expressing appreciation for the professionalism of our inspectors, and so on.

A lot of the small firms don't even respond, and it goes across the spectrum – from small firms with completely clean reports – to small firms that need to be referred to our enforcement division. We can't really tell why small firms choose to respond or not. And then there's this group in the middle where – some of them take an approach similar to the big firms. And, in fact, some of those small firms – they look to our inspectors and our remediation staff as free consulting. But, then others challenge us on every single finding. So, I see the whole spectrum. I'd love to read that study.

It's not my study.

Okay.

Can I ask a follow-up question?

Yes.

So, the discussant came up with even a different theory. He said that you guys are all gaming us. In other words, you guys have to keep tension between you and the accounting firms so you can game Congress so they don't come down on you. Any comment on that? That you guys are gaming us?

I believe we use pretty consistent criteria when we're dealing with firms, so we're not trying to game the firms. I don't like some of the wording that we use in our inspection reports. I came from GAO where we tried not to use certain charged words in reports. In fact, we often found we could make our point much more effectively by not using certain language.

And so, it was a real shock to me to come to PCAOB and see how those inspection reports were written, especially when the inspection reports were saying that – if your audit is included in Part One, it's an audit failure. To me, that was over the top – and we've discontinued the use of that language. But, there's still a lot of language in our inspection reports that refers to failures of the firm. Almost every paragraph starts off the firm failed to do this, the firm failed to do that – I don't think that's productive language. But, I'd be curious to see these correlations.

Any other questions on inspections or standards or – yes – and this won't be your last chance. I just figured we'd talk about these issues before I go on to some of the other things we're doing.

On the auditors reporting model – I've noticed – and this is pointed out in the re-proposal – there's a lot of inconsistency across jurisdictions on some of the things for the reporting model. To me, one of the minor inconsistencies is around materiality reporting. You see the materiality is reported on the 10-K in the Netherlands, but not in the E.U. and the PCAOB's proposals. Can you talk a little bit about that, and why that is?

I think that reporting materiality – just putting in a number – is somewhat misleading. When you are doing an audit you start off with the planning materiality – which is used for determining other levels of materiality and other levels of testing – and then depending on what you find, you might decide you have to adjust your materiality for a certain area. So, let's say you're finding indications of fraud – you're certainly not going to use your planning materiality for your deep dive into that area. And then, when you're evaluating deficiencies and errors, you're using a test level of materiality. And when you're deciding whether the financials are fairly stated along with the disclosures in all material respects, you're bringing all this in, and comparing it against whatever your adjusted materiality might be at the end of the audit after evaluating everything you've learned. So, which number do you put in there, and what conclusions are outsiders going to make about that?

Many people think that materiality means if there's something below this amount, the auditor's not looking at it. And that's not true. So, to me, it would be problematic and misleading, and I'm not sure what outsiders would gain from disclosure of a particular number. If we're worried about audit firms not using proper materiality, I think that's better handled through the inspection process. Maybe we'll see evidence from the U.K. that this is valuable.

Additional Remarks

Alright, let me move on to a few other things that we are doing. This morning I mentioned our outreach and dialogue with audit committees. We have found this to be very valuable. We can learn what issues audit committees are seeing – maybe, unintended consequences that are happening on their audits or concerns that they might have about PCAOB oversight. They tell us what the audit firms are telling them about the PCAOB. And, frankly, it's good for the firms to know we're talking to their audit committees. That level-sets and keeps everybody honest.

And part of that started with the ICFR issues – when we started drilling down on ICFR auditing– auditors, in some cases, had to change their approaches. And that made issuers question – why they were doing that. And, in some cases, the audit teams said – well, the PCAOB is making us do this. So, we had to have some dialogue and explanation.

There will always be tension in the system, and there should be. That's what an audit is all about, and, frankly, that's what a PCAOB inspection is all about. So, we need a healthy level of tension out there. I think we're getting closer to that level, but we'll have to keep this dialogue going – because as new problems crop up, we'll probably continue to see new forms of tension.

We're working on developing a permanent broker-dealer inspection program. The Dodd-Frank Act gave us the authority to inspect auditors and audits of SEC-registered brokers and dealers. The Act directs us to determine the scope of the program. And we're taking our time on this. There have been significant adjustments in the industry with broker-dealers and auditors, and we're letting those adjustments happen.

You know, it's just fascinating that many broker-dealer auditors were unaware that they were required to follow the SEC independence rules. I had one auditor in a small business forum stand up and argue with me, and he quoted to me the AICPA independence rules. And the problem was – those weren't the rules he was supposed to be following. So, we've seen some improvement in that space and some auditors of brokers and dealers who have said that they are not going to do that type of audit work anymore.

Some of the small firms were doing the accounting and the auditing and, they had to make a decision as to what to do—the accounting or the auditing, but not both.

Our staff are trying to develop a proposal for a permanent broker-dealer inspection program board action late this year. Again, I think it's okay that we're taking our time here. And, whatever we decide, there will be some political views on that as well.

We're integrating economic analysis into standard-setting, as I mentioned. Chairman Doty established the Center for Economic Analysis where we are bringing in economists and others to help us with this. There was a reorganization between the economists in our Office of Research and Analysis and the Center, and we're still working some things out. We still need to figure out how this is going to work at the PCAOB. But right now, the staff are cranking out the work, but I think we've got more work to do in terms of – how do we best use our research and analysis functions? We'll be working on this going forward – trying to rationalize some of this. But the staff is doing a great job in moving forward on economic analysis.

We've also done a deep dive into the analysis of risks to audit quality presented by the audit firm business model. We're looking at everything from profitability to partner compensation to dilution of the audit business in relation to everything else – and the issuer pay model – all those tensions that put pressure on the auditing business itself that could potentially impact audit quality. We're hoping to publish something on this, but I think it won't be anytime soon. These are sensitive issues, but we we've got research papers that we received from our staff on this, so stay tuned for more from the board on this.

And we're taking a look at the impact of data analytics and big data on the audit. We heard a lot about that this morning, and the real public policy question is – where should regulation and standard-setting come in? We don't want to do anything too early in the process – otherwise, we might stifle innovation. Or, we might simply miss the boat because we don't know enough yet. On the other hand, we need to be ready to go if, in fact, our standards need to be changed. We don't want our current standards to stifle innovation and to prevent new innovative techniques, because maybe a firm would need to do additional work under the old standards in addition to the new, innovative approaches– and do clients want to pay for that? We're trying to be nimble and on top of this so that when the time is appropriate we can jump on this.

So, we're staying in close touch with the firms on these issues. The firms have been very good about sharing with us what's happening. This will be a difficult issue once it hits. And, if we decide we need to have standards in this area because things are changing so quickly in the area of technology – will the standards be outdated before they're out? So, these are important questions that we're going to have to face, and we're also looking at what kind of talent we need to do that.

I mentioned that we just had our Standing Advisory Group Meeting over the last couple of days, and we discussed current and emerging audit issues – and many of these we've already talked about today. But, I'll let you look at the list of items up there.[iv] The one that we haven't talked about is whistle-blower activity. The audit firms and the internal audit community are considering this an area of emerging risk – because whistle-blower activity is increasing as companies are putting in place hotlines and internal communication programs.

And companies are investigating complaints through those mechanisms – often bringing in external law firms to do the investigation. And many of those investigations are done under privilege, so that's impacting the internal audit community, because they're not getting access to the issues under investigation. They're not sure to what extent this is impacting risk that should be included in their risk assessments. For the external auditor – often the internal auditor is concluding on this, and then passing that along to the external auditor. So, certain risks could be masked by the time they get to the external auditor.

The other potential risk is that these investigations take a long time, and if they're ongoing while the audit is underway, and there might be a tendency to say it's not going to be material. Yet, there are still risk factors involved, even if it's not material to the financial statements. So this is something we're monitoring.

We decided that we don't need to do standard-setting efforts on many of these issues right now, but that we need to continue to monitor and stay on top of these things in case we need to put out guidance – or have outreach with firms and audit committees about any of these issues. So, we talked a lot today about the audit of the future. I hope I was able to give you a flavor of what PCAOB is worrying about. I'm happy to take any other questions about any of these or other topics.

Questions and Answers

Anybody worried about the future of the audit? Yes, one right here – okay, yes, go ahead.

Okay, just a quick question on the big data area. To me, it kind-of divides into two parts, and maybe you have an opinion on this. But, one is the – everyone now uses the term one hundred percent sample. You know, you can just go to the database and look at everything. So, is a hundred percent sample considered a sample under the auditing standards which say you have to have a representative sample?

And I looked up – I'll give you the second part so you can answer both together – looked up – you know, the accounting firms not really using the term big data correctly. You know, if they were using it correctly, they would start moving into a lot of non-accounting data.

You know, census data, social media data, and all those kinds of stuff. Now, where's the standards on this – on that area of big data?

Well – it's interesting. This is why we're not in any position to issue standards right now. When people talk about data analytics or big data – they're talking about different things. And so, I think we need to parse out what these different buckets of analysis are that we're talking about. Data analytics is one thing. Big data would apply to something else completely. But let's just talk analytics for a moment. The question is what are you doing in the analysis? And what is being done in the analysis would then determine how the analysis would be characterized as an audit procedure – maybe a risk assessment procedure – or maybe evidence. It depends on what is being done in that procedure. To me, that's the key question.

I don't really buy this hundred percent sampling as being the end-game. I think you always have to do something else besides running a big body of transactions through some procedure that maybe gets you part way there, and maybe it identifies anomalies. It may result in stratifying data and risk – maybe into low risk and high risk categories. I don't think you'll ever get to no risk – and to be able to say – okay, that's a hundred percent audited, so we don't have to do anything else there. And if you're stratifying your risk, and you find the high-risk bucket – well, you're going to have to do – obviously – more work there.

The firms are worried about what happens when that high-risk bucket is too big or too many anomalies are detected through an analytics procedure. Then they're going to have to audit those transactions or do something – and maybe it would have been more efficient to just take a random sample. So there are various dilemmas involved.

And so, I think we need to better define what these data analytics procedures are and how they fit into an audit. And big data is different, and might be more of a generalized risk assessment, but not necessarily an audit risk assessment.

Thank you.

Jeanette, there's two things I'm going to talk about in the next speech that were on your SAG list. And so I'd like to get a little color about the issues that you talked about at that meeting.

Not surprisingly, one of them is the impact of the FASBs which are currently out there as proposals.

And the other's auditor's role in non-GAAP measures.

It was a very interesting meeting, and I think we decided that the PCAOB is going to stay on top of issues related to non-GAAP measures and the new FASB rules, but we're not considering any rule-making anytime soon. And, in fact, the FASB and the SEC are the right parties to deal with this, for now – and the SEC guidance on non-GAAP measures is going to be helpful. I think we're better off waiting to see how the SEC guidance helps to change behavior. Frankly, I think the SEC guidance gives auditors some teeth to go back to the client and say – you better clean this up. And the SEC staff at the SAG Meeting said that companies should begin to self-correct second quarter.

The one potential auditing change that we could consider is to potentially expand the scope of the auditor's read and consider requirement to cover any information that is furnished – but not filed. But, I don't think we're there yet. And then, the other one was the materiality proposal?

Yeah.

We're not thinking about that right now, so – I mean, we're certainly monitoring it, and I'll be curious to hear what you have to say about that.

Alright, yes.

With Tom being here – and I wonder if Tom will be able to talk on the revenue recognition transition – but, the proposal fraud study indicated that, in their sample, sixty percent of the cases that they reviewed, revenue recognition was involved in terms of the financial reporting fraud risk. So, is the PCAOB going to be looking at that very carefully in terms of maybe even issuing a standard dealing with auditing revenue recognition?

We issued a Practice Alert a couple years ago on that, and I think we're in wait and see mode on this. Obviously we'll be monitoring it – a lot of others are monitoring it. Jay Hanson is on the task force that's dealing with this – what's the name of the task force?

The TRG – the Transition Resource Group.

Yes. So, we're staying on top of this – but for the moment, we don't have a standard-setting project in mind. But, this could result in some kind of guidance, if we see immediate practice problems.

I'm just more concerned because auditing a new standard. It's got a lot of expectations that will be happening. And then, with the accounting being so closely correlated with the possibility of fraud – a particular – sort-of – risky kind of area.

Right.

That's why.

I think that's always been the case – and will continue to be the case. And so our Practice Alert talks about the need for high levels of professional skepticism when auditing revenue. And, frankly, I'm hoping that – in the transition – issues with revenue get cleaned up a little bit. So, if there were some shady practices or borderline practices – in the clean-up – that those would go away or be detected at least.

I always found when I was an auditor – anytime standards changed, it gave a really good reason to go do a really deep dive and to clean things up if necessary. And the client would have that leverage to also say – we need resources, we need to change how we're doing things. So there's always something healthy involved in these kinds of transitions and changes – but there's risk as well. We could see new types of fraud emerging. The professional skepticism and the emphasis on management's judgments and estimates – that are going to be involved in the transition to the new revenue standards – are also going to add risk to this area.

Alright, well, hope I gave you a few things to worry about.

I always get into trouble when I bring this up, but – since we have time – the audit standards say that the auditor is supposed to be knowledgeable about GAAP, GAAS, and the client. And I get into trouble when I've mentioned this. I've had senior partners yell at me for bringing this out, but...

What part of that don't they like?

Basically the part about understanding the client.

Well, they, literally, they give me examples like – well I, I audit such and such a company – it's too complicated. Oh my God, you know – you can't say that to me, right? Or, at least, you better not say that publicly. But, so I think going back to the audit quality measures, standards, and stuff – is something needed in this area to kind of – I don't want to use the work mandate, but at least something to look at that particular issue – about understanding the client. Because clients are – even mundane clients – are getting more complicated – just because of the integrated electronics and stuff. So, there's no such thing as a simple big client any more.

Yes. Good audit partners would make the effort to understand the client. There might be some out there that say – oh, this is too complicated for me, I'm not going to bother. Well, they shouldn't be audit partners if that's truly their attitude. The interesting thing on our ICFR findings, the root cause of many of the ICFR findings that we had was that the audit team did not understand the flow of transactions. So, even at that lower level, the teams were not gaining a sufficient understanding of the flow of transactions to understand what were the key controls – and where were the risks were so that they could identify the key controls and then test them properly. So, understanding the client is key to the audit.

Alright well thank you so much. Oh, I've got one more – okay. I think I've got time, right? Yep, one more.

I don't know if you'll be able to answer this, but I was wondering what impact, if any – of the PCAOB's dealing with the public audit company market – what impact that has had on the private company audits?

We do hear about this – from the Chamber of Commerce and others sometimes – that some of the ICFR standards that teams get accustomed to using on public company audits are being followed on a private company as if it was an audit of a public company. So, we hear that does spill over into the private company market. I think that's probably the biggest impact. There's always a dilemma for companies that want to go public – and that is at some point they need to have an audit under the PCAOB standards. And so, sometimes if they wait, they have to go back and do re-work. So, that kind of dilemma exists as well. Those are the areas that I've heard of.

Alright, well, I'm very happy to be here, and I thank you for your attention, and I'll be around for a little while if you have any other questions.

---

[i] Transcription Note: The original transcript has been edited for flow and ease of reading. Any changes to content were not intended to change the overall message associated with the applicable discussion.

[ii] Transcription Note: This refers to the slides associated with the presentation – please refer to those slides.

[iii] Transcription Note: Please refer to endnote ii.

[iv] Transcription Note: Please refer to endnote ii.

Tom Linsmeier[i]

Opening Remarks

Thanks John. Wait to save the clap for until the end – to see if it's worth it. It's a challenge here for a finance reporting person to come and think about getting deeply into auditing considerations. But, frankly speaking, during my time period – almost ten years on the board – auditing has become more and more important to the standard-setting discussions on the financial reporting side. And what I'd like to do today is share with you five of those areas where auditing considerations have come to the floor. That's not the entire list, but it's some of the more interesting items.

And I think it – and perhaps as a result of the creation and existence of the PCAOB – perhaps more interest in documentation of judgments and estimates, concentration and internal controls for financial reporting, and the inspection program – causes people to worry – entities to worry – when they come to implement new financial reporting – what will be the auditing implications of that new effort in financial reporting? So, today, I want to talk about recent financial reporting areas that potentially were influenced by auditing considerations.

First, I'll talk about what some think is a very controversial proposal related to materiality – and hope to indicate to you that there was no intent to be controversial. That doesn't mean that – at times – we have intended to be controversial. The surprise was we had no intent here, and it became controversial. I want to weigh in a little bit about GAAP and non-GAAP presentations – since it seems to be the issue du jour in the papers every day now, and how I think audit committees could – potentially – really think about the presentation and non-GAAP measures. I also want to talk about accounting conventions versus full compliance with GAAP, and the actual movement away from being comfortable with accounting conventions. Some issues that came up with insurance loss development tables, and I'll close with the going concern issue – where there may be disagreement about the threshold between the PCAOB and the FASB.

So, let's start with the materiality and application to disclosure decisions. We've been undertaking since almost 2008, I believe – and we move really fast in FASB-land – to work on a disclosure framework project. Because – and this started with our Investors Technical Advisory Committee. So, it started with the users, who are saying – I pick up financial reports and I can't identify the wheat from the chaff. I'm going to look at three hundred pages of guidance – of reporting – and I don't know what I should be concentrating on, and I've got limited cognitive capabilities, and I'm not going to be able to process everything equal. We need improvement in disclosures to make them more effective.

So, we started out a long process to try to change the disclosure regime related to FASB disclosures – to improve the effectiveness of disclosures. Not – some of the preparer community thinks it's an effort to reduce disclosure overload – that's never been the idea behind the project. It is to make disclosures more effective, and we have two prongs to that approach. One is to improve the board's decision process. When I got to the FASB, disclosures were something we did at the end of a standard-setting project. Oh, by the way, we've got to do disclosures – let's make some up – is almost what the process was. Surprisingly, over the years, there was some consistency in that process – but it was by luck in some way.

And so, we started with the Board's decision process, and the first part of this project was a conceptual framework chapter proposal to more consistently think about how to develop disclosure requirements. That was proposed several years ago, and we're – instead of going final in that – what we did is decide before going final, to apply that decision process to four vexatious and challenging disclosure areas – to see what the implications would be. That's really not of import to this discussion, but it is, in some respects, importance to the controversy. Because, as we applied the disclosure framework to four areas, at least two of them – thought to be having over-disclosure – the outcome of applying the board's decision process was to increase disclosure requirements, not to decrease disclosure requirements – though the controversy is a belief that we're trying to decrease the information available to users in lines in the U.S. market.

The more important part, though, that I want to concentrate on today is the entities' decision process. Where we want entities to appropriately exercise judgment when assessing disclosure requirements. When I vote for a disclosure requirement, I think it may be relevant to entities in the reporting economy. But, perhaps not all entities, because that aspect of the disclosure requirement will not be all that germane to the business activities of some entities relative to others. And materiality is a way that could move forward to say – even though there's a requirement, if it's immaterial – that aspect of the disclosure is immaterial for the entity – they don't need to provide that disclosure. That runs against the checklist mentality that many audit firms have related to disclosure.

We started the entities' decision process by doing a field study to try to understand how materiality was being applied in decisions about what should go into 10-Ks and 10-Qs. And we use the word materiality because that's the word we've always used, but we thought people were – entities might be – having trouble applying that to qualitative disclosure. So, what we did is rewrite it and reframe it – call it entity specific relevance – which was supposed to be the same condition. And what we ended up finding is when people re-did their disclosures, thinking more carefully with a redefined materiality, they reduced and made more effective their disclosures.

But also in the field study was a recognition that even if that is the objective – in making disclosures more effective – there are constraints in the system that make entities not want to streamline disclosures to emphasize the things that are materially most important, and those constraints are audit, regulatory, and legal – all of which introduced some second guessing in the system about decisions entities might make about removing disclosures. And, a belief that sometimes – why bother with that fight? Let's just put it in immaterial things into the financial statements. And so, that's where we started on the entities' decision process – with that concern.

We proposed, recently, changes to the codification to try to address that issue. First, we said if each – before each disclosure area in the standard – say provide the disclosure only to the extent material – to let entities realize that materiality can be applied to each disclosure requirement. Don't think of materiality as – if the event, transaction, or circumstances are material, it gets you into the codification for that particular topic. You got to do everything. That's not what we implied. What we wanted to make sure people understand is – materiality could be applied disclosure by disclosure.

Of course, we made things worse because often – when I started on the board, we started disclosure requirements by saying – this is the objective of the disclosure. In meeting that objective, provide this information, and – oh, by the way – if that doesn't meet the objective, provide more. That's not language that promotes some discretion moving forward, and disclosure requirements were changing that. And then we added guidance – the controversial guidance – in applying materiality.

This is the guidance. This is the first item – it's not controversial – materiality should be applied individually and in the aggregate. You can't just get a pass if individual things are immaterial, but in the aggregate – across the entity's financial statements – becomes material. We said it was a legal concept – that caused some controversy – I'll explain that in a moment. We also said it should be applied equally to both quantitative and qualitative information. And, lastly, where I thought the controversy would be here – but it's not seen so controversial – omission of a disclosure requirement – omission of a disclosure because of its immaterial – is not an error.

Why did we do that last thing? It had to do with auditing, okay? Non-compliance with disclosure requirements that are more than clearly trivial – but are less than financial reporting materiality – are reported to audit committees as an error. Entities generally indicated, as I said before, that they prefer not to have to have that discussion with their audit committee. Don't be questioned on it – let's just do it rather than be questioned on it. In effect, moving materiality from financial reporting materiality to more than clearly trivial, if that were the case. That lowers the threshold, and is a source of potential disclosure ineffectiveness. And so, we proposed that recently.

The bigger issue is – we defined materiality within that proposal, and changed how we defined it – with the interpretation that that change was some nefarious action by the board to try to reduce the material disclosures for users. Not the intent at all. And this slide[ii] helps you to see this going forward. What we had before we changed materiality in 2010 – in Concept Statement 8[iii] – prior to that, materiality in the United States was defined similarly by the US Supreme Court, by us and Concepts Statement number 2, in SAB 99 of the Securities and Exchange Commission, and in AS 14 – all defined similarly.

Our proposal moved away from that – and the reason we moved away from that is – we are trying to converge our conceptual frameworks with the IASB, and we need to concentrate on that change in two big chapters we issued. And just said – well it's easier to go their way and we need to concentrate on it – and we – our belief – put noise in the system. Because our definition of materiality isn't even in the codification – it's in the conceptual framework. It has no authoritative status, okay? So all we're doing is trying to reduce the noise in the system and go back to how materiality is defined and applied throughout the system.

CON 2, SAB 99, AS 14, and the Supreme Court generally – key word on that line – generally – defined material base – materiality – based on whether there is a substantial likelihood that inclusion of the information would make a difference in reasonable users' decisions. What we did in CON 8 in 2010 – was change the threshold to whether there is a reasonable expectation that inclusion of the information could make a difference in reasonable users' decisions – clearly moving from substantial likelihood to reasonable expectation – and from would to could – lowers the threshold.

But, interestingly, if that was going to be controversial – to go backwards – the CON 8 change I said was made to converge with IFRS, and resulted in no observable increase in disclosures in the United States. So, no one was paying attention to that change – particularly in making their disclosure decisions, okay? The recent proposed change to CON 8 that was made to reconcile – I already said that. Then, the language generally conforms with what we said in CON 2, but generally conforms with the rest of the system. So, I wanted to at least give you that explanation if you've been following the controversy, and wondering what those crazy people in Norwalk were doing.

So, here's the feedback that we got on that proposal. An objection – we said materiality was a legal concept. People reacted to say – you're taking accountants out of the system, and lawyers have to be involved in every decision then – if you call it a legal concept. The problem with writing standards in words. What we're trying to say is – and we have no other choice – we wanted to say – materiality is a living concept that can change through the courts, or administrative, or executive action. It's legal. It's living. It's changing. And therefore, we can't lock it down because it will change over time. But people overreacted and said – you're privileging lawyers, you're not saying it's an accounting concept, and you tied it to the U.S. Supreme Court to fix – decision – which is about anti-fraud provisions – without, and that was, again, poor writing on our part – because we were primarily tying it to what is for federal securities laws and decisions by the SEC and for auditing the PCAOB.

Omission not an error – nobody thought that was all that controversial – they thought that was a good thing. Burden of proof – when we said that it had to be that you didn't have to provide it – you had to provide it to the extent it was material – the reaction to that was that means that we have to prove its material before we put it in. That's not the intent. Again, I think we'll change the language – you don't have to put it in if it's immaterial, right? And the definition I already described to you – some would like us to step up and put the definition in the codification – to say that we have the authority to define that in their system. I think that would be just a nicer effort to conform with everybody else's words, but I don't think it will change much of how people apply materiality.

The next steps in this process – project – are to issue Exposure Drafts. Remember, I said in the first phase – the board's decision process – we're applying that process to four areas of disclosure. That's what's listed on this slide.[iv] And defined benefit plan disclosures are criticized as being too voluminous – especially for frozen plans. Fair value measurement disclosures are criticized as being too voluminous, especially if you're not a financial institution. So, we wanted to apply those in those areas, but we also wanted to do it in two areas where there's some criticism that the disclosures were not sufficient. The income taxes disclosures don't tell anything about earnings that are locked up in another foreign country that have difficulty coming back. And interestingly enough, we have little or no inventory disclosures at all.

And so, we've applied that, and we're going to put those out to show people what this process means. The outcome will show there will be more disclosure requirements now, at least. We're going to hold a roundtable to try to quell the controversy in the fall – bringing all these aspects together to see how people – so people understand the implications of the full project. We'll re-deliberate materiality, then decide what it means for interim disclosures – in the United States.

Because what interim disclosures says is – okay, you don't have to – unless specified in the interim disclosure topic – repeat an annual disclosure – unless there's been a material change. And so, we to lock down materiality, and think about whether or not we could remove some disclosures from the list of always having to do it every quarter. If we think change will come forward – through the materiality provision – and we'll keep on moving forward – and in all the aspects – to try to reintroduce better disclosure effectiveness within the system. But auditing considerations clearly affected our conversation in that area.

Let's move to GAAP and non-GAAP presentation. There's a - I wanted to write re-proliferation – I can never say that word – re-proliferation of non-GAAP earnings, but I don't know if that was really a word. Because we had non-GAAP earnings, right? Reg G went out. They went down for a while, and now they're proliferating again, okay?

According to Jack Ciesielski – he's got some very interesting data, if you're interested in this area. He had a two part study called a Non-GAAP Earnings Epidemic.[v] What he's shown is that non-GAAP earnings reports were issued by sixty-seven percent of S&P 500 companies in 2014. He's just issuing a new 2015 report – that percentage goes up.[vi] Note the reported adjustments create a net increase of over twenty percent in non-GAAP earnings when compared to GAAP earnings. And seventy-six percent of the adjustments increased reported results. The question that comes to mind for me is – could this directional bias in the adjustment be related to the fact that non-GAAP earnings are not subject to audit or attestation?

Let's think about and revisit – if I were involved with an entity – I'm going to put myself in the shoes of the audit committee – and I've looked at what Reg G and item 10 says in this regard. What I think audit committees ought to be thinking about in applying the guidance that exists today – because I don't think all of us understand some of the teeth that are in that guidance. But, maybe that was brought up this morning. Reg G requires public companies that disclosed non-GAAP measures to include in that disclosure a presentation with equal prominence of the most directly comparable GAAP financial measure. One thing – got to link it together – and you have to reconcile the non-GAAP measure to the directly comparable GAAP measure. Interesting – Regulation G also requires disclosure of further material information, if any, as may be necessary to make that Non-GAAP measure not misleading.

How can a non-GAAP measure be misleading? It can be misleading either by containing an untrue statement – not probably as likely – but it also can be misleading if a material fact is omitted. And I want to exploit that particular guidance in my evaluation of some common non-GAAP measures in a moment. That's Reg G – people also don't understand there's also an item 10 attached to the Reg G guidance – rulemaking – for both Regulation S-K and Regulation S-B. It prohibits, amongst others, adjusting non-GAAP measures to eliminate – or smooth – identified non-recurring adjustments that are identified as non-recurring, infrequent, or unusual.

If you expect this same thing to occur within the next two years – or the same thing occurred in the past two years – you can't call it infrequent, non-recurring, or unusual – unless it doesn't occur over a four or five year span.

Presenting non-GAAP financial measures on the face of the statement is prohibited; face of GAAP statements or in the notes – is prohibited. And using titles or descriptions for non-GAAP that are confusingly similar to GAAP titles can't be done. But even more importantly, in my evaluation of non-GAAP measures, this – item 10 – requires a statement disclosing why management believes presentation of the non-GAAP measure provides useful information to investors regarding either financial conditions or results of operations – and the justification for the use of the measure must be substantive to provide a non-GAAP measure. That's the framework that exists today. I'm not sure it's being followed.

Here are some examples of issues for audit committees to consider. If the justification for a non-GAAP measure is to provide a cash measure of operating earnings – a common justification – is it misleading to report non-GAAP measures that makes adjustments for only the following three items – depreciation, amortization, and stock-based compensation – a very, very common non-GAAP measure? I would have trouble saying that's not misleading in the following aspects. Are there not other revenues and expenses included in operating earnings this period with the associated cash flows occurring in other than this period? If that were the case, you're not consistently measuring cash operating earnings, and therefore there's an omission of a material fact in meeting what you're justifying.

In addition, if – think about it – we're saying cash operating earnings. Is it believed misleading to report – over time – a measure of cash operating earnings that never deducts amounts for property, plant, and equipment – and intangibles – depreciation and amortization? I would think that's misleading. This is a timing issue – cash preceding the expense amortization, but the measure never deducts the costs of property, plant, and equipment; and intangibles. And finally, if an entity buys back stock this period – which almost all entities paying stock-based compensation do – they don't go and take it out of treasury, because they don't want to dilute their earnings per share. So, what they end up doing is – before they pay the stock-based compensation, they go buy the stock in the market, and then issue it to pay the stock-based compensation. Isn't that equivalent to a cash outlay for that expense? I think that of those decisions could be misleading and evaluated as being inappropriate.

Let's say it's not cash operating earnings that entities are trying to do when adding back depreciation, amortization, and stock-based compensation – what they're trying to get a better measure of operating cash flows – that could be another justification. I don't understand, necessarily, why they would do that. I think there really is an operating cash flow measured in the cash flow statement – but if that's what they're trying to do, let's evaluate that. Is that non-GAAP measure being reconciled? If that's the case, the reconciliation should be from the non-GAAP measure to the operating cash flow measure – not to the operating earnings measure – if that's what they're trying to do. In addition, if the non-GAAP measure closely tracks operating cash flows – again, why then do it twice?

Or an interesting – more interesting – question is – GAAP prohibits a per-share presentation of operating cash flows. But, it's very likely that the non-GAAP measure is being put forth on a per share basis. Is that problematic – relative to GAAP? Finally, to avoid being misleading, if non-recurring expenses or losses are being added back – remember those first statistics – seventy-six percent of the adjustments improve earnings – so it's the expenses or losses that are being added back, not the revenues or gains often being reversed out. So, if expenses or losses are being added back to arrive at our non-GAAP measure of recurring net income, are adjustments being made for all non-recurring items? Or, are only certain expenses and losses being added back?

I would say you could assert – if I was looking at it from an audit committee perspective – that's a misleading set of adjustments if I don't do it for all non-recurring items. And there is guidance within Reg G to say that's a problem, okay? Another interesting question is – are they adding it back net of tax or are they just doing it gross of tax? Because the net income number – if they're trying to come up with a net income equivalent number – is net of tax. But you could inflate the non-GAAP measure by adding it back gross of tax. Those are all interesting things that I would believe a good audit committee should be challenging the entities they're working with in providing non-GAAP measures. And I know that some, high-quality audit committees I'm familiar with are doing just that. But that's an interesting take on that particular issue, or at least I found it that way when I started exploring it this week in developing the materials.

Let's move to a common thing – accounting conventions versus full compliance with GAAP. What do I mean by accounting conventions? Here are some long-standing accounting conventions – accepted in applying U.S. GAAP – a capitalization policy for property, plant, and equipment; and intangibles. Obviously, they exist almost in every entity, right? They take a number and say – if I buy or obtain an intangible below that amount, I don't have to capitalize it – I expense it. That's a quasi-materiality assessment built into an accounting convention. It's acceptable today in U.S. GAAP to report royalty revenue on a one-month lagged basis, because often you don't know what the royalty is going to be in the month – associated with the revenue of that month – until the next month. That's acceptable in applying U.S. GAAP.

Under the equity method of accounting, recently, we just – we discovered that all of us who teach it in intermediate accounting – and you have this basis difference that you have to amortize under the equity method of accounting – many, many entities don't amortize the basis difference. And I think that could be acceptable as an accounting convention – if it was consistent with not making a difference because it's immaterial, okay? Now, over my time period of the board, these are things we've had to put into the literature recently. Why was standard setting rather than accounting convention needed for these three items?[vii]

There's an exception in IFRS 16 – on leases from recognizing in the balance sheet low-value leases. How is that not distant accounting – the capitalization policy applied to leases? Why did the IASB have to write it down? Why did we have to write down the exemption and Topic 606 – that's the new revenue recognition standard – from assessing whether promised goods or services are performance obligations if they're immaterial in the context of the contract with the customer. We are forced to write down to make it work – that if it's immaterial – the performance obligation's immaterial – you don't have to separately account for it. I don't understand why we had to do that.

Well, people who are actually claiming - I think some of this has to do with top technical offices in Big Four accounting firms having fun with us after standards come out – they're claiming if there was a number on this bottle[viii] which you could call in for reporting quality problems – that was a separate performance in settling it off – even though it wasn't – anyone can call in. It's not a commitment under the contract with the customer. Anyone can call in, but we're having that sort of silly conversation in trying to apply Topic 606 moving forward – why?

We had to introduce a practical expedient in Topic 751 that allows an employer with a fiscal year end – other than month end – to measure a defined benefit pension plan's assets and obligations as of the month-end date that is closest to the employer's fiscal year end – an alternative measurement day. Why did we have to write that? Couldn't we just say there's a convention – that if it's close enough and it doesn't matter? It doesn't work.

What's causing this sort of analysis and questions to increasingly be brought forward to the board? Are recent audit considerations that focus on the documentation of judgments and/or adequacy of internal controls creating a demand for changes in how financial reporting guidance is written – rather than relying on accounting conventions that permit non-compliance in material situations? That's an open question – that's not an assertion, okay? Or, is there another reason that's going on? I mean it could be that people resist change, and every time you have to change something, they have parade it as something now new – but some of these things are looking backwards, not brand new things that we're dealing with.

But this makes standard-setting more troublesome, and for me it's troublesome that I have to write – in certain instances – immateriality guidance in part of a standard – isolated – because that immateriality guidance should apply throughout the whole system. Why do I need to write it specifically – in limited places – that might imply it doesn't apply elsewhere? And that does not make sense to me.

We developed insurance loss development tables recently, and – to require for short duration contracts. So, Update 2015-09 disclosure about short duration insurance contracts requires – for annual reporting periods – that an insurance entity disclose, in a tabular format, on discounted information about claims development by accident year – including separate information about incurred claims and allocated expenses, and paid claims and allocated expenses. The loss triangle people talk about in short duration contracts – being very useful. We're putting it into GAAP.

This disclosure should be provided for the number of years for which the claims incurred typically remain outstanding, but – we said – not to exceed ten years. So those – that data – could be 10 years long, plus – in aggregate – for things beyond 10 years. All claims development years should be presented together to best communicate the development trends to users. We had to say that in the standard, okay? What is the auditing consideration that caused us to wait – to delay the issuance of this by over nine months? All periods presented in this disclosure, all claims development that precede the most recent period, shall be considered supplementary information – it took us nine months to come up with this solution to an audit independence problem.

The decision – that decision about calling all the years but the most recent one supplemental – is due to independence concerns that might arise upon changing an auditor. If the new firm had to audit all of the years included in the claims development table – what is that independence issue? It arises if the auditor that wanted to bid on the job was doing consulting for that company in the prior nine years, okay? The board did not prescribe a particular location for presenting the supplementary information – the required supplementary information could be in the note – all put together – but then clearly indicated that nine of the years are supplemental and not subject to audit. Very awkward sort of presentation if you're reading that footnote disclosure – you put in an XBRL or you put into data aggregators – what's going to become of that, alright? The board did not preclude the entire development table from being audited, but there's another auditing consideration that complicated financial reporting standards.

Let's go to the fifth – and most complicated of our decisions – going concern. I started on the board three months after we signed a Memorandum of Understanding with the IASB. One of the silly things on the Memorandum of Understanding was – IASB had going concern guidance for management in IFRS – we didn't have it in U.S. GAAP. We put that down on the short-term list – short-term projects to get done. And it took us nine years to get that darn thing done, right? Why was it controversial? Let's start first – what is the GAAP for the basis of accounting? What does GAAP say about the basis for accounting? Continuation of reporting entity as a going concern is presumed as the basis for preparing financial statements until the entity's liquidation becomes imminent, right? That's GAAP – and we have to write that in the midst of doing going concern – just to make everybody make that clear.

When an entity's liquidation becomes imminent, financial statements are prepared under the liquidation basis of accounting – meaning you record assets to net realizable value and on liabilities at expected settlement amounts, okay? Even if an entity's liquidation is not imminent, of course, there may be conditions or events that raise substantial doubt about the entity's ability to continue as a going concern. In those situations, even when there's substantial doubt – before liquidation is imminent – GAAP says continue the going concern basis of accounting, alright? That's the basis in GAAP.

Let's move to going concern because its – Bill Kinney and Jeanette and I were talking at lunch – this all started in the auditing literature and moved to federal securities laws. It didn't start in financial reporting. So, what do auditing standards and the securities laws say about going concern reporting? They both require that the auditor – not management – the auditor evaluate whether there is substantial doubt about an enemy's ability to continue as a going concern. Now – we're going to different with this in our guidance – for a reasonable period of a time not to exceed one year beyond the date of the financial statements.

So, guess what happens with that rule in the private company community? You don't issue financial statements if there's a going concern problem until it's one year past the financial statement date – and then no one has to do a going concern opinion. But no one gets to see the financial reporting on difficult entities for over a year, okay? So, that's the basic - in both auditing standards and securities laws.

And auditing standards – the standards also require an auditor to consider the possible financial statement effects, including footnote disclosures and uncertainty about entity's ability to continue as a going concern. The auditors have additional responsibilities not just that's in the report, but perhaps causing changes in financial statement amounts, or, at least, in disclosures. The SEC also has guidance on disclosure that it expects from an entity – when an auditor's report includes an explanatory paragraph that reflects substantial doubt about the entity's ability to continue as a going concern. So, the SEC says – auditor moves, entity might have to do something, okay? But, that's the basic going concern guidance for the players in that guidance.

So, after eight years of struggle – and real struggle of the audit community, okay – about what the threshold should be, and whether we're going to cause the demise of very entity in the United States by having management having to do this – and whether management will really ever get involved with doing this. Not recognizing that the auditor – when they're responsible – has to have a relationship with the client in making this evaluation. The Update 2014-15 requires management to assess entities' ability to continue as a going concern by generally incorporating and expanding on certain principles in current auditing literature, okay?

First, we provide a definition of the term substantial doubt – so, the original guidance started in the '80s, and there was no agreement with what the term substantial doubt meant. To my chagrin, our board decided substantial doubt does not arise until it's probable that the entity has an inability to consider – continue – as a going concern. So, about a seventy-five percent level, okay? Not that precise, but about a seventy-five percent level. Academic research had demonstrated that – without defining substantial doubt – there's a wide variety of how its interpreted, in application, in the U.S. markets – but, on average, it's about sixty to sixty-three percent – but it could be as low as fifty, and it could be as high as seventy-five, right? That's where it was, but a lot of noise about what substantial doubt really meant in the system.

We require an evaluation every period that is interim and annual. There's some stuff in three, four, and five[ix] about how you handle if management – once there's substantial doubt – takes action to alleviate it – what it means in the disclosure. And if they take actions and still alleviate it – what it means in the disclosure. But more importantly – the last thing number six – we're requiring an assessment for a period one year after the date the financial statements are issued or available to be issued. So, it's not the financial statement date anymore – whenever you wish to do financial statements, it's got to be for the next year. So playing the game of the delays is not going to work anymore, because you're still going to have to make the assessment when you issue financial statements.

I dissented to this decision, okay, and I'm going to give you two primary reasons I did. First, requiring management to disclose when it had substantial doubt about the entity's ability to continue as a going concern – to me and to my fellow board members in the concept statement on note disclosures – are outside of scope of what should be announced in financial statements. Let me elaborate. Instead, future-oriented disclosures about an entity's overall ability to continue as a going concern, from my point of view, should be required and remain in SEC filings as a part of management's discussion and analysis – primarily because that allows us to be subject to, say, harder forward-looking information. You put that information in the financial statements and the safe-harbor goes away – which I think is a huge constraint. With this view is also consistent with what I described as the Board's decision process for financial statements – what you are going to disclose in your financial statements.

We had to decide what the scope is. Where is the FASB's boundary for disclosures, and when do we move outside that boundary for the SEC? And a lot of people will say it's been caught – forward-looking information should be the division. That's a vacuous statement, because everything we do in financial statement measures has embedded in it forward-looking information, okay? So, our decision was – it's okay to disclose forward-looking information within GAAP reports if that forward-looking information is embedded within measures or in the notes within the financial reports. If it's outside that, it shouldn't be in financial reports, and should be in the SEC's purview. So, we decided that – or proposed within the document – and then, as a board, chose to ignore it when we finalized the going concern issue.

Second, require disclosure only when it's probable – that high of a threshold will provide information about going concern's uncertainties that is too late to be of significant benefit to users. All the users told us that – at probable – they've already known there's a going concern problem. This is after the fact reporting when you wait that long – making the disclosure at best confirmatory, and having little or no predictive value. So, I thought we should be emphasizing ways to get – within financial reporting – knowledge that there's a problem about the going concern, and how you might think about it within the financial reports, okay? So, any disclosure about financial reporting implications of a going concern – not that it's a going concern for financial reporting implications.

To me, at minimum, should be at a threshold of more likely than not – greater than fifty percent – or, more tied to the SEC's threshold – reasonably likely. Now, somehow reasonably likely in words is interpreted as like thirty percent – I don't know how we get these numbers with these words, but that's how it's interpreted within our system. The PCAOB seems to have similar concerns – or at least is struggling with some concerns – about what the threshold should be, and whether it should be changed. The Practice Alert that they put out – the PCAOB put out – said continue doing and following the auditor literature guidance – which does not define substantial doubt. And it – it doesn't define substantial doubt – it's not like it's an improbable – it could be that they'll be – the auditors would be – making the call before management makes the call. I don't know that that's fully resolved, but that's a possibility.

What's my conclusions of this journey of five auditing issues - auditing considerations - that affect financial reporting? During my time at the FASB, auditing considerations have had increased importance to both financial reporting and standard-setting decisions. This might suggest that the FASB be U.S. auditing standard setters – not just the PCAOB – but the AICPA's Auditing Standards Board should explore mechanisms for promoting consistent consideration of auditing issues in our standard-setting activities, and facilitate more timely discussion so we do not find ourselves in disagreement with each other as we move forward in the system. I've often, at – I was on the Standing Advisory Group of the PCAOB for a period of time – and I asked regularly that we talk more closely as we make decisions, not after it's done.

And, I think that would be something that would be very useful to go forward, because I do not think auditing considerations – and their effect on financial reporting standards-setting – is going to go down.

The auditing considerations and their importance are going to go up, and I think we have to find a way to do it consistently. Interestingly, we just put up – we will be putting out next month our final credit loss – expected credit loss model – which will require, by issuance year, underwriting standards for five years going backwards through time – of credit risk exposure over each of the five years by year of issuance of asset. No discussion was had as to whether we ought to be worried about auditing issues and independence problems with auditors in that particular disclosure. The two, I think, the system – one of the things that the system – that the CIFR[x] Committee on Users said – is we needed coordination between all the players in the system to develop consistency in how we think about things. I think we've had a lost opportunity about not doing it, as well.

Happy that take some questions.

Questions and Answers
Yes.

What was the final vote count on the going concern?

Five – two.

Five – two – okay.

Larry Smith and I declined to vote for it.

Tom?

Yes.

I think what you concluded is actually very significant. Because in 1999, I was a member of the AICPA's financial taskforce in the aftermath of FAS 133 – accounting guidance for hedges – and I was actually appalled at the lack of coordination – the lack of conversations – between the FASB and the, then, AICPA's Auditing Standards Board. So now, what I'm hearing from you is – whereas some of these things have come to a head, that you cannot avoid talking to each other, which I think is a good thing.

And to be fair, we do talk to each other on a quarterly basis. Some of our board members and staff talk to the chief auditor and his staff on a quarterly basis. So, it's not like we're not doing it all the time. But I'm suggesting that we do – have some advantage to do it more deeply.

And I just want to comment that the SEC oversees this process now. I think especially since the going concern opinion issue happened. And, that – the going concern reporting – was kind-of an odd one as well. Because the final rule was much different than what, I guess, what we were seeing coming down the pipe. And so, that's, I hope, an anomaly – we're in a complicated spot right now.

Yeah, I agree – that why I dissented.

Yes.

The field study that you mentioned during the materiality discussion – is that something that's publicly available?

I don't know the answer to that. The person you should contact at the FASB is Nick Cappiello.

Okay.

He is the project manager on the disclosure framework project. He will be very happy to receive any contact from you, and he will give you the appropriate answer – then I will.

Alright.

Because I'll make it up.

Tom.

So, I read an article not that long ago talking about how going concerns were not very informative, and I believe there's at least one faculty member in the room that has a paper that suggests that they are not very informative now. But now we have what appears to be an inconsistency between the reporting it by management at 75%, and the substantial doubt of the auditor – so, what are we to conclude if we get this conflict?

Should we, I mean, this also follows up on the idea that if we get consecutive going concerns – which are also, sort-of, not really informative – so is this conflict – are we going to not see any more consecutive going concerns if management finally pulls the trigger and says – oh, we have a problem – but it's too late to do anything about it?

Well – what Jeanette just said – we put them in a tough position. Now they've got to decide whether they conform to our threshold level of probable in our definition of substantial doubt, or keep some differences within the system. And, that's their struggle. I would suggest that moving up from substantial doubt will define between being between fifty and seventy-five percent – average sixty to sixty-three – to seventy-five percent within the financial statements – we're making going concern statements less useful.

And we've published some data out on this as well, and there's a difference between large companies and small companies on this reporting rate. So, at a small company level, there is a higher incidence of that. At the larger company level, it's actually under-reporting rather than over-reporting on going concerns. So, it does depend on company size.

Yes.

I have some questions. First, why did the FASB decide to use the phrasing substantial doubt – couldn't they have come up with some other wording so that there wasn't a conflict with auditing standards?

Well, all along, we didn't think we'd end up conflicting with auditing standards. So, we were dancing together, believing maybe we could both come to a conclusion that we liked. And that's right, because what we were saying before we went final – perhaps would have come to a threshold for substantial doubt that was less than probable.

Yeah, that was actually my second question - was to follow-up on Jeanette's point - is did you - I like the – not that it matters what I like – I like the early warning that you had in the Exposure Release, or whatever you call it. And then, that kind of went away. I'm wondering, do you have any insights on why that was decided – why it was decided to get rid of that? Because, that would have given investors, obviously, earlier warning.

We were so naive – we added this, because we thought we'd just copy what the IASB did, and just print it out. I will tell you that the reaction to making these calls by either auditors or management is stepping on the third rail. And since we're involved with both, it was like standing on to two third rails, okay? And so, the resistance to the whole thing was amazing through the process. Because they were also concerned about self-fulfilling prophecies. We're going to destroy businesses in the United States. Can management really make the decision as if the auditor is not involving the management in the decision? Is it as it is now? I mean, it would – the hyperbole in the comment letters was at a high level. By the way, I didn't say the disclaimer at the first – I just said that I disclaim.

Yes, Bill.

This issue's a long-standing issue, as you know. In the early eighties, there was concern by the people – this, Bernie Sanders, the people, the masses – wondered why nobody told them the company was about to go bust. Surely the auditor knew it, surely the company knew it, and the auditors had taken it up because – even though they thought that management – around this, I guess one more question. Getting up – because you have strong views here, obviously – and in your heart of hearts, do you think that the management of the company has an obligation to tell stockholders that we may not be able to pay our bills for the next twelve months or not?

And, if not, then do you think – well, answer that first one, could you please. Because if it's not management's responsibility, then I can reconcile myself just to get my position. I found I reconciled myself to the idea that management was very difficult to predict their own demise...

Right.

...but the subject – the going concern paragraph says that the auditor now believes that his or her client is likely – more likely than not – to go bust in the next twelve months, and that seems to be information. If it doesn't have a going concern paragraph, then you should be able to

sleep well at night. And no matter how bad the numbers look, the auditor doesn't yet think – or at least is not yet feel compelled – to say the company is going to go bust within twelve months.

So, I think that you're hitting on some of what was the controversy – actually having to predict potential demise rather than saying something less so – is something that both auditors and management are not very comfortable with. But more so, they have a great deal of discomfort about having hindsight bias in evaluating – when they didn't do it – and the company went under. Because some companies go under – like that. Very quickly, and has a legitimate explanation for how it can happen very rapidly; or other ones could be a long build-up over time. So, in hindsight bias, company goes under, you didn't make the call, and I think that implies that you should have been able to see it.

That was a lot of the noise and concern – not noise – legitimate concern in the system in making that call. I skipped over one of my slides of what my preference would be. I think that management should have to make a call that – there, substantial doubt will remain. But I also don't think, in a going concern accounting model, when there is substantial doubt you ought to be able to say – I'm amortizing my property, plant, and equipment over twenty years, or depreciating or amortizing it. I think you, at least, in the accounting policy footnote should say – we're following the going concern basis because it's GAAP. If we last that long, it's going to be – we expect this asset to last twenty years – but there are issues here of the quality of this estimate, because of other factors that exist with the company.

So you tie it back to the accounting and not failure in prediction per se.

That's right.

A consistent man – good.

Thank you very much.

---

[i] Transcription Note: The original transcript has been edited for flow and ease of reading. Any changes to content were not intended to change the overall message associated with the applicable discussion.

[ii] Transcription Note: Please refer to the slides associated with this presentation, which are also included in the web-site where this document was located.

[iii] Transcription Note: Specific references to regulatory items have not been specifically cross-referenced to an applicable reference, but those should be available publicly from the applicable regulatory body. While this endnote is only included here (as there are a significant amount of references) – for reference, it applies to all applicable transcripts from the symposium.

[iv] Transcription Note: Please refer to endnote ii.

[v] While it appears this information can only be purchased or accessible if a client of the service, it appears to originate from a research service noted as "The Analyst's Accounting Observer" (at the following web-site - http://accountingobserver.com/) – and part one of this study is called "Volume 24, No. 9: Where It Lives In The S&P 500: The Non-GAAP Earnings Epidemic, Part 1" and can be obtained at the following web-site - http://accountingobserver.com/product/volume-24-no-9/; while part two of this study is called "Volume 24, No. 10: The Non-GAAP Earnings Epidemic, Part 2" and can be obtained at the following web-site - http://accountingobserver.com/product/volume-24-no-10/.

[vi] Again, it appears that the information can only be obtained by purchasing it or being a client of the service, but the subsequent reports are the following (with the web-sites following): Volume 25, No. 4: Wonder Bread: Non-GAAP Earnings Keep Rising in the S&P 500 (http://accountingobserver.com/product/volume-25-no-4-wonder-

bread-non-gaap-earnings-keep-rising-sp-500/); Volume 25, No. 5: Wonder Bread: Non-GAAP Earnings Keep Rising in the S&P 500, Part II (http://accountingobserver.com/product/volume-25-no-5-wonder-bread-non-gaap-earnings-keep-rising-sp-500-part-ii/).

[vii] Transcription Note: Please refer to endnote ii.

[viii] Transcription Note: If the memory of the transcriber is correct, the presenter was referring to a beverage bottle in this case.

[ix] Transcription Note: The references to numbers in this paragraph appear to be referring to the slides associated with the presentation. Please see endnote ii.

[x] Transcription Note: This appears to refer to the work of the SEC's Advisory Committee on Improvements to Financial Reporting – a related website is the following - https://www.sec.gov/about/offices/oca/acifr.shtml.

Beverley Bahlmann[i]

Opening Remarks[ii]

So, first of all, we always work in the public interest. So, we have a due process, we have our mandates, and everything that we do is always in the public interest. We have a large range of stakeholders and set standards for the world. Also, there's lots of jurisdictions – lots of rules and laws and regulations. So, when we are looking at standards – it's not just one jurisdiction and one set of rules and regulations. So, it makes it a little harder for us. We do try and keep them principle-based for that – so that they can be applied to large range of circumstances. But, we've done a lot of work to try and identify what the key public-interest issues are.

And probably at the top of that – is fostering a perfectly independent and challenging skeptical mindset – and which will help the auditor to be a kind of critical challenger. And, as you'll see, we have a big project out on professional skepticism, and I'll talk about that a little bit in a while. And that project cuts across a lot of other work that we do as well. Now, as we all know, professional skepticism isn't something that we can write into the standards – there's lots of different facets to it. And before we actually start standard-setting in that area, we want to think a little bit more about how we can try to help the auditors to be more, particularly, challenging. And as we do, we believe that that is one of the areas that will improve or enhance audit quality.

We're looking at things like documentation. So, as we go through all of our changes, we gather information about what needs to be documented to gain or enhance audit quality. Very important – we are looking at keeping our eyes on this – it's precious. There's an evolving environment where the way businesses are run, where the way audits are put together – it's all changing. And the standards need to be flexible to be able to be applied to all the different circumstances. So, we going through and thinking about the exact dates – and I'll talk about that again a little bit later.

We are looking at transparency, and there's a lot of talking – there's a lot of jurisdictions around the world that are requiring more around transparency. We've just finished our audit reporting standard, which will come into effect at the end of this year – a little ahead of the PCAOB – and one of the things which has come out of that was a little more transparency into the audit. But then, there are other things around transparency as well that we are looking at on the contract side – on the audit firm side. So, in some jurisdictions there is a requirement now for transparent reporting – certain things that need to be reported. And, with a little role in the standards for us to put something in the standards related to transparency.

And we're focusing on the firms and the quality control at the firm level. We are looking again at our quality control standards – and that includes networks. So, there's lots of different arrangements out there with regards to the different types of networks that you get. So, again, very hard for us to write something very specific in the standards. But, we are thinking about what can be done, and for the way that firms can be better off. We've looked at monitoring and remediation. Obviously, very important to the regulators, and I'll talk about that in a bit. And then, reinforcing the need for relevant communications.

So, those are the areas we sort of identified as our public interest issues, and they cut across all of the projects. So, each one that we talk about and think about – we are thinking about all of those to make sure that those are embedded in the work that we do.

So, in moving on to – how we got to where we got to. We've done lots of work to try and identify areas where we need to focus our resources. And we differ from the PCAOB – so we have a voluntary board. And so, it's made up of 18 volunteers – except for a full-time chairman – and we meet four times as year – for five days. So, we have limited time to be able to discuss these issues. We work in project groups, and the board members – and we bring in specialists as necessary. And, as we go through, I'll talk a little bit about how the PCAOB is involved with some of those project groups as well. And that's – we do have limited capacity as to what we can do, so we are very careful of what we take on. And we did a lot of work to try and determine what it is that we needed to do.

So, in 2009, we finished what we called the clarity projects. We re-wrote all of the ISAs – we re-structured them. Some of them were bigger revisions than others. For example, the standard on group audits was a much bigger revision than some of the others – they were just refinements and enhancements in those standards. But we did agree to do a first implementation – of which we did carry out – in 2012 and 2013. And we said – our objectives met – all of the changes that we've made – are the standards being consistently applied and implemented? And people – a lot of people – write to us and said – this is all fine. The standards aren't broken, but these are the areas that you need to think about again, and that's what's resulted in the projects which we have up there[iii] – as well as doing lots of outreach.

So, our chairman and our board members go around the world speaking to people about where there are areas that we actually do need to pay attention to. And, we then put together a strategy, and, again, consulted on this. We said – we think these things are a good idea to task – do you agree? People said yes, but I can also think about some other areas. And we came out with six projects that we think are our priority for the next, probably, five years – relating to standard-setting, relating to the ISAs. So, we have professional skepticism, quality control, and group audits, and I'm going to talk about those in a little bit in more detail, because those are the ones we've been consulting on recently, and those'll result in standard-sitting in the very near future.

At the same time, we recognized that there was work to be done financial institutions. The IASB had released IFRS 9 on financial instruments, and the auditing standards are a little bit behind being able to be used in relation to IFRS 9. So, we embarked on a project to look at our standards on auditing fair values and estimates, and we've accelerated the work in that area, and hopefully we'll have the Exposure Draft on that out by the end of the year. So, making some refinements related to IFRS 9, and some other issues that we've identified relating to auditing fair values and accounting estimates.

Audit data analytics – it's a big topic. Every time we listen to anything anywhere – there's always a lot of talk, and I'm sure you've probably spoken about it a bit at this conference. And, it's very important. The standards have been a little bit left behind with regard to data analytics. They still can be used, but at the PCAOB SAG, this week, there was the comment on – that perhaps an audit is done using the auditing standards and then the other work is probably done using data analytics – and it's not really right. It should really be combined. So, we are thinking about how we can build data analytics into the audit, and we think a little bit more about how we actually going to get that work done.

And then, ISA 315 – which is the risk standard – so, how we identify risks and how we address those risks. Again, there was some significant issues that were identified in that standard, and we are trying to go through them, and then also draw some of the work that we are doing on some of our other projects. So, the way to identify risks, obviously, affects the work that's going to be done on the auditing fair values and estimates. So, some of the work has to be done before some of the other work can be done. So, we're sort of trying to run these projects in tandem. So, those are the major projects that are in our agenda at the moment. And there are some others, and I'll talk about those yet.

Well, first talk a little bit about our ITC[iv], and we'll start with professional skepticism. So, our invitation to comment closed on Monday, and we've probably gotten about 70 responses. A lot of our responses have only kept on professional skepticism. There's a very big interest in this topic, and it cuts across various areas, and so it's not only audit that gets impacted by it. So, we also are looking at it from an ethical standpoint, and from an educational standpoint. Because we have recognized that it's a more realistic solution to try and get people to think more skeptically. We can write in the standards a hundred times – it's not necessarily going to change behavior – because it's about behavior.

So, the professional skepticism project is probably a little bit behind some of the other projects in that we've got more thinking to do before we actually decide what it is that the appropriate actions are to address the issues that have been identified. And so, we have established a direct working group, and the working group consists of two people from audit, two people from education, two people from the ethics side – and they will work together to try and work out what it is. And, it's not necessarily standing-setting. It may be others that may be needed to actually put into action some of the responses that they decide need to be done.

This is an area where we are going to be looking at a lot of academic research, and I'm sure that there is a lot of academic research on the topic. So, if there is anything that you think may be of interest to us – we'd love to hear about it. I've got some – oh, sorry, let me change the slide[v] – and so, moving down the slide – on the right hand side – we have had some discussions about professional skepticism, and we think that it's an attitude. It's affected by professional judgment – so we're not going to be doing a project on professional judgment necessarily. It will link in – embedded – in the way that it impacts on professional skepticism.

So, we're not going to do a professional judgment framework – we're just going to think about it in the context of professional skepticism. And then, again, thinking about how this can all be documented and demonstrated. So, that's what the regulators are looking for – that's what audit quality is looking for – is how we can demonstrate that professional skepticism. So, it our invitation to comment, we did ask some questions about professional skepticism, and there were two parts to the invitation to comment. There was an overview document – which is very high level – intended for investors, for those charged in governance – people who didn't want to read the detail of what it said in ISA blah, blah, blah. So, the questions that I've got up here[vi] are the ones that are from that overview document.

You go into the more detailed document – which is a very long document – it's about a hundred pages – there is a lot more detailed comments on each of these topics. So, with regard to professional skepticism – and we're looking at the definition because there's not a common definition of professional skepticism across the auditing standards and the ethical standards and education standards.

So, again, it's quite a hard thing to look at – to try and get everyone in common agreement with what the defined understanding is of what it means. We're looking at what the drivers and the impediments are, and then we're looking at whether there's others that should be taking action. And not that we would necessarily be responsible for that, but we could try to drive to take action as well. If everyone worked together, we could get people to have some – be more professionally skeptical and demonstrate that in the audits that they undertake. And I do believe that will then help us to enhance audit quality.

And the second topic that is in our ITC is quality control. So, in quality control, we're looking in particular – so we have a quality control standard which sits above all other standards. So, it applies to all of our audit and our assurance engagements – it's called ISQC 1 – it's a quality control framework for all audit and other assurance engagements – and we're considering how ISQC 1 can help – first, design more effective systems of quality control that are perfect for the lines of financial services that they provide and the associated risks that they have.

So, we're looking at, in particular, things like firm governance and the tone at the top. And, we've done a lot of outreach and our invitation to comment. And we've had a lot of coming about through governance and tone and the top – and also how that drives down to tone at the middle – making sure that the quantity comes all the way down – and then, obviously, down to the engagement level. And, so we're looking at how the quality control system can be adaptable to the rapidly changing business environment. So, the firms are changing the way that they do audits. So, what used to be a very traditional structure – now they're looking at different ways of doing audits. There's shared service centers offshore and onshore and those kinds of things. So, how does quality control work in all of those circumstances? So, we need to write a standard that can apply in these various circumstances – and, again, with the changing circumstances.

So, we've come up with what we think is adding – at the very beginning – a new sort of approach to quality control – we call it the quality management system – or the QMA – and we haven't done a lot of thinking on this. We wanted to get some views before we go too far down the path of developing anything. We wanted to see whether the people did have an appetite for something that was more adaptable. We do believe it will probably be a little more scalable.

So, one of the issues that we often have on our quality control standard is for SMPs.[vii] And they say – well, it's kind of hard to use for SMPs, because it's quite structured the way it's written now – where it – if it's – enter all the risks of that particular firm, it's most likely going to be more scalable. So, we're looking for views, and from what we've heard so far about whether to continue exploring down this path or not – and it's very mixed reactions. People will think – well, it's probably a good idea to think a little more about it, but we don't know what it looks like so we can't really give much comment – which is a fair comment. And so, we are trying to do a little bit more work about what it, perhaps, could look like – and then we'll probably look for more views on that.

So, the way that the quality management approach would be is that you would set-up quality objectives. So, taking a look into the circle that's up there[viii] – you would perform your quality risk assessment; you'd design and implement processes and address those risks; you would then look at the quality control activities; in four, we'd look at the communicating and documenting all of those; and then you would monitor it – very importantly. And, it's a continuous circle because – when you want to try it, and you find something that's wrong, then you go back to the start of the circle. And so, you carry on going around. This is all, obviously, overarched by the leadership responsibilities and accountabilities – their firm governance at the – or the tone at the top. So, we are looking at restructuring our quality control standards, and, obviously, that will have enough of an effect into a lot of the other standards as well – particularly, the quality control at the engagement level. So, we'll see what needs to be done there.

Regardless of if we go down the quality management approach, we – if we did go down that – which we're not going to lose any of our time or talents. We do think that it still gives a good base of policies and procedures and controls with quality control at the firm level. And, in fact, it actually provides a way for us to actually look a little bit more.

And we've been looked at – asked to look at – the role and responsibilities of the engagement partner. Is there enough in the standards to be able to drive the engagement partner to do what he needs to do – he or she needs to do – on the audit? That also then runs into the responsibilities in a group audit situation. So, there's a lot of different circumstances where, for example, work may be done in one location, the engagement partner may be situated somewhere else – sometimes they call it the litter box situation – and there's nothing in the standards that says – is it okay? Is it not okay? So, we can try and be – sort-of, clarify what the responsibilities of the engagement partner are – and that's also for group audit situations.

As I said earlier, we are going to be looking at transparency reporting, and whether we should be putting something into the standards for transparency reporting. Bear in mind, that a lot of jurisdictions don't actually have a requirement yet. We're looking at the impact on audit quality of these evolving audit delivery models. We call them audit delivery models – I'm talking about onshore, offshore, shared service centers – so, how do you ensure that the quality control of people that are doing work for your audit is what you need them to be – for your auditor to be able to sign-off.

When I was listening to the PCAOB SAG – their new proposals on other auditors – they also state to consider how quality controls are impacted there – and they're a little bit more definitive about what forms part of the engagement team, and who's not a part of the engagement team, and who's considered other auditors – and they give it a little more balance. So, we'll probably note very carefully at what their proposals are so that we're not too much out of sync with them. And, we're looking at other auditors that are not component auditors. You might have a situation – where it's not in a very important situation – but for some reason you're using another auditor. Again, there's no guidance in the standards that tells you what to do, so we are considering whether we need to put something in for other auditors.

We're looking at networks, and, again, at the PCAOB SAG, the question was asked about – how the reliance on the quality control procedures and policies of network firms is impacted at the firm level – or the individual firm level. But I think I have – just a quality control situation and a group audit situation where you're placing reliance on somebody else's policies and procedures. What do you need to do in relation to that? And, does it make a difference if it is part of your network or another network firm? And as I said earlier, the networks are all structured very differently. Some of them are much more integrated. Some of them are just associations of firms. So, we need to be able to distinguish in the standards between these different situations, and what reliance can actually be placed on those policies and procedures.

Monitoring and remediation – very much a hot topic for the regulators. They want the firms themselves to try and monitor – look at the policies and procedures, find where the gaps are, and then remediate then. And so, the process goes on. And we do think that the QMA will help with that process, and, in particular, if there, it will be a lot more documented. An engagement quality control review – so in the U.S., you have a separate standard for the engagement quality control review. In the ISAs, they are embedded within the standards – so we've asked the question – should we have a separate standard to focus people on it? But people are asking for more from an engagement quality control reviewer. Who that person actually is? What do they actually do? And, what the function is? But, at the same time, you need to always maintain the balance between the EQCR and the engagement partner. We wouldn't want the balance to go out.

So, if we do strengthen the requirements for the EQCR, we do need to think about what the engagement partners themselves do. So, as we're going through this, it's also iterative. As we think through one thing, that may impact something else, and we may need to put in some more requirements. So, those are the major topics that we're looking at in quality control. There's some various other words, but – human resources and whether you can link the newer generation with audit quality or not – those kinds of things. So there are a couple of other, sort of, lesser ones. I haven't noted them up there, but they are detailed in the ITC.

We just asked some questions – I'm not going to go through them. Those are just some questions about the QMA and then the audit quality control standards – and in all the questions that we ask, we ask – is there anything else that we've missed? So, while we are opening up the standard, if there is something in there that we haven't actually noted, we'd like to hear about it. Because once you opened it up and we've done our work, it's going to be quite a while until we open it up again. So, we want to do as much as we can.

And then the last topic that was in our ITC is group audits – which, group audits was a standard that was brought in in 2009. It was one of the bigger revisions in the clarity project. It went through three different exposures – so just a very difficult standard to write. And I think it has improved the audit quality – quite a lot – in group audits, but there are still are some problems in it. It's quite definitive about definitions and what you call a component and what isn't a component, what's a significant component and what isn't. So, it's not very flexible – and, in particular, today with evolving practice and the big complex ones – they find it quite difficult to apply the standard down to some of these.

So, we're trying to think about having more of a top-down approach to assessing the risks within the group, and making it easier to be able to apply the standard to the various different kinds of structures that we are looking at. Sorry, so that's the top-down approach. And we're also looking at, as I said, at the roles and responsibilities of the group engagement partner – but also the group engagement team – to try and, again, very similar to what the PCAOB's doing, we're trying to gain a draft – the engagement team – to be more involved in the audit, and to drive the risk assessments off, and to do more evaluation of the work that the component auditor has done.

We're going to be looking at things like acceptance of the group audit. Again, there's access issues – there's access issues everywhere in the world for various different reasons. Probably the most obvious examples are in equity and accounting investment, where you may have access issues. And in that case, we are considering which – it hasn't – there's not a lot of appetite in the responses I've seen so far. But we are considering, like the PCAOB, to be able to make reference to another order in an auditor's report. So we don't have that in our current standards, but we are thinking – or we have asked – whether the people do have appetite for it. But, it's coming back as people not really wanting us to open that up. When accepting a group audit – there's been questions about how far you need to go to be able to understand the group, and then, obviously, audit them – and pass in certain circumstances – not even accepting it.

On the real acceptance side, we need to start thinking about mandatory rotation. So, there's various jurisdictions in the world that have now mandatory rotation, and, again, that is also impacting the way that group audits are carried out – around replacing your component auditors, etc. – so you want to start thinking about what we can build in – trying to make sure that there is audit quality in the group audits.

Materiality – so we're not actually starting a project on materiality. We'll think about whether we can do a little bit of guidance on component materiality. It's very inconsistently used – inconsistently understood. At some point in time, we will start a project into materiality in the very near future. We are waiting for the IASB – who's doing some work on materiality. Once they have progressed their work sufficiently, we'll start thinking about what we can do on materiality. It's a standard that comes up with all of our projects, and it's a standard that comes up as problematic. But, we don't want to do work before the accounting standard setters themselves have actually done work in that area. Otherwise, it's – we might need to go back and make changes at a later point in time.

We're thinking about work on components that are not significant. So, we've got lots in the standard about this component is significant, you to do all of these procedures – so we depart happy. But very often, there's lots of other components which are not significant – which if you add them all up, they may still be a material number. So, we want to think about a bit more guidance around those situations – and what you actually do on those other components. And there could also be some structures as well where there are no significant components – they're all non-significant, and, again, the standard doesn't give you a lot of guidance as to how you would bridge those situations. So, we will be doing a little more about that.

We're thinking about what we need to do on consolidation procedures – and there's not a lot in the standard as to how far you go on consolidation procedures. So – some of these really big complex groups have several layers of consolidation. So, as the group auditors are at the top, how far down do you actually need to go? How much reliance can you place on the work that's done on the sub-consolidations? So, we're having a look at that.

At least the – probably one of the most important things in a group audit is the two-way communications. So, we are trying to think about how we can enhance the two-way communication so that there's proper instruction going from the group auditor to the component auditor, and there's proper feedback coming back from the component auditor to the group auditor. And, on the other side of it, we're thinking about the component auditors themselves – whether we need to have something in place for them. It's a little bit more difficult to put requirements and guidance for the component auditors, but they have no guidance at the moment.

So we often get the comment that – a big company is audited by a Big Four auditing firm, and they – a tiny little company situated, say, in Australia – and they get the same instructions as some big subsidiary in the U.S. – and a lot of it's just not applicable, and I have to do a lot of extra work. So, how do they push back – there is no guidance for the component auditors themselves. So we'll be thinking about – either it will go into the group audit standard or whether we actually need a separate standard for requirements and guidance for the component auditors themselves. And then, that was actually asked at the PCAOB SAG this week as well. Somebody asked – what about giving some guidance for component auditors? So, obviously, they'll start thinking about it as well.

And then, just under group audits, questions – again, I'm not going to run through them as they're very general questions. Currently there's about a hundred questions if you take all the sub-questions that we have. So, there's a real lot of technical detail in the group auditing standard, and most people are trying to avoid the group audit – because it's very technical. But, we have gotten back some feedback so far from some of the firms and some others.

We also ask some general questions just around our public-interest issues – and whether people feel that we have the right things to do. We have asked if anything else that people think we should be doing, and I'll talk a little bit about how we'll do a consultation on our future work at the end of this year – but we did ask the question anyway. So, ignoring all these topics that are in the ITC, is there anything else that you think that we really should really be working on? So, if anyone's got anything to add, then we'd like to hear about it. And then, and very importantly, and this obviously affects most of the people in this room, if published, planned, or unwritten research that is related to the topics that we've been talking about. So, it's very helpful for us to know what's out there, and because, then we can have a look –often we can refer to that. So, it's very helpful when we're setting our standards.

So, it closed on the sixteenth of May. So, the consultation – we are still taking responses for another two or three weeks. So, if you do you feel like there's something you feel strongly you want to write to us about, we'd are happy to listen. We take – obviously, read all the responses that come in, and it helps us to having informed opinion and informed discussion at the board level. So, from now until December, we'll be analyzing the comments. We'll discuss those with our board and our Consultative Advisory Group - which is very much like the PCAOB SAG.

In December 2016, we'll be looking at project proposals to start studying standards for quality control and group audits; however, at the end of 2017 or 2018 having Exposure Drafts for changes after those standards. Again, it depends on what work is done on ISA 315 and 540, we may have to slow things down in order for some of that work to be done first. And, with regard to professional skepticism, towards the end of the year, and I'll have big discussions about what they think the appropriate way for it is. There may be some standard-setting, but, most likely, the biggest response won't be standard-setting. We'll be thinking about what we can actually do to address some of the issues relating to professional skepticism.

And then, just some of the other work that we're doing. First of all, auditor reporting. So, your PCAOB here have just recently provided their revised auditor reporting proposal. Our auditor reporting standards came out about 18 months ago. They are effective for years ending after – for periods ending after – December 15th of this year.

So people have been doing dry runs – actually there's some countries in Africa – that the whole country had to do a dry run – a list of companies and what they deemed to be public-interest entities – had to do a dry run. And, it's a good learning, and we're getting common messages of the areas where people are finding it lacking and where they're finding it good.

And so, generally the feedback has been positive, and there's much more communication between those charged with governance and the auditors. People are thinking more about the disclosure. So, we have a meeting with the IASB recently, and they said that they can – that they think that there will probably be a marked effect to the quality of disclosures – because people will be looking more carefully at the disclosures themselves, and then, obviously, the auditor is going to be reporting on them. The auditors themselves are thinking a little bit more about what they do. So, when they were actually making conclusions on key audit matters, they've been thinking about – did I actually do that? And was it appropriate that I did that, because now I have to put it in a public report. So, there is an increase – or we expect there to be an increase – in audit quantity.

The hardest part is, obviously, putting the plans together without making them too technical – so that you can actually understand what they are. So we'll carry on monitoring, and we do plan to do a post-implementation review of the auditor reporting standards. So, again, if there's any research in this area of the main, sort-of, two or three years, it will be very helpful for us to be able to determine whether the standards are working as we intended them to work, or if we need to go on in and make some changes again.

There is – on Monday – we'll be publishing on our web-site, a document which compares our requirements to the PCAOB's proposals. So, it'll be a press release and a document sort of saying – these are the similarities and these are what the differences are between the two proposals. It's fairly high-level, but it should be able to give you a good indication of what the differences are. So, that will be up on Monday.[ix] And we are doing lots of other implementation – we're providing the auditor reporting, we've done a lot of outreach – that's been going on. We've been doing some work at the World Bank to try and get some figures done – to be able to help people with the implementation of the new audit reporting standards.

And our other big project, as I said, was the auditing of accounting estimates and fair value – ISA 540. IFRS 9 has made an essential that we actually go into standard and make some changes quickly. So, we put it on an accelerated timeline. We're hoping to have an Exposure Draft out by the end of the year – it's a lot of work. I mean, obviously, it's a very complex topic. We are doing lots of outreach. So, we're speaking a lot to the PCAOB, Basel, the IAIS[x] – so people that are relevant in that space – trying to find out what needs to be done in that standard. At the same time, trying to think of SMPs – because we can't make these standards too complex. Working for banks and financial institutions that are going to be applied to those people that have much simpler financial instruments. So, there is a lot of work that's going on and in that area.

We did publish a – we called it a project update – in March, and this really included material on audit issues regarding the move to Expected Credit Loss accounting. So, we sort of set out how current standards can actually be used for the trenches in IFRS 9 – about that standard and we're going to think a little more about how the standards need to change. So, for the people who have adopted IFRS 9 early, there is a little bit of guidance – and that's also to get some feedback back on those documents.

When this project started, it started as a financial institutions – so we were looking at banks and insurance companies – obviously recognizing there that ISA 540 should be opened up and to get standards more than just for financial institutions. So, it is covering all types of entities, and it will be a revision of the whole standard. And then just some of the challenges that we have identified – I've probably already gone through those – they're pretty standard. So, all those that are an auditor would understand them. You can see there – on professional skepticism – so this is one aspect of the project on professional skepticism that has been moved forward. Because we are opening up ISA 540, we don't want to open it up and then have to open it up in two years again when we decide to do something on professional skepticism. So, they are thinking about how it can be bolted to the standard.

So, we're looking at the way that the requirements are worded, and then they require an audit to be critically challenging. So, are we actually requiring just to get corroborating evidence, or do they need to question whether the evidence is sufficient or not? So, the way that the requirements are written may start to change and as we go forward. And, whether that happens or not, that's, sort-of, one main concern at the moment. So, that's subject to discussion. At this point, we've got a June board meeting – there are already some proposals for how professional skepticism can be built into the ISA 540. Obviously, it's a standard then we – where professional sketches is very, very important – and, hence, we brought that aspect of it forward.

And then just some other work that we're doing – the Ethics Board has made some changes in relation to non-compliance with rules and regulations. And we've had to make consequential changes for that – so, those will be approved at our June board meeting. There are some new requirements for group auditors to now report on non-compliances. So, again we'll have to look at past to look for evidence of how people understand when they need a report and when they don't need a report.

I've spoken a little bit about 315, and it has just commenced – the work will probably be accelerated – due to us trying to get some of these other big projects done – everything is based on the risk model. So, they are looking at what they actually need to do to improve how people identify risks, because we've got risks and we've got significant risks – and people sort of track them in buckets. And we're not sure that's working so well. The concept of significant risks needs a little bit more thought. So, we are looking at, perhaps, a new risk framework. So, it's still going to be the audit risk model, but the way that you get to the heart of the risks that you actually audit might be slightly different.

We're doing some work on agreed upon procedures. So, again, this is a project that's a bit of a hangover from our last strategy. And due to the auditor reporting project, it was pushed back. But it's used by lots and lots of different people, and it's also seen in different ways. So, some people use it for assurance, and if that doesn't actually give you any assurance. Some people use it with other procedures to give you some assurance, and do some procedures that don't give you any assurance. So, sort of multi-scope, or hybrid, engagements. So, we've got a discussion paper, that will probably be released after our September board meeting, with some thoughts about what we think AUPs actually are and what some of these other engagements are. And trying to determine whether there is a need for keeping the AUP as it is, and then creating something for these other types of engagements; or whether people aren't actually using it inappropriately, and the AUP standard is fine. So, there will be a discussion paper coming out a bit later in the year related to that.

Data analytics – as I said earlier, we are thinking about what else we need to do on data analytics and how we can pull that into all of our projects – in particular, with ISA 315. So, as the risk standard project takes off, it will become more important. Because, obviously, it will be driving the way that auditors do their risk assessments.

Assurance on integrated reporting – again, that's very important in some jurisdictions – probably less important here. There's some jurisdictions that already require integrated reporting – and we're looking for the need for what type of assurance we might need on those integrated reports. Whether they are being assured at the moment, and what's being used make them assured. So, we have a greater standard for assurance engagements – ISAE 3000 – we're trying to work out whether that is appropriate to use for assurance on integrated reporting – we might need to do a Practice Alert on that, or we might need a whole new standard. So, after – a discussion paper is going to our board at the June meeting – so that will be published just after the June meeting – discussing some of our considerations and thinking about what we can actually do on assurance on integrated reporting, and whether there is a need for it.

We continue to monitor the environment. We continue to do outreach – so, we engage very closely with the IASB – always monitoring the accounting standards to make sure that our standards are kept up. So, the financial institutions – or the 540 project – is very much because of the changes that the accounting standard have made. If they make changes to materiality, that will drive us to do a project on materiality. So, we are in constant contact, and we have regular meetings with them. It's the same with the PCAOB – so, we do have meetings as well to understand what they're doing. They have started to join some of our working groups to provide inputs to our projects. So, ISA 540 – or our fair value and estimates project – has a member that is from – representing the PCAOB. And our quality control – sorry – the 540 is actually as an observer, but they still provide the feedback. Our quality control project also has a member that is a representative of the PCAOB. So, we are happy to sort of get that input into our projects.

But, we have a separate group that monitors the environment to have a look at things – developments in things like cyber security or corporate governance – or those types of things. Once those things kind of fall out, we can look at whether we need to put them into our work agenda or not.

So, on our work agenda, we have work plan that was 2015 to 2016, which was all those projects you saw. They're all very big and all only just started. They most likely will run for the next three to five years. It was a very full agenda already. But, we still going to consult – because we have 2017 to 2018 work plan. We'll send out a survey to say – do you think we should still be doing work on these projects? Is there something that's more important than the work that we're actually doing? So, it's a choice – we can't add to our work program at the moment – but we could replace. We could slow down – there's various things we can do when something else important comes up. So, say, for example, integrated reporting does become really important for us, we would have to slow something down to be able to fit in. But, it takes three to five years to set a standard. So, if it's getting important now, we need to start working in that area.

So, we are going to be doing some consultation on our agenda – explaining this is what we do – so very much what I've explained to you now – and, in fact, if there's anything else? And we're always looking for input as to what that something else may be. And it may be something here, and New Zealand may have the same issue, and Ghana may have the same issue. So, once we see that it's global – a global issue – we can start bringing it onto our agenda. So, that will have to be finalized in December 2018.

So, I think that's a quick update on everything that we're doing. So, thank you for your attention, and are there any questions?

Questions and Answers

Is your presentation going to be publicly available on your website?

It isn't, but I'm sure they could sent it out.

Yep.

Do you have any thoughts on what the guidance on data analytics would look like? I'm having trouble envisioning what that...

I'm not sure it's going to be guidance necessarily. It may be – they're still in the very, very early stages of trying to work out how data analytics impacts the audit. And thinking about how we have audit quality over that. So, it may actually be built into the standard itself – as they revise 315 – they may roll some guidance into the standard itself. I'm saying – when you are looking at evidence – so, things around evidence and what you would be looking for in testing controls would be different when you are testing controls using data analytics. Sufficient, appropriate audit evidence – those kinds of things.

So, it's still very, very initial stages. It may be something that's outside of the standards – like a Practice Alert – that says – if you are doing an audit in a very complex IT environment, this is how you would apply the requirements in blah, blah, blah standard. So, at this point, it's still very, very open. But, it is a very big topic for us – and everywhere we go we are hearing about it. So, there will be some changes coming because of it.

You mentioned that you are looking at the audit risk model and how to adjust it. What kinds of things are you looking at doing? Are you looking at academic work in that area too?

Obviously, we're looking at work. We always do – if there is something. But, in particular, we're looking at physical controls. So, the way that our standard is written is very cumbersome in relation to controls and the way that we are able to understand the business. I did some work on a disclosures project, and we looked a little bit – looking at disclosures that, in fact, are generally systemic. How people out there understand them. It became very clear – even our board members, and we had two board members from two different Big Four firms – had fundamentally different understanding of what that one requirement meant. So, we're looking at understanding the business – and how does that feed into – how do you assess your risk, and then, the work that you need to do?

So, we've got this concept of significant risk. So, we're looking at whether that's still appropriate – whether should we call it something else – explain it a little bit differently? So, we're not going to change the way we do an audit. It's just more clarifying what some of those things are – and in particular – the controls testing section. We have a lot of comments from SMPs – going, do we even need to test controls? We're never going to rely on them. So, do we even need to document the system? And there's always some element of controls – so it just would be a much simpler documentation. So, one thing that we have been asked, in particular, and has come out from – we had a lot of – we've had roundtables in Paris, Kuala Lumpur, and in Africa – and what has come up, very much, is that people are looking for more examples. So, whether those go into the standards or we do them as separate staff documents – or non-authoritative type documents – people are looking for more examples, and what good looks like. So they say – please provide more examples, so the people can actually see what it is that they need to do.

You know, you were talking about monitoring and root cause analysis – things like that. Are you going to do guidance to follow – I'm sorry – what is that?

Yeah, very much so. I suspect it's going to become requirements. So, there's a very strong push – and there has been for a while – from the regulators – that part of our QMA would be the monitoring. So, then doing a root cause analysis, understanding what the issues are, and then putting something in place to remediate that. So, very, very likely – I'd probably put money on it – that it will become a new requirement in some way, shape, or form. And then there will be guidance as to what that actually means for different types of firms.

I have a question that maybe a little outside of your scope probably, but you're a lot closer to it than many of us are. Could you give us your thoughts on what your constituents and issuers are saying about mandatory auditor rotation?

Yeah, it's a – our Ethics Board has actually gotten to the issue of mandatory auditor rotation, and because we have so many different jurisdictions where the requirements are also different, they've decided not to actually put anything into the ethics standards in relation to mandatory auditor rotation, but they are doing auditor association. So, they're typing it up – and the requirements to think about – when you've had a long association with another auditor – I'm sorry – with an audit client. So they're not going to quite put in there – you can only be an auditor for five years and you have to roll off after five years – so they're not going to quite make that strict. But, they will be typing it up a little bit – so that's on the ethical side, and I think that's even in the works at the moment.

I'm interested in your term critical challenger for – am I assuming that you've adopted the presumptive doubt approach over the neutrality approach to professional skepticism?

That's actually our Chairman. So, I'm not sure if it's his term. I think he has adopted that. So, we haven't – it should still be very much subject to a lot of discussion. So, I think maybe it's a little bit extreme to call it a critical challenger. And where we get – I'm not sure – in relation to the different types of approaches. But I am – the audit – the professional skepticism working group is actually headed up by an academic out of Germany – Professor Annette Köhler – and so she has been looking at all of the different models. And I'm sure that she's being providing lots of input to them. So, it's not – again, very, very early days of the professional skepticism – so, we use it, and maybe we use it a bit tongue and cheek at this point in time.

So, you talked about component materiality – what are your thoughts on what the guideline would be on audit materiality?

We're still going to have a good look at it. So, again, one of our largest projects – and one of the biggest issues in disclosures – was how do you apply materiality to disclosures? Because, it's not a number – very often, it's not quantitative type information. And what we find when we started looking at it was that we actually had to go into the actual principles behind materiality, and we didn't want to start touching some of the principles without doing a more holistic review of the standard. So there, again, when we look at group audits, we're going to look at what we can do. We may not be able to do very much, because we're probably going to need to think more holistically about materiality before we actually get to guidance for component materiality.

What we will do, though, is that we'll probably look at what the firms have in place for component materiality. They must have put some guidance in place – and see if there's anything useful in what the firms have developed, and perhaps, put that in as guidance. But it wouldn't necessarily be any more requirements – it would just be trying to bring a level of consistency in the way that component materiality is applied.

What kind of assistance – in terms of data or funding – can you provide to researchers?

Oh, he went there. We do have some things in place, and I would probably need to find out exactly what it is. So, we do – we have – we are currently in the process of commissioning some research on specific topics to the IAAER.[xi] We also have IFAC themselves – it's an International Federation of Accountants[xii] – which we subsist under – they have a research body, which also – they sort of commission a lot of the research that we do need done. And we do have some funding in our budget for academic research, but, at this point, I think it's gone towards the specific areas that we've commissioned at the moment. But, if you are interested, I can – we have somebody on my team that deals more with this, and I can get her to, perhaps, send an email detailing what it is.

So, you're working on similar projects as the PCAOB is. Is there – how much overlap is there between your projects? Or, what things are you doing that the PCAOB is not doing?

So, there's more and more overlap as we go. So, I said there's their guidance on group audits – we will look very much at what they do on other auditors – and I think that probably will have an impact on what we're doing with group audits. There's some in there that are the same, and then there's some that are slightly different. But obviously, we do consider including what they'd be doing. So, as we move forward – we're not converging as such, but we are trying to make sure that the standards are roughly the same.

On the auditor reporting, again, very similar concepts as to what we've got in our new standards, but there's slight differences in the way they describe certain things. So, we, again, are monitoring that – when we then we do our post-implementation review, we'll see whether that, perhaps, works a little better – or if it's an area that's not working for us. Just going back to our projects – so I think – I don't think that they are working on quality control at the moment – which we've started. They're not looking at the risk standard necessarily – which we have now started work on. I'm talking about the auditing ones here. So, I assume they're not doing much on agreed upon procedures and integrated reporting – I actually don't know – so, I'm not going to answer on that.

Data analytics – obviously they're considering – and we probably are looking at the same things, and some of the comments that I heard at the PCAOB SAG are very similar to the comments that we get and that we've been getting at our roundtables that we've been having for our ITC. On professional skepticism – I think we're doing work on professional skepticism, and I'm not sure if they have commenced work on that area. So, they are quite a lot of big areas that we are working on similarly, and then there are some projects – and I haven't looked in detail and what their agenda is – what they doing that we are not doing at this time.

[i] Transcription Note: The original transcript has been edited for flow and ease of reading. Any changes to content were not intended to change the overall message associated with the applicable discussion.

[ii] Transcription Note: Her initial comments were inadvertently missed – for purposes of recording for this transcription – so the remarks begin at the beginning of the recording obtained.

[iii] Transcription Note: This refers to the presentation slides, which are also included for reference in the symposium web-site.

[iv] Transcription Note: ITC is the invitation to comment that is discussed elsewhere in the document. Also, as mentioned in an earlier transcription, specific references to regulatory guidance are not included here, but would be able to be located through the applicable public channels.

[v] Transcription Note: Please refer to endnote iii.

[vi] Transcription Note: Please refer to endnote iii.

[vii] Transcription Note: Based on a review of the web-site associated with the IAASB (http://www.ifac.org/), SMPs appears to indicate small- or medium-sized practices (or practitioners). Another term used appears to be SMEs – small- and medium-sized entities.

[viii] Transcription Note: Please refer to endnote iii. Also, to reduce the duplication of this type of endnote, all other similar references to the slides associated with the presentation also correspond to the information contained in endnote iii.

[ix] It appears that it can now be located at the following link - https://www.ifac.org/publications-resources/new-auditor-s-report-comparison-between-isas-and-pcaob-reproposal.

[x] Based on the following link (http://www.iaasb.org/projects/accounting-estimates-isa-540) this appears to be referring to, in addition to the PCAOB, the Basel Committee on Banking Supervision's (Basel Committee) Accounting Expert Group and the International Association of Insurance Supervisors (IAIS).

[xi] This appears to refer to the following – the International Association for Accounting Education & Research – and this appears to be their web-site - http://www.iaaer.org/.

[xii] Here is the web-site for this body - http://www.ifac.org/.

Panel Discussion[i]

Participants – In Alphabetical Order By Last Name (*With Identifier*)
Cindy Fornelli – Moderator (***CF***)
Jeanette Franzel (***JF***)
Scott Marcello (***SM***)
Roger Martin (***RM***)
Jeannine Strandjord (***JS***)
Joe Ucuzoglu (***JU***)

Opening Discussion
CF: Okay, ladies and gentleman, I know people are still gathering, but we are going to go ahead and get started, because I have a fantastic panel as evidenced by three of my panelists are giving addresses. You've already heard from Joe Ucuzoglu, you will hear from Scott Marcello immediately after this, and Scott is the Vice-Chair of Audit at KPMG, as well as the Americas Leader for Audit at KPMG International. So, you'll be able to hear from him, and have some time of Q&A with him as well. And, of course, to my far right, we have Jeanette Franzel. Jeanette is one of the PCAOB board members, and one of the only two that has a CPA designation, and I was telling Jeanette, not only is she one of the two CPAs on the PCAOB, she and Jay Hanson, in my mind are the only two practicing CPAs in the history of the PCAOB – so they have that expertise on the board. And you'll get to hear from Jeanette right after lunch.

And to round out our panel, to my far left, I have Roger Martin, who is at the University of Virginia, but perhaps more importantly for today, he is a KU alum – so welcome Roger. And then last, but certainly not least, to my right we have Jeannine Strandjord, who is the Audit Committee chair at MGP Ingredients, Euronet Worldwide, and sits on a number of other boards as well, including the Kauffman Foundation – which those of us from Kansas are very well acquainted with. And she, too, is a KU alum – so we're very pleased to have KU alums on our panel.

So, we've got a lot to cover today. We're going to cover three main topics. We're going to talk about the PCAOB's as well as the CAQ's audit quality indicators projects. We're going to talk about what audit committees want to know about audit quality. And, we're going to talk about some of the bigger topics that you heard Joe touch on – ICFR – internal control over financial reporting – in the audits, as well as the use of non-GAAP and other non-financial information in the marketplace. We will leave time for Q&A. We will do that at the end as Joe did with his discussion, and so I'm going to go ahead and get us started.

The subject, or the theme, of this year's symposium is increasing audit quality. And, of course, I think if we're going to talk about that, to be true to the theme, we need to talk about what comprises audit quality. And so, the PCAOB has had a major project going on over the last couple of years, as has the CAQ, in trying to develop a set of metrics – or a set of indicators – that could help audit committees, and others, trying to ascertain audit quality – also known as audit quality indicators or the AQI project.

So, I'm going to start with you Jeanette, and if you could, give us a little bit of an update. First of all, maybe explain what the PCAOB did - you had your Concept Release that went out last year. I think the comment period closed in September of 2015 – so you got a number of comments. I know that at the PCAOB's SAG meeting – the Standing Advisory Group - you also had a discussion in November about AQIs. So maybe some of the findings, some of the thoughts, and then we'll open it up to the panel to get to both the academic, the practitioner, as well as the Audit Committee perspective.

JF: Sure, thanks Cindy. Before I get started, I have to tell you that the views that I express today are mine alone, and do not reflect the views of the Board, or the Board members, or the PCAOB staff. As Cindy mentioned, we've had a pretty robust discussion about this topic in our November 2015 Standing Advisory Group meeting - we had a breakout session where people could have small group discussions to make recommendations and provide their thoughts. And we had reporting back out, which is publicly available. It's out there on the web if you want to watch it. I did a presentation to Audit Committees in February, and I actually re-watched that session of the SAG meeting in preparation. I mean, this is getting really nerdy. Whenever I do that, I get so much more out of it the second time around. We really did a deep dive into some key questions at the meeting in November. We talked about AQIs and their content. Can a standard set of AQIs even be assembled? Which AQIs might be most effective? How would audit communities use them? Are they useful? And we discussed use of AQIs by investors. And, so those were the themes of our different breakout groups, as well.

There was general agreement that PCAOB should continue to perform work and study this effort – that this is a worthwhile effort. There was support for narrowing the list of twenty-eight [potential indicators]. When the staff proposed putting out that Concept Release, they said let's just go broad and get the feedback, and so, that's a good principle to operate by, but twenty-eight is way too many. I think, we need to come up with a set of useful ones, and that doesn't mean that everybody has to use all of them. And that maybe audit committees and firms should figure out what works in their context.

We also got the message that we should not mandate the use of AQIs anytime soon, and I totally agree with that. In fact, if somebody asked PCAOB put out a proposal to mandate the use of AQIs – I don't even know what we would do right now. So, we're going to keep studying this, obviously, and observing, and let experimentation happen. I think that is so important. We certainly applaud the efforts of the CAQ and various audit committees out there, and the firms, too – to the extent they are looking at this. So, we want to continue to let this develop and go down the path to see what happens next. Some investors did say that ultimately they want something mandated, but they were even saying it's too soon right now. So, that was, in a nutshell, what we got from the November SAG meeting.

CF: Excellent. So, Roger, I'm going to turn to you now. I know there is academic literature on audit quality in general, and, could you share a little bit? What's some of the components or metrics of audit quality that researchers use to try to get that – get your hands around what are those components?

RM: Sure. And I'm pleased to see so many practitioners, because, I think my role here is how to simplify the academic research into terms that you can make sense of given what you do. There are experts – my academic colleagues – that are experts here who do really detailed work in everything that I'm going to talk about. So, what I'll do is I'll irritate them, and, hopefully, present it okay. I also ask to remember that I'll have to remember – so, Cindy hasn't confessed it, but she's a Kansas State graduate. So, one of my challenges is that I'll have to use small words so she can understand.

So, audit quality. I think that any paper dealt with audit quality in the past decade, or longer, the authors claim they are researching audit quality. So, I'm not intentionally ignoring anyone's research. What I did – just to get a quick view for this panel – was that I did look back at the last fourteen years of research – looking for terms like audit quality or auditor quality or things like that – and found 220 publications in what I would call the top eight auditing related journals. Almost two-thirds of those are what we call archival – which means we use observable market data – it's available to the public – to find things that we might, or might not, be able to learn about audit quality. Most of our research is based on what we can observe. So, remember, we can't observe the process very much – we observe outcomes – and that has its advantages and it has its disadvantages.

The ways we have evolved to assessing audit quality focus on four things. One, two of these are really black and white measures. So, one is going concern opinion – going concern uncertainty – was or was not issued, and in hindsight we decide it should have been or should not have been. So this is a two-by-two matrix if you think of either the auditor issued the going concern opinion or they didn't, and it turns out – in hindsight – that was good or not good. So, one measure of audit quality is whether they got that right.

Another very coarse measure is a measure of after-the-fact misstatements. So, we discover after an audit opinion's been issued – in two or three or five or how every many years – that it turned out in the issuer having to restate their financial statements. So, that also implies that the audit must have had something peculiar about it, and what we – all we can observe in research is – well, it looks like the auditor got that wrong. But, we have to remember a couple of things. The auditor was only providing reasonable assurance, so we don't expect them to be correct one hundred percent of time. And, we can't know what happened at the time. So, the condition of the world that happened at the time of the audit that five years later looks very black and white – remember, at the time of the audit, that's not true at all. So, they're making judgments and there's some uncertainty around those judgments. We know that some of those are going to be correct and some are going to be incorrect.

In academic research, we're relatively comfortable lumping large numbers of these together and looking at averages, because we're trying to make observations about this very big population of auditors and opinions they're giving. I'm not sure how helpful that is on the ground. Because, if I'm an audit committee member or an auditor, I don't think those averages help me – because I only care about one. I care about my audit, and so I think we have to remember that. Academics, sometimes – and now I'll really insult my colleagues – I think we take license, and pretend like – well, if this is true on average, it must be true sixty percent of the time for this client. Well, that's not helpful to that client.

Two other measures that I think are a little finer – or maybe a little more helpful. One is we look at accruals. So, we think we know and we think that we can predict the types of accruals that companies make, on average, based on their business model, based on their financial health, and things like that. So, we go in and we can compare basically cash flows to earnings numbers, and we try to estimate what we think the accruals must have been going on that time.

The second thing that we do along these lines is we compare actual earnings to expectations. So, expectations can be analysts' forecasts, expectations could be prior-period earnings, but the idea is – we have an expectation of what earnings will be, and then we look at the distribution of, well, what were actual earnings? What did they turn out to be? And if earnings always just barely come in slightly better than last year, and that happens year after year after year – that begins to look a little bit suspicious, because nature probably has a little more volatility than that. So, we offer that maybe that means something's going on there.

Now, again, this is very hard to help a specific audit engagement. Joe mentioned this earlier – and I think we need to remember this on the academic front – this might be a great risk assessment tool. So, it might be that we could come in – that an auditor could come into – a specific client. And, say that it seems like there's a lot of unusual things going on with the accruals here – of course, the auditor is going to audit those accruals, but this might be an attention-directing tool that they could use in the spirit of risk assessment.

CF: So, Joe and Scott, I'm going to turn to you now. Based on those metrics or those data points that Roger just mentioned that are frequently used in the academic literature, do you find those as real drivers of audit quality or measures of audit quality? And if not, what do you use in the firms? Because I'm guessing you have your own.

SM: We do.

CF: Don't fight each other for who goes first.

SM: We're going to have to fight this out.

JU: So, historically, there has obviously been a focus amongst multiple constituencies – academics, the firms ourselves, clients, investors – on some measures of quality. But they tended to derive what I would characterize as output measures. So, after the fact, when the financial statements were determined to be wrong, the regulator came in and issued a criticism that the audit was deficient. And those things are clearly helpful and relevant, but they often come too late.

And I think part of the impetus for the project that the CAQ undertook, and the PCAOB studied – and that us as firms have been looking at for the last couple of years – is if there are more forward-looking indicators – and many people refer to those as input measures. And just to put this down at a plain English level, I'll give you a couple of examples. So, in executing an audit, we found a high level of correlation between moving work up and avoiding a disproportionate number of hours coming at the very peak – after the issuer's fiscal year-end. So, we can measure milestones and percentage of hours that are incurred in various phases the audit. It's an important metric. Leverage, similarly – what's the makeup of the team, what's the percentage of the hours coming from the partner, the senior manager, and all the way down to the first-year professional.

Now Greg Jonas – who was at the PCAOB and led this project – I think he said it best. None of these indicators actually give you the answer – they just give you very good questions to further pursue and explore. Is there an anomaly? Is there a potential cause for concern at a time when you can still do something about it? And so, we do use those types of metrics internally, and we look for anomalies across our issuer base. And, to the extent that there are issues that look like they're above a certain level of concern around the sleeve of measures that we use, were able to go in and be more invasive up front. And whether that's getting the staffing corrected or whether it's getting the right specialists involved, we can do something about it before we wind up with an output measure after the fact.

SM: Yeah, and I guess I'd add – not repeating any of what Joe said – I got a couple of additional points. One, it's a little uncomfortable sitting right here between Roger and Cindy – just for the record. But in all sincerity, the one thing that's interesting – and often quoted in fact – is when you have an audit bust, you can't necessarily conclude that the audit was flawed. And, a lot of times financial statements go through and are perfectly fine right in front of us, and you have no way of knowing whether the audit was good in that case – or not either. So, in some ways, it's kind of a very bad situation for an auditor to be in – because you can't demonstrate to the public, to the stakeholders, to your regulator the value of what you do very easily because there is no strong easy way to measure the lack of – a failure of – audit quality.

Having said that, I absolutely think that we've got a vision into having the metrics – we do have to make sure that we're thinking about full alignment. In my mind, that alignment is to really believe certain things drive quality, and we'll keep refining those things as we move through time. We do have to measure – I mean – we have a hold ourselves accountable. And what accountability means is how to compensate people, how to recognize and reward people, how we evaluate the performance, you know.

And it has to be not just engagement specific – this does get to part of what the CAQ and the PCAOB have – it has to be the tone and the leadership sense of the organization. Are we actually driving the right behaviors? You know, to use Joe's analogy – or if you're thinking utilization of staff matters in audit quality and over-utilizing staff, except in rare situations where it's warranted, is bad for audit quality – are you holding the people accountable that schedule those staff to make sure they're in position to do the right things to make sure that they're at the right rates? And if not, you're going to have a problem down the road. And so, that's one piece of this.

The second is the notion of root cause analysis. We have to constantly ask ourselves – I think we fell in the trap, I know we did as a firm – I can't speak for the rest of the profession – of just thinking we could solve all of our problems by improving our training – giving a few more processes and changing some methodology – and our people would do better. But, I equate that to – it's kind of like the tourist who doesn't speak the local language deciding to yell a little louder hoping that the person will get it. Our people – it's not that the training doesn't work, it's that they need more than that, and so holding ourselves accountable to really understand what was causing issues in engagements – whether it's findings from the PCAOB or others – and then really fixing the core – to me, is what's really important. So, that's how I think of this whole notion of audit quality indicators being valuable in that context.

JF: If you don't mind, I'll just follow-up on what Scott said about how he's not sure whether the other firms have gone through the same process – first fix the training, then fix the methodology, and then realize that it's really some of these input and process factors that are impacting quality. Many of the other firms also have gone through that process, and when you look at the standards in the history of the profession, it is interesting because the requirement for a monitoring function was really the after-the-fact internal inspections. That's how the profession thought about monitoring quality, and that was way behind the curve in terms of other professions and industries that have traditionally measured quality through the process. So, I'm thrilled that the firms are getting to these input and process measures.

RM: So, I'll jump in there, too, just to add one thing. So, when I said that two-thirds of the papers I looked at were archival, that leaves a very important one-third where we, in academic research, actually get into some of this decision-making judgment process. And, I certainly don't want to understate the importance of that research. Because, I think, that research can really inform how our auditors thinking, how are they making decisions, and also how to inform the firms about how to analyze that. Because it's very difficult to figure out how someone made a decision. Even with all the work papers in front of them, and all the information that they had at the time, you can't get into their head to think about what are all the factors that led to them making this choice. And I think academic research is making very good progress. I'm thinking about that audit process, and the firms and the PCAOB could benefit from really stopping to think about – alright, if we're learning from academics that these things are affecting the judgments and the decision-making, how can we use some of that? And that, I think, is very applicable – maybe more so than the archival, after-the-fact output measures.

CF: So, Jeannine, I want to get you in on this. Because you are the audit committee chair on the panel, and, ultimately, you are, in a sense, the ultimate judge of audit quality. And, certainly, these indicators of which we're speaking are meant to help you in your role. So, what do you think of the indicators that Roger has mentioned – or some other ones that Scott and Joe and Jeanette have shared with us?

JS: Well, certainly I think those are important indicators; however, I care about the ones that are the input indicators – the ones that are going to keep us from having a bad audit. I am not concerned about the going concern – if we get to that point we've had – I no longer have a problem, I have a serious problem. So, I care about things like tone at the top; really understanding of the integrity of the CEO and the CFO, how geared they are to compensation; and then what that compensation plan does. I do care about – I look at the deficiencies every year – whether they're significant or other deficiencies – and are those going down year after year, and are they getting better? Is a deficiency ever coming up in the second year? That matters to me.

Certainly the quality of the public accounting firm and the partner – and I don't care about the whole firm – I care about the group that's on our audits. That's what's important to me. So, as much as I understand the PCAOB – you know, they always bring in, talking about the PCAOB, audit of the whole firm – certainly that's important. But, I really care about what happens with this particular audit, and what happens with this group. The audit partner. Is the audit partner - and when I talk about qualified, I'm really talking about really understanding the company. What makes it run? What are the risks from lines of this particular company? Industry experience would be very nice, because then they understand, you know, if it's a small transaction or large transactions, diversity of risk, etc. And it's very important to me that they understand the business. And so, we ask a lot of questions. I ask a lot of questions of them about what do they think of the finance staff, the internal audit group. Ask the internal audit group and the CFO of what do they think of the outside firm – and how good is the partner? I mean, that's very important. So, spending some time with the partner before the partner comes on the job – and really looking at the resume and what kind of experience they have. And, is it something that's going to help in this particular company? Any problems that come up during the year – and I'm not talking about the problems, the serious problems that are a significant restatement – I'm talking about the little problems that come up and what got missed. How did that get missed? And then, again, understanding the business – and that's something I'd also expect of the audit committee. They have to understand the business and what drives risk. So, those are mine.

Oh, by the way, to go back to Roger's point, we wouldn't count the number of accruals at quarter-end. We – in my audits – we actually forecast out ninety days. And to just give you a little rebuttal here – in the last forty-eight quarters, we've only missed earnings – that one-quarter earnings forecast – twice. And, we've always either exceeded or been on the forecast. Now, ninety days is not much. This is a company, by the way, that has get input from almost a hundred different groups – because we operate in 45 countries, there's three businesses, we get a hundred different people coming in with forecast – but they forecast out eighteen months. They do it every month, and they're very good at forecasting. But, we wouldn't be counting the number of accruals at quarter-end. It would be a monstrous job. And I think, to me, that's getting a little bit into the weeds. But, you know, you have to really understand the business, again, to understand whether it works or not.

CF: Well, Jeannine, you touched on some of the issues that will take us to our next session. Our next big area that we want to focus on – and that is what you really want to know about your audit. So, what we did at the CAQ is after we put out our quality indicator approach, and the PCAOB put out theirs, we had a number of roundtables over the summer last year. And then, we've had a couple of workshops where we brought together audit committee members to talk about, really, what do the audit committee members really want, and how do you go about assessing the quality in a real tangible way. And so, highlights from those discussions that we have had. And, in fact, we had the latest workshop just this week. What we heard from audit committee members, as I over-generalize and summarize, is that while they value the quantitative indicators that both the CAQ and the PCAOB put out, what they really would like help with – or what's really valuable to the audit committee – is those qualitative measures for those qualitative aspects of audit quality.

How do I get – you mentioned several times that what you really care about is your engagement team – your lead engagement partner and your engagement team – how does an audit committee member get a sense of the independence, objectivity, communication skills – knowing how and when to ask the hard questions, knowing how we went to follow up with the audit committee member? And so, I would like to spend a little bit of time, and I'm going to turn back to you, and ask you – how do you get down a little deeper? So, all of these quantitative things – the hours and the workload – important, but can you did a little deeper, and what questions do you ask? What do you look for?

JS: Well, I think it's somewhat subjective, but I think it's getting to know your audit team, getting to know the partner who's on your job. I do talk to the partner outside of the regular audit committees, obviously, and even though you have your four audit committees a year, you also have the earnings committee meeting before that. But, in addition to that, it's becoming pretty common to meet with the audit partner before you actually have that meeting for earnings release, and talk to them, understand what they're doing, understanding how they're looking at the company. Again, understanding if that audit partner really understands the mechanics of the business – what makes this business tick? Does he understand – does he or she understand the real ethics of the leadership team? How is that…

CF: The company's leadership team?

JS: …the company's leadership team. And they have to know them well enough to know what's driving them. And, again, they should understand the compensation plans. Is there anything in that compensation plan that's driving that CEO – or if that CEO then drives the CFO, that drives the CFO to try to do something? I mean, I feel much better when I see a CFO stand pat on – we're not going to get the same type of bonus this year. On one of my committees, they didn't make any covenants for two years in a row – and they stood pat and said – you know, we didn't make it, so this is how it's going to be. When they're willing to do that kind of thing, you have much better feel that they're the kind of person that's not going to try to fudge the books, and make it look better so that they can get that next bonus. And that's, I think, very important. So, those are some of the things that I look for.

CF: So, I'm going to turn back again now to Joe and Scott. You and your role as assurance leaders in your firms meet with, and have had over the course of your careers, many opportunities to meet with audit committees. Do these issues that Jeannine just raised – are those what you're hearing when you're in with the audit committee? What questions do they ask you? How do you feel they're trying to assess the quality of both you as a lead engagement partner and your team? Should I make Scott go first this time?

SM: I'll go first. I can think very, very much in line with some of Jeannine's comments. I think that it's part right – an audit committee is assessing individuals and their characteristics, and by the way, most of the time they interact with those people, there's really no stress. There's really no big issue – there's nothing to judge, right? You really want to know what they're going to do when things are difficult, when they have to make a tough call, etc.

So, one thing is when new partners are assigned, I'm seeing the audit committee is much more engaged in the selection of that new partner than they were five years ago or so. I think many years ago – five or more – they would have relied on the firm to assign the right person. Now they really want to go interview different candidates. They want to understand, well, who else I could work with. They'll want to talk to the prior CFO, the CEO, the controller, people they've interacted with to get a sense of communication style, etc. They also want to interview them and really ask them questions about – how do you know about our business? What do you think about it? How do you intend to engage with me and communicate? And I will say it's a really important balance they're looking for, because what they want are people that can make difficult decisions, but they're also not looking for people that'll cause issues or problems or chemistry problems when it's not necessary, right?

Because at the end of the day, the best, I think, teams work very well with their engagement team, management, and others to get to the right answers - to get the right information - but not so close that they can't be skeptical and objective and ask hard questions when it's the right time to do that. I think the other things they really do is they really want to drill down and understand. So, when you're talking to management, what are you hearing? Who on my team isn't that strong? Because you can come back and say – look, you got the perfect finance team – you're probably not being totally candid with me, right? So, who is it really that our auditing team should worry about? What are some risks that are keeping you up at night? I know you've got the big presentation you have to present to the audit committee as the audit's through, but if you had to pick the one, two, three things that are really, as the lead engagement partner, making you concerned each and every day, what is that? And how do you think about those things? And then, how can I as an audit committee chair do a better job in that regard around it? Those kind of interactions, I think, are the things that audit committees use to help assess their engagement teams.

CF: So, Joe, can I pick-up on that last point that Scott made? Because we are talking about audit quality indicators as it relates to the auditor engagement team, but, of course, there are many different factors that go into audit quality. It's not just the audit team, right? There is the financial reporting team. There's the internal audit of the company. The CEO. The CFO. And, even the audit committee, right? The robustness of the audit committee. The skill sets of the audit committee have an impact on audit quality. So, how do you see that whole mix, and what do you do as the external auditor to try to get your arms around that as it relates to audit quality?

JU: Why, I echo Scott's comments - specifically as it relates to audit quality indicators. I actually have seen the proliferation of discussion around AQIs over the last year or two as a significant positive in trying to achieve these objectives. Because there's so much discussion in the broader regulatory community around the fact that audit committees need to set the tone that audit quality is paramount. And, that audit quality should be the primary basis on which an audit firm is selected and compensated and retained.

And yet, that's asking a lot of an audit committee if an audit committee doesn't have anything at its disposal that's sort of tangible with which to evaluate that level of quality. And in the absence of that, at times, the conversation moves to price, because that's one very tangible number. Am I getting a good deal on this? And if we really do want to come back – commoditization – and demonstrate that the audit – it is a value-added exercise where there is true differentiation – you know, a really good audit adds a lot of value for the corporation and shareholders – then we have to have metrics that allow for a dialogue that's more focused on quality than price. And AQIs give us the ability to do that.

Now, I know that Jeanette mentioned that there's no regulatory mandating on the horizon, and I whole-heartedly agree with that, but this is actually an area where the marketplace is working. So, contrast that to, earlier, we had a dialogue about why have investors not demanded more forms of assurance on certain measures and metrics, and I suspect that part of the reason is because the investment community is very diverse, and it's hard for them to get together with one voice and demand things. Well, audit committees – that's a bilateral engagement – the audit committee engaging with the auditor. And, as word gets out that there’s a tool that may, well, be effective at helping audit committees accomplish the very significant statutory responsibility they were given under SOX – to directly appoint, oversee, and compensate the independent auditor – audit committees are asking for this now.

So, I was with an audit committee yesterday before I flew out here, and we had a discussion about regulatory developments. And, this topic of AQIs came up. And the audit committee chair – this was not one of the engagements where we piloted it last year – but the audit committee chair said – you know what, that would be very, very valuable for me to receive on an annual basis in connection with me evaluating your performance. I'd like you to start reporting that. And as it gets more and more exposure in forums like this – as the PCAOB’s out talking about it to audit committees, as firms are out talking it to audit committees. You know, we go to the annual audit committee symposium, we had an entire panel on AQIs. The market pull from audit committees will naturally result in a proliferation, in my view, even in advance of any type of regulatory action.

CF: So, Jeanette, I know part of your role at the PCAOB is that you, particularly, are interested in liaison with and in dialogue with audit committee members, and that you have made that an area of focus for yourself over the last year or two. What are you hearing about audit committee’s use of either a subset of AQIs that the PCAOB has put out, and/or any of the qualitative components that audit committees look at?

JF: I think the feedback we’re hearing is very consistent with what's already been said. I do want to emphasize, though, were talking about big company audit committees here, for the most part. We ought to distinguish between what we're seeing with Fortune 500 companies versus mid-cap companies and small companies. We’re hearing from audit committees they want to know about their own audit – they want to make sure the audit firm has assigned the right partner and the right team; that the firm is providing enough resources to the team, but with the right amount of balance. They don't want the engagement partner to have to call the firm’s national office every other day. So, there's kind of a balancing act there.

I find it very interesting and positive that audit committees are even using the word professional skepticism. I don't think five years ago audit committees were doing that. So, how does the engagement team exercise professional skepticism? That's a qualitative issue, and you hear that they want to use metrics but it needs to be done in context with other qualitative issues.

One area that Jay Hanson, my CPA colleague on the Board, and I have been really pushing with audit committees, and I think we're seeing some traction – and we've been pushing the firms on this a little bit, too – is how many hours are the staff working at the end of the audit, because that's a critical point where quality often suffers. And so, we're seeing firms move some of the work to a point earlier in the audit and having dialogue with audit committees about that. Jay Hanson found an article that said if you are sleep-deprived you are basically as impaired as if you are drunk, and that really resonates with audit committees. You don't want drunk auditors. And I recently spoke at one of the big firm's training for new seniors – these were the seniors where it was their third year, they all just got promoted, they just survived busy season, and I talked to them about this concept of drunk auditors. If you're sleep deprived, you are basically going into the office drunk, and that really resonated with them.

It is interesting to see audit committees are now worrying about the staff working too many hours at the end of the job. So, we have some positive movements there. There is variability in audit committee performance out there, even across the big firms, the big companies. But I'd say, for the most part, the big companies who participate in NACD and in some of these other professional organizations are doing a good job.

The next tier of firms in terms of market size – we talked to them about how audit committees are working, and it's a tough, mixed bag at the mid-cap companies. There are some very good audit committees, and there are some that really don't have the expertise to oversee the audit. And for the smallest companies, we've actually surveyed some of the auditors that attend our small business forums on their interaction with audit committees, and their views on audit committee oversight, and I was just amazed at how candid those small firm partners and staff have been with us about the level of quality or lack thereof in some of those audit committees. So, across the different sizes of companies, I think there's still a lot of work to do. I'm glad that the bigger companies and the bigger firms are leading on this.

CF: So, Roger, picking up on what Jeanette just said – the interaction between the auditor and the audit committee – the dynamic there and how it might differ between larger-sized companies and smaller-sized companies – is there any research that has been done or can be done on that dynamic, or are there impediments that just make it very difficult to do that?

RM: Well, I've been distracted there for a minute just thinking how introducing alcohol might affect, or stimulate, the decision making process.

CF: I suspect there's a Kansas State joke in there somewhere.

RM: I tell you, I just move to Aggie-ville and the problems solved. Well, obviously, what they described is a really interesting calculus, and that makes it very hard for researchers to make progress in this. I think this is right for what we call a field study approach – where we can't simulate this in a laboratory. We can't take a simplified case and try to simulate what an audit partner is going through or what an audit committee member is going through. So, field basis research is basically where we get agreement from parties to basically walk us through how this works, and we do this with interviews, we do this with observations of behaviors and outcomes, and things like that. That's a very difficult and long, live research approach, but I think that's really the way – at some point – we can make contribution to that.

But, also, as an educator – because the rest of the academics are also educators in the teaching sense – this is exactly why I jump up and down in front of my class room – and I say this is why auditing is so cool – because this is really complicated. You know, we could pretend like auditing is all about that introductory textbook, and here's your forms of evidence, and here's your management assertions, and go out and do good in the world. And that's fine for a year or two, but that's a pretty boring view of auditing. I also don't want to scare them off and say this is all done behind smoked mirrors, because that's not true either. It's a very interesting buyer-supplier relationship where there are quality expectations and there are users of this output from the auditors. And I use this to motivate students – that this is a life-long type of learning process, and you have to learn some basic skills – the accounting and the auditing, the evidence, and the data management, and things like that – but you also really need to be thinking about what's going on around you.

And I think that's what I hear you guys and ladies describing. Let's not pretend this is objective and we're simplifying this. This is very complicated, and the more we understand those nuances, the better off we're going to be. In research, we can only tackle one of those nuances at a time, so we're in there – I think we're making contributions – but I'm not sure that we can get near the complexity that you all deal with in reality.

JU: And I have to tell a really quick story on this point about the ills of working the staff too much late in the cycle. This is not a new issue. We found in the archives a letter from Deloitte to a client in 1912 that accompanied the delivery of the reports. And, literally, the cover letter reads – please find attached these reports. As you know, the figures are off by twenty-six cents, but, as you know, the reports were prepared late at night under great duress. A hundred years ago – same issue – we're making some real progress.

CF: Right.

JU: It just took a while.

CF: Right, what did you say that the next five years are going to exceed what's…

JU: Happened in the last fifty.

CF: …happened in the last fifty years, so maybe there's more to come in the next while?

JF: Yeah, so working 22 hours a week, right?

CF: As opposed to 22 hours a day.

JU: That letter was actually written under a Kansas City office.

CF: There you go. Well, now I'm going to shift this to our third big topic area, and talk about some individuals that have been in the news – at last at the accounting end and auditing news – and I want to talk about ICFR. And then, also pick up a little bit of – on the topic that you touched on, Joe – about non-GAAP measures.

So, Jeanette, let me start with you. Over the last several years – in the PCAOB inspection process – there have been the citation of deficiencies in the audits of internal controls. In fact, I think so much so, that in October of 2013, the Board issued Practice Alert Number 11 that highlighted some of the areas around ICFR that you we're seeing in the inspection process and some concerns that you had. So, tell us – where the status of the ICFR audit today? Are you still seeing the same concerns or have things improved?

JF: So, first I have to level-set us as to where we are in terms of our inspection cycle, because I always get confused as to which year I'm talking about, because there's a lag.

SM: So do we.

JF: So, for the Big Four firms, the latest year that we've got public information out is the 2014 inspections, and those reports came out in 2015. We're done with the 2015 inspections, and currently preparing the reports – so those will be out soon, but I can talk a little bit about 2015 – just generally. So, I think 2013 was probably the peak year for these findings, and we did see, for three out of the four firms, a significant decrease in deficiencies between the 2013 and 2014 years – in the reports issued in 2014 and 2015. And ICFR findings were driving the overall audit deficiency rate in those reports.

So, of course, the ICFR deficiencies were coming down as well. I asked the staff to slice and dice these numbers so I could try to figure out any trends, and I couldn't. And part of the problem is that we're only dealing with four firms – and each of the four firms were in slightly different places – and some not so slightly different – but were all in different places for the most recent year. There was still one firm that did have a fair amount of findings related only to ICFR issues, and so that was driving the numbers on the "ICFR-only" findings. Well, the good news there was that they were not also having extensive substantive audit findings in the same audit areas. And so, hopefully, if they can fix their ICFR findings, their overall results will come out better.

We did have one interesting trend, though. Between 2013 and 2014, the nature of ICFR deficiencies that decreased were those associated with testing design effectiveness and operating effectiveness. So, auditors are getting better at actually testing the design and operating effectiveness of the controls.

The deficiencies related to selecting the right controls to test remained constant, and that was an interesting finding. If you don't pick the right control to test, it doesn't matter if get the other part right. We are expecting to see a further decrease in ICFR deficiencies across the board for the Big Four in 2015 inspections, and I haven't tried to analyze those numbers yet. But, the good news is – there's been a tremendous amount of improvement in this area. I will say, and

I've said this in other forums as well, I think in some cases these weren't necessarily isolated auditing problems. They also involved ICFR design and implementation problems at the issuer – problems that the issuer needed to take care of. And that's why the auditors were struggling. I think we've seen improvement across the system, and we'll continue to see that.

CF: So, let's pick up on that point, though, about the issuer's design and implementation of their internal controls, and what that means from the audit perspective, and the difficulties that that can provide you all – particularly since AS 5 requires auditors to take a top-down risk-based approach to the audit of their internal controls. So, how do you go about assessing that – particularly if there hasn't necessarily been any error? What are some of the challenges that you all see? And I'm looking at Scott and Joe.

JU: I'll go first.

CF: It's your turn – to go first.

JU: I think it's important to start with the macro context here in terms of what is trying to be achieved – with the objective of what the legislation was when Sarbanes-Oxley was enacted. There is a tremendous benefit to the company having a robust system of internal control, and, ultimately, the process can't work in an optimal way unless there's an alignment between the company's implementation of its controls, the quality of the auditors that were around auditing the controls, and then the audit committee's oversight process in its entirety. And, as we work to instill a very rigorous standard and achieve those benefits – there's obviously some bumps along the way. And, communication is absolutely essential.

What we found is that when we sit down with our clients, and we talk through what the objective is – and then, we come up with common sense ways in which they could meet the objective, and we can meet the objective – we get to good answers. When there's a big push late in the cycle – it's already December, the company is trying to close its books – and then you come in suggesting there's a bunch of things that are, you know, that need to be modified – that that rightfully creates a level of consternation. So, getting that benefit early on in the cycle is critical.

The other piece of this – you mentioned Cindy – the objective is to take a top-down risk-based approach, and to focus on that which is important and material. And so, my own belief is that – for those controls that are most important – that sit atop the highest risk elements of financial statements, the most subjective estimates – having an increase in the level of effectiveness of the company's controls, the documentation of controls, the execution of those controls, and then elevating the level of our work that we do to make sure that the intricacy of those controls is appropriate – that's well worth the cost. Now, if you take that approach and try to peanut butter across the entire population and you start focusing on things that are less important, then you can understand where frustration would come in. So, communication early in the cycle and a focus on that which is important are absolutely essential. Maybe one comment on the whole issue of the quick factor – I can certainly offer some thoughts as well.

SM: Sure.

JU: But it is a particular challenge.

SM: Sure. And one thing I'll say is – our firm, I took my role in the firm this past July, and I was welcomed to the PCAOB report that is the outlier in what Jeanette was describing – the ICFR comments, and…

JF: I was trying to be discrete.

SM: It's public information. In fact, it is one of the things I said to our leadership team is we're going to fix this immediately. Now one of the frank things I also learned, being a little naïve, is it's hard to change an audit firm immediately because the cycle is pretty long, but we've already been making significant progress. And I say that because – one thing I learned in this – just to build off what Joe was saying – you can't audit better than your client's environment will allow. And one of the things that I've often had to really get my partners to get their head around is – let's make sure we're having those very difficult conversations.

Your skepticism starts at the very beginning of the audit by evaluating the environment and planning what you do. You've got to really challenge management where they're not doing it right in the right areas. We're not going far enough to make sure they are. And I'm not talking about material weaknesses – but I am talking about their willingness to come along and be part of the audit in a way that allows the audit firm to do the high quality work they need to do. It's one of these metrics we put in place to really measure how our clients are performing – and really challenging them to make sure they're getting better and we're getting better around that.

Now, having said that – to Joe's other point – one thing that continues to be a challenge, I believe, is going ahead and calling a material weakness when the only thing you have is the control review and no other evidence, right? No, there's been no audit adjustments, there's no passed audit differences. Having that conversation – that's the one that really matters, right? Detecting the material weakness in internal control or a significant deficiency before there's any causes – well, the cause is known, but the outcome is not – is hard. Because, in essence, it's very judgmental, right? You're calling management up and saying – I believe either the design of your control won't capture something that could be material – that could be a very, very difficult and judgmental conversation. Or, we agree on the design, but we don't think that way you've effectively executed it actually would have caught an error. And, again, we didn't find and error – so to get into that very difficult conversation.

But if you don't get this right, you're never going to get the audit quality side of this right – because you're always going to deal with the fact that – it's never a problem until you have some kind of failure. That's not the world we want to live in, right? We want to get into a world where helping our clients prevent failures, where we're making sure we're calling the issue before they become a problem – and if that means clients dealing with the disclosure of material weaknesses or having to make significant changes to their control environment before they've actually committed deficiencies, that's the way the world should work. But getting there is not as easy. It is a process of evolution, if you will – getting all clients to act with the same mindset.

JF: We know there was a pretty dramatic SEC enforcement case recently…

SM: There was.

JF: …on this very issue – where the contracted internal auditor detected some deficiencies, nobody was willing to call it a material weakness. There was a restatement subsequent to that, and the new firm that came in found fourteen material weaknesses, and the SEC went after everybody involved. They went after management, the internal auditor, the external auditor – so that's a very instructive case.

JU: It's caught people's attention – as it should have. And this gets back to the very intent of the statute. Material weakness reporting was intended to be an early warning system that – even before there was a financial statement misstatement – investors would know there's something amiss that could potentially cause a problem that would ultimately impact their investment decision. And when you look at the research that's been done on the actual reporting of material weaknesses in the decade plus since SOX was enacted, the preponderance of material weaknesses are only reported after a material restatement – a material error – has been the detected. And so, it's backwards relative to the initial intent.

And to Scott's point, this requires a mindset shift – it requires an approach by both the audit firms and the corporate community. But, we are seeing an increase in the instances of material weaknesses being reported upon in advance of the financial statement error. I can't speak to the statistics across the entire population, but, anecdotally, in terms of eyes that come across my desk, it's becoming more prevalent.

SM: Absolutely.

CF: So, Jeannine, is this hitting the boardroom?

JS: Yes.

CF: Do you have these discussions?

JS: We do. And I guess I think companies have the self-interest in getting their control environment in great shape because errors are costly. You know – whether the error causes some kind of problem. But, even a problem with the books, and you have to go to the street and talk about a significant error – that's costly to the company. So, they should have a strong self-interest in getting a strong control environment. As I mentioned in the company where they are in 45 countries – most of the problems that they had in the early days of the company were because of problems in their control environment. Maybe not the books, but for the control environment, they lost money. You can't afford that kind of thing.

So, I think you have serious reasons to want to bring down the number of deficiencies you have every year. And in the recent companies I've been associated with, we have brought them down every year. And we talk about that – how can we get to fewer numbers of significant? How can we get to fewer numbers of other? Haven't had a material weakness, thank goodness. But, how can we keep bringing these numbers down?

CF: So, Roger, generally about academic research, some of the academic research that's out there. And I think there is both some quantitative and experimental research on ICFR – give us a little flavor of what's out there in the research, and what might be coming.

RM: Well, certainly we're seeing the same lack of material weakness identification prior to misstatements in research, and that's been true pretty much since the beginning of the ICFR reporting. Jeanette, I can't remember where she gave a speech where you have a lot of statistics on restatements versus the material weaknesses…

JF: Yep, AAA last year.

RM: Was it at the AICPA?

JF: No, it was the AAA Annual Meeting last year.

RM: The AAA – I encourage my academic colleagues to look at that speech, and that's an interesting class exercise that helps students understand what we're talking about. Where she gives the statistics where you can basically figure out how many companies are getting material weakness reports and how many were getting misstatements after the fact, and the overlap of those. And that's really interesting, I think, for students to see the challenge of exactly what Joe and Scott are talking about – and that is how do you know a problem could happen – because it hasn't happened yet?

And I think that research – at least my view is – you talk about a change in a mindset, but that's a real education challenge, too. And not necessarily on-campus education, but how does that expertise get developed in an auditor that the partner has? A partner can sit there, and anticipate what bad things could happen, but I don't think a senior has a chance until they've seen enough calamities to begin to piece together evidence that says this could lead to this bad outcome.

We know a little bit about how hard it is to do that with analytical procedures. We've done a lot of research where we look for patterns – the ability to identify patterns in analytical procedures that might indicate an underlying misstatement. I think the research might be moving in that same direction. What is it that an auditor has to experience before they can say – well, given the control design, here are the things that can still happen that are not very good? And firms are challenged because you have to develop that experience under fire. In terms of us understanding that process, I don't know that we have a really good insight yet into the firms and that level of decision-making, but I think that would be very productive in the future.

CF: So, now I'm going to turn and talk more about the non-GAAP measures agenda you touched on in your presentation. And, Jeanette, I'm going to turn to you first, because we just had your SAG Meeting earlier this week, and you're fresh off of that, and I know this is a huge topic of conversation. And one of the benefits of SAG is that you get the various constituencies, right? You got audit committee members, investors, preparers, auditors, academics on the SAG.

What was the nature of the tenor of the discussion, and what are same takeaways that we should think about?

JF: It was a very interesting discussion – and we also discussed it at our November SAG Meeting as an emerging issue – but we did a deep dive over the last two days on it. And we heard this morning about the proliferation of the use of these numbers. The use of non-GAAP measures is increasing; and it's all kind of going in one direction – and people are getting more creative about how they are using these. And so, that's also caught the SEC's attention.

And the SEC – just this week – updated its compliance and disclosure interpretation on non-GAAP measures. They've become very clear on specific examples of types of non-GAAP measures that may be misleading; whereas, before the guidance was more open-ended – and that allowed for some of this creativity. The SEC also included specific examples of when the staff will consider a non-GAAP measure more prominent than GAAP. The SEC staff presented at the introduction to this section of the SAG Meeting, and sent a strong message – saying that the SEC will start challenging these measures. There will be more comment letters, and companies should self-correct this quarter. So, the SEC is coming out pretty strong on this. They also said that the SEC intends to curb some of the bad practices associated with non-GAAP measures.

The SEC is doing what it needs to do, and that's where this effort should start. We had discussions about what the auditor's role should be. Should there be assurance over this? Should the auditors be looking at it at all? And I think the biggest concern that came up was the difference between whether these are included in 10-K filing – in which case the auditor has to read and consider under our current standards whether there's some material misstatement of fact or whether they're materially misleading. And those same measures, if they're put out in other types of communications – like press releases and so on – even though these later get furnished, for the SEC they're not filed – so they don't come under the auditing standards. We had a lot of discussion about the potential for our auditing standards to be expanded in scope to address the furnished information.

I think the general consensus was that we all need to stay on top of this. Right now there's really no rule-making role for the PCAOB, but we should keep our eyes on it and see how practice changes. I thought the one suggested change – for just bringing some of this into the read and consider requirement under our auditing standards – might be an interesting proposal. But, as Joe mentioned, there's no real framework for presenting this information. You can't really audit this – so it would have to be under the read and consider – and that's already a mushy standard. So, we're going to keep our eye on this.

CF: And so, I want to get to the practitioners' point of view on all of this. First of all, is any use of non-GAAP measures – any of this in the control environment – in the ICFR audit? Jeanette mentioned the 10-K?

SM: That's probably one of the biggest questions audit committees should be asking. Because, it's mixed. Some companies have very strong controls around non-GAAP measures. And if you think about it, logically, if you're going to tell the market that way – that these are the most important measures that I use to manage the business and, in fact, that I use them equally – usually they have to be able to say – because they need to to comply with a rule with other measures when I disclose them – the next logical question is – okay, well what controls do you have around them to make sure, when you report them, they're accurate?

And some of them are fairly obvious and easy because they are adjusting earnings for certain items, and hopefully the companies do have good controls. Others are operational statistics – a lot of companies would say it's more important we know, for example, my sales and not my audited revenue. If I have long-term sales contracts, you know – that the flow, the pipeline of new sales orders – that's more important. Well, okay. What controls do you have around what you're reporting? What systems does it come out of? Etc. Several really important questions.

I also think that one of the difficulties about non-GAAP measures is, in some sense – and Joe said really well today – the notion that people want different, more current, more relevant information is true. And you can't cut that off. On the other hand, the question really isn't as much about the accuracy of the information, I think. It's the context of the information, and can I as a reader really understand the context of what you're telling me? Or, are you spinning to me? And it's hard – I don't care how smart you are as an investor – it's pretty hard to know what the motive is and what management is trying to do. I will say that a red flag that I would look for is how often do you change the composition of your non-GAAP measure? If every quarter, you're adding a slightly different tweak to it – that feels a lot like you're trying to continue tell a story. And you laugh a little bit, but there are companies that periodically keep updating those measurements.

And I will also, last thing I'll say – there's a herd mentality. That I'm in an industry and my five best competitors have that thing and they adjust for that particular item – like the fair value mark on derivatives, because that doesn't really count in their earnings. Well, I got to do the same thing is not that unusual. So, I think those are things that audit committees and others need to stay focused on, because it really is a difficult area, quite frankly.

JU: It comes down to a race to the lowest common denominator. I think from a technical standpoint, if we accept that these measures are being reported in the 10-K, they arguably do fall within the company's obligation to certify their disclosure controls and procedures – which is a more expansive population of controls that ultimately is audited. It's more expansive than the internal control over financial reporting; but nevertheless, companies should have their own controls to support their certification. If the numbers are reported outside of the 10-K, then they're arguably under the statutory requirement for controls to be applied. But, we've seen a significant increase in the focus of audit committees demanding that company management have as robust a system of internal control over the preparation of that information.

In terms of our requirement – so, as Jeanette mentioned, if something is sitting in a document filed with the SEC, under the current audit literature dating back to SAS 8, we have an obligation to read and consider it, and to do something if we conclude that it's materially inconsistent with the financial statements that we've audited. You used the technical term mushy – which in spirit – so if a company reports a metric, and it's earnings before nine different charges, but those charges which were taken from the underlying financial statements, and they equal the amounts from the financial statements. We can argue whether it's a good metric or a bad metric, but it's not inconsistent with the information in the financial statements.

And so, the technical obligation of the auditor, in that case, is somewhat limited. We've had more and more audit committees say – I don't care whether you're technically required to be reporting on this or not, I want to hear what you think. So, I want you to look at it, and if there's something that looks out of bounds to you, you need to sit here and look me in the eye and tell me. And that's certainly an effective mechanism. And, there's shades of just how far astray some of these measures have become.

So, last week, I was sitting in an audit committee meeting, and there was a discussion that centered around some of these metrics. And one of the audit committee members looked across the table and said – these aren't non-GAAP metrics, some of these are anti-GAAP metrics. And so, we looked at him and said – what do you mean anti-GAAP metrics? And so, there are certain adjustments that are being made and are not just stripping out a particular item and non-recurring, but they're actually changing the basis of accounting. The accounting rules have a certain measurement and recognition framework – it tells you to take the revenue and spread it over time – and the non-GAAP metric is actually undoing the accounting principle, and putting back in as if you followed some different accounting principle. And that's one of the things that the SEC highlighted…

JF: Right.

JU: … in this CE&I interpretation this week – as out of bounds.

JF: I hope that the SEC guidance helps the process. The advice that I would give to audit committees is – ask your audit firms, if appropriate in the audit, how do our non-GAAP measures that we've been using stack up against this guidance? And do a good scrub down, and hopefully the firms will also be telling the audit committees that they need to do this. And, you know, we'll have to monitor this.

CF: So Jeannine, are you having more of these kinds of conversations in the boardroom?

JS: Yes, and I think that the audit committee should be asking – why are they using the information? Is it something to help the investor understand the business better? Is it what we're using internally to understand the business better? So, and does it tie? And we use numbers on the boards I'm on – where they tie-back to the financials. I mean, you can see the numbers that we either take out or put in – in the financials. They're in various places – they're audited, very auditable. And, in those circumstances, I do believe non-GAAP makes a lot of sense. I think it has to be consistent. I wouldn't understand any numbers that changed or where we change the formula quarterly or even annually. When we have changed it after a couple years because you found something better – that's different. But you can't just go back and forth to what looks best this quarter.

JF: You know…

JS: It doesn't make any sense.

JF: There was one very interesting investor analyst perspective in one of our closed meetings. That was – no, I don't want this regulated. I love seeing the messiness that these people put out, because I can judge the integrity of management by what they are…

JS: Yeah – right.

JF: …doing with these things.

JU: Great point.

JF: It was really an interesting perspective.

JS: Yeah, right – that's probably true.

JF: Yeah.

JS: And, I think that's a case where you go overboard with it. I mean, if people go overboard, you start wondering, too,…

JU: Yep.

JS: …what exactly are they trying to do?

CF: So, I have a lot more questions that I want to ask the panel, but I think this is the part of our session where I'm going to open it up to the audience. I want to make sure that we leave some time for you all to ask questions. So, any questions for the panel?

Questions and Answers

CF: We'll start here.

What I'm listening to right now is that you have to read and consider information to determine if it's materially inconsistent with what's reported in the financial statements. And say if a non-GAAP measure takes seven exclusions with all the exclusions tying back to the financials – then it's not inconsistent. But that's only the quantitative side of materiality.

Has anyone argued that on the qualitative side? For example, in the audit, anything that turns a loss into a gain is universally considered qualitatively material. Well, if your non-GAAP financial measure ties back to the financials, but turns a loss into a gain – that's materially inconsistent with the financials.

JU: I mean, these are exactly the questions that are being debated right now. To start with, many of these metrics fall outside of the 10-K, and therefore they never even get into the realm of this dialogue. To the extent that they do fit within the 10-K – the auditor has to make this determination. Again, it's not a question of whether the numbers materially differ from the financials – it's a matter of whether it's materially inconsistent with the financials, and the preponderant interpretation to date has been that if these numbers are transparently disclosed – in terms of what's in or out – and they tie back to the financials.

Let’s just say that the income of the company on a GAAP basis was a hundred, and there was two hundred dollars of stock-based compensation – and it's very common that some companies in certain sectors report a non-GAAP metric that excludes stock-based compensation – and when you back out the two hundred of stock-based compensation it turns the number to a one hundred loss. The two hundred is an audited number that is sitting in those financial statements, and the use of it is not materially inconsistent with those financial statements. Now, if the standard were different – if the standard was, you know, does it produce a materially different outcome in the financials? Maybe you’d get to a different judgment. Right now the standard is – is it materially inconsistent?

SM: I think the other thing to remember – or to think about – is what is the SEC guidance to management on non-GAAP measures? And, up until the recent discussion, it really was pretty straightforward. It was – it can’t be materially misleading, it can’t be any more prominent than the GAAP information that you're presenting, and you have to reconcile it. And, basically the SEC learned, and would say – if you do those three things, you're within the provision of the rules.

So, as an auditor, basically, when you apply that standard, it would be hard for us to say – yeah, but you know what, we really just don't like that particular disclosure because it just doesn't feel right. Given that that's what the rule says – and that's part of the issue. I think that's where the audit committee becomes really important, though. That's where you have a conversation – a very open conversation – with the audit committee, and say – look, this is totally appropriate in the sense it follows the rule. It is not materially inconsistent with the financial information that’s presented. But, I will tell you, that you're an outlier compared to what I would think is good practice in this area – and really ought to challenge management and understand it. Now frequently – I really haven't found that the case very often – but when it is, you've got to be able to have this conversation.

JF: And I think that the new SEC guidance will also help identify certain types of items that shouldn't be…

JU: Yes.

JF: …used.

JU: Right.

SM: That would be helpful…

JU: Definitely.

SM: …because it will narrow the field at least to take away some – I would almost call them – egregious, if you will.

CF: Yeah, and another, I think, ripe area for exploration – and could give us a little more insight into this – is the SEC has a Concept Release out right now on Regulation S-K that gets into some of these issues, too. And while I don't think the SEC is going to do anything with all the information they gather, the comment letters that they receive might be instructive, and might be an area to explore what some of the issues are – and might even lead to ideas for research.

JS: There's a lot of questions.

SM: It's going to take a little bit of time.

JS: Yeah.

Really enjoyed this panel this morning. I really appreciated Roger Martin's bringing up the question about how we educate students on recognizing that a problem would happen before the problem actually becomes found. And, basically, I see this as a pattern that could represent a problem. And, I play a lot of chess, so I know when my king is in trouble – that that presents a problem. So, I think, from my own experience as an auditor, the best way to develop the given ability is actually working on – not smooth but – messy audits. That's how you develop the experience.

So, my question is to Joe and Scott. What are the firms doing into simulating these messy audit scenarios in their training, because that's where I think you should be doing it.

JU: It's a tremendously valuable tool. So, we've actually taken earlier audits that have been messy – audits that have been inspected by the regulator where deficiencies were identified – and we sanitize them and put them into case study format. And that served as the underpinnings of a significant amount of our training, because you don't learn a lot going through an audit where everything's been done right and found nothing. You learn a lot by going through the messy situation and having to make the real world judgments, and take a stand, and push back, and refuse to issue until the underlying matters have been corrected.

And that's actually – and, Scott, you mentioned earlier on the panel – one of the great PR challenges of the profession. In most professions, the public can see both the good and the bad. They know when a profession messed up. You can also see the airline that got you there or the drug company that helped cure somebody – either themselves or with the help of somebody else. With the auditing profession, the only thing that ever really gets seen is the stuff that went wrong. And when we stand up, and we do the right thing, and force the particular issues to be corrected before the numbers go out – were precluded under the professional standards for making any mention of that publically. Were bound by confidentiality, and so it really is a difficult spot to the end of my PR standpoint.

SM: And I would just add, I think we're doing exactly the same. The one thing we're really looking at is scaling – we do it merrily now, but making it scalable – which is truly doing experiential or simulation irk-mines, where we're putting the young senior in an environment where it's basically – here's the pattern, and we're making it intentionally go down that path, right? So, we're trying to help them learn about scoping a large, international engagement – which areas they should audit? We know that that's a challenge for a lot of teams, and we're simulating certain information where it's going to be very easy to miss a very important fact. And, as a result, is going to be an audit failure – and, as a result, is going to be a messy thing. And, hopefully, they catch it. But, if they don't, they'll learn even more from the fact that they went down that path, and have that experience. So, that's one of the things that we're trying to scale, if you will.

CF: Okay – one more quick question. Right over here – you've got the microphone. I hope you don't mind, I'm sorry. Go ahead, you've got the microphone.

Can everybody hear?

CF: Yes.

Yeah, this is basically a follow-up question to something that Joe mentioned in the earlier session, but I think this is a question that can be posed to any of the members who choose to answer it – which relates to – Joe mentioned about the benefits of having CEO, CFO certification of the financial statements on issues like fraud and so forth. And I just wanted to draw an analogy, give a perspective on each partners' signature on the audit report.

Now, there are, of course, regulatory disclosures that can be made in identifying the engagement partner, but I wanted to get your input – as well as the panel members input – on whether there's any incremental benefit of audit quality of actually having engagement partners sign as many other parts of the world – and many other capital market – they do, and they have found benefits associated with that.

So, I was trying to get the analogy in terms of not just the disclosure versus signature – and whether audit quality in the perception or in fact – in terms of the processes that go into the conduct of the audit – changing as a result of some of the action of putting the signature on the audit opinion.

CF: I know you directed the question at Joe and Scott – I'm actually going to redirect it at Jeanette as the PCAOB has just issued their new standard on partner identification, and, in fact, the SEC has finalized that rule – so that is going into effect. So, give us your perspective on that question. Was it done to improve audit quality or were there other reasons that the PCAOB put that forth?

JF: That's actually a very messy question and, that's why it has taken so long to get this thing out. The ACAP – the Treasury ACAP report in 2008 – had a recommendation to the PCAOB – the ACAP was the advisory committee on the auditing profession to U.S. Department of the

Treasury – a recommendation that the PCAOB look into whether the auditor should sign the report.

And, because of the liability scheme in the United States, it became very problematic for auditors to actually sign the report. So, unless the liability issues could be fixed, and we at the PCAOB could not fix those – we decided to do something that was within our control. There seemed to be a demand for, at least, disclosure of partner names, since this is available in other countries – and so we went down this path of disclosing through a form. And we'll see what happens. Some of the research that was done in other countries I don't think was really relevant to our environment. So this might be a good experiment for researchers going forward, and I'd like to see us do a post implementation review on this particular requirement to see what kind of benefits we gain – or not – from this.

I will tell you I spent twenty-three years of my career at GAO where we signed our audit opinions. And we were in government – so nobody was going to sue us. I did sign a lot of opinions, and, yes, it does focus you, but there were a lot of very high profile audits that I did where our Comptroller General wanted to be the one signing rather than Jeanette Franzel. So, I was heading up some audits where the Comptroller General signed. I was equally focused on quality in both of those situations – whether I was signing or whether the Comptroller General was signing.

CF: Okay, I'm sorry to cut this off, but I do want to be respectful to the rest of the program. So, I'm going to ask all of you to join me in thanking Jeanette, Jeannine, Joe, Scott, and Roger.

---

[i] Transcription Note: The original transcript has been edited for flow and ease of reading. Any changes to content were not intended to change the overall message associated with the applicable discussion.

Research Session 1 – Timothy Seidel[i]

Questions and Answers

There seems to be a bit of a disconnect between your research questions slide in H1 – and that the research question slide said, if I remember correctly, this audit report date difference provides an indication of lower audit quality because of the decreased time pressure.

And, so then, I thought that it would be like a two-part hypothesis – where you have this H1 test where you have an association, and then you eventually tie it to that pressure – versus some other factor that delayed not only the completion of fieldwork, but, you know, not necessarily pressure itself. And so, I'm sure you'll get to that in your design, but – so data and the research question's not going to be…

I got you – so there needs to be a better link between the two – problems with semantics – okay.

I think I might have the same question – I'm not sure. But, I think conceptually I'm having a hard time doing – and first, let me say I didn't see the schedule until yesterday – so I haven't seen your paper or any paper – but, are you interested in deadline pressure in a time frame or in disclosures – what's your construct?

So, this is an interesting project. Where it really started out with - time pressure - that was our interest. But, as we got into it a little bit, we found that there was quite a bit of research already out there, and really where we felt the biggest contribution would be – with the research – and perhaps we need to flush this out a little more – make it more clear – was really trying to see whether, or not, it was really the effect of this disclosure. Whether or not there was change in practice – where it really wasn't the disclosure – it really was just the change in practice that occurred as a result of this disclosure. Whether or not the ability to identify auditors under this time pressure has changed as a result of this accounting standard.

That was really where we thought there was more contribution, and so, we probably still need to work on making sure that is clearly indicative of what we were interested in. We feel like though, however, before we can make that leap, we have to really nail down that – any association that might be there pre-FAS 165 – really, probably was due to time pressure. I don't know if you feel like – I don't know if that's necessary – but we feel like it's necessary. So, let us know if you don't think it is.

Yeah, I think it's just hard to know if you change the deadline – if it actually means we have less pressure or more pressure. It could be that they were just trying to avoid subsequent event disclosures – in terms of the audit addressing those or not. So, it could be something else that you may be measuring or picking up, but I'll think about it.

Yeah – okay – keep thinking about it, especially as we get through some of the research design to see if that maybe answers some of your questions – and, again, maybe it's just some of our writing – our framing – that just needs to be cleaned up.

Joe.

Hey, the big question here, I guess – so, after 2004, we know with AS 3 that audit report dates where pushed back. So, how do you know it's, I guess, 165 versus just the change in the PCAOB definition and what relates to the actual audit report date? How much of your pre-period includes prior to 2004?

And I'm not being critical in the sense that maybe we look at the change in AS 3 in combination with SFAS 165 as, maybe, audit report date was meaningless; whereas prior to 2004, there was a large, rich literature in audit report lag, and it was a lot of meaning with that variable. But now, we're in a world where – we had a sorting mechanism before to infer who had issues versus those that didn't. And now, everyone's been thrown into the same report date.

You know, I think that's a great question. In fact, I'm going to skip ahead now - just to answer that question - to this particular slide.[ii] So, what we did, over these next brackets, as you can see – we split the sample based on pre-FAS 165 and post-FAS 165. So, with FAS 165, it was effective for fiscal years beginning after June 15, 2009. So, that was kind of the timing. And so what we did is we calculated the difference, in days, between the audit report date and the filing date – so when the company actually filed – in both the pre-period as well as the post-period. And we thought it was really interesting, because this was straddled right on the accounting standard that came out.

And so, this was the pre-period. I don't know if you can see – it's really small – but you can see that less than fifty percent of the sample observations in the pre-period were within four days on average, but then you see this really long tail and the average number of days – overall for this distribution – was ten. So, there was an average of ten days between the audit report date and the actual filing of the 10-K, the annual report.

Tim, you should show a boxplot, year by year, with the difference, right? So, if you have the boxplot of the days, and then you show since ever, since available, since 2000-09 – then you can say that it's not the AS, but it's the whole thing.

Perfect – yeah, okay, now that's a great…

Just show the trend.

…suggestion. Now, this is the post. So, and this is zero right here – so over ninety percent – it was actually over ninety-five percent – now there's no difference. It's on the same day. And so – but yeah, I think that's a great suggestion.

I have a question – can I ask you a question?

Sure.

Just in addition to my suggestion. Alright, well, first, I think the thing is backwards, right? Companies that have bad quality tend to result in longer audits – it's not the other way around, right? So, you will never be able to disentangle that relationship. So, maybe, the tone of the paper should be that – with the current rules or the current practice, we have lost the information that date. And then you don't have to show us causality, because you will probably never get to that, right?

Yeah, now that's a great point.

And then, I think it circles back to then you don't have to make it all about this FASB disclosure – it's just saying – we're in the new world of regulation, and we've lost this signal, right?

Yeah.

And I think that's a big – you know, that way you're not getting like – I have to prove it's 165 – because then people will be like – oh, I don't know if it's...

It might be subsequent events…

...right – which speaks...

Which you can – and I, to another thing that we talked about before – about these fee restatements. So, how sometimes – about ten percent of the time – in year two, the next year's fee disclosures restate last year's fees, because we didn't even have time to tell them the fees. And then, there was actually a restatement of the fees. So, really, an interesting question is – whether these fee restatements are informative even in the current period when the date is not important.

Okay – no, great. Thank you.

But, then, this is – you have pre- and post-, right? But, in reality, what the data shows is – a decline, decline, decline, decline, decline – right? When the ICFR opinions came by, then the audit report got longer, and then longer, and then longer, and now it's a 10-K date, right? So, maybe it'll be nice to just – not only pre-, post- – but actually do something about the years.

The years.

Right - you have a lot of data, so you can add year to your data, right?

Yeah – good.

So, can you speak to the – I think – there are two things that I'm a little confused about. Maybe you already addressed them. So one is when you say it's time pressure. So, do firms consistently have – particular firms – have time pressure all the time? And, looking at the distribution of those date changes would be helpful to see whether or not you're actually picking up people who are consistently having time pressure.

The second one – issue – seems to be that – wouldn't it be the distribution of the clients in a particular office, and how closely tight the fiscal year ends are of those clients? That might be a better measure of how high pressure is actually applied – it would be consistent. Because you have a lot of filers at the same – near the same date – so some distribution of – the standard deviation, let's say, of days in that office would be an indicator of time pressure. I mean, maybe you've dealt with both of those, but both those seem to be getting more at time pressure than just looking at these individually.

So, I think that's a great suggestion. We do control for that exact variable in all of our misstatement models. So, that is one of our controls – is that workload compression at the audit office level. So, that is in there. That is, obviously, a source of pressure. I guess we were focusing on the engagement level for now where they're right against the wire. There may be an interactive effect as well – so that might be something. Again, the time pressure piece – we were really trying to establish whether or not that – you know – is this consistent with prior research? I think our more interesting or the area where we contribute more is really whether or not this potential signal is now changed as a result of…

Just as a follow-up, it would seem that if you have offices that don't appear to have a lot of pressure because there's a lot of time between filers – did they move their dates consistent with your arguments about the fact that these date got moved because of these subsequent events? That would be also informative about what's going on with that movement of the dating.

Okay, now look across the board, again, in that post period across all fifty thousand observations - there is now ninety-five percent…

Right.

…there is now no difference in the time, but yeah, that's something we can look at.

Now, can I as quick question over here – we're a little neglected over on this side of the room?

Yes.

So, I'm a little bit troubled by your significant coefficient on the within a week variable, since you're also controlling for the last day. If an audit partner makes the decision that he's okay signing off before the last day possible – is there any time pressure at all? And if there's not, the fact that you get a significant result there makes me question the significant result on the last day variable. It seems like maybe you're picking up on something else.

What do you think it could be?

I don't know the answer to that question, but if there's no time pressure in the case of the last week – and I would argue that there's not – and you're still getting a result there, then I don't know what that's capturing.

So, would it be better if we – instead of using the full week – we drill that down to maybe two or three, four days, something like that? Because, I would argue that, even when you're within a couple of days – like in our situation – the anecdotal evidence that I gave before we started.

We weren't filing on the last day. We were filing – I don't know – we probably ended up filing four or five days before the actual deadline. But, as we got closer, the pressure mounted and we started working around the clock, so I think that there is obvious – I think that there is pressure. I would argue that there is.

Okay.

Audit partners in the room, you know, they may…

I'd be really interested to hear that as well. My experience was that we never – we basically never had it done before the last possible minute because we always wanted – the answer to how much audit work should you do is always more than you've done. And so we wanted as much time as we possibly could to do as much as we could possibly do before we had to put pencils down. And so, if we made a decision we'd done enough two days early, then that – it didn't seem like time pressure.

Yeah, and what you need to remember to is that – we see this change where there's no difference between the filing date and the audit report date, but there's a still a lot of companies out there that file much before or even a few days before the actual required filing deadline. We're trying to get the proximity of the audit report date and the required filing deadline. So, these guys are kind of pushed out further into the process.

Okay.

But that – it's something to consider.

---

[i] Transcription Note: The original transcript has been edited for flow and ease of reading. Any changes to content were not intended to change the overall message associated with the applicable discussion.
[ii] Transcription Note: This refers to the presentation slides, which are also included for reference in the symposium web-site.

Research Session 1 – Ann Backof [i]

<u>Questions and Answers</u>

Can you go back to the previous slide... [ii]

Sure.

...could I have that? So, could you clear up for me – why that estimation inaccuracy production also does not – I'm trying to get some sense of why does it not getting it right not affect your competence – why isn't a signal of competence?

Well, so we tested – we actually went through it, and I'll show you the results. We ran a few different models to test the linkages – to see if it would load on competence or not. But when we originally hypothesized this, we thought that estimation inaccuracy direction – so, if we sit and look at the magnitude of the error itself. Then that tells whether or it's accurate or not. And when we're thinking about competence – the same level of competence to get you the same magnitude of the error – but when we're thinking about the direction of that error – that's when we thought that management's incentive would come into play here. So, we would have a greater impact on perceptions of trustworthiness rather than competence itself.

Yeah.

So, we felt like estimation inaccuracy direction really impacted perceptions of trustworthiness. And so, when I present a bit more and H2, I'll go through the prior literature that talks about and has looked at this idea of trustworthiness with respect to management's provided evidence, and why we believe that it's going to play out the way we predicted – okay?

Yes.

Two comments – and I'll actually have two more contributions for you.

That's wonderful, and Ashley is taking notes – so this is great – thank you.

So, the comments are that – you might want to do an analogy that is continually done in the bank – financial industry – that I'm familiar with. So, we normally do stress testing of models. This is, you know, running models through several analyses and look to see what they're able to accomplish – stuff like that. But we also do what is called back testing and that's very common.

Right.

So back testing is basically look at what was done – with the physical model – but now that more time has passed – you have more information, you can know how well you dealt with the uncertainty at the time you made those assumptions, etc.

Right.

So you may want to use that technology, because – you understand?

Right.

You can learn more.

Thank you.

So now, in terms of the contributions. Those are a very timely – time, because the PCAOB is looking at all the issues about estimates and are looking very closely. They are going to be coming out with proposals – for auditors, auditing estimates. So, while they're doing this, it's going to be directly relevant, so get it published quickly, because there's a contribution. If management comes to know that auditors are looking – actually do that testing – it is going to constrain their behavior in playing hooky and acting loose in the future. So, it's having a disabling effect on management's behavior in the future.

Okay.

So that deterrence, in my opening, raises audit quality.

Right - okay.

That's one contribution.

Okay.

The other is – everything that you talk about in relation to management is also done by specialists. And as you know, there are good types of specialists that are either management-provided specialists or even the auditor provides specialists – if you do it at once. And, you could potentially do the very same thing with a specialist's work also – and that would have a disabling effect on the specialist's work...

Right.

...but you better get it right – I will be checking on you.

Thank you, and, so, that is a limitation. We're just looking at management and what they say. But we do acknowledge, certainly, that specialists are playing a very large role in the estimation process – so thank you for that. Okay, so back to each one, and hopefully I can give you a satisfactory answer to this linkage here.

Yeah, Marcy.

I just have a clarifying question – I'm curious about the materiality of this inaccuracy. Is this estimation uncertainty resolving over time? Is that what this error or inaccuracy is? And is it within reasonable range?

So, I can show you – basically what we have in the actual materials itself – it was a valuation of a trademark, and it's a revenue growth rate assumption that we're looking at. And, in each setting, the assumption is either over-stated or under-stated by one percent. Now – if I jump, I can show you what it looks like actually.[iii] So, this is the analysis that they received – a sensitivity analysis – and in the box up there it highlights the impact of this estimation inaccuracy.

And so, we ran a few conditions here to see how close you had to be – how much of a cushion – if the cushion actually impacted whether or not the direction had an effect. And so, in this setting here, the cushion went up from a hundred and forty thousand up to two hundred and seventy-eight; the other side down; and then we ran a mutual condition. And, to see if the trend of these impacted it – and we did not find that the trend actually had an impact – it was still the direction of that inaccuracy.

In terms of materiality, we did make a setting where it is relatively close – and so, this is the setting where the assumption was under-stated – and so it was inconsistent with management's incentives – they were conservative basically. In the setting where it was consistent with management's incentives, we presented a trend where it was going down year over year – that cushion was shrinking. So, it was definitely a strong manipulation. But we tested to see if that affect went away – if we didn't have a trend but we just had noise in the prior two years, where we did not see the cushion continuing going down – we still saw the impact of the direction of the inaccuracy. Does that answer your question?

I'm not sure – I need to read the paper.

Okay – it's on SSRN.

Okay – any other questions? Yeah.

What are management's incentives? Like, did the people know what management's incentives were?

So, it's set up as an impairment analysis. And so, what we do in the actual background – we set it up and say – you're auditing, or you're planning the audit, of the current year impairment analysis. And it's an impairment analysis for a trademark. And so, basically, the incentive is to ensure that the fair value exceeds the book value so you don't have to write down the trademark itself.

And so, if you look on this discounted cash flow – which is what we give them – which is their valuation model – up top, we have a fair value estimate on the first line, then we have the book value, and then we have that cushion. So the incentive is to ensure that the fair value estimate exceeds the book value, and in all of their conditions, it does. It just approaches that idea of an impairment if management had overstated prior period assumptions based on the current year-to-date results. Does that answer your question?

Yes, it was just a lack of clarity – you probably bring it up in the paper. But, it's not entirely clear that if you – you might understate one year in order to overstate the next year versus – and so, what's your incentive is at a different time – it's not quite clear.

So, we already had, in this setting, the overall incentive is to avoid recording an impairment loss – regardless of what year you're operating in – you would not want to have to take that loss onto your income statement. That's what we're using.

Yeah.

How do you manipulate the evidence specificity?

So, we manipulate evidence specificity – right here.[iv] So, this is actually the less-specific condition. So, there are three key assumptions – there is a location growth rate – so how many stores are they going to open in a given year; there's a revenue per store growth rate; and then there's a discount rate. The assumption that we manipulate is the revenue per store – or per location – the growth of that revenue. So, it's key assumption two. And so, in this key assumption two, this is presented as the prior year workpaper, which includes management's justification for their assumption.

And so, in the less-specific condition, we state here that they expect the revenue to grow annually at eight percent – and that is based on their argument that they are going to increase sales prices, as well as increased customer demand. And what's important is in both of these conditions – so we say that they're going to increase sales prices, and they believe that they can do this based on the results of recent market research. Where – they say they're going to increase customer demand – and they're going to increase that by instituting a new marketing campaign. So, this is the less specific condition.

In the more specific condition, we simply expand on the actual research – the market research – that supports the ability to increase that price, as well as the type of marketing campaign that they are going to engage in. So, we try to hold the generic information constant across the specificity of the evidence. They know that there is marketing research that supports the increased price, and they know that there's a new marketing campaign – the more specific evidence goes into the details of that.

I don't want to neglect this side – so you won't feel I do. Yes.

So, that doesn't sound like specificity to me in the context of a complex estimate. I was thinking of something like you have a point estimate – or you have a point estimate and a range and a trend – and here, I mean, when you hold the information constant. Or, you had same – a same store growth – you can have lots of different same stores that made up that. But here, it's kind of like more supported or - I don't know. Specificity makes me think about precision and that's not what you're – and I can see how that could kind of relate to it.

So, let's go back to this idea of support. So, it's basically going back to the support theory literature – that how good are you in support of a hypothesis or a prediction? And so, what we're arguing here is that the evidence acts that support, and the specificity of that evidence is what we're manipulating. So, we're not manipulating the specificity of the actual data that they are using to – so for – I think what you were saying we have multiple data points…

Right.

…that we're aggregating, right? We're not manipulating that by any means. We're actually looking at it – in terms of the justification provided by management.

So, it's more or less justification?

Yeah. So the question was – is it more or less justification?

Yeah, I just think in the context of complex estimates study paper – I mean, I flipped through and found that you had made particularly of that. It didn't seem like specificity to me – I don't know what else you want to want to call it.

Okay – certainly, we can think about that. Thank you. Yep.

Where you talked about the incentives of management, you said it could be interpreted as a persuasion attempt?

Uh-huh.

But, it's not directly in your models – so, are you interpreting the persuasion attempt as part of whether the trust aspect that comes through?

Yes – exactly. So how does the trust come through – and we also gather measures of how they perceived the evidence. Did they perceive it as biased? Did they perceive it as providing more or less support to justify that idea of – is it perceived as a persuasion attempt? So, those are the underlying constructs, but we have the evidence to look at that.

Okay – I was just wondering about that.

Thank you.

I'm wondering – let me first make sure I understand the results, and then have a question.

Sure.

Sorry – so, when it's inaccurate and consistent with their incentives, they combine with the increased risk and increase effort.

Right.

So, I really like it because this is showing that auditors are doing a good job – like you think they should. Is your assumption that they should be increasing risk with this condition?

So, in this condition, we don't make more of a statement about if it's over- or under-stated, what is the more appropriate risk assessment. What we do find is – that when the prior period assumption is overstated – it appears aggressive – they do react to that in their reliability assessments and in their risk assessments.

What I'm wondering about is – rather than compare it to the other condition – if your control for – you know, it seems like it could potentially compare to zero. Like, what percentage are increasing or what percentage are not increasing in that condition? Just thinking that would be interesting, because you could almost make an argument that they should all be increasing – and compared to – I'm curious about what percentage...?

So, actually at the planning judgments – so the planning judgments, not the reliability assessments. You want to look at the risk assessments and the planned audit effort – is that what you would go straight to?

Yeah, I just think it's just a totally entity, independent measure – so, it seems like you could make an argument that they should be increasing – because this is consistent with the bias versus what percentage is not increasing in terms of – maybe, if you're thinking about if auditors are doing a good job – there may be those that are arguing that they're not. And I'm curious about how that – how big that...

I can certainly look into that. I don't know, but I can certainly look at that. Definitely. Yes.

I'm curious if we have a measure of the belief of – that you have a measure of the belief in the ability of the company to achieve those objectives. For example, the increase in the market share and increase in price, because, to go back to Brian's question about specificity, I actually think you may have captured this pretty well - as far as the original support theory, right? Because, Tversky and Kahneman[v] look at unpacking things, right?

Yes.

So, you have a probability of – for example, death by natural causes – and in this case increasing market share.

And how are you going to document that into the process?

Right – and so, if you start specifying for the company the number of ways that we're going to increase market share. If you can show that unpacking factor actually increases – that would be the perfect process for this.

So, we have – like I said – we did measure their perception of the support that the evidence provides. But you would want to look at a justification measure, or what exactly?

So, if you asked the auditors for a probability that they can or that they could have increased market share under both of those conditions, you can actually calculate the unpacking factor.

Right, I don't know if we asked that, but I'll see what we get. I'll look through the instrument to see if had anything that we can certainly – I can see that. So, looking at the actual underlying components? Okay, thank you – I'll see what we have to measure that.

Last question.

Oh, last question – so, let me put up a pretty graph – okay, there we go.[vi]

So, this is a question that I hate to ask, because I know how hard it is to do an experiment, and to change anything in the experiment. So, my question is – why did you choose just to measure audit effort in total? Because, the standards – as I read them, the current standards – I know they're going to be, potentially be re-written. But we have three methods for testing estimates – subsequent data, testing management's process, and doing your own independent estimate.

Right.

When I see this and I see management may be incompetent or not trustworthy – I think – well, then maybe I won't test management's process, I should go do my own independent estimate – we'll go get some quick data. And I know some firms are kind-of interested in doing all three as much as they can, so maybe that would be a way that you argue – why you measure effort.

Right.

But I think it would be cool to see if – and not to tell you to do a follow-up study – but to see when does this get so strong that they revert away from testing management's process and not doing something totally dependent – which I think they are already doing. But, I think it would be an interesting – a little bit different twist. Because, a lot of this, I think it makes sense, but I would like to see the ah-ha. What's totally surprising – what do we really gain?

So, I think your scope – the scope of your project – is all about testing management's process, and that's fine, but I think of maybe as the next step – what I would like to see – is that next – what change in your procedures that would actually...

And we can certainly do that, but I will leave you with something interesting,[vii] and encourage you to go read the paper.

Yeah.

So, if you read the paper, pay attention to the additional analyses, and look at what happens when it's more specific versus less specific. And the grayed-out boxes are changing the actual process. So, it's more specific, we're finding that estimation inaccuracy direction is impacting directly the reliability of management estimation process – their perceptions. But, when it is less-specific, we're finding that auditors are taking a little bit different cognitive route getting to their planning judgments.

---

[i] Transcription Note: The original transcript has been edited for flow and ease of reading. Any changes to content were not intended to change the overall message associated with the applicable discussion.

[ii] Transcription Note: This refers to the presentation slides, which are also included for reference in the symposium web-site.

[iii] Transcription Note: Please see endnote ii.

[iv] Transcription Note: Please see endnote ii.

[v] Appears to be referring to Tversky and Koehler (1994) – which includes references to other works by A. Tversky and D. Kahneman – with this reference (as included in the paper – but it's also possible the applicable study was not located in the transcription process): Tversky, A., and D. Koehler. 1994. Support theory: A nonextensional representation of subjective probability. *Psychological Review* 101 (4): 547–567.

[vi] Transcription Note: Please see endnote ii.

[vii] Transcription Note: Please see endnote ii.

***Research Session 1 – Ganesh Krishnamoorthy*[i]**

<u>Questions and Answers</u>

What's the bias – bias with respect to what?

Bias in the sense that it's not – it's an incomplete picture of the audit quality of the firm, right? Because the inspection reports are only disclosing the deficiencies found. It's probably not looking for strengths – which is a different discussion altogether – but if the signal provided by the inspection reports is that all you're reporting is deficiencies.

But, it's just deficient with respect to no deficiencies. Not deficiency with respect to you did an awesome audit and ninety-nine terrible ones.

Yes, but it all depends on what you're thinking as what the baseline is, right? Deficiencies versus no deficiencies – that point's taken. But, in the sense that – if you do – if an inspection is only focused on deficiencies and you find only deficiencies – yes. But, if you're going to have a viewpoint where you're looking for a lot of evidence – which might provide evidence on strengths – which is also useful in the audit process. So, this certainly doesn't make the argument that this entire argument for making inspections – that it's a signal of audit quality to the outside world. It's a way of improving the audit quality – that point is well taken.

Okay, sure.

What we are examining here is a different view of the world where some of the information that's gathered in the information process is potentially wasted away. Because, there's a lot to be learned from the strengths as well. And so, it's not – we're not questioning what the current regime is – just saying that if you shift the regime to one that is more balanced then what kind – does it matter to investors? That's really the question here.

Well, maybe it's just the word bias – it's such a loaded kind of word. You're really just talking about perspectives. So, maybe it's just the word bias, because that's more like a human kind of thing. The inspectors went in, and they have a bias – it sounds bad. If their job was to locate deficiencies – so there really wasn't a bias – that's their job. It's like if you took your car in for an inspection – you expect them to come back with one tail light is out, and, you know, whatever, whatever, whatever. So...

But your mirrors are good...

...or your headlights.

You don't say that your mirrors were good.

Yeah, you know – I think that's right.

So, it's of course right, but you probably haven't heard it.

Now, that's a fair point, and, again, I think the idea here is that if you're only focusing on deficiencies, you might be losing a good part of whatever else they could find which could be potentially useful.

And as you've said deficiencies every time, but you've got significant up there – do you mean significant? Or are these just deficiencies? I don't recall any gradation that the PCAOB – insignificant deficiencies they'll let pass – they won't let anything pass. But, I think it's just the auditor didn't satisfy that particular inspector, and if the firm – the audit firm – can't talk him out of it, it's a deficiency. And significant has nothing to do with it. They do this for internal control, but not for deficiencies. So, if you strike that, would it change your presentation?

No.

Okay, just go for it.

The reason is that – I think – our manipulations are essentially based off of the deficiencies that are actually reported in the inspection reports. So we essentially, you know, take those and then use those as manipulations.

Are we going to get to individual companies – knowing inspection results for an individual company - or for all of KPMG, together?

Okay, the way we have structured it here is that – it is going to be a firm report – similar to what the position is right now – with no disclosure of specific companies. In other words, it's going to be Issuer A, Issuer B – which is how it is currently disclosed. So, we don't make any recommendations in terms of making drastic changes to – for example – providing specific information about the company that the investor's making judgments on – or not even the industry in which that relates to. So, we are still working within the parameters – the disclosure parameters – in that regard.

So, all of KPMG's clients are either praised or tainted by this report – you're going to consider the direction of the information. It's more demerits – it's more deficiencies than expected. And that, you think, has all the clients are going to have a change in their investment desirability based on that report?

Yeah, I mean it's very hard to disentangle what you're probably referring to – is this contagion effect, right? I mean, basically, the report is essentially saying Issuer A had this, Issuer B had this, and so forth. And, the question is – to what extent does an investor take that information and apply it in the context of a specific question? So, that's part of what we are not able to disentangle – the contagion effect. This is a firm-wide effect – that is typically being communicated in these inspection reports. And, essentially, these problems are then, in some ways, investors trying to assimilate this in terms of making decisions about - based on where the inspection mattered…

You know, ninety-five percent of KPMG's clients were not inspected that year.

That's correct.

Okay, just to understand - this is kind of a strange land, right?

Given the nature of the inspections, they're going to list a bunch, and there's going to be a lot of positives and a lot of negatives – how's that going to end up being – how do you expect an investor to weight that? You're not just going to get all good or all bad – it's going to be fifteen different companies with some good, some bad, and in different areas. How are you going to best base on that?

Well, what do you mean by good and bad? Maybe there's something about…

Well, you talked about having information about a good audit – how are you going to see seventeen different inspections with good and bad – and make an individual investment decision on one company based on all these conflicting sources of information?

Well, we are talking specifically here about in - when you look at a real world report – a mix of deficiencies and strengths – you could potentially have seventeen different companies with a mix of deficiencies and strengths…

Right.

Now, unfortunately, in an experimental sense, we can't. The package would be messy. So, what we're working with – and I'm going to – when I get to the manipulations I can tell you exactly what we did – we have, essentially, focused on one company – Company A – so taking one of those companies – an excerpt from the report, and essentially leave that out as having deficiencies or a mix of deficiencies and strengths. So, in that respect, it is sort of focusing on just one company among – but, you know, it's sort of there – I'm happy to hear your suggestions, but it becomes very messy to be able to communicate that in the experiment setting.

I get that, it's just, in reality, they're not just going to get one company. So, how can I extrapolate that to when I see KPMG's inspection report? Because I'm going to see more than Company A.

Understood, but there's always a trade-off you got to make between, you know, how externally balanced something is going to be vis-a-vie being even bigger. Then you're turning so many different dials here. I mean the alternative could be for us to be able to provide – once we get to how we manipulated this, maybe you have some thoughts on how we could have done it differently?

Yeah.

Can I ask you – is it known as you go from no deficiencies to some to a lot of deficiencies – just take the deficiency side, don't bother about the strengths – is it known that more deficiencies, the investors punish KPMG's clients?

Well, that – that's what we're trying to figure out here in the sense…

But, you got strengths in there to complicate it further. If it's not known whether deficiencies – more deficiencies – matter, which it may or may not. But, Deloitte didn't go bankrupt when they had a Part Two – and neither of the other firms – and KPMG looked good for a while, but now they've got more than anybody else.

So, what you're asking is – is it just the number of deficiencies – does that matter? Or is that?

Well, you're saying – does deficiencies and strengths matter? And I'm just saying – if deficiencies alone – which is the real world now – would – is that known already? More deficiencies would lead to worse results from investors?

No, we don't know that.

Okay.

And that's not – we are not trying to address that in this. But, you're right – we don't know if more deficiencies are going to do it. What we are looking at here – so that that's a different question.

But it's related to your H1, isn't it? It's a piece of H1 – half of it.

Progressively, we are going – the only complication here is that all we did was three different deficiencies – you know, that's not exactly like it – we have three deficiencies, and then – so, here's the – before I jump into it.[ii] So, it's a three by two experiment. So, in one condition, we have three deficiencies only – no strengths. Second, we have two deficiencies, and one of those deficiencies actually gets converted into a strength. And, the third one, we have one deficiency, and two of those deficiencies remaining get converted into strengths.

So, we wanted to keep the strength of all things constant, so, as you can see, it is basically take the same pieces of information and just turn the deficiency into strength. So, to answer your question, the copying – we can't address that simply because our results are based on the joint effect of decreasing the deficiency and adding strength. Does that make sense?

Yeah.

Yeah.

And so, one of the things that bothers me a little bit about this – and I think this goes to Bill's point – is that regulations are written not to give out, for example, traffic certificates or tickets that say good driver – it's to give tickets for having violated something, right? So Bill's point, I think, is a good one.

That, in fact, you have to know whether – given that almost every regulation in the United States is written in the negative form – is this regulation actually changing their views about the quality without adding the complexity of strength. Because, we just don't give out good awards when we have a government regulator overseeing someone's behavior. It's always are you doing something that's in compliance or not? We don't go, turn around, and give you a badge for doing a good job.

Understood – I mean, I think that I'm not debating what's the practice. What we are asking here is that during the inspection process, it's very hard to imagine that they don't – they either don't observe, or have the potential to observe – things that are also going right. The strengths that the firm has – and that feedback loop – at least, based on the inspection reports – is lost. So, your point's well taken in the sense that that's the current regime.

But, if you step back and say – well, there is this other piece of information that's potentially gathered during the inspection process right now – or could be potentially be gathered – to reinforce. For example, firms could say – well, Issuer A, B, and C – well, you have these deficiencies, but you also have these things really good. So, the firms can come back and say – okay, maybe that's feedback we can use in terms of getting things right – maybe reinforcing things – and so forth. So, that feedback – as it relates to strengths – is a potential – that if that feedback were there, it's of some benefit.

[iii]And so, to answer your question, Bill, essentially we took these three findings – deficiencies – and turned the same deficiencies from an actual report – and turned that into strengths – and that's the only way we knew to be able to keep the weight constant across – the information value constant.

[iv]*Let me just say that - I think that what you just ended with – is where I would begin. Because, I think, after looking through all of what you've done, what you're trying to do is take the current inspection report, and say – what could we do differently? Or, what could we do with the inspection process differently, and would it make a difference to investors?*

And I think, for me, it took a while to get to that point – where I can see where you're going. There's some questions on how you do it, but I still think that maybe if you were to present it as a comparison of the current regime to the options, and what investors – I don't want to say prefer – but use. I think that might be a good way to sell it.

That's a good point. I mean, this is one of those things where you start out, we think – oh, this is a neat idea. But when you start – and you start to operationalize it – there are still problems with respect to some of our manipulations, like I said. One of our big problems we're facing now is that there is no way around the fact that our reporting – disclosure of deficiencies versus strengths – is encumbered with audit quality differences, right? So, we don't really know whether it's the balance or it's the audit quality. That's a way that we might be able to try to fix that.

At the present time, I think, basically, what the big message here is that these – we can always debate about whether these alternative views that we put together – they are all valid or not –

whatever. Already some of them have been debated – and some of them – there is some argument for why some of these alternative regimes that we put are – over the other five – sells. Maybe they're legitimate sells. And what we find here is that this – at least, again, you don't want to think about sub-optimal behavior, because certainly you need some benchmark. But, certainly, there appears to be a least favorable type of judgment that is associated with the current regime. Which means – that it's potentially biasing investor judgments to the downside – and maybe significantly – and that's sort of the big message. And, again, struggling in some of the other things, but if that message is of some value, I think we have some value in this study.

---

[i] Transcription Note: The original transcript has been edited for flow and ease of reading. Any changes to content were not intended to change the overall message associated with the applicable discussion.
[ii] Transcription Note: This refers to the presentation slides, which are also included for reference in the symposium web-site.
[iii] Transcription Note: This comment was made by the presenter in some later remarks, but is included as it references back to a prior question.
[iv] Transcription Note: The question and answer presentation, as included in the remainder of this document, continues here (following the deviation noted in endnote "iii" above).

Research Session 2 – Joshua Gunn[i]

<u>Questions and Answers</u>

Hi, good morning. I was wondering – how did you get the data to measure your foreign sales by country and city? So, maybe I misunderstood.

We didn't measure the foreign sales my city – we measured it by country. We got that from Worldscope. So, in the test where we need to have the foreign sales by country, we throw out any observations where they defined it as a region. Say, like Europe foreign sales – we take those out because you can't do it there. So, then they have to disclose it by country, and that's in Worldscope.

Where do I start? Well, first of all, it's, honestly, almost unbelievable that any of the Big Four would lack expertise to do worldwide audits – I doubt that. I mean, these clients are large, right? They just do an audit over there with the PWC Dublin office. I mean, they – all of the Big Four – say that they're multinational firms. That's what they sell.

That's what they say everywhere, right? They have expertise to do it for the largest clients, right? The top – 498 of the Fortune 500 are audited by the Big Four. So how can we say that Big Four Mr. A – that has a little more of a market share – has more quality than Big Four Mr. B? Where does the difference in audit quality come from?

So, from my perspective, it comes from the experience from doing other similar types of audits. So, there's a lot – if you think about – so, here it was yesterday, one of the partners mentioned that they have trainings just trying to decide – trying to train up their auditors on how to select components for which ones to get audits, and what the extent of the procedures were, and how sometimes they miss things – that they select the wrong one – or they put them into rotation plans.

So, these and they – you know, he talked about the fact that they wanted them to make that mistake in the training as opposed to out in the real world. I think the fact that they're doing that training – I think – I don't think it's too far of a stretch – to say that some of them will be making that mistake in the field. And – as they have the expertise – they are a little less likely to.

Yeah, maybe that's an engagement – a big one engagement – for which maybe the personnel of the Dublin office of PWC would be better, but how can you say that, on average, these areas are a trend. I mean, the findings – they clearly show that all these specialty measures are crap. They're all negatively correlated with each other. I'm just now sure what they're showing there – and to other people. I mean, it's just – it's just...

I hear you.

I'm just not sure what I can take from this – that's all.

I mean – we thought it was an interesting question, and we're testing it the best way that we how to.

Maybe.

Yeah, Nick.

So, following up on that, actually, I would be really interested to see how many of the Big Four offices are – Big Seven – and how many of those firms are actually measured in your sample. How many of them have no experience with a multinational firm? Is it many, do you think?

I'd be honest…

At the office level?

That's a good question. I don't have that stat off the top of my head, but that's something that we can definitely take a look at.

My anecdotal evidence tells me that some offices are going to have zero.

Yeah.

Like – very, very little. And so, from an engagement team to engagement team point of view, I can absolutely see the development of some expertise in this area.

Yeah, that's a good point – I think that works. I think that will help – help our case. That's a good point. Thanks.

So, I'd like to make a recommendation on perhaps how you can reframe the paper, and improve the contribution. The other auditor proposal that recently came out from the PCAOB – in the economic analysis, they must justify a need for regulatory intervention. The only evidence they have to justify it right now – as far as I can recall – is inspection data. And, we can't even, really, verify that because it's not in the Part One – it's in the Part Two.

However, your paper, perhaps, offers evidence that there is large variation in audit quality in these multi-jurisdictional audits. And, therefore, perhaps the media does serve as evidence that there is a problem – and a need.

Okay - thank you.

I know that you're just trying to tie it to the normal industry specialization and measures, but did you try looking at just the number of multinationals that you have in each office, and are the results pretty similar? And, I know there's a problem with – the more clients you have, the more multinational audits you'll have. Just also control for the number of clients in the office – just that that might get…

Okay, yeah – we do as a robustness – we do have a linear measure that just separated them into experts – experts and non-experts – we have a linear measurement, and we found similar results. But, it's a good point to control for number of clients.

Just to rebuttal Miguel, my friend, for a minute. I don't see any problem – I still need to read the paper, so I guess I don't fully understand what you're measuring. So, you're saying that, like, the Atlanta office – its international expertise – compared to the Oklahoma City office of a given Big Four. Does that?

For example, it could be – yeah.

Okay, I mean I don't see why that couldn't be the case.

But we have firms, not offices.

Look, the offices – those partners go over to those countries often. I mean, they don't just outsource the whole thing – they're intimately involved in the engagement.

Yeah, I mean, I did a lot of these audits as a practitioner, and I – honestly, the approach varied. You know, so some really big clients – it was extremely well-controlled and lots of visits from the auditor; a lot of other audits it was pretty much just – send some instructions and take it back and check the box.

You could get some more variation – if you look at some of the UK reports that have been coming out – where they discuss some of the approved audit methods. There is wide variation and how they describe their groups. How often departments go off and they don't go, whether they're actual visits or periodic phone calls. There's some insight you can gain from those reports. Just anecdotal – to suggest that there is a wide variation in how these group audits approach the audit.

Thanks.

Yeah.

Do you throw out the office – I mean, this goes to his point about how much experience – do you throw out the offices with no foreign experience, and then test within the set of offices that have foreign experience? Because, that's actually a stronger test of that expertise, because you should still find variation within the people who have experience in the foreign – rather than comparing against people who don't have any. Is it a variation of the group that works and has a lot of international experience?

I mean, if we're going to argue this on multinational experience, it would be unfair to compare it to somebody who has no foreign experience, right? So, the notion about people who have no foreign experience I think is a good one.

Yeah – no, I was just thinking about that a little bit, and that's a good – I think I answered Nick's question a little bit incorrectly – because we throw out any firms that don't have any foreign sales. At least in our sample there wouldn't be anybody who has absolutely zero. Now, it doesn't mean that there's not any that don't have absolutely zero, but there – because our test variable doesn't make sense unless they're are multinational audit.

So, that's the approach that we took. But I'm sure there's a lot of different ways that we could separate that out – and maybe somebody who only has one versus somebody has more than one multinational – there could be a lot of different ways to do it.

I'll just comment on a possible falsification test – I'm not sure this makes sense. But, you could take clients that don't have significant foreign operations – okay, get a whole sample of those. Now, the quality of their audits should not vary with the foreign expertise of the offices and firms, right?

Sure.

And if it does, then you've got something else.

We've got something else – that's a good idea – I like that. We can give that a try.

Yeah.

One more thing to take into account in your cross-sectional test – Phil Lamoreaux's dissertation looks at PCAOB access to workpapers internationally.[ii] And that's going to, probably, have a large part of how well did these big group auditors get involved with the component auditor process.

Yeah, we had the same thought. I started to look at it. I don't know the results - it's not in the paper, but we do have some…

And that could tie you back to the comment here about this proposal – to also look at the group audits subject...

Yeah, we've done a couple of other things that aren't in the paper – like English language and that kind of thing, and it seems to work out. Thanks.

---

[i] Transcription Note: The original transcript has been edited for flow and ease of reading. Any changes to content were not intended to change the overall message associated with the applicable discussion.

[ii] A reference to this document is the following – from ProQuest - Lamoreaux, P. T. (2013). *Does PCAOB inspection exposure affect auditor reporting decisions?*(Order No. 3597831). Available from ProQuest Dissertations & Theses Global. (1459215700). Retrieved from http://search.proquest.com/docview/1459215700?accountid=14556.

***Research Session 2 – William Buslepp*[i]**

<u>Questions and Answers</u>

Can you go back to one of the slides?[ii]

Okay.

Yeah – this one. Thank you.

Okay. So, a couple of comments. You need to probably add – one of the important factors is the complexity of the audit – especially if it involves extensive use of specialists. That would, usually, raise audit fees – one of the factors – so that's an important position. And then, here's an argument for you to show why audit fees actually sometimes are not a good measure at all of audit quality – that's why you're looking for something better.

And probably why they've invented this – the PCAOB in its audit quality indicators Concept Release, right – which you cite at the end – are highlighting certain factors for me. So, the first four factors of audit professionals are staffing leverage, partner workload, and management and staff workload. So, that's where you're going – so that's good. So, let me give you an example – sort of a counter example – as to why audit fees may not be a good measure of audit quality.

So, imagine a company that has sold off one of its business units, but the rest of the company – that's still under audit – has been of the same risk. So, the risk hasn't changed. But, because one unit has been sold off, the audit fees will probably come down. Does that mean that the audit firm's displaying lower audit quality? No, it doesn't mean that at all. So, that's a unique counter-example that you could use to say that we do need to come up with alternative measures like you're doing.

Thank you.

Thanks. So, I worry some that what you're picking up on is basically the average client size that's been audited by these firms.

Okay.

Because, it's going to be really hard to get out – I know you control for like the client size – the individual client size.

Yeah.

But, you might try controlling for, like, the average class size of the firm.

Well, we do break out the results. We do break out Big Four or, well, the top – the annually inspected – at the end, and we do find results when we get rid of the lower ones as well. Because that was a big question the first time we got our comments was that – are we picking up just these little, piddly little ones that have one client? So, we do break out the Big Four and the BDOs and such – stuff like that.

Okay, so there's still quite a bit of variation in client size, even within the Big Four. The other thing I would say is you might check – so you showed in one of your slides – I think it's a couple forward, about, if you find it[iii] *– and you showed that some of the firms are actually giving hours worked by their staff, right?*

Yep.

Could you, perhaps, validate your measure by comparing it for those firms where it's available?

Well, our measure isn't an hour-based measure.

It should correlate.

Yeah, it should correlate. That's a good idea. Yeah, we hadn't thought about that, I guess.

I would be much more likely to believe you're getting what you think you're getting if it does highly correlate with those firms that are putting that out there.

Yeah, but really the only one that really does that – that gives you the number of hours – is Ernst & Young.

You showed two, I think it was.

That's just overtime, so the PwC is…

So then add 40 hours.

Yeah, I guess we'd have to add – try to – let's see if it would work.

So, it seems to me that you're not doing a real test of the abnormal fees here, because your slide[iv] *says fees is equal to rate times hours, and you're estimating workload, which, obviously is hours. And then, you're putting it – so you have to endogenous variables on the right-hand side of your equation. And now, you're having results that look strange – or abnormal fees that are inconsistent with the proper literature – and I think you need to go back and think about how you are going to control for that endogeneity.*

And you're making arguments about – on one of your last slides, you don't put any stars next to abnormal fees, which has about the same T-statistic as your workload measure. The very last slide[v] *I think it was – 1.49 or something. So, I think you really need to be careful that you're not making statements seriously – so you've got a negative sign and you've got the opposite signs. So, you've got something going on with this endogeneity that you're not controlling for.*

Well, we don't find different results if we exclude abnormal fees – I can tell you that.

Well, it's still – I mean, what I'm saying is if you're going to do this, either orthogonalize the abnormal fees from the workload, or use another method to control for that endogeneity to assure yourself that, in fact, what you're picking up is a measure that's different from what you would be getting if you were using fees.

Yeah.

You want to assure us that you've actually gotten workload – that they're not picking up something else.

Yeah.

So, you have an audit firm-level measure, and you don't have a lot of years. But, how sticky is that over those years that we do have?

It does change over time. On average, you find that the – consistent with what we saw yesterday – that workload is decreasing, but it is sticky – I will admit that.

And so, I notice that did you – it looked like you did – a changes?

Yep.

Or just the changes in accruals - why not do that with restatements as well?

Well, can you really say it when you have a logit model, that if it's a change that that leads to higher restatements? I don't know.

I don't know. I'm just not very convinced with the accruals. And the going concern measure – you just look at whether or not they issue a going concern, right? But you don't really tie it out to the accuracy of the going concern? It seems like almost ninety percent of the missed going concerns are on the conservative side.

Yeah.

Which, for me, it doesn't necessarily indicate lower audit quality – it just indicates that they're being more conservative.

Yeah, but that's like a going concern. That - I think a first time going concern suggests that they did something different though, doesn't it? Versus that – if, I could understand if it's just in continuum – oh, I do issue my going concern the same way I did last year, you know? That would – but, if you look at the first time they issue a going concern, it suggests that they did something that they didn't do it the previous year.

Yeah. I still think that the changes measures. So, if you go the changes and workload – and you can throw that into a logit model. You don't have to a change in restatements – it's just whether or not there was a restatement or, after they were hired, there was a restatement or a restatement on the same years. Then you have a change in workload with that – it would just strengthen, I think.

Yeah, that might be – we might be able to do a t-test like that, but it kind of worries me.

I don't know if you can do this with your data or not, but I don't think your hypothesis is as linear as you're saying it is. In other words, you can't always say – degree of workload on audit quality. I think there is – there must be some kind of curve in there. Just like that optimal point.

Yes.

Because a low workload could also mean low audit quality – as well as for a high workload. So, you need to think of somehow you could see if there's a curve in your data – and some kind of optimum point. That this workload had the lowest level of restatements, the lowest level of accruals, whatever.

Yeah.

I don't know if you can do that in your data, because – but I don't think it's linear.

I think we run it as deciles and as a high-low variable – we get similar results when we run that – yeah. So, to try to take something that's quintile – because I know it – yeah, I don't think it's as perfect as anyone says it is, but we're just saying that higher equals – probably, more likely – equals worse.

You are treating all the restatements as the same. Maybe you can get some interesting results if you do sub-sample analysis. You can differentiate fraud in these statements – as well as non-fraud.

But this is a good question. Do you expect that higher workload is going to detect worse fraud? Or they're going to be more likely to miss bad frauds? Or are they going to miss - more likely to miss minor frauds? My guess is they're going to be more likely to miss minor frauds. Because, you know…

That's an interesting question.

…my guess is that an auditor's smart enough that if it's a high-risk client, they're going to change their workload. Our results are on average results, but, you know, the workload is probably going to change when there's significant factors that affect that.

One of the other things that, you know, we didn't find a lot with meet or beating – I will tell you that. But why? Because I would have guessed that if you're a smart partner, you know that that's going to be a higher risk than if it's just one where it showed consistent profit or where it's not really at the high risk level.

Okay, do you have any suggestions for the quality of a workload or the quantity of workload from a member?

No, I don't think have any suggestions regarding quality or, because there, obviously, I wish we…

Because your paper is showing that more workload results in worse…

Yep.

Maybe they can adjust workload to be a little more smart?

Yeah, I wish we could, but I don't think we have that – enough information, or else…

So, your measure is calculated at the audit-firm level, right?

Yep.

And you're trying to compare – so, for example, PriceWaterhouse to Deloitte & Touche to try to compare within or between firms?

Yep.

Am I right? Why do you use office fixed-effects then?

We were told in a previous review that we need to control for variations in the offices.

So what you've done is you've stripped out the differences between the firms – which is what you're trying to test. So, all you're capturing now – when you have office fixed-effects – is within office – which is the same – since your variable is calculated within firm – it's within firm variation. So, you're really comparing, say, for example, Deloitte & Touche to itself.

Within the office.

But within the office.

Right, within the office, but the variable's calculated at the firm level. So, really, by controlling with the office fixed-effects you're doing the same thing as controlling for firm-level fixed effects. So, I don't know that these can be interpreted in the way that you want them to be.

Okay.

You should think about it.

Yeah, because we were beat up last time – it was kind of funny because we don't know if you need office fixed-effects, and now we're talking about it again – because it's funny.

So, if you look at Appendix A, there's substantial differences between the Big Four firms and the rest of the smaller firms – and it's a big factor of difference. I mean, could that be driven by the leverage that the Big Four firms use on their engagements? Like the relative balance between staff and partners – do you have any evidence on that?

And then, also, you're sort of making the implicit assumption – by using the percentage of fees – that pay for audit services against the number of accountants – that the fee structure is similar across services and then across firms across services. So, do you have any comments on those – getting more comfortable with the metric?

At this point, yeah, I wish I could come up with something that's better. You know, I don't admit having anything that go across – you know – there might be higher rates at certain ones. But, all I can say is, you know, we've tried it with – and I probably should include it – we tried it with tri-annual – we tried with annual separately – and we get kind of the same results. So, I don't know if – I understand that there'd be differences across firms.

All the way at the back, Will, for you.

Oh, sorry.

So, I don't know if this was what Scott was saying, but if you look at the descriptives – the distribution of your variable of interest – I think it infers that Grant Thornton was five times more busy than Ernst and Young. Which would suggest that what Nick was talking about – there's got to be something else – client size, risk, complexity – something else driving the distribution of that variable. You're going to have to take it into consideration.

Yep.

So, I was thinking about it a little bit – and you might consider looking at just the Audit Analytics data base, because then you'll have a lot of private firm coverage. And they also have information about the size of those private firms, which is the missing link here.

Yeah.

That we're talking about. And so you could – if your goal here – which is an admirable goal – is to get an actual measure of workload that includes private clients – which is extremely important - you might try looking at the private client coverage with Audit Analytics. And then, comparing that to your measure – and maybe there's something you can do with that data – to help sort of clean your measure up. I'm not sure – it's sort-of a vague idea, but...

Yeah.

Maybe one more?

He's got the mic, so...yep.

One of the things that you're saying is – in the governance literature – that more literature is based on how many boards do you serve on – whether you're actually busy or not. Because, part of the argument is – if you serve on more boards – or you have more clients per auditor – you can actually better handle that. So, you self-select that.

So, if sit – I have five clients, and the other one has three – I have those five clients because I can actually handle those five clients. So how – looking at the literature in comparison to what you're doing – how can you try and parse from – okay, you're saying it's lower quality, but maybe it's actually better quality because that guy can handle five and that guy can only handle three. Do you understand what I'm saying?

Yeah.

So, you're saying a blanket statement if you serve all – if you have five clients, you're worse than the guy who only serves three – but maybe that guy who actually serves the five is doing that because he can better handle the five than the guy who can only can handle three.

That's good though – it would help support the alternative hypothesis – so, I hadn't really thought about that.

[vi]*Okay - thanks Will.*

---

[i] Transcription Note: The original transcript has been edited for flow and ease of reading. Any changes to content were not intended to change the overall message associated with the applicable discussion.
[ii] Transcription Note: This refers to the presentation slides, which are also included for reference in the symposium web-site.
[iii] Transcription Note: Please refer to endnote ii.
[iv] Transcription Note: Please refer to endnote ii.
[v] Transcription Note: Please refer to endnote ii.
[vi] Transcription Note: This final comment was included to note the presentation had ended, for reference purposes.

Research Session 2 – Michael Ricci[i]

Questions and Answers

Why did you have them listen to the interview rather than read?

So they didn't have a transcript of the interviews –they just listened, and after listening, they came away to create documentation. We thought this would be a strong setting to capture the dismissiveness variable - as they decide what they are going to take away from the inquiries.

Can you talk a little bit about your decision to choose a goodwill impairment task, and whether you think your result would have been different if you chose something that had a little bit more judgment to it?

Because it seems like the outcome of that - the preference of management - they don't really care about the number, as long as it's not impaired. But if there was something where there was maybe a little more wiggle room, and they were trying to just nudge the auditor along – they might get caught up in motivated reasoning a little bit more.

Yeah, so it's an interesting question. We actually chose the setting because we thought this was a setting in which motivated reasoning could operate well. And so, while I agree that management may not be concerned about the exact number - as long as it exceeds book value, the computation of the fair value estimate, the discounted cash flow model, the revenue projections embedded in that model, the assumptions underlying those projections – all have substantial wiggle room. And we felt, with that ambiguity, it was still a good setting for motivated reasoning to happen.

So, in the real world, a lot of these motivation and confirmation bias effects might disappear because of several triggers that I can think of. I was just wondering how you managed those triggers. They could be all the way from - having in your mind – look, we have a new client and this is what's going on – and I need to look tough. You just want to look more skeptical. It could be if the client had a history of aggressive accounting treatment, and you're aware of that. Now, you'll look at it different – absolutely.

The PCAOB, as you know, is thinking about coming out with a standard in this very area – auditing accounting estimates. So, absent a standard here, maybe this might go on. But once a standard comes through – who knows, maybe auditors will change – pay more attention to this. The other thing I can think of is– do you think there might be some reason, on the part of auditors, to avoid getting into a documentation scenario. And so, perhaps, the auditor is – now every little - if they look at it, they have to document it. And so, what do you do to make it cognitively inexpensive and also less laborious? Because, now it's like they're going – is it okay – let's move on then – whatever.

Yeah, so there may be a few questions embedded in that – and I'll do the best I can to address a couple of those points. First I think you're asking if there are potential factors in the world that moderate the effects observed here. One thing that I think is interesting is that we find this effect even in a setting where accuracy goals are very strong, so I think this is consistent with the notion that auditors are focused on being accurate in this setting that has received a lot of scrutiny. But they also may, simultaneously, pursue a goal – or have a goal - to accept management's position, especially in these ambiguous areas - due to various conditions in the audit environment - deadline pressure, budget pressure, incentives to maintain client relationships - all those things may simultaneously exist.

And then I think your second point is 'what's the message to regulators?' We show a potential benefit of focusing on preference inconsistent evidence while documenting. But we don't capture all the costs and benefits. So, there may be costs of doing this related to litigation. And, if audit quality were held constant, I would expect this increased documentation to perhaps increase litigation costs. But we also show an improvement in audit quality related to this. We don't capture a net effect and we can't do that in our study. So, additional research will be needed to evaluate the costs and benefits of having auditors engage in this type of documentation as they're evaluating evidence.

---

[i] Transcription Note: The original transcript has been edited for flow and ease of reading. Any changes to content were not intended to change the overall message associated with the applicable discussion.

Research Session 3 – Ikseon Suh[i]

Questions and Answers

I have not read the paper, but I think in your theory section you mentioned something about hindsight bias - can you, kind of discuss, with your results and experiment – how that affected it? I'm just trying to think of hindsight bias and fraud risk.

Okay - so let me go back to, probably, to this model.[ii] So, what we propose is that generating many alternative explanations increases auditors' perception of past difficulty or complexity. So, the more they pursue the task of generating many alternative explanations, the more difficulty they perceive – or the more complex – they perceive the past. That's when companies do – that's when auditors will – that's when they kind of fall back on the existing hypothesis. So the initial hypothesis on the client explanation, so…

Anchoring more than hindsight bias – that's not how I think of hindsight bias.

So, hindsight bias would be the initial hypothesis that clients provide as part of the explanation, right? As to why gross profit margin has increased substantially from one year to another.

Hi. I was curious about something here. In the experiment, what was the order in which – did they assess fraud risk after giving their agreement with a client explanation? The order?

So, the order was: first, that we gave them information on either high or low control risk; and after that, they read the result – or preliminary result – of the analytical review procedure; and after that, we gave them explanations on – we gave them the CFO's explanations on why the gross profit margin increased from one year to another.

Okay.

And then we used this – so, the case material – this case material that we used for our study – is same as the one used by Quadackers et al. (2014).[iii]

I was curious on the structural model there. Why there – or maybe it was tested and just isn't significant – but did you try the link between the number of ideas directly to the fraud risk assessment?

Yeah – we did, and we didn't find any significant path.

Okay. I was just curious about that, because my experience in practice is that we tended to sit down and do the fraud brainstorming prior to – or, if that didn't work, just prior to – the risk assessment. So, a lot of times the – what we came up with in that fraud brainstorming would directly inform and make part of that risk assessment, so I was kind-of looking for that direct link to test against that.

---

[i] Transcription Note: The original transcript has been edited for flow and ease of reading. Any changes to content were not intended to change the overall message associated with the applicable discussion.

[ii] Transcription Note: Due to copyright issues, the slides are not available – but this is the related discussion during the Q&A portion.
[iii] This reference refers to the following study (as obtained from the reference section of the paper itself): Quadackers, L., Groot, T., & Wright, A. (2014). Auditors' professional skepticism: Neutrality versus presumptive doubt. *Contemporary Accounting Research,* 31 (3), 639–657.

Research Session 3 – Aleksandra Zimmerman[i]

Questions and Answers

Congratulations on finding a really interesting data set. The one question I have is on your going concern analysis. When I look at your descriptive statistics, you've got – N is a hundred and seventy-two and gender you've got ten percent. So, you have seventeen women in your going concern - in your distressed sample?

Right.

So, I don't know how you can – I don't know how many of those had a going concern opinion of those seventeen women? So, I guess my point is just – I wouldn't hang my hat on that analysis.

Right. It's hard to tell because there's not – perhaps not enough power.

Yeah, you're really looking at a really restricted sample.

I hear you – point well taken – yeah.

And then we could – oh, go on Miguel.

No, I really like the SEC comment thing – it's really nice and new. Now, just with respect to expertise and fees – like what kind of the no association? I mean, so maybe what would be interesting is – under which circumstances are firms able to charge for the experience on the engagement, right? So, maybe – what here would be interesting is – when am I able to turn A partner's expertise into B level hours, right?

So, maybe you got cities or an environment with a lot of competition and then with less competition, and then it becomes interesting, because I know a lot of very good partners that are able to charge more because the environment is very competitive. Then it becomes interesting – not just – it's sort of obvious that more expert partners are associated with client that often pay more. But what is not obvious is how much of that – those rents – are you able to pass on the client through the competition.

So, if I hear what you're saying correctly, you want to kind of examine what, perhaps, MSAs are driving this effect or where do we see that it's not…

Yeah – on average effect…

Yeah.

Is, perhaps, obvious to some people – but it's not obvious that I'm able to pass those rents, given the competitive nature of quality. And in the going concern part, I mean, if you think about the drivers of quality, right? Litigation, penalties, expertise, and independence – it's not obvious that more expert people are more independent, right? You sell the idea that going concern – going concern is a test for independence, all else equal. So, more expertise does not necessarily make people more independent. But if you're going to go that route, you're really going to have to beef it up.

Ok, great - thank you for your advice. I appreciate it.

Thanks. Do you know anything about the distribution of these partners across audit firms? Are they mostly Big Four?

So, our sample here is all Big Four.

Okay.

Yeah, sorry – I didn't mention that at the beginning.

No, maybe it's in a slide and I just missed it – okay. So that's interesting. I am curious about – so, if it's all Big Four, then I suppose most partners are promoted around the same time. I think that changes a little bit outside of the Big Four. Are you dropping the non-Big Four? Or do you just not have any?

We do have non-Big Four observations that we do an additional analyses. So, we focus on the Big Four for our main analyses.

Okay, that's probably fine. Alright, well that's…

Because there's a lot less observations, so – yeah.

So, I apologize that I didn't get a chance to read the paper, but – so, from the quality perspective, did you look at accruals or restatements or other measures to kind of get at that? Because, I think with going concern is that – it could be independence, but it could also be that the firm – or whatever – they're trying to protect from litigation – so they're just putting out going concern opinions. So, I was just wondering if you were considering other measures of audit quality.

Yes – so what we did look at abnormal accruals, and we didn't find anything for experience or gender there. We did look at abnormal working capital accruals, and did find some effects there. So, we have to do some additional analysis to see what's going on – why we are not finding an effect.

So, is it currently in the paper, and I apologize?

No, it's not in the paper. So just the going concern analysis is there.

Yep.

How does the deal with the comment letter get resolved? I mean, you have the comment letter data – use the comment letter, right? The test for quality here is – do these comment letters get resolved quickly and swiftly.

I hear what you say – okay. Now, the comment letters aren't necessarily something that the auditor has power over. Because it may be just – but it could be.

Yeah.

Yeah – good point. So looking at the period in which the comment letters get resolved as a measure of quality?

Yeah.

Okay.

Can I?

Yeah.

I don't want to pick on your results, but, you see what I have so say – does partner experience matter? I would ask – does partner experience matter materially? Your qualification is .006 – you could drop that out of the equation and it wouldn't make any difference in the results. So it – so I don't know – I can't get too excited about .006 as being materially answering this question.

That's per year, right?

It's per year, as well, on the left hand variable as well.

Yeah, for every year of experience, there's a .006 effect with the coefficient – yeah – on pricing. And you'll have to remember, this is the effect on the natural log of fees, yeah.

So it's a half-percent per year?

Here it's hard to tell with the coefficient on going concern is because you're really looking at the odds ratio. Point well taken – is it economically significant? Yeah.

So, I had the same comment, I guess, as Miguel. I think it's – so, it's very creative. I really like the setting – the sample. But it's from comment letters – so, obviously there was something with the SEC – pointed out, that was concerned about – disclosures or what not with the company. So, if not use the comment letters as, sort of, a measure for quality – at least make sure that you control for the severity and maybe the number of those deficiencies within those comment letters when you're doing your other quality measures.

Okay – good point. Thank you – controlling for potential issues and accounting errors. Although that could potentially be a separate paper. I know at the SEC – I think there's some work being done in that area.

So, something Miguel said, I think, was – it's no secret that the types of firms that get assigned experience partners are going to pay higher audit fees, in general. One thing you might be able to do to address that is – look past the period that we know a partner should have rotated off, and then see if you still find your effect, right? So, we know there's a new partner there – are you still seeing the effect here. And if so, maybe it's a firm effect and not a partner effect. And if not, you've got really strong evidence that what you found is specific to the partner.

Okay. I'll have to see if we have data to do that – but that's a really neat idea.

You should though – you can follow the firm. You don't know who the new partner is, but you know it's not the old one, right? After a certain period, you know that the partner has rotated off – they have to.

I don't know if the data tells us when that is. Because I know there's a separate paper by Miguel – Alastair – right Miguel?

Yeah.

That looks at audit partner rotation.[ii]

It's not my paper. He didn't invite me to be on that paper, by the way.

So, it's not like we know, every single year, who the partner is.

No, but you know there's a mandatory rotation period, right? And if you go that many years out – then you know it's not the same partner.

Okay.

So long as you have – as long as the first year is that many years from the end of the data, right?

Okay.

From now, basically.

Okay – great. Yeah. Thanks.

So, I'm a little concerned that you might have a non-representative sample. I mean, because you're conditioning upon – if you get tips on a bad outcome – to narrow it down. And then, I think forty percent of your firms are getting going conerns – even in the main sample. So, how much can we generalize this to partners that aren't included in this? Because it doesn't look to be the average firm that you've looked at.

No, I agree with you. This is a little limitation of the study – that it may not be representative of a sample. But, it is representative of, you know, population that is a little bit more distressed. So, unfortunately, that's the data that's available – so it's always going to be a limitation of the study. What we can do is, kind of, do some boot-strapping and kind of take different slices of the data to see if we're still finding it in different types of firms. Do you have any suggestions on how to overcome this limitation?

No, I'm sorry – it's probably a bad comment if I don't have a good suggestion. But my main comment was that – do you think it's generalizable? If forty percent get this – get a going concern in a sample. You know, that's very high. SEC comment letters indicate that something probably went wrong. So if we see a...

But that's not necessarily true. I think, maybe, we should do a better job of describing – like, what the nature of the SEC comment letters are. Because, many of the companies in our sample are pretty representative of the population of public companies in the U.S.

To add to what Rob said – or maybe to rebut what he said a little bit – I wonder if they are firms that have some sort of problem, this is a rich setting for the auditor to have a bigger impact – and their experience to matter more – in helping to resolve the comment letter. So, if you take Rob's comment and you take Miguel's comment, and put it all together, I think – if you're sort of – what's the word – harvesting the power of the sample by doing that.

Yeah, and to your point – I guess the fact that the firms are copying the audit partner means that the audit partner matters, right?

So, I guess that would be my point – is that...

You know, the audit partner...

...you know, the audit partner did something in order to be present in the sample. So, if you did something to make you present, what do we, you know?

Conditional...

You've already – yeah – conditioned on the outcome to be present.

And another thing along those lines – since Rob brought up the going concern thing – it looked like in your full sample the percentage of clients that were getting going concern was the same as it is in your distressed sample?

Yeah, all about the...

What does that tell you about before you've even identified distressed firms?

I mean - they're all stressed.

They're all stressed.

Well, they're all distressed, and we don't even need to – for the going concern analysis – you don't even need to condition on distressed firms.

You know, you bring up an interesting question. I didn't do the analysis part – Al did – so I'll have to go back and do – talk that over with him to see if that's true. Yeah, okay.

I have a question about the gender issue before our male students get passed over for partnership. Convince us – or speak to – how you might have tried it through the ringer that this was not picking up client characteristics. If this is truly a twelve percent premium that's being charged by female partners?

Because that's what it is.

We, I mean, we did the best that we could – based on prior literature – in terms of developing the audit pricing model and controlling for audit characteristics then – I don't know if you have something else in mind in terms of controlling for client characteristics? I mean we can't really rule out the fact that – maybe audit partners might be placed on more difficult audits and that's why they're getting higher pricing. There could be a self-selection issue, but if there's something we can do in this model to convince you? I would…

One suggestion I would suggest is to do some sort of matching procedure. So, it's unlikely that they're randomly assigning females to – or males even – to certain clients. So, you might try to match on the industry characteristics and the…

Okay – do a matched sample?

Yes.

Yes. Before question, I'm sorry, because I didn't read the paper. Anyway, I have a question. What is the correlation between audit partner experience and client size? Because, I think, even though you control for the client size in the regression – I mean, if there is a very serious correlation between partner experience and client size, my opinion is that significance may be resulting from the size effect. Or how about, I mean, another way is by client size. For a big group – a big size group – and a small size.

So, do a separate analysis for larger firms versus smaller firms – or do some buckets by quartiles? Now, we do look at VIF factors to see if the correlation was too high between partner experience and client size, and it wasn't. There were no multicollinearity issues – but I like your idea – slicing by client – the data by client size – and re-running our regressions that way.

Would, go ahead – no, go ahead.

On the gender thing again – and this isn't particularly specific to your paper – but it's really hard to swallow this fee premium thing. Because, you know, it's not like the offices are loaded with women partners. So, when a woman partner rotates off – I mean, does the fee go down? And then what happens – you know, the male partner rotates off – now we've got Susan. Okay, now you've got to pay 10 percent more. It's just – the story doesn't ring true. And, it's not really a criticism of your paper – just kind-of a general thought.

No, it's a great research question – once the data comes out – to answer. I mean, when you have enough years, you can look at that. But, our data can't – unfortunately – answer that.

Go ahead.

Because we don't have enough observations for that rotation analysis yet.

So, I think about five minutes ago I was going to say – or two or three minutes ago – I was going to say you haven't got any questions about gender – so maybe you don't need it – all your questions are about experience, and that might be controversy, and maybe there's more you can with experience – and maybe cut out gender as a control variable. I'm not sure if the new questions are shooting that down or not – maybe you need to look at it more. But, at least, they're skeptical questions.

The thing about the experience is just that – I think I agree and disagree with Miguel's kind of premise that – it's not that surprising that there's a fee premium. I agree that there's not surprise that there's a fee premium. I don't think that fee premium is what he characterizes as extract of rents. Because I think what happens is – you're assigning more experienced partners to firms that need the experience. They're getting more, but they're also getting paid more for it.

And it's – so I think a couple more interesting question is – what are the characteristics both – which experiences, you know? I mean, clearly client size, client age are going to be related to experience. But, what are the situations that experience is being – more experienced partners are getting assigned to harder clients? I think we could learn a bit from using that data that way – that we haven't had it before.

I mean, obviously, we're going to have it a lot more specificity in a couple years, but that might be something that you can do that – to drive home the experience in addition to the fee premium to come and see what it is that it's being paid to do. I don't think it's just extracting rents because their experience, but I think it's paying for them to do something – like look at losses or look at foreign sales data – you know, that their expertise is being used in that manner, or something like that.

So, if I hear you correctly, you're saying look more and see – how does partner experience match up with the client? You know, where are the more experienced partner assigned? Or is it kind-of all around the client type?

Yeah, and I think if you do a couple matching procedure, you're going to see that – where you're not going to be able to – so there's going to be some buckets where you just got all experienced partners. And so, learning what those buckets are might be pretty interesting.

Great - thank you.

---

[i] Transcription Note: The original transcript has been edited for flow and ease of reading. Any changes to content were not intended to change the overall message associated with the applicable discussion.

[ii] The only likely related paper I could locate was listed in Alastair Lawrence's CV – in the following manner: "U.S. Audit Partner Rotations" (co-authored with Henry Laurion and James Ryans) (2016). *Forthcoming at The Accounting Review.*

Research Session 4 – Joseph Schroeder[i]

Questions and Answers

So – two issues. First is your estimated cut off probability. I know the Hosmer - Lemeshow[ii] trick for doing that. But that – your cut-off is like twenty-two percent, but your sample rate of misstatements is only eight percent. Do you incorporate that eight percent in the twenty-two percent? Because, if I were doing this, I'd say anything, in particular, over eight percent would have the likelihood of having a material weakness as opposed to over twenty-two percent, which I believe is what you're saying.

And second, the PCAOB is really concerned about material weaknesses being disclosed at the same time as the restatement is disclosed. And so, if you're arguing that they're relying more on internal controls, did you check to make sure that the material weaknesses were not disclosed simultaneously? Because, the PCAOB is saying that auditors are ignoring, missing, or whatever which would not be reliance moves.

Right.

In fact, poor quality of internal control audits that show up the goal. I have one of these when I have a restatement.

Yeah, so…

What about those issues?

So, with respect to the second one, we make sure that we're picking up the original internal control audit opinion, because a lot of times they'll be multiple in the file. So, you can see that they do re-issue the opinion when they have a restatement. So, we're getting the – what was it at that time – for that model. And, for the second one - so you're suggesting using eight percent as the cut off…

Yes.

…to get it. I – so, I agree – and then on the flip side of that – we're not necessarily sure if that material weakness disclosure is accurate. So, there's a lot of recent research that says that that percentage is actually lower than what the actual true material weakness outcome is. So the model tells us that maybe it should be about twenty-two percent material weaknesses as opposed to eight. But, you know, as a sensitivity, we could - we could run the eight percent cut-off, because…

Because the Hosmer – Lemeshow example uses a model that has a prediction rate of fifty – that assumes fifty percent.

Yeah.

You clearly do not have that.

Yeah.

So, I want to make sure you have a cut-off rate that reflects that actual sample rate.

Okay. Yeah – I think that's a great – you know – that we can consider the eight percent cut-off.

Yeah – Brian.

So, you went over those kind of fast, so I was wondering if you could should spend a little bit of time talking maybe a little bit more carefully about what you did in the pre-404, kind of sub-sample check, because – now as you were going through it, I don't have trouble believing that those firms that are subject to those integrated audits have lower financial statement quality.

In fact, that might be why they are subject to these additional screens. But it seems like the idea that it's because of over-reliance – it is a harder sell. And, so, I wonder if that pre-stuff can be explained a little better, but also maybe even integrated more into the main analysis to say – hey, look – firms that were subject to it before – or weren't subject to it, but would have been subject to it – actually had better quality, suggesting that they would have had lower quality – or something.

Yeah.

So, A – can you tell me about that, and B – would you consider making it integrated into your...?

Well, there are a couple of different ways you can do it. You can either use just the market value of equity cut for '01 to '03...

Sure.

...and we'll throw it that way. The way that we did was – we went to '04 and said – did you have an internal control audit in 2004 versus not have one. And then we used that classification and take it back to '01 to '03 for those same firms, then run the analysis on that. So that's how we've classified them. We've also run a market value of equity cap, and we don't find any significant difference when we do it. It's not that they're better quality at that time – it just means that they have similar, you know, quality during those periods...

So take those that would have been subject to would not have been subject – had the same quality?

They have the same, and then when we switched to the '07 to '12, and then we've done analysis with '05 and '06 on those as well – that's what we find – that there's, you know, statistically different. So, one other thing we could do is, maybe, to incorporate a difference-in-differences design or something.

Yeah.

Use that as a way to kind of bolster some of the results. So, that's all we've done at this point – we haven't done the difference-in-differences. Yeah.

Going back to your story a little bit – do you know if the same auditors are performing internal control audits that are performing the financial statement audits? And, maybe there's a lot of research talking about integration of specialists and auditors that could be affecting your story?

Well, but my assumption is that the firm is doing both – the engagement team is both. Now, there could be different personnel doing the different things, but I'm not aware of too many instances where – like Ernst & Young would do the financial statement audit and Deloitte would do the…

It has to...

I don't think you have...

...you can't separate that, right.

Yeah.

No, I guess my point was just to help you build your story in a sense that, perhaps, the integrated audits are worse off because there's poor integration between more people, more teams...

More teams…

Yeah.

You know, that could be another problem out there, right? So, we're putting for the theory – I think that's another example where you just have more people on the team – or more people – more, you know, more cooks in the kitchen, you're going to have really bad food, right? I mean that's usually what happens – that's what I might guess. Yeah, it might catch on – cooking pizza and audit and all that kind-of stuff. So, I think that's a similar argument that it would be – I don't think it would be inconsistent with this over-reliance or, if you think, a different mechanism that's meeting our H2 prediction, right?

Yeah.

So, Joe, I have some research in this area too, and one thing I found is that not all material weakness are created equal. There are certain types that are going to have a higher likelihood of misstatement after the fact. So, entity-level – what else – there was revenue that result in more of a misstatement after the fact, relative to other areas and such. And so, I guess the only concern I might have is to make sure that that's balanced between the two groups that you have

– to make sure that it's – does one group – the accelerated filers – just have entity-level controls, more of these revenue-type of internal control weaknesses that are just leading to that result that you're…

Is that from your dissertation?[iii]

Yeah.

Yeah, so can you send us a copy of that – that's forthcoming in CAR?[iv]

So, we'll check…

Yeah.

But, yeah – no, so that's a good point. As Nick said, that's another difference that…

And you could show that in univariates…

Yeah, no that's – yeah, great, yeah.

Tom.

Just one more point – so, also, the pushback is that the auditors have been pushing material weaknesses to significant deficiencies. And again, that goes against your over-reliance on controls and their clients pushing back – so, I think at least mention that that's where some of the noise results are going to come from, and you're still finding - you're still finding your result even though that's occurring.

Uh-huh.

I just think you have to be careful about bringing that up.

So, yeah – so that's interesting because if they're incentive is to push a material weakness down to a significant deficiency, then they might actually then start relying on the controls when they should have had max control risk. So, the firm…

You may recognize that it's bad.

Yeah.

But they're exceeding the client demands that they don't get the material weakness. So, I don't know that I would call that relying on them.

Okay.

In fact, reminding of that could be problematic.

Yeah. I think it's back to that incentive, right? It's – we've only got so much fees, and it's like I did an internal control audit – I get to the financial statement audit – and it's like we ran out of budget, pencils down, we're done – right? And the whole point of the financial statement audit, you know – you're going to find a lot of misstatements there. When you switch to this reliance strategy, you're assuming these controls are catching it. But, you know, my partner used to say – if you peel back the onion, you begin to realize it stinks. You know, it's like – let's just not peel back the onion, and just rely on controls, right, so – opinions.

Yeah.

Which partner was that?

Well, he's retiring – so I don't even know if he'll be around to be in the partner database, so – and you can be assured that I'll be running regressions to see which of my former partners are the best, so…

Remind me of your sample period.

Our sample period is 2007 to 2012.

So, one thing that concerns me – if you go back to the diff-in-diff analysis that we talked about a little bit – it would really concern me. It concerns me even though your sample period is slightly removed from the actual implementation of SOX. There was a lot of change in who was auditing who over this period, because of this implementation.

And so, if what's happening – in that market – is actually big auditors are focusing more on their larger clients, and the auditors at the bottom of the distribution that are still getting integrated audits are now shifting from what used to be a large auditor's high quality to somebody down the market some, you're going to see over that period that their quality is going to change. Whereas the people who were already in that down market group may not so much – they may have a pretty level level of audit – accounting quality.

Yeah.

So I don't – I don't necessarily have a good recommendation for you – other than to just be really clear about who's auditing who and maybe carve out groups that are alike – in terms of auditors – that my help to address some...

So, one thought is to, you know, anyone that has a turnover during the sample period – throw them out.

You drop...

Yeah.

Which is going to be…

Which is going to be, I suspect, a really large portion of your sample.

Well, '07 to '12 – the turnover – the portfolio rebalancing that occurred was '03 and '04, predominately.

That doesn't spread out until later…?

Yeah, so – I've got – done the research in the area and those turnovers started to dissipate after AS 5.

Okay – well, that's good.

But, yeah, the bulk of that – you know, the Hogan - Martin 2009 studies[v] and rebalancing – about all that – that occurred pretty much with Sarbanes-Oxley Act, you're going into 404(b), and the Big Four firms had a massive rebalancing that sent everyone down to Grant Thornton and BDO. But after that rebalancing, it's kind-of just reverted back to the turnover rates that you would expect.

Okay.

But, it's something to consider – yeah.

I mean, I reckon if you…

It's an interesting time period, because the '03 – '04 rebalancing doesn't necessarily say that, you know, anything about the quality or nefarious. It's just – you know, look baby, I love you – but you've got to go to the smaller person, right? Yeah – but, yeah.

---

[i] Transcription Note: The original transcript has been edited for flow and ease of reading. Any changes to content were not intended to change the overall message associated with the applicable discussion.

[ii] This refers to the text that is included as the following reference in the references of the associated paper: HOSMER, D.W., AND S. LEMESHOW. *Applied logistic regression*. 2nd edition. New York, NY: John Wiley & Sons., 2000.

[iii] The following is reference to this individual's dissertation – as obtained from ProQuest: Seidel, T. (2014). *The effective use of the audit risk model at the account level* (Order No. 3621991). Available from ProQuest Dissertations & Theses Global. (1545892834). Retrieved from http://search.proquest.com/docview/1545892834?accountid=14556.

[iv] A reference to this version can be found at the following reference from SSRN: Seidel, Timothy A., Auditors' Response to Assessments of High Control Risk: Further Insights (May 2016). Contemporary Accounting Research, Forthcoming. Available at SSRN: http://ssrn.com/abstract=2430869 or http://dx.doi.org/10.2139/ssrn.2430869.

[v] One example of what he's referring to here is from the Curriculum Vitae of Chris Hogan (obtained from the following site - https://bps.broad.msu.edu/media/documents/57602cfd10edd5dd37071fd5.pdf), with the following reference: Hogan, C.E. and R.D. Martin. 2009. Risk Shifts in the Market for Audits: An Examination of Changes in Risk for "Second-Tier" Audit Firms. *Auditing: A Journal of Practice and Theory* 28 (November): 93-118.

***Research Session 4 – Sridhar Ramamoorti*[i]**

<u>Questions and Answers</u>

Well, very different presentation, and I know this is a very complex area. I was wondering if – there is so many different points, so many different metrics – quantitative, qualitative – is there a way that you think that we can come up with a composite measure of audit quality? And what do you hear – of that idea being discussed about?

Well…

Well, we're going to have ten factors…

Right.

How do you go through all that to come up with whether it is high or low? Because you cannot say ten different things – and it's very complicated – so how do we determine what is good or bad?

Right. No, that is very fair.

So, that's one…

Okay.

And the other one is – you keep mentioning root cause analysis.

Right.

This is a very complex area given the different assertions and accounts and, you know, pieces of evidence – we're looking about all kinds of things – it's a big mess. How do you come up with some kind of a framework – where you say – well, if you find this unusual thing, here is how you go about finding the root cause. Can you comment on that?

So, on your second question. As far as, I think, the PCAOB is actually doing the root cause analysis probably for some time now, and I do know that they – what we're going through with their inspections teams to – and I'm also sure they'll be collecting some sort of database to look at, you know, how to put all that together. But, other than the fact that they're doing it, and that they are getting insights out of it – not very much of the sharing a couple of the details – at least not with me – on the Standard Advisory Group. So, I can't comment very much on that.

But, on your first question, I completely agree with you that – having a composite measure would be very helpful. The only thing that had been discussed – not specifically a composite measure – but they have talked about how companies, perhaps, define indicators – that's it – just an ad hoc number – five, okay? And take that to audit committees. And having audit committees engage in a conversation with their external auditors around those measures. And coming up with a pretty customized interpretation of those five audit quality measures and how that impacts, you know, that particular engagement. So, that's one thing they've thought of – not composite – but just in customizing it to a particular entity. And what they are really kind of doing – to get the conversation to move away from getting the cheapest auditor possible. So, if you don't want them to talk about competing on cost, but let's compete on quality. That seems to be the theme of that conversation – so, that's a good thing.

Anyone else?

Well, obviously, I'm one of those people who enjoys philosophy – so I appreciate all those comments, and I'm taking a number of them along home. And there are a lot of different applications where I can see that they apply. For those of us that aren't currently in practice environment, the analogy I like think with a little bit when it comes to this issue – which I've had lots of questions about from its inception – is defining good teaching – measuring good teaching. That is pretty close to home, and you can find that's context specific. There are a variety of methods at work. I have yet to see an evaluation system of the quality of the classroom experience that I have any – that I place any reliability on. And that's a little simpler than audit.

But to me, for those of us not currently in the practice environment, have any of you participated in the assessment of learning exercises to this point? You got a lot of – do you put a lot of reliability in this things? And so, I can kind of place myself – even though I'm not currently in practice environment – I can kind of place myself in this dialogue from my own experience in the academic. I haven't seen the AAA define quantitatively or qualitatively what good teaching is – yet.

Thank you, Jack. The only comment I have on that is – many, many years ago – more than twenty years ago now, I remember Tom Cech, Nobel Prize winner in chemistry[ii] from the University of Colorado – Boulder – was our keynote speaker at our teaching conference – telling us that it is because of the measurement issues that Jack alluded to that we do not have a Nobel Prize for teaching, why you do have a Nobel Prize for research. He'll contend there's a way of evaluating, independently, you know, whether somebody's research is high quality. And, on that basis, you are able to be awarded the Nobel Prize. But – teaching – it would be impossible to do that. It's highly local, and school evaluations are not really reliable – all those issues come – with the applicable measures.

Anybody else? Yeah.

Just a comment – yeah, it seems like there are situations where you need to have other dimensions other than composite. And now, when you look at the reports – the audit reports on sustainability – so you can't have just one dimension to say that – yes, this is my opinion – because each dimension is unique, and – same thing as the IFAC[iii] was wondering about audit opinion. You have ten, fifteen, twenty line items that are balancing. It is just unreasonable to say that all of them are fairly stated, because, no matter how much work you do, some accounts – like financial instruments – you cannot have the same high level of comfort that everything is fine.

So, they are thinking that – why not we have a metric – metrics – where we have each line item and you get – which is that control level – your high level, high level, high; medium level; low level. Because, you cannot be high level of confidence that that instrument is fairly stated – you can't do it.

So, it's the same thing when it comes to audit quality. They give you five dimensions that are most important, and then, seriously, the probability of this and that – high, high – that they see. The same thing – teaching. Teaching – there may be also delivery method, there will be counting method, something else – there may be three dimensions, and then, how you're doing in each dimension – high or low. So, sometimes it's great to come to one composite measure which consists of different periods – different dimensions – all along. That's just something to think about.

Well, that's certainly an interesting thought – yeah.

Anyone else?

Do we got time for one more?

Sure.

I would say – you know, I'm kind of one of those guys that – I would prefer to have more data as opposed to less, but more data is preferable to none. And right now we're in a setting where we really don't have anything. So, I think that as the input data and the output data are produced, the market will take over. We'll sort of gravitate towards the ones that are more meaningful and move away from the ones that are less meaningful. So, I think that what you might do in your paper is, sort of, instead of just sort of ending – it was a great thought piece, I thought – it just sort of ended. But, make some suggestions about – we're going to have these audit quality indicators – now, so suggest what they might look like.

It reminded me of the article in the Economist,[iv] *about ten years ago, you know, about the illusion and exactitude of accounting information, and sort of that – and what you're saying here is that, you know? These are going to be inexact measures, but I'd prefer to have some of the RBI numbers and on-base percentage numbers than to have nothing at all to be able to look at. It's not really a question – just sort of a way you might think of how to end your paper.*

Yeah – you know, I think that's a great idea about the whole sort of market response, and how they might, kind of, whittle down these measures to what they find most useful from their perspective. And yeah, that's also a service, in that sense, to the investing public, right? They are telling you what they want in terms of these measures, etc. around them – you know – anyone mandating anything. And – but, I guess one of the issues though is, Scott, that the PCOAB's very nervous about mandating anything at this point. They just don't want to go down that path. But, that's why they're saying this is what they'll do – you know – talk about it.

And, meanwhile, what you're saying – which would be very helpful is – perhaps audit committees might be able to pick up on this audit quality indicators Concept Release, and at least – for their own purposes – might be able to ask the firms to come up with their own measures. Hey, I mean, as an audit committee member – I can do that. I can ask my auditor to do that. So – it's so easy, right? I tell them – you don't do it, you're fired. I'm going to pay someone else to do it for me, right? So, you know, as an audit committee member, I do have that ability. So, that sounds like a terrific suggestion, actually.

And then, back to point on mission. Yeah, I can pick and choose what I want out of that – but, where are we going to get everything? You know, and the PCAOB has already done us a great service by undertaking this project, and carries along all of these measures. Even though they may not be perfect – you know – it's a start, and it's better than nothing. So – yeah, thank you for that.

---

[i] Transcription Note: The original transcript has been edited for flow and ease of reading. Any changes to content were not intended to change the overall message associated with the applicable discussion.

[ii] See the information regarding this award at the following site - https://www.nobelprize.org/nobel_prizes/chemistry/laureates/1989/.

[iii] This refers to the International Federation of Accountants, with their site - https://www.ifac.org/.

[iv] The article referenced appears to be the following – this is a citation from ProQuest - Special report: True and fair is not hard and fast - the future of accounts. (2003, Apr 26). *The Economist, 367*, 72-63. Retrieved from http://search.proquest.com/docview/224029205?accountid=14556.

Research Session 4 – Nam Ho[i]

Questions and Answers

While I like the idea, I do have a couple of concerns – because I keep thinking about who's making the decision to hire the auditors – do you think it's the audit committee? Do you think that it's executives that might have some influence in there? It seems like – if you don't have those in the model – their affiliations – then you might have a correlated omitted variable in there.

Because they may be affiliated with the firm as well and that's what's driving them in hiring other affiliates, you know, below them. Just something to think about that you might want to make sure you add to your models is the affiliations of the executives as well as the audit committees.

Yeah, so we thought about this actually quite a bit. It tends to come off that people are concerned about audit committees a lot, and the response to that goes – in terms of talking to industry people – and no offense to anyone who's on audit committees in this room or who will become as well – is that a lot of audit committees that appear to still rely heavily on management to make a recommendation for the auditor. Not all – but some of them still do rely on management to give a recommendation in terms of the auditor that they'd like.

And, as well, one thing that we did look at fairly closely because we were concerned about this as well – was for CFOs. We looked at affiliated CFOs when they arrived at the firm – we don't find evidence that affiliated CFOs are overly promoting their former firm. And we also don't find that CFOs are taking to hiring a lot of their old pals, unless that firm was already audited by their affiliated firm. So, if you have a new Deloitte CFO come in, we don't actually see more Deloitte alumni jumping on board – unless Deloitte is also that external auditor. And then we were looking specifically for firms that were matched with Deloitte before that CFO was hired.

How's it going? In one of my discussions – when I was talking to tax partners – they told me about one service that's growing in prominence a little bit – both with audit and non-audit clients. But they were talking about services in which – so tax – a consulting service – in which they help the client put together their internal tax function or improve the internal tax function.

So, you know, internal controls surrounding taxes and the structure of the department – but also they give suggestions as to who to hire for tax director jobs. So, if you can look at the choice of the auditor – plus do they provide non-audit services – maybe tax services – would that also incrementally increase the number of the alumni that they hire? So, another thing you could try.

Yep – great – thank you for the suggestion. What we're – actually, we're currently working on revising the paper, and we're looking at non-audit services and that. So, that's exactly the kind of feedback that we're looking for in terms of what else to integrate into the paper. So, thank you for that.

So, I'm a little bit confused about the conclusion that you drew at the end of your presentation, given the results that we've seen in your presentation. Because I don't, again, I don't think a lot of us have actually read the whole paper yet. But, you don't find any results, at least not two-tailed, for switching. The graph that you showed us was particularly revealing, I think, in that there's really no preference for the auditor that has a connection with the majority alumni at the firm – at the hiring firm.

It's the hiring that is driving this result, and yet, in your conclusion, you say that – you know, there's this circle back where firms send their people out into the world, and then they are hired by those clients who are picking those guys up. Do you – can you make the connection for me?

So, I guess it would be – the thing that we like to show in that graph – I can bring it back up here.[ii] So, what we look – the kind of plan showing the previous period laying out before the switch. So, what you would expect is that the current – the reason we're not being concerned about all the reasons why you might choose to switch, right? So, presumably, in this world, you would have already aligned your current staff with whoever your current auditor is.

And then, leading up to the switch, we don't see any signs of preparation to switch to a specific auditor. So, we don't see this kind of twenty-five percent for the incoming auditor to be particularly damning, because we're also considering the fact that it's unlikely that you would have already pre-optimized your alumni – you want things that work for the incoming auditor.

So, here's the way I interpret your results – and this is just my own personal, sort of anecdotal, story – but it is a lot easier for an accounting department to hire from the pool of people that they know than to go out and do interviews with people they have no experience with whatsoever. And so, I don't see this trend – this hiring trend – as so much like we're trying to get some synergy between our accounting department and our auditor – it's just easier to hire people from your auditor, because your auditor can vouch for them – they've been on the engagement team. They're may be some issues there because you're not actually allowed to go to your client – right away at least.

It just seems like the hiring effect – which is most of what you're finding – is it totally shocking? Because the costs are lower to hire from your auditor. And I don't know if you can rule out that interpretation somehow – if that's not the one you want to make – but it's the one I draw, looking at this graph at least.

Yeah, so we started off with thinking that it's either choice of people who are going there or people that we'll bring in later on, and, the more we look at it – that we're starting to think about framing this paper. And so, in terms of hiring as being kind of the significant result that comes out of it. And so, I would agree with your interpretation for the most part on that – in terms of I do think that the hiring thing is the most glaring aspect of the results – that, for sure, you would say is likely going on. And even, yes, in terms of the cost of hiring your auditor – you kind of know their qualifications already, and it kind of circles back to why familiarity is preferred – but, maybe, preferred post-choice rather than pre-choice – yeah.

I had a similar, kind of real interest in this hiring, but what I was thinking of was a little bit different. So, related to this cooling-off period, I would kind of think that once a relationship with our former auditor was terminated, we've got a pool now of people – and maybe a year later, and maybe a couple of years later. So, do you know – but, on the other hand, we just fired our auditors. So, big firm – let's just pick on one – Ernst & Young – we just fired them – man, they left a bad taste in my mouth. I'm actually going to decrease my percentage or not increase it as rapidly.

And so, I'm kind of curious if you looked at something like this – but not the old auditor or the new auditor – to see if, a year or two removed, at least, the hiring for that old auditor either increased or decreased or if it stayed the same – as a percentage of the firms?

So, we've looked preliminarily – not heavily invested – I guess I would prefer that I would go back and look at it a little more before I tell you too much about this. But, from kind of the preliminary look at this, what we've actually found is that it's the decrease in – of alumni rates of the other firms that they chose – that they have chosen that they want – is fairly spread out among the other available options.

Okay.

You don't see, kind of, two holding steady – one goes up and one goes down.

So, I – similar to some of the other comments – Nick's – I think the hiring is the thing that is the most intuitive to me from your results. One thing that I was wondering is – instead of looking at auditors switching, if there's a way to look at firms that switch less than you might expect when they have a whole lot of these alumni.

So, for example, after a firm has a restatement, we know that auditor switching goes up as they replace that auditor. Maybe when they have a lot of alumni, they are less likely to switch when we would normally expect them to. And that might be a little bit more of an indication of, you know, an aspect of this – a consequence of this hiring.

Yeah, I think that's a really good idea. Actually, I'm kind of hoping that we have the kind of necessary data to do something like that. With that, and still have power to – since we don't have that many switches to start with. And then, once we get down to switches that specifically follow a restatement – probably pretty small pool in terms of these switches that we could actually draw inference from. But, I think it's a great comment. And I'm eager to try it, and hope it works. So - thank you.

Okay – I was going to say never mind – but I guess who gets the mic gets the last question. So, you got your data from LinkedIn. How do you get comfortable that that data is complete? Like, they're there seems to be a selection issue with some people posting to LinkedIn where you may not. You know, that may mean that systematically certain characteristics – like that they choose not to disclose.

Okay, so it's sort of our Wikipedia, right? So, it's not going to be perfect, but we do, kind of, rely on its reliability to a certain extent. So, there are a lot of surveys out there that say – you know, this certain percentage or this certain percentage of the accounting and finance industry has a LinkedIn profile. And, the average user updates it blank number of times or uses it for these types of activities. And based on those surveys – the survey results look good – that say around ninety percent, if not over ninety percent, of accounting plays have a LinkedIn profile. And on average day, they log-in once a week, and then they're fairly updated.

But, of course, there's always going to be input error or, you know, we are subject to people just falsifying information on there – and we're kind of at mercy of whatever exists on the service. But, to the extent in the large scheme of things in terms of – we don't believe that that number that is either misleading on purpose or potentially misleading is driving our results. So, they're not really strong enough in terms of – we got really close to kind of the borders of significance. I'd worry about it more in terms of – where we are in terms of the results that we see.

And then just one more – maybe this is a suggestion – additional test you could add. Something that I thought about that might be kind of interesting – if you can get at it from the LinkedIn data to see how long they were with that particular firm?

I know a lot – at least at the Big Four – after you were with the firm for four, five, six years, you had a pension. It was maybe small, but then you have these economic incentives to kind of make sure that the firm exists into the future – and so you may be more medically to want to make sure that that firm, you know, continues to have clients. I don't know if that's something you can get at or not, but it might be interesting to see the proportion of firm alumni that have been with the firm for more than six years or so.

Yeah, so we're a bit hesitant to go too far back. So, in terms of being able to say that – yes, he worked at a place – were a little more comfortable than saying he worked at a place for this long in length in the mid '90s or the early 2000s. Because some people aren't updating for – or are completing their – that timeline – in an accuracy that they are from the time that, supposedly, they would have joined LinkedIn going forward. But that's something that we're starting to look at in terms of – we can kind of do some sort of analyses with it. We might not want to hang our hat on it, but it's definitely something interesting to look at.

---

[i] Transcription Note: The original transcript has been edited for flow and ease of reading. Any changes to content were not intended to change the overall message associated with the applicable discussion.

[ii] Transcription Note: This refers to the presentation slides, which are also included for reference in the symposium web-site.

Research Session 5 – Brant Christensen[i]

Questions and Answers

Well, I mean, I...

Just talk loud, we're all right here.

Yeah.

It seems like chicken and egg – I'm assuming you're going to get into that.

So, we look at the timing.

Yeah.

We look at the timing – yep. Okay, we actually – yeah, we'll get there – but yes, we look at the timing.

Yes, Elizabeth.

I had the same thought on the last paper – to what extent do you think that's strategic? Because, they know things like – I know what the materiality threshold is, and I know how much they're going to look at certain accounts. Like, they know what their mythology is – because, as an auditor, that was my biggest bane of my existence – was when I found an employee at my client who was an E&Y person. They're like – oh, well this isn't material. Why do you care? And they refused to answer the question. So, have you thought about that at all?

So, from the client's perspective they'd rather keep them because they know what to expect?

Yes.

I mean that would – that's sort of the nefarious side of fit, right?

Uh-huh.

That's maybe the downside of fit.

Right.

That they may know what's coming. I guess you could view it as a positive – they could work together better. That's part of the fit story.

Okay.

Just maybe the darker side.

The darker side that works with…

Yeah, it works with the theory, right?

Yeah.

So, there's that better fit – they're going to work together better. Well, there would potentially be fewer head-butting, right? If they knew what to expect – if they kind of knew what was coming. They knew how the inventory observations worked. They kind of knew what to expect as far as client requests, okay? That could go the other way, too – from a quality perspective, right?

Right.

In that it could actually hurt quality. So – and we'll look at that a little bit later on.

Yeah, Marcus.

I don't know much about partner's retirement plans but I have heard that they retain some sort of the vested interest in the well-being, financially…

Excellent.

…of their former firm, right?

Uh-huh.

I don't know if that speaks against your theory here, but almost like a complementary factor there that they literally have a financial interest in making sure their former firm goes on.

So, there's a rule about that, okay? And this is a great point. So, partners have to sever their ties to the firm. So, there is a cost to being an audit committee member on a company audited by your former firm. You cannot hold a financial interest in that firm. You have to liquidate your interest in the firm, okay? And so, we talked to a couple former partners, and we're like – so does this happen? Because that – I mean, it's pretty big choice, right? Basically, cashing out your pension.

And to the partners we talked to – it depends on the attractiveness of the pension plan. And so we actually – so we looked into some pension plan attractiveness – attractiveness of the pension plans for these firms, and two are rated really highly. Deloitte and EY are actually – have some of the more attractive pension plans in the country. And not just in the accounting industry, but overall – whereas KPMG and PwC do not. And so, part of the reason that we run a regression firm by firm – because the willingness of partners to sever those times likely differs by firm. So, that's a really good point.

Yeah, Josh.

Does any – in that situation, if it's the pension plans – so, the partner's only one member of the audit committee. So, if the audit committee decided that E&Y was the best auditor to switch to for that firm, does it ever happen that that E&Y partner will just leave the audit committee, instead? Like, have you looked for that, maybe?

We haven't – that's an interesting idea. So, we do look and see – and we require the affiliated member to be the chair – if it holds.

Okay.

But we haven't seen if they switch away – that's interesting. Is that – that would be another option, right?

It seems like it would corroborate the kind-of story that you're telling everybody.

Yeah – no, that's a good idea. That's a really good idea. That's very doable.

Yeah, Nick.

So, I'm going to echo the comment Josh made for the last paper – before the break – thanks. So, you pitched this just now as – hey, an audit committee knows what they're supposed to do, they are involved and selection of the auditor. I worry, though, that there are not actually though. This could have bad consequences if they're not changing auditors when they really probably should after a restatement or after some controversy happens. That would make a really interesting additional test. I don't know how full the paper is at this point, but, I think...

It could always be fuller, right?

Of course, it always...

It can always be fuller – you change the font size, right?

Exactly.

So, we were 12-point; now were down to 11. So, we've started to look at that. We've looked at – we've got univariate so far that suggests that the switch. So, the – so Hennes et al.[ii] find audit firms are terminated following restatements, right?

Uh-huh.

What we've seen so far in the univariates is that that is moderated by this affiliation factor. But, we don't find an audit quality effect, okay? We don't find that audit quality goes down. And so, even though they may be more likely to keep them when they could have been fired, audit quality isn't suffering. And so, we're not seeing that they're being rushed, right? We don't see that they're being enriched. We don't see that the affiliate auditors are enriching their former firm. When we look at restatements, we actually only find a positive effect for KPMG – we don't find any negative effects across the four. We do find some positive effects with audit quality on KPMG. And so, even if that did come through with the – when if it doesn't, it looks like an error, right? That they're keeping them after a restatement. We're not finding that's harming quality in any way, so – and you could argue that, from a pure standpoint, that maybe the auditor shouldn't be let go if there's a restatement, right? It's not always the auditor's fault. So, just because they keep them after everything doesn't mean that's bad.

Yeah.

That was actually my point, is that – you know, we see that – if we see that auditor turnover is higher after restatements, we don't necessarily know that audit committees aren't over-reacting to the restatement – if the restatement had some measure of noise, and there isn't a signal of audit quality. We're not always certain that it does.

Or they're getting fired because they forced the restatement, right?

Right, because...

Yeah.

Yeah, right.

Yeah, it's kind-of hard to know exactly why – yeah.

So it's – so we'll look into that. Yeah – so for audit quality, we're finding low rates of restatement for KPMG. One of our next steps is looking at that moderation effect after restatements. We also want to look at lawsuits in order to see if there's any perceived independence concerns for investors. If there's an accounting related lawsuit, are they more likely to name the audit firm as a defendant? And the client thinking – hey, you guys were buddies – we're going sue you because we don't think you did a good enough job. So, we're going to look into that as well.

Yeah, Joe.

So, there's a paper coming out in JAR[iii] *– if not, it's already out in JAR, and I think Knechel's on it – and the other guy was at Arizona State. And they were looking at, I think it was, item ones in the 10-K – or looking at the 10-K disclosures – to see how similar they are. So, you know, what they found was – that if you're an odd duck at one firm, and then there's another firm in that area – metropolitan statistical area – that's more similar to you, you just naturally gravitate to them.*

And I'm wondering, again, in this case – and I haven't read the paper – but, is it possible that they're naturally gravitating to the firm that is more similar to themselves, and they just happen to also hire partners from that firm, because they want audit communities with expertise? And this – I don't – you know, thinking about that paper, and think about how that paper shows this natural evolution over time. Is this, maybe, part of that mechanism?

So, would you want us, then, to control – so Lennox and Park[iv] has like a match variable – to try to match on characteristics of that client to the audit firm character – portfolio – would that – controlling for that – would that kind of appease…?

Well, they have the significant – they have the measure that they use in that paper. So, it might be something interesting to see.

Okay.

You know, if that's part of the story – or may you can add to that paper. But, as you're presenting, it's just something that came to mind – you know – that recent paper that came out.

Okay – thank you – okay.

A comment and a question, I guess. Correct me if I'm wrong – you said, statistically, the coefficients on the management and the audit committee are not different?

Correct.

That is, I think, interesting that the audit committee, of course, is the one that's supposed to be making the decision. And so, one would hope that those coefficients would be different and they're not. So that might be an additional finding – as much as a non-statistical difference can be a finding. The other question was – have you looked – although they're statistically the same – have you portioned any part of that sample to look when those two conflict? So, when management is EY and the AC[v] is PwC to sort of – who wins?

No, we haven't set like a battle – anything like that. We have dropped observations where management's affiliated to make sure it wasn't driven by that, and everything still holds. We haven't run any sort of battle – any of those comparisons. What we did do – this is kind of interesting, different head-to-head – and all the practitioners are gone, so we can kind-of do this. Is we – so, right now, everything's run firm by firm.

So what we did – we kind-of pooled it all in order to see if there was, like, dislike effects. If EY really hated PwC, and so they're like – we're not going to hire them, okay – former EY partner. And we do find some evidence – so Deloitte partners didn't like anybody. PwC doesn't either. Okay, so if you have a former partner of a given firm – and it makes sense that if they're more likely to hire their firm then they're less likely to hire from the other firms, right? It kind of goes hand-in-hand. But we do find some evidence of - we call this preference, alright? A revealed preference of former partners on audit committees that they not only favor their firms, but they favor them over certain firms. And so, we don't do the management versus audit committee, we do kind of pit the firms against each other. So, does that kind of answer? I thought you'd find that interesting.

I'm just – I'm very interested in this idea of independence and the auditor. I guess – I feel like as a profession – I'm going to get on a soapbox for a second – we've lost sight of the client, and we did so a long time ago. Even the regulators refer to "the client" as management right now. So, I'm very interested in this idea of who actually is in control – if it's the audit committee or management.

So, one paper that you'd probably find – Beck and Mauldin[vi] – they look at a power struggle between management and audit committee as far as fees. And them – they do find that when one has low power, the other dominates, right? And so, when there's a mismatch, the strong – the stronger team wins. And oftentimes, that's the CFO – in driving the fees. And so, there's been a little with that done that's interesting.

Yeah, Joe.

Back to the table where you had the four firms.[vii]

Oh, the battle. Yeah.

Yeah. So, you said Deloitte – is it Deloitte and KPMG that don't have any preference?

So, PwC prefers PwC over all others. Deloitte – just doesn't like anybody, right? So, the Deloitte effect was weaker – to begin with. And so, they just had a dislike – it appeared they had a lack of preference for PwC and EY.

Again, I guess, my only thought on this was the market dynamics. Like Deloitte and KPMG, I think, tend to be a little bit smaller, you know, presumably; whereas EY and PwC would be bigger – so they're might be more available audit committee type people – but that's just something to be, you know, careful about in some of the metropolitan areas. The supply of audit committee...

Right.

...partners is going to be lower because they're smaller offices, presumably. But, if you have just – that's something that kind of sparked my mind when you talked about that.

Yeah, well, right now, we don't really do a lot with this.

Right.

We kind-of hold it out mainly as a robustness test saying – hey, even when we run a pooled multinomial-ic model the story's the same.

Okay.

So we hadn't found nothing wrong with the – yeah, Nick.

So, just really quick – why is the coefficient negative – like on EY audit committee when EY is on the left hand side – you know, shouldn't it…?

Yeah, EY hadn't, doesn't relate in the firm-by-firm either – it doesn't come through…

Okay – so, it is positive when it should be positive? They all look negative.

Well, you got to see – so it's the diagonal, right?

It's insignificant in the…

It's insignificant in the firm-by-firm.

I see.

And so, the interesting thing that we find with this is – the management effects. So, if you look on the diagonal, right? On PwC, the management effects go away when you run pooled. Only PwC comes through for the main manipulations, which…

But the diagonals are all either not significant or negative – except for KPMG.

KPMG and PwC comes through strong – still comes through strongly in the global – yeah.

And those are the ones that came through…

And those are the ones that came through strongest in firm by firm as well. And those are the ones as well – where the firm pension plans – where they're not as lucrative as Deloitte and EY.

Sure.

But I think the story…

I just think the story looks weird.

Yeah, I mean.

Regarding the pension plan…

Yeah, so I think we can look at the support…

Not really – so, if you're an audit committee and you don't want to resign – the negative story actually makes sense. If that – if you buy the pension thing, the negative story actually makes sense.

Sure.

You're less likely – because you don't want to leave.

Sure.

So – thank you Brian – good point. So, any third party…

I don't know that I buy the pension thing, but if you do…

No – but you do though – because you just offered up an explanation.

[viii]*When we've had conversations with partners – that that is the reason.*

It's basically…

Because they're…

Yeah.

Once they get – and some of them are vested very early – and so they'd be walking away from a large sum of money.

So, okay – thank you very much.

---

[i] Transcription Note: The original transcript has been edited for flow and ease of reading. Any changes to content were not intended to change the overall message associated with the applicable discussion.

[ii] This appears to refer to the following study, which appears to be referred to in the paper itself, but was ultimately published with the following reference, as obtained from the journal's web-site: Karen M. Hennes, Andrew J. Leone, and Brian P. Miller (*2014*) Determinants and Market Consequences of Auditor Dismissals after Accounting Restatements. The Accounting Review: May 2014, Vol. 89, No. 3, pp. 1051-1082.

[iii] While not clear, it appears that the question is referring to the following article from JAR (reference from the journal's web-site – in the June 2016 issue): BROWN, S. V. and KNECHEL, W. R. (2016), Auditor–Client Compatibility and Audit Firm Selection. Journal of Accounting Research, 54: 725–775. doi:10.1111/1475-679X.12105.

[iv] This appears to refer to the following study, and the following reference originates from the paper itself: Lennox, C. S., and C. W. Park. 2007. Audit firm appointments, audit firm alumni, and audit committee independence. *Contemporary Accounting Research* 24 (1): 235-258.

[v] Transcription note: The participant appears to be using the acronym "AC" for audit committee.

[vi] This appears to refer to the following study, which appears to be referred to in the paper itself, but was ultimately published with the following reference, as obtained from the journal's web-site: Matthew J. Beck and Elaine G. Mauldin (*2014*) Who's Really in Charge? Audit Committee versus CFO Power and Audit Fees. The Accounting Review: November 2014, Vol. 89, No. 6, pp. 2057-2085.

[vii] Transcription Note: This refers to the presentation slides, which are also included for reference in the symposium web-site.

[viii] Transcription note: While these last three italicized comments in this transcription were not made by the presenter, they were made by another co-author on the paper – Thomas C. Omer – who was also in attendance.

Research Session 5 – Nicholas Hallman[i]

Questions and Answers

So, it seems that finding a meaningful difference between those computations for the overall population and just the population for auditor A – it kind of depends on the amount of overlap between auditor A and auditor B. And maybe you'll get to this, but what evidence do you have there is meaningful – or that there's a meaningful separation between the clients of auditor A and auditor B, for example?

So, it's not in the paper anymore – this is one of the symptoms of going through the dissertation process. There's a lot of stuff that gets put in and then discard – and it's still around somewhere, and I'm debating about whether to put it in, so – thanks for asking the question, because I may put that back in the paper.

What I've done is I've actually graphed for every audit firm and every audit office, the 75th and the 25th in that range – for the risk of their clients, and then set them out all next to each other, and the variation is a lot more than I expected. I suspect more than you would expect as well. Because, you're right – if these two auditors are stacked right up on top of each other – both stacks centered on the full distribution – which is real important for me here – there's going to be no effect. My zero – if they're stacked right on top of the distribution – so it's going to be zero.

Zero.

Right, and if there all stacked on top of each other, there's not going to be any variation. And so, it's important that there is variation in the portfolio, and I can tell you – there is. That's not in the paper now – perhaps it should be.

I was not in the dissertation committee, but I would think that would be really important to show up front. Because, let's say they're not stacked right on top of each other, but they're close – you could start to observe differences that aren't meaningful. And so, I think showing it in meaningful separation there – is important.

So, when you say you think I can start to observe differences that aren't meaningful, what I would expect – if they're all stacked on top of each other – all, first, set centered on the distribution – is I just wouldn't find any results.

If they're exactly centered – yeah, the calculation would...

Be zero.

...literally give you the same number on the calculation. But, if you started shifting that a little bit, you're going to get different numbers there, right?

The differences will be small, but yes.

Right.

Yeah. So, I mean, I don't have the summary statistics in the slide deck, but the variation – like the standard deviation for that measure is like .3 – and given the theoretical maximum and minimum is -1 and 1 – a .3 standard deviation is pretty high. There's some significant variation in this number – both on average across offices and firms, as well as across clients as well.

So, one of the things – you'd get at this without graphing necessarily – is just test – do a non-parametric test on the ranks across your portfolios. And pick – for one – pick the portfolios out of the middle that seem to be close together, and pick the end points and see if your results hold in the middle and across the end point.

Yeah.

And you can get at the same point. Might be easier – I don't know if it's easier than a graph – the graph sounds good – but, nonetheless, it will be another way to support the idea that you're getting certain differences.

Certainly – and I will say one other thing – again, not in the slide deck, but then – these effects that I'm predicting are different depending on whether the value is negative or positive. And, depending on what the DV[ii] is. And I might talk about that later, if we've got some time.

Can you just – I'm a little bit confused – is the contrast set by audit firms as they classify clients from one group to another? How is this contrast set or measured?

So, here's the idea. Maybe – I think I probably didn't articulate it well to begin with. If you're auditor A up here, and you're used to looking at a very same set of clients – client X is your most risky client. So, by contrast with the rest of your portfolio, they look risky – despite the fact that if you get a higher perspective – a broader perspective – they really are just a middle-risk client, right? And vice versa for auditor B – by contrast, with the rest of auditor B's portfolio, that same client looks like they're really safe. Even though they're not really that safe – they're middling again. It's just a contrast effect?

So, how you measure it? How do you know? What type of archival data are you able to access – to make sure this?

So, it's just Compustat and Audit Analytics.

Okay – on the auditor...

So, I calculate F-score and bankruptcy risk[iii], which you can do with very available data. And I just ranked them within – and I'll do this both at the firm, and the office, and industry-office levels to see where this effect is really taking place. But, you can do it with available data.

So, Nick, this is almost assuming that all the engagement level partners – and those that are working on these engagements – have visibility into the entire firm's portfolio.

So - continue and then I'll answer.

And so, I think – and that might be just be a drawback – but it might be a good – I don't know if you can get to this or not – I mean, maybe doing it at the office level is good – but, at the partner level would be great. I mean that's where you would really expect to see – because then, if you know who those partner's clients were, then you could get – it seems a link better up with the experimental evidence that you were talking about before. Now, I don't know if you can get to that or if you've thought of that, but just something…

I've certainly thought about it – and, as you probably suspect, I can't easily get to it. I might talk to Brant – he's got a little bit of – he's not some nice partner data from his dissertation.[iv] But, I do do this at several different levels. And, the problem is a lot of partners have one major client. And so, you can't get at this effect anyway even if I did have the data. In fact, what I find is – when I use the firm level, it doesn't really show up – because, as you'd expect, any partner at the firm probably didn't have a lot of visibility with the rest of the firm's clients. At the office level, it shows up really strongly.

When I dig a little bit deeper into, like, the office-industry level – where I suspect you've got a pretty homogeneous group of auditors all sort of exchanging ideas. Really, where I expect this to happen the most – the effect shows up sometimes – but starts to go away – because I suspect the denominator in, if I – I've set down my remote here – the denominator might measure it's really small.[v] So, if I want – if I think about what my equation is here, right? The rank in the office over the rank of – in the full distribution are in the group. That group rank is like one out of three in an office-industry, and so it gets to be a really course measure, and there's just a lot of noise in it. And so, when I get sort of a broader measure – I get like maybe ten in that denominator – I think I get some more accuracy and some more precision with the measure.

So, I think this gets at Tim's point, too – but, and I don't – sorry, I haven't read the paper – if you just took a factor analysis of your ranks and the fees in that office, and found that they both positively loaded on the same construct, you'd be able to get around the individual auditors not knowing the whole spectrum of clients. But, the office is ranking them and charging fees consistently, and that would be a way to strengthen the argument that this ranking system works very well using Compustat numbers and they're looking at the engagement. If the whole office, overall, is all looking at the same construct – which is risk in your case – their belief about risk of pricing should follow that, and the rankings you're using should also follow that same construct.

So, a different method of getting at the same thing is I put fees on the left hand side of a model where this is the predicted variable - the variable of interest…

That's fine.

…and I get exactly what you're expecting here. So, not only are they changing their behavior in the audit, they're also charging more when a client looks riskier than it actually is. That's controlling for the client's actual risk by the way – so it's incremental.

But this is – well, I mean, I'm not going to argue my preference, but by telling me what those loadings are, I feel a whole lot better about the fact that you're capturing this same construct – putting it in the regression, I'm sort of treating it independent of everything else that you're putting on the right-hand side...

Yeah, that's true.

...and so, it would be really nice – and that's a footnote – it would be a really good way to solidify what – the question that Tim has about the partners being able to see everything.

Yeah - I like that a lot. Thank you.

[vi]If that's the case, as Tom suggested, I should also see this show up in pricing. So, my second hypothesis involves audit fees – where I put audit fees on the left-hand side. I put different controls but the same test variable on the right-hand side. And I find, in fact, that it does load through a fees model as well.

Help me out with something – I might just be missing something here – but when you have abnormal accruals on the left-hand side there?

Uh-huh.

Connect for me the auditor's misperception or bias in the risk assessment to the firms, then, abnormal accruals.

So, here's – so, can I get back to that when I actually show you the result?

Sure.

Okay, which is just like the next slide[vii] – so I'll come right back to that. I told you ask questions during, then I'm putting you off to the end – I'm sorry.

That's alright.

[viii]I'm going to go through, sort of, my main results, right? So, in that first test where I've got abnormal accruals on the left-hand side, and I use my bias measure, it loads negatively, right? And to answer your question, the idea there is that if you've got a client that looks riskier than they actually are to their auditor, the auditor is going to take extra precautions and constrain those abnormal accruals as much as they can.

Now, interestingly, one of my concerns – my major concerns – around when I did this study was that I was going to conflate perceived risk with actual risk, and I can be pretty certain in this case that I haven't done that because the actual misstatement risk variable loads very significantly in the opposite direction of my perceived misstatement risk variable, right? So, a client that actually has a lot of misstatement risk – that's going to be a client with a lot of high abnormal accruals, as you would probably expect. But when, independent of that, when that client looks like they've got high misstatement risk, those abnormal accruals are going to be constrained by their auditor. That's the story – you can…

So, I'm a better auditor on my most risky clients?

You are a more conservative auditor on your most risky clients. I don't know that low abnormal accruals is, in and of itself, necessarily bad.

Right.

It's conservative, I think.

Nick – I think maybe one way to sort of get it this is to relate it back to the audit risk model, similar to, kind of, what Joe did in his presentation. So if you've got this risk – this perceived risk. So, if you think audit risk equals inherent risk times detection risk. If they're perceiving that it's higher risk than normal, then they need to increase their audit effort in order to get that detection risk in order to achieve the same audit risk.

Yeah.

And so, as they're making a mistake in over-estimating the risk on a particular client, then they're also going to over-estimate the amount of effort that they need to put forward.

Yeah.

Does that kind of get at what you're asking?

We're focusing on the over-estimation side – I think we actually likely more need to talk about the problem with the under-estimation side.

Yeah, it's the same – yeah, flip side…

Flip-side of the same coin.

Are they over-estimating? I mean it's kind of the context – this is your contrast, right? In their portfolio, they're estimating what the risk is relative to their portfolio – not to the spectrum of risk. So, I don't know if we could – maybe it's just a choice of the word over-estimating, but, based on their portfolio, they have an assessment of what the risk is in their portfolio and what they're going to be subject to. And, that's all they know.

Yeah.

And so, what we don't know – or and what we do know is that we don't know if they look outside of their portfolio – which I suspect they don't. And that's our bias. We can look outside of their portfolio and say – hey, wait a minute guys. You're over-estimating this. But no, they're protecting themselves, based on their own reality if you want to call it that – that's their own reality.

So, I'm making an assumption here – that the right decision is to get as broad a perspective as possible. That may not be the case, and that's sort of an assumption that is embedded in my measure. But as you say, it could be like – these things might not – they might be a little more local. The right answer might be more local. I tend to think not, but it's a good point.

So, do the fees change? So, when you get your...

I change the model for fees.

Yeah – so, when they move from client auditor error – or A to B – do their fees go down in the new audit realm?

So, I have not looked at that. So, what I have that is if you've got a high – a high value for this measure. So, you're being treated very conservatively because you've followed the top of the distribution in your office – when you switch, that measure – it goes down a lot. So, you're switching to a new office where you don't fall near the top of the distribution – correcting this problem – a problem in quotes here.

But then the fees should have a respective – given that context, the fees should have...

I agree – that's…

I mean I think you should see something. Not – I don't know if it would be big or not, but certainly, if you're now the bottom of the totem pole whereas the next auditor...

It should change.

They shouldn't be judging – I mean that may be how they got you.

Yep, they've decided, right?

But they took because you're – for them – you're the easy guy, of course.

Yep, so it's a great prediction and it's easy to test – I will test it.

Brant.

If you go ahead and test that, you might want to be careful, too, because the first year under any auditor, you're going to have a lower...

That's true.

...and so you may need to capture the first two years versus the past two years to see if there's really a change above and beyond the first year fee cut.

That's true – yeah – in the back.

The other thing is that they might switch to a non-Big N auditor, too, so you'd lose that fee premium and all that, so...

So, I'd have to control for it.

Yeah, and then...

Or maybe just limit it to within Big Four switches.

Yeah, right – so just being careful on that when you work it out.

Okay.

[ix]Yeah – please.

So, are you sure that the other firms haven't implemented something like this?

No – in fact, I'm almost certain at this point they had, but the only assumption necessary here is that they didn't implement it simultaneously.

So, I like the test if Deloitte is the only one that implemented. So you kind of have – I mean I wouldn't – you know, it's the shock right? So the shock would be to see if it works.

Yeah, and so...

Assuming that you can confirm that Deloitte was the first mover, and then in your post-period the other Big Four firm in your control group hadn't, right?

So, help me think about this though. I don't think that I need to assume that nobody else implemented it on even – on either side of my event date – so long as they didn't implement it on my event date – so, simultaneously with Deloitte. If I can confirm that, I think I'm good on the diff-if-diff test, right?

Well, if you did three years before and three years after, and say a couple of firms entered in year t+1 or t+2, it – I guess it would bias against you, yeah.

If it was really, yeah...

So, it would be nice to have a couple of clean years to look at.

So, I've reached out to some of the other firms and basically just gotten dead air.

That's what happens.

So.

Sorry Tim.

Let me understand the test. So, you've got all the firms in this test, but do you...

All the Big Four – I limit this to the Big Four.

So, what happens if you just do Deloitte's offices that you have in your sample? I mean, you should see this from their Deloitte offices, right?

I'm confused by that – so I'm assuming common distribution that's tested across the offices – in roughly the same time period.

But each office has its own set of biases, right?

Uh-huh.

So, what you just told me is that they would change – so after the change, that bias should go down across the board. You should see a pre- and a post- effect of – just for Deloitte. Because, shouldn't everybody adjust their view of their clients based on this new tool?

That's what I'm seeing. That is, in fact, what I'm seeing. And I'm still calculating bias here at the office level.

Okay.

But for all of the Deloitte offices – or, at least on average for the Deloitte offices – the bias goes down relative to all the other firms.

Then that's – I think that's a good test.

Okay – good.

I think it's a good test.

Matt.

Could you not go – so, go within Deloitte and then – so, Deloitte's offices are going to have different – like, some of them are going to be towards the middle of the actual spectrum. Some of them will be towards the end of the actual spectrum. Test whether the bias is reduced on the ends. The ones in the middle shouldn't change much, if at all.

Yeah.

Then you don't even need to worry about when the other firms put this in. And so, you know for sure when Deloitte did it. You know which offices in Deloitte it should have helped the most. And see if it helped them.

That's a good point.

So, here's an idea – it might be messy – but, moving it forward – maybe a year – and getting to look at a sort of quasi difference-in-difference by the firm – or by the clients that switched to Deloitte in that year two.

Uh-huh.

Almost – so you're kind-of getting a group then that was not with Deloitte – that was with Deloitte in that second year, but then you have Deloitte clients.

So then I do have to assume the other firms didn't implement before in order for that to work.

Yeah, then you would just have to check to make sure. But, that would be something you'd have to do. But that might be a quasi difference-in-differences.

Sure. So I think I'm out of time, so I'm going to call it. But thank you very much for all the questions and feedback. I really appreciate it, and go home.

---

[i] Transcription Note: The original transcript has been edited for flow and ease of reading. Any changes to content were not intended to change the overall message associated with the applicable discussion.

[ii] Transcription Note: Given there are multiple dependent variables in the presenter's tests, DV appears to be referring to dependent variable.

[iii] From the paper (both the information and the references) – F-Score originates from the following paper - Dechow, P. M., W. Ge, C. R. Larson, and R. G. Sloan. 2011. Predicting Material Accounting Misstatements. *Contemporary Accounting Research* 28 (1): 737–779; while the bankruptcy risk measure originates from the following paper - Zmijewski, M. E. 1984. Methodological Issues Related to the Estimation of Financial Distress Prediction Models. *Journal of Accounting Research* 22: 59–83.

[iv] This appears to be referring to Brant E. Christensen's dissertation, which can be accessed at the following reference: Christensen, B. (2015). *Mandatory partner rotation and audit quality: Evidence from U.S. audit firm archival data* (Order No. 3738136). Available from ProQuest Dissertations & Theses Global. (1739152679). Retrieved from http://search.proquest.com/docview/1739152679?accountid=14556.

[v] Transcription Note: This appears to a reference to or towards the presentation slides, which are also included for reference in the symposium web-site.

[vi] Transcription note: this comment is included because it refers to a prior point and ultimately leads into the next question that occurred in the presentation.

[vii] Transcription Note: Please refer to endnote v.

[viii] Transcription Note: This comment ultimately responds to the prior question – so it is included for reference.

[ix] Transcription Note: Since this appears a bit abrupt, just a note for reference that this follows further discussion of an additional test performed by the auditor.

PCAOB
Public Company Accounting Oversight Board

RELIABILITY

INTEGRITY

QUALITY

Trends in Audit Oversight and Audit Quality

University of Kansas Auditing Symposium

Jeanette M. Franzel, Board Member
Public Company Accounting Oversight Board

May 20, 2016

PCAOB: Protecting the Public Interest through Audit Oversight

Disclaimer

- The views I express today are mine alone, and do not necessarily reflect the views of the Board, other Board Members, or PCAOB staff.

PCAOB 2

PCAOB at a Glance

- Statutory mission areas
  - Registration, inspection, enforcement, standards
- Staff: 876 (budgeted for 2016)
- 2016 Budget: $257.7 million
- Registered Firms: 2,100 (1,200 U.S., 900 foreign)
  - 950 report no activity subject to PCAOB oversight
- 2016 Inspections (estimated):
  - 10 annual, 140 triennial US, 62 triennial foreign
  - 75 broker and dealer auditors

PCAOB 3

Equity Markets Around The World

Global Equity Market Cap $62.8 T

Global Equity Market Cap for U.S. Traded Companies: $32.6 Trillion

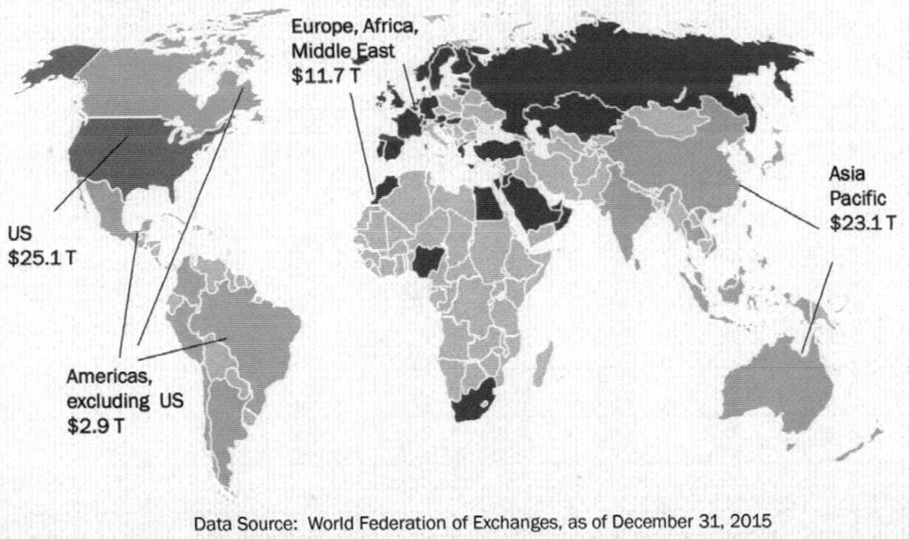

Data Source: World Federation of Exchanges, as of December 31, 2015

PCAOB 4

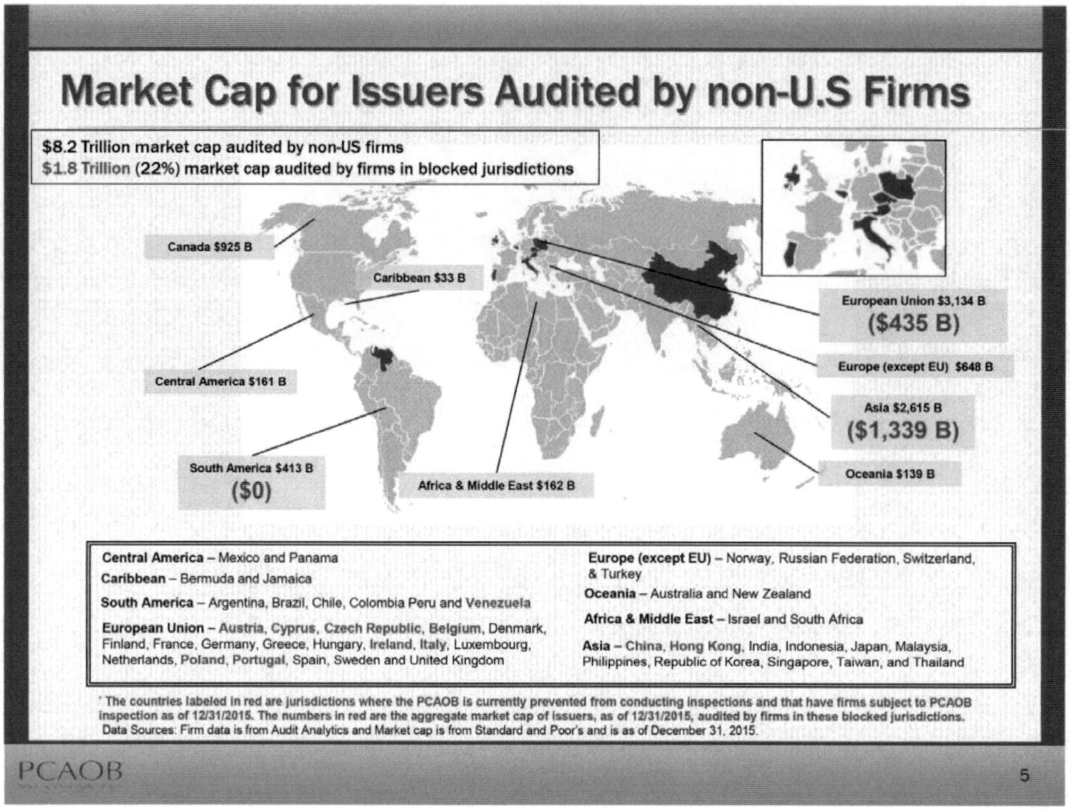

Market Cap for Issuers Audited by non-U.S Firms
$8.2 Trillion market cap audited by non-US firms
$1.8 Trillion (22%) market cap audited by firms in blocked jurisdictions
Canada $925 B
Caribbean $33 B
Central America $161 B
South America $413 B
($0)
Africa & Middle East $162 B
European Union $3,134 B
($435 B)
Europe (except EU) $648 B
Asia $2,615 B
($1,339 B)
Oceania $139 B
Central America – Mexico and Panama
Caribbean – Bermuda and Jamaica
South America – Argentina, Brazil, Chile, Colombia Peru and Venezuela
European Union – Austria, Cyprus, Czech Republic, Belgium, Denmark, Finland, France, Germany, Greece, Hungary, Ireland, Italy, Luxembourg, Netherlands, Poland, Portugal, Spain, Sweden and United Kingdom
Europe (except EU) – Norway, Russian Federation, Switzerland, & Turkey
Oceania – Australia and New Zealand
Africa & Middle East – Israel and South Africa
Asia – China, Hong Kong, India, Indonesia, Japan, Malaysia, Philippines, Republic of Korea, Singapore, Taiwan, and Thailand
' The countries labeled in red are jurisdictions where the PCAOB is currently prevented from conducting inspections and that have firms subject to PCAOB inspection as of 12/31/2015. The numbers in red are the aggregate market cap of issuers, as of 12/31/2015, audited by firms in these blocked jurisdictions.
Data Sources: Firm data is from Audit Analytics and Market cap is from Standard and Poor's and is as of December 31, 2015.
PCAOB
5

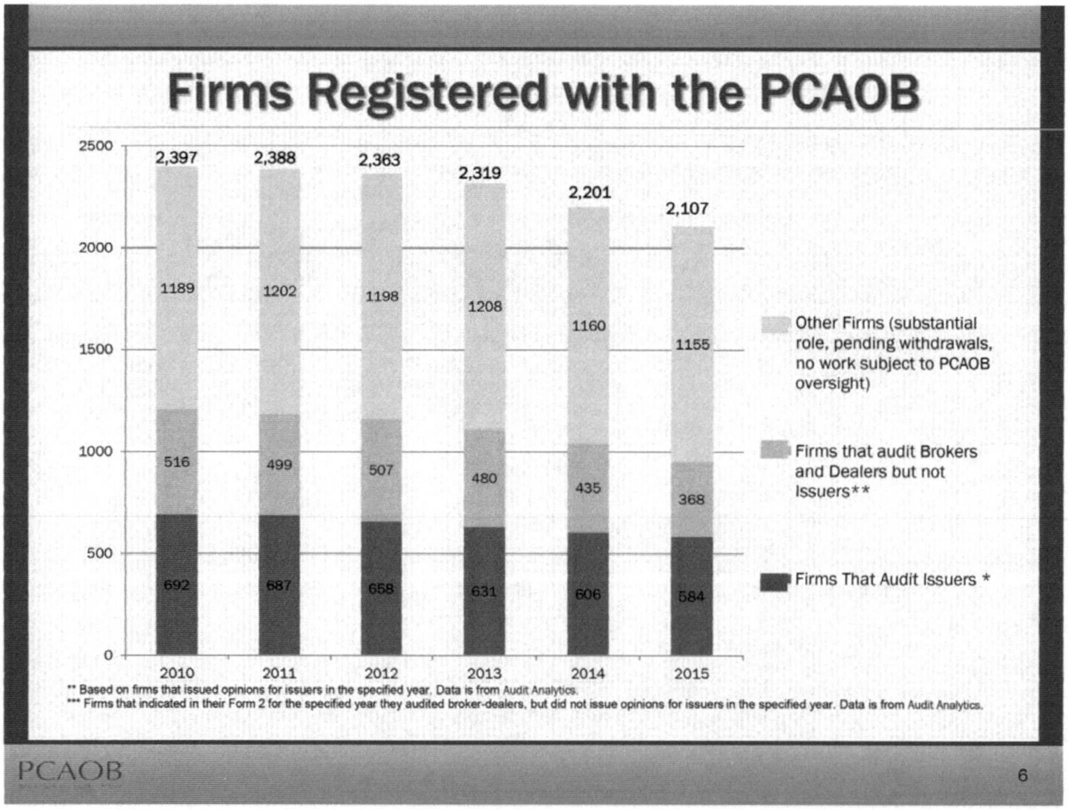

Firms Registered with the PCAOB
2500
2000
1500
1000
500
0
2,397
2,388
2,363
2,319
2,201
2,107
1189
1202
1198
1208
1160
1155
516
499
507
480
435
368
692
687
658
631
606
584
2010
2011
2012
2013
2014
2015
Other Firms (substantial role, pending withdrawals, no work subject to PCAOB oversight)
Firms that audit Brokers and Dealers but not Issuers**
Firms That Audit Issuers *
** Based on firms that issued opinions for issuers in the specified year. Data is from Audit Analytics.
*** Firms that indicated in their Form 2 for the specified year they audited broker-dealers, but did not issue opinions for issuers in the specified year. Data is from Audit Analytics.
PCAOB
6

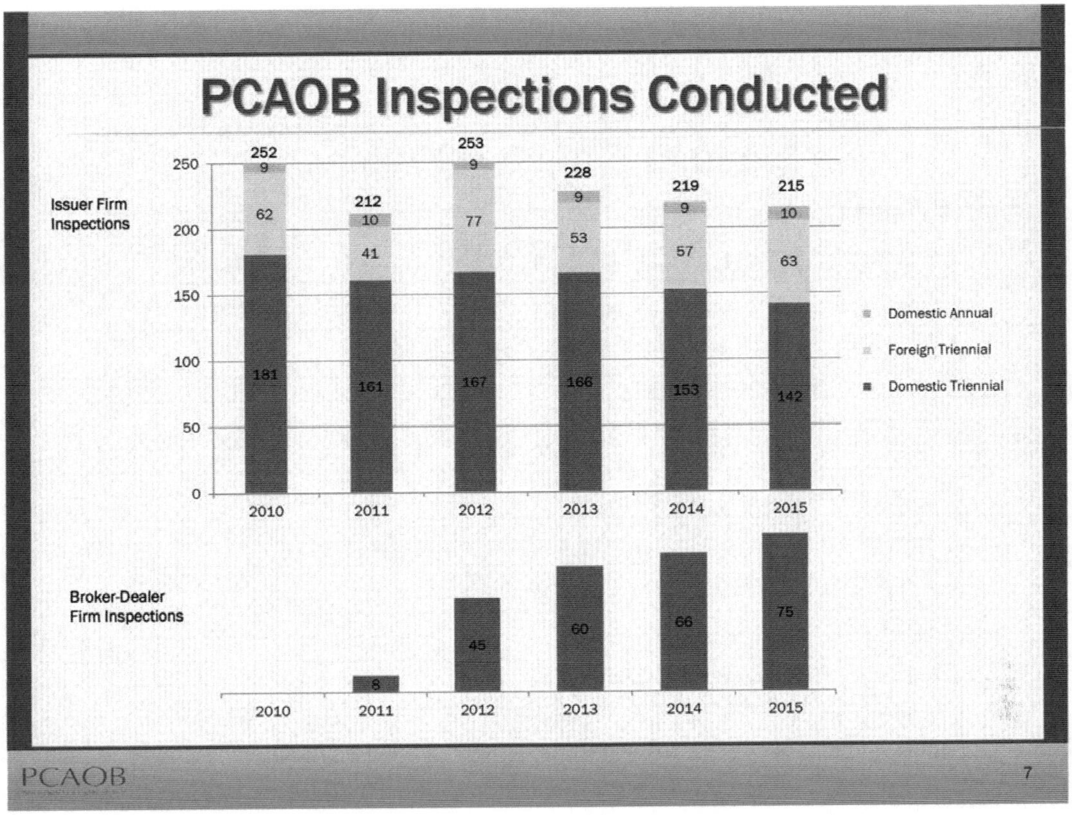
PCAOB Inspections Conducted
Issuer Firm Inspections
250
200
150
100
50
0
252
9
62
181
212
10
41
161
253
9
77
167
228
9
53
166
219
9
57
153
215
10
63
142
2010
2011
2012
2013
2014
2015
Domestic Annual
Foreign Triennial
Domestic Triennial
Broker-Dealer Firm Inspections
8
45
60
66
75
2010
2011
2012
2013
2014
2015
PCAOB
7

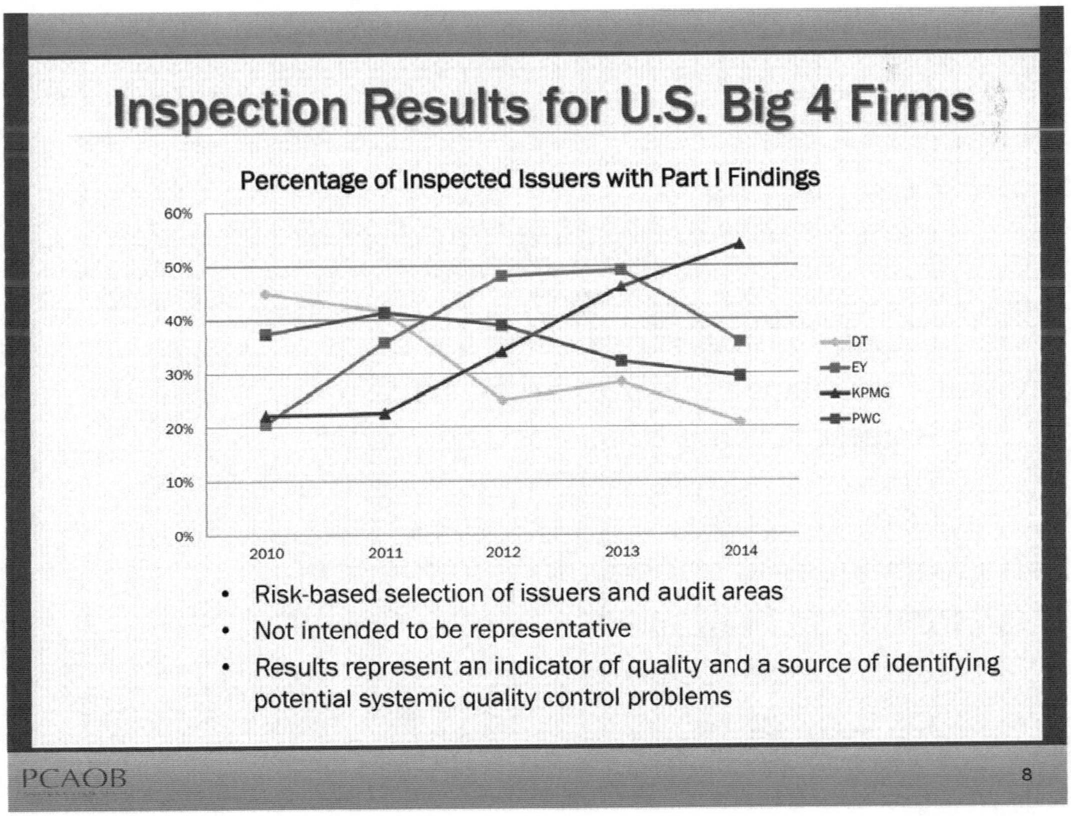
Inspection Results for U.S. Big 4 Firms
Percentage of Inspected Issuers with Part I Findings
60%
50%
40%
30%
20%
10%
0%
2010
2011
2012
2013
2014
DT
EY
KPMG
PWC
• Risk-based selection of issuers and audit areas
• Not intended to be representative
• Results represent an indicator of quality and a source of identifying potential systemic quality control problems
PCAOB
8

PCAOB Inspections: Areas of Frequent Findings

Audit Areas:

- Auditing Internal Control (AS 5)
- Auditor Response to Risk of Material Misstatement (AS 13)
- Auditing Accounting Estimates (AU 342)
- Audit Sampling (AU 350)
- Auditing Fair Value Measurements & Disclosures (AU 328)

Financial reporting areas:

- Revenue
- Accounts receivable
- Inventory
- Business combinations
- Goodwill

PCAOB 9

General Improvements at Large Firms

- Tone at the Top
  - Focus on audit quality backed by actions and resources
- Improvements in firms' systems of quality control
- Training in complex audit topics
- New practice aids and checklists
  - Professional skepticism
  - auditing fair market value and management estimates
  - ICFR
- Coaching and support to audit teams
- Monitoring of quality

PCAOB 10

State of Audit Quality

- Large U.S. firms have made significant improvements in audit quality
- Continued remediation is needed to strengthen QC systems and monitoring to prevent audit deficiencies
- Need for increased focus on quality across the global networks and at affiliated firms
- U.S. triennial firm results are nuanced due to the changing mix of firms inspected each year and changes in client base
- Implications for future inspections approaches
  - Addition of non-risk-based selections ("randomization")
  - Potential for shifting inspection focus to testing of a firm's QC system

PCAOB 11

Audit Quality Indicators

Treasury ACAP 2008 Report, Concentration and Competition

- Recommend that the PCAOB, in consultation with auditors, investors, public companies, audit committees, boards of directors, academics, and others, **determine the feasibility** of developing key indicators of audit quality and effectiveness and require auditing firms to publicly disclose these indicators.
- **Assuming development and disclosure of indicators of audit quality are feasible**, require the PCAOB to monitor these indicators
- "A key issue in the public company audit market is what drives competition for audit clients and whether audit quality is the most significant driver."

Final Report of the Advisory Committee on the Auditing Profession (ACAP), Oct. 6, 2008, pp. VIII:14-15

PCAOB 12

PCAOB's AQI Project

- PCAOB Concept Release, July 1, 2015
  - To seek public comment on the content and possible uses of a group of potential "audit quality indicators."
  - May provide new insights about how to evaluate the quality of audits and how high quality audits are achieved.
  - Taken together with qualitative context, the indicators may inform discussions among audit committees and audit firms.
  - Enhanced discussions, in turn, may strengthen audit planning, execution, and communication.
  - Use of the indicators may also stimulate competition among audit firms focused on the quality of the firms' work and, thereby, increase audit quality overall.
  - 28 potential indicators: audit professionals, process, results.

PCAOB 13

PCAOB's AQI Project – Next Steps

- Encourage voluntary use and experimentation with AQIs
- Monitor voluntary use and related market developments
- Outreach and feedback from audit committees and other stakeholders
- Continue the development of AQIs and advance thought and practice in their usage
- Potentially publish additional information related to AQIs
- Other issues
  - Time horizon for next steps
  - Linkages with quality control standards project and root cause efforts
  - Assessment of qualitative factors and context
  - Public reporting vs. use by firms and audit committees
  - Highly concentrated audit market

PCAOB 14

Standard-Setting

Projects:

- Transparency about Participants in the Audit (Approved)
- Audits Involving Other Auditors (Board Proposal, April 12, 2016)
- Auditor's Reporting Model (Board Reproposal, May 11, 2016)
- Going Concern (PCAOB Practice Alert No. 13)
- Auditing Estimates, Including Fair Value Measurements (Expected Proposal, 4th Qtr. 2016)
- Auditor's Use of the Work of Specialists (Expected Proposal, 4th Qtr. 2016)
- Quality Control Standards (Research and outreach)

Effort to improve process:

- Top to bottom review of process
- Use of environmental scans and improved research approach
- Integrating economic analysis
- Project-based coordination with IAASB

Additional PCAOB Focus Areas

- Outreach and dialogue with audit committees
- ICFR dialogue with preparers, auditors and audit committees
- Development of the broker-dealer inspection program
- Integration of economic analysis in standard-setting
- Analysis of risks to audit quality presented by the audit firm business model
- Consideration of the impact of technology, data analytics, and "big data" on the audit.

Standing Advisory Group, May 18, 2016
Discussion of Current and Emerging Audit Issues

- Economic Developments
- Use of data/ data auditing
- Auditor's role – non-GAAP measures
- Impact of FASB materiality proposals
- Revenue recognition transition
- Cybersecurity
- Auditing forward-looking assumptions
- Disruptive technology changes
- Mandatory audit firm rotation in the European Union
- Whistleblower Activity

PCAOB 17

Audit of the Future

PCAOB 18

Auditing Considerations and Financial Reporting

Thomas J. Linsmeier
FASB Member

2016 Deloitte / University of Kansas Auditing Symposium
May 20, 2016

FASB FINANCIAL ACCOUNTING STANDARDS BOARD

1

Recent Financial Reporting Areas (Potentially) Influenced by Auditing Considerations

- Application of Materiality to Disclosure Decisions
- GAAP vs. Non-GAAP Presentation
- Use of Accounting Conventions vs. Full Compliance with GAAP
- Insurance Loss Development Tables
- Going Concern

FASB FINANCIAL ACCOUNTING STANDARDS BOARD

2

Application of Materiality to Disclosure Decisions

FASB FINANCIAL ACCOUNTING STANDARDS BOARD

3

Disclosure Framework: Two Components

Improving the effectiveness of notes requires both:

Consistent considerations by the Board in each standard-setting activity	Appropriate exercise of judgment by reporting entities when assessing disclosure requirements
↓	↓
Phase I: Board's Decision Process	**Phase II:** Entity's Decision Process

FASB FINANCIAL ACCOUNTING STANDARDS BOARD

4

Entity's Decision Process

Field Study Provided Insights on

Effectiveness of notes after applying two different criteria for non-compliance with GAAP

- Materiality
- Entity-specific Relevance

Constraints of reporting system on entity's ability to exercise judgment

- Audit
- Regulatory
- Legal

FASB FINANCIAL ACCOUNTING STANDARDS BOARD

5

Entity's Decision Process

Proposed Changes to the Codification

- "Provide disclosure to the extent material"
- Eliminate language that limits judgment
- Add guidance on applying materiality

FASB FINANCIAL ACCOUNTING STANDARDS BOARD

6

Proposed Guidance on Applying Materiality

- Applied individually and in the aggregate
- Legal concept
- Quantitative and qualitative
- Omission not an accounting error

The last item was proposed because
- Non-compliance with disclosure requirements that are "more than clearly trivial" but are less than financial reporting materiality are reported to the audit committee (AC) as an error
- Entities generally indicate that they prefer to provide these disclosures rather than to have discussions with the AC to justify their exclusion
- This lowers the threshold for disclosure and is a source of potential disclosure ineffectiveness

Defining Materiality in Financial Reporting

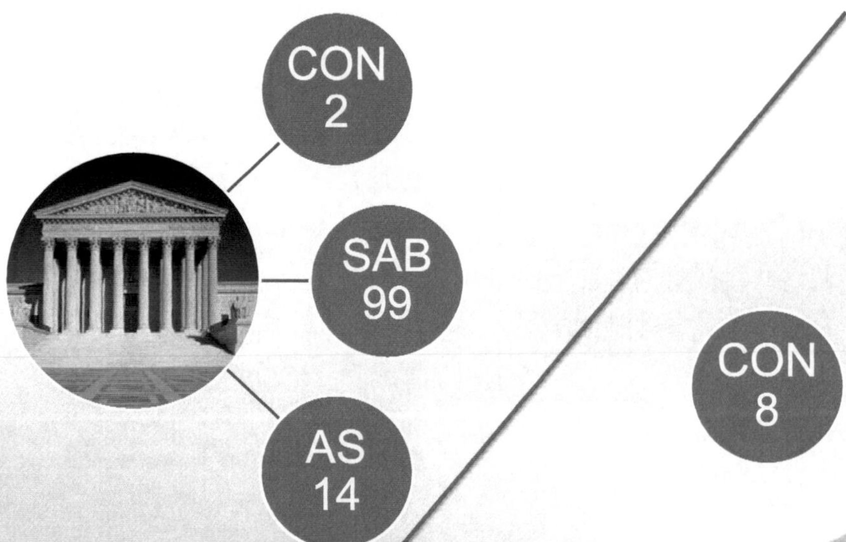

Defining Materiality in Financial Reporting

- CON 2/ SAB 99 / AS 14 generally define materiality based on whether there is a substantial likelihood that inclusion of information would make a difference in reasonable users' decisions
- CON 8 generally changed the threshold to whether there is a reasonable expectation that inclusion of the information could make a difference in reasonable users' decisions
- CON 8 change was made in 2010 to converge with IFRS and resulted in no observable increase in disclosures in the U.S.
- Recent proposed change to CON 8 definition of materiality was made to reconcile FASB's definition of materiality with that of the SEC and PCAOB. Language generally conforms with original CON 2 definition.

FASB FINANCIAL ACCOUNTING STANDARDS BOARD 9

Materiality -Comment Letter Feedback

Legal Concept
- Lawyer involvement
- Accounting concept
- Anti-fraud

Omission Not Error
- Support for the statement
- Reduced communication concerns

Burden of proof
- Prove materiality for inclusion?

Definition
- Concerns over departure from CON 8
- Absent from Codification

FASB FINANCIAL ACCOUNTING STANDARDS BOARD 10

Next Steps

- Issue Exposure Drafts Applying Board's Decision Process to Disclosures on
  - Income Taxes
  - Inventory
- Hold Roundtable on All Aspects of Project
- Redeliberate Materiality and Deliberate its Application to Interim Considerations
- Redeliberate Proposed Concepts in the Disclosure Framework
- Redeliberate Proposed Revisions to Disclosures in 4 areas on this slide

Defined Benefit Plans

Fair Value Measurement

Income Taxes

Inventory

FASB FINANCIAL ACCOUNTING STANDARDS BOARD

11

GAAP vs. Non-GAAP Presentation

FASB FINANCIAL ACCOUNTING STANDARDS BOARD

12

Proliferation of Non-GAAP Earnings

According to Jack Ciesielski's, 2015 two-part Analyst's Accounting Observer report entitled "The Non-GAAP Earnings Epidemic"

- Non-GAAP earnings reports were issued by 67% of S&P 500 companies in 2014
- The reported adjustments resulted in a net increase of 22.2% in non-GAAP earnings when compared to GAAP earnings
- Seventy-six percent of the adjustments increased reported results
  - Query: Could this directional bias in the adjustments be related to the fact that non-GAAP earnings are not subject to audit or attestation?

FASB FINANCIAL ACCOUNTING STANDARDS BOARD

13

SEC Guidance on Non-GAAP Reporting: Reg G

- Regulation G, requires public companies that disclose non-GAAP financial measures to include, in that disclosure
  - A presentation, with equal or greater prominence, of the most directly comparable GAAP financial measure
  - A reconciliation of the disclosed non-GAAP financial measure to the most directly comparable GAAP financial measure
- Regulation G also requires disclosure of further material information, if any, as may be necessary to make the non-GAAP measure not misleading
  - Misleading measures contain either an untrue statement of a material fact or omit to state a material fact

FASB FINANCIAL ACCOUNTING STANDARDS BOARD

14

SEC Guidance on Non-GAAP Reporting: Item 10 of Regulation S-K and Regulation S-B

- Prohibits, amongst others
  - Adjusting a non-GAAP performance measure to eliminate or smooth items identified as non-recurring, infrequent or unusual, when (1) the nature of the charge or gain is such that it is reasonably likely to recur within two years, or (2) there was a similar charge or gain within the prior two years
  - Presenting non-GAAP financial measures on the face of financial statements prepared in accordance with GAAP or in the accompanying notes
  - Using titles or descriptions of non-GAAP financial measures that are the same as, or confusingly similar to, titles or descriptions used for GAAP measures
- Requires a statement disclosing why management believes presentation of the non-GAAP financial measure provides useful information to investors regarding financial condition and results of operations
  - Justification for the use of the measure must be substantive

FASB FINANCIAL ACCOUNTING STANDARDS BOARD

15

Examples of Issues for Audit Committees to Consider

- If the justification for reporting a non-GAAP measure is provide a cash measure of operating earnings, is it misleading to report a non-GAAP measure that makes adjustment for the following items only?
  - Depreciation/amortization
  - Stock-based compensation
- Are there not other revenues and expenses included in operating earnings this period for which the associated cash flows occurred in other than the current period?
- Is it misleading to report over time a measure of cash operating earnings that never includes deductions for the operating assets purchased?
- If the entity buys back stock this period to pay the stock-based compensation, is that not the same as a cash cost incurred this period?

FASB FINANCIAL ACCOUNTING STANDARDS BOARD

16

Examples of Issues for Audit Committees to Consider, cont'd

- If instead the adjustments (on the prior slide) are reported to provide a non-GAAP measure of current period operating cash flows
  - Is that non-GAAP measure being reconciled to GAAP operating cash flows (not GAAP operating earnings), which is the most directly comparable GAAP financial measure?
  - If that non-GAAP measure closely tracks operating cash flows, is that non-GAAP measure being reported on a per share basis?
    - Recall GAAP precludes presentation of a per share operating cash flow measure
- To avoid being misleading, if nonrecurring expenses or losses are being added back to arrive at a non-GAAP measure of recurring net income
  - Are adjustments being made for all nonrecurring items (revenues, expenses, gains and losses) or are only certain expenses and losses being reversed?
  - Are these adjustments being made net of tax?

FASB FINANCIAL ACCOUNTING STANDARDS BOARD

17

Use of Accounting Conventions vs. Full Compliance with GAAP

FASB FINANCIAL ACCOUNTING STANDARDS BOARD

18

Longstanding Accounting Conventions Accepted in Applying U.S. GAAP

- Capitalization policies for PP&E and intangibles
- Reporting royalty revenue earned on a 1 month lag
- Ignoring the need to amortize basis differences when applying the equity method

FASB FINANCIAL ACCOUNTING STANDARDS BOARD

19

Why Was Standard Setting (Rather than an Accounting Convention) Needed Here?

- Exception in IFRS 16 from balance sheet recognition of leases of low-value assets
- Exemption in Topic 606 from assessing whether promised goods or services are performance obligations if they are immaterial in the context of the contract with the customer
- Practical expedient in Topic 751 that allows an employer with a fiscal year-end other than a month-end date to measure defined benefit plan assets and obligations as of the month-end date that is closest to the employer's fiscal year-end (alternative measurement date)

FASB FINANCIAL ACCOUNTING STANDARDS BOARD

20

Use of Accounting Conventions vs. Full Compliance with GAAP

Queries:

- Are recent audit considerations that focus on the documentation of judgments and/or on the adequacy of internal controls creating a demand for changes in how financial reporting guidance is written rather than relying on accounting conventions that permit non-compliance in immaterial situations?
- If not, what is the reason for the change?

FASB FINANCIAL ACCOUNTING STANDARDS BOARD

21

Insurance Loss Development Tables

FASB FINANCIAL ACCOUNTING STANDARDS BOARD

22

Update 2015-09, Disclosure about Short-Duration Insurance Contracts

- Requires, for annual reporting periods, that an insurance entity disclose in a tabular format, as of the date of the latest statement of financial position presented, undiscounted information about claims development by **accident year,** including separate information about
  - a. Incurred claims and allocated **claim adjustment expenses**
  - b. Paid claims and allocated claim adjustment expenses.
- The disclosure should be provided for the number of years for which the claims incurred typically remain outstanding, but need not exceed 10 years
- All claims development years should be presented together to best communicate development trends to users

FASB FINANCIAL ACCOUNTING STANDARDS BOARD

23

Auditing Considerations

- All periods presented in the disclosure about claims development that precede the most recent reporting period shall be considered supplementary information
- This decision is in response to independence concerns that might arise, upon a change in auditor, if the new firm had to audit all of the years included in the claims development tables
  - Independence issues would arise for auditors that provided consulting services to the entity in the predecessor years, limiting the ability to bid on the audit
- The Board did not prescribe a particular location for presenting the supplementary information
  - Required supplementary information may be presented as a schedule outside the audited notes or within financial statement notes accompanied by a clear distinction between supplementary information and other disclosed information
- The Board did not preclude the entire development tables from being audited

FASB FINANCIAL ACCOUNTING STANDARDS BOARD

24

Going Concern

FASB FINANCIAL ACCOUNTING STANDARDS BOARD

25

GAAP for Basis of Accounting

- Continuation of a reporting entity as a going concern is presumed as the basis for preparing financial statements until the entity's liquidation becomes imminent
- When an entity's liquidation becomes imminent, financial statements are prepared under the liquidation basis of accounting
- Even if an entity's liquidation is not imminent, there may be conditions or events that raise substantial doubt about the entity's ability to continue as a going concern
  - In those situations, financial statements should continue to be prepared under the going concern basis

FASB FINANCIAL ACCOUNTING STANDARDS BOARD

26

Going Concern: Auditing Standards and Securities Laws

- Require that an auditor evaluate whether there is substantial doubt about an entity's ability to continue as a going concern for a reasonable period of time not to exceed one year beyond the date of the financial statements
- U.S. auditing standards also require an auditor to consider the possible financial statement effects, including footnote disclosures on uncertainties about an entity's ability to continue as a going concern
- The SEC also has guidance on disclosures that it expects from an entity when an auditor's report includes an explanatory paragraph that reflects substantial doubt about an entity's ability to continue as a going concern

FASB FINANCIAL ACCOUNTING STANDARDS BOARD 27

ASU 2014-15: Presentation Of Financial Statements – Going Concern

- ASU 2014-15 requires management (rather than auditors) to assess an entity's ability to continue as a going concern by incorporating and expanding upon certain principles that are currently in U.S. auditing standards. Specifically, it
  - (1) provides a definition of the term *substantial doubt*
  - (2) requires an evaluation every reporting period
  - (3) provides principles for considering mitigating effect of management's plans
  - (4) requires certain disclosures when substantial doubt is alleviated as a result of consideration of management's plans,
  - (5) requires an express statement and other disclosures when substantial doubt is not alleviated
  - (6) requires an assessment for a period of one year after the date that the financial statements are issued (or available to be issued).

FASB FINANCIAL ACCOUNTING STANDARDS BOARD 28

My Dissent: Reason #1

- Requiring management to disclose when it has substantial doubt about the entity's ability to continue as a going concern is outside the scope of the disclosures that should be required in notes to financial statements
- Instead, future oriented disclosures about an entity's overall ability to continue as a going concern should continue to be
  - Required in SEC filings as part of management's discussion and analysis
  - Subject to a safe harbor for forward-looking information
- This view is consistent with the FASB's recent proposed Concepts Statement, *Chapter 8: Notes to Financial Statements*
  - This document proposes that future-oriented assumptions and expectations that do not affect the measurement of numbers recognized in financial statements generally should not be considered by the Board for disclosure in the notes to the financial statements

FASB FINANCIAL ACCOUNTING STANDARDS BOARD 29

My Dissent: Reason #2

- Requiring disclosure only when it is probable that an entity will be unable to meet its obligations will provide information about going concern uncertainties that is too late to be of significant benefit to users
- Users indicate that when disclosures are provided only when it is probable, they typically already know about the uncertainty
  - Making the disclosures at best confirmatory
  - Providing little or no predictive value
- Any disclosure about the financial reporting implications of a going concern uncertainty should be required when going concern issues are
  - At minimum, more likely than not and
  - Preferably even earlier when those issues become reasonably likely
- The PCAOB appears to have similar concerns

FASB FINANCIAL ACCOUNTING STANDARDS BOARD 30

My Preference

- We should not have brought auditing guidance on going concern into GAAP by making management also responsible for making the going concern assessment
- Instead when it is reasonably likely that an entity will not have the ability to continue as a going concern, we should have required disclosure about how that uncertainty bares on estimates and assumptions used as inputs to measurements recognized in financial statements
  - For example, if there is substantial doubt that an entity will have the ability to continue as a going concern, this uncertainty should be required to be
    - Discussed in the accounting policy footnote for PP&E in relation to estimated useful lives

FASB FINANCIAL ACCOUNTING STANDARDS BOARD

31

Concluding Remarks

- During my time on the FASB, auditing considerations have had increased importance to financial reporting and standard setting decisions
- This might suggest that the FASB and U.S. auditing standard setters should explore mechanisms to
  - Promote consistent consideration of auditing issues in our standard setting activities
  - Facilitate more timely discussion so we do not find ourselves in disagreement with auditing standard setters
    - As is potentially the case currently with the PCAOB relating to the threshold for reporting going concern issues

FASB FINANCIAL ACCOUNTING STANDARDS BOARD

32

Questions

FASB FINANCIAL ACCOUNTING STANDARDS BOARD

33

The Informational Value of the Audit Report Date and the Effect of SFAS No. 165

Steven Glover
Timothy Seidel
Brigham Young University

James Hansen
Weber State University

Brigham Young University

Motivation

Prior research suggests that individuals adjust their actions to avoid the penalties associated with missing deadlines (Mano 1990)

In the audit context, prior research generally finds that deadline pressure negatively impacts audit quality (e.g., Rhode 1978; Alderman and Deitrick 1982; Kelley and Margheim 1990; McDaniel 1990; Ragunathan 1991; Choo 1995; Willet and Page 1996; Glover 1997)

"one of the biggest impediments to auditor skepticism, however, in my view, is the calendar. Public companies have ***filing deadlines to meet, and they are rarely missed. When they are missed, the consequences can be serious, including declining share prices and harm to investors***. If potential issues are discovered late in the audit process, or an issue is not resolved in a timely manner, ***auditors may feel pressure to cut corners. We have seen it in inspections and enforcement matters***: Auditors recognize that there may be a problem with management's estimates or conclusions but allow themselves to be talked out of doing anything about it." (Jay Hanson, PCAOB Board Member)

Brigham Young University

Motivation

The current audit report provides little insight regarding the quality of the audit performed beyond the name of the firm performing the audit

Report of Independent Registered Public Accounting Firm

The Board of Directors and Shareholders of Wal-Mart Stores, Inc.

We have audited the accompanying consolidated balance sheets of Wal-Mart Stores, Inc. as of January 31, 2016 and 2015, and the related consolidated statements of income, comprehensive income, shareholders' equity and redeemable noncontrolling interest, and cash flows for each of the three years in the period ended January 31, 2016. These financial statements are the responsibility of the Company's management. Our responsibility is to express an opinion on these financial statements based on our audits.

We conducted our audits in accordance with the standards of the Public Company Accounting Oversight Board (United States). Those standards require that we plan and perform the audit to obtain reasonable assurance about whether the financial statements are free of material misstatement. An audit includes examining, on a test basis, evidence supporting the amounts and disclosures in the financial statements. An audit also includes assessing the accounting principles used and significant estimates made by management, as well as evaluating the overall financial statement presentation. We believe that our audits provide a reasonable basis for our opinion.

In our opinion, the financial statements referred to above present fairly, in all material respects, the consolidated financial position of Wal-Mart Stores, Inc. at January 31, 2016 and 2015, and the consolidated results of its operations and its cash flows for each of the three years in the period ended January 31, 2016, in conformity with U.S. generally accepted accounting principles.

We also have audited, in accordance with the standards of the Public Company Accounting Oversight Board (United States), Wal-Mart Stores, Inc.'s internal control over financial reporting as of January 31, 2016, based on criteria established in Internal Control-Integrated Framework issued by the Committee of Sponsoring Organizations of the Treadway Commission (2013 framework) and our report dated March 30, 2016 expressed an unqualified opinion thereon.

/s/ Ernst & Young LLP
Rogers, Arkansas
March 30, 2016

Brigham Young
University

Research Questions

Research Questions:

Does the proximity of the audit report date to the client's required filing deadline provide an indication of lower audit quality as the result of heightened deadline imposed time pressure?

Has the informational value of the audit report date in identifying auditors under heightened deadline imposed time pressure diminished following a change in practice of dating the audit report as the result of an accounting standard (SFAS No. 165)?

Did market participants understand the information conveyed by the proximity of the audit report date to the filing deadline and has that changed post-SFAS 165?

Brigham Young
University

Prior Research

- In general, experimental evidence finds that deadline pressure negatively impacts audit quality (e.g., Rhode 1978; Alderman and Deitrick 1982; Kelley and Margheim 1990; McDaniel 1990; Ragunathan 1991; Choo 1995; Willet and Page 1996) although there are specific contexts where time pressure does not affect or can positively affect auditor judgment (Glover 1997)
- Archival evidence also provides some evidence of a negative association between time pressure and audit quality (e.g.,Lambert et al. 2014; Blankley et al. 2014), although not entirely conclusive (Krishnan and Yang 2009)

Brigham Young Universitv

Hypothesis Development

According to Auditing Standards, the auditor should date the audit report no earlier than the date on which the auditor has obtained sufficient appropriate evidence to support the auditor's opinion or the end of fieldwork (PCAOB AS 3110, paragraph 1)

Public companies are subject to a compressed timeframe in which to obtain sufficient appropriate evidence

Category of Filer	Revised Deadlines For Filing Periodic Reports	
	Form 10-K Deadline	Form 10-Q Deadline
Large Accelerated Filer ($700MM or more)	75 days for fiscal years ending before December 15, 2006 and 60 days for fiscal years ending on or after December 15, 2006	40 days
Accelerated Filer ($75MM or more and less than $700MM)	75 days	40 days
Non-accelerated Filer (less than $75MM)	90 days	45 days

Brigham Young Universitv

Hypothesis Development

- Effective for fiscal years ending after June 15, 2009, the FASB issued SFAS No. 165, Subsequent Events (ASC 855) which requires companies to evaluate subsequent events through the financial statement filing date
- Although there are no auditor-related requirements in the standard, auditors began dating their opinions on the date the financial statements are filed with the SEC

Brigham Young University

Hypotheses

H1a (H1b): Pre-SFAS 165, an audit report dated within a week (on the date) of the client's required filing deadline provides an indication of lower audit quality

H2a (H2b): Post-SFAS 165, an audit report dated within a week (on the date) of the client's required filing deadline does not provide an indication of lower audit quality

H3a (H3b): Pre-SFAS 165, the market reacted negatively to information conveyed by an audit report dated within a week (on the date) of the client's required filing deadline

H3c (H3d): Post-SFAS 165, the market does not react to information conveyed by an audit report dated within a week (on the date) of the client's required filing deadline

Brigham Young University

Sample

- Comprised of client-year observations with a fiscal year-end between December 2003 and May 2014 with sufficient data from Compustat and Audit Analytics to construct our model variables
- We exclude:
  - Foreign filers subject to different filing deadlines
  - Companies that delist from a stock exchange after the filing date
  - Companies filing after the permitted extension period (15 calendar days after filing the NT 10-K)
- We identify the required filing deadline for each company-year observation adding the number of days to file based on the company's filer status and fiscal year to the fiscal year-end date, adjusted for holidays and weekends

Brigham Young University

Sample

- We reconcile this to the Audit Analytics Non-timely Filer Information and Analysis database
- We manually adjust the few discrepancies identified

Sample Selection and Composition

	N
Observations (non-foreign filers) with a fiscal year-end between December 2003 and May 2014 with the available data for tests	95,139
Less: observations with missing data for model variables	(46,544)
Less: observations where delisting due to bankruptcy, liquidation, or other events (where Compustat variable DLRSN equals 02, 03, 07, 09, or 10) occurs in the year subsequent to the filing date	(52)
Less: observations where company files after the extension period (NT)	(1,084)
Sample	**47,459**

Brigham Young University

Sample

Audit Report Date Proximity to Required Filing Deadline		
Variable	**Mean**	**N**
ARDbeforelastweek	42.0%	19,937
ARDlastweek	36.5%	17,326
ARDlastday	11.3%	5,371
ARDNTperiod	10.2%	4,825
Total	**100%**	**47,459**

Pre-SFAS No. 165

Difference between Report Date and Audit Report Date

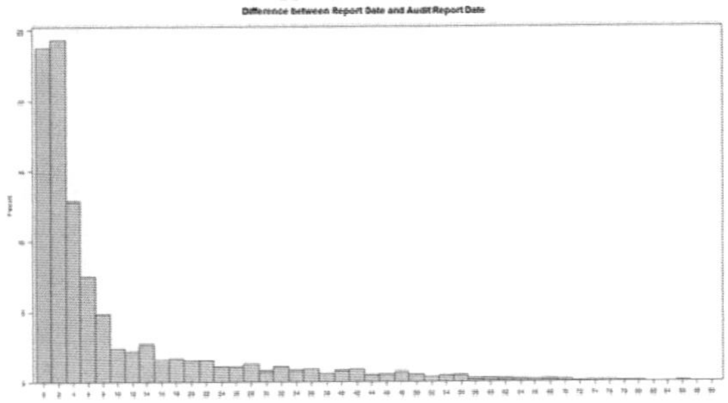

Brigham Young University

Sample

Audit Report Date Proximity to Required Filing Deadline		
Variable	**Mean**	**N**
ARDbeforelastweek	42.0%	19,937
ARDlastweek	36.5%	17,326
ARDlastday	11.3%	5,371
ARDNTperiod	10.2%	4,825
Total	**100%**	**47,459**

Post-SFAS No. 165

Difference between Report Date and Audit Report Date

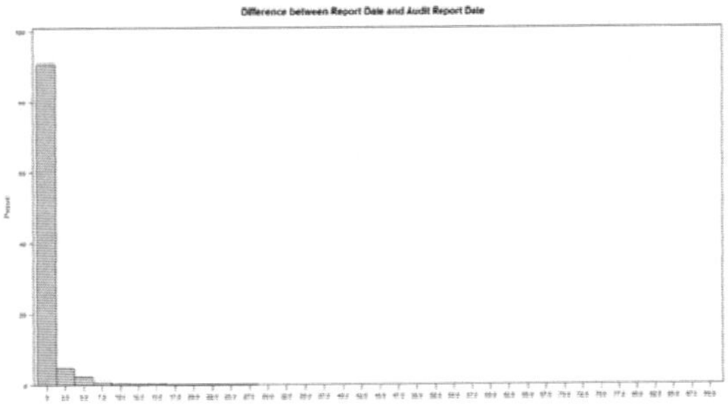

Brigham Young University

Sample

Proximity of Client Filing Date to Required Filing Deadline (N= 47,459)

	Pre-SFAS 165		Post-SFAS 165		
	N	%	N	%	Diff.
File10Kbeforelastweek	7,621	27.6%	6,675	33.6%	6.0%***
File10Klastweek	16,556	60.0%	11,782	59.3%	-0.7%
File10KNT	3,410	12.4%	1,415	7.1%	-5.2%***
	27,587		**19,872**		

Proximity of Audit Report Date to Required Filing Deadline for File10Klastweek group (N=28,338)

	Pre-SFAS 165		Post-SFAS 165		
	N	%	N	%	Diff.
ARDlastweek	8,672	52.4%	8,262	70.1%	17.7%***
ARDlastday	1,998	12.1%	3,105	26.4%	14.3%***
		64.5 %		**96.5%**	

Brigham Young University

Research Design

- Audit Quality Proxy: Misstatements (as revealed through subsequent restatements)

$$Pr(Misstate_{it} = 1) = \Upsilon_0 + \Upsilon_1 ARDlastweek_{it} + \Upsilon_2 ARDlastday_{it} + \Upsilon_3 ARDNTperiod_{it} + \Upsilon_4 POST_{it} + \Upsilon_5 POST_{it}{*}ARDlastweek_{it} + \Upsilon_6 POST_{it}{*}ARDlastday_{it} + \Upsilon_7 POST_{it}{*}ARDNTperiod_{it} + \Upsilon_8 BigN_{it} + \Upsilon_9 Specialist_{it} + \Upsilon_{10} ICMW_{it} + \Upsilon_{11} LnAssets_{it} + \Upsilon_{12} Leverage_{it} + \Upsilon_{13} MTB_{it} + \Upsilon_{14} FIN_{it} + \Upsilon_{15} FREEC_{it} + \Upsilon_{16} M\&A_{it} + \Upsilon_{17} ROA_{it} + \Upsilon_{18} Loss_{it} + \Upsilon_{19} ARINV_{it} + \Upsilon_{20} FSCORE_{it} + \Upsilon_{21} Busy_{it} + \Upsilon_{22} OfficeSize_{it} + \Upsilon_{23} AUD\_WLC_{it} + \Upsilon_j Industry\ FE + \Upsilon_k Year\ FE + \varepsilon_{it}$$

Brigham Young University

Research Design

- To test *H1a* and *H1b*:

$$Pr(Misstate_{it} = 1) = \gamma_0 + \gamma_1 ARDlastweek_{it} + \gamma_2 ARDlastday_{it} + \gamma_3 ARDNTperiod_{it} + \gamma_4 POST_{it} + \gamma_5 POST_{it}*ARDlastweek_{it} + \gamma_6 POST_{it}*ARDlastday_{it} + \gamma_7 POST_{it}*ARDNTperiod_{it} + \gamma_8 BigN_{it} + \gamma_9 Specialist_{it} + \gamma_{10} ICMW_{it} + \gamma_{11} LnAssets_{it} + \gamma_{12} Leverage_{it} + \gamma_{13} MTB_{it} + \gamma_{14} FIN_{it} + \gamma_{15} FREEC_{it} + \gamma_{16} M\&A_{it} + \gamma_{17} ROA_{it} + \gamma_{18} Loss_{it} + \gamma_{19} ARINV_{it} + \gamma_{20} FSCORE_{it} + \gamma_{21} Busy_{it} + \gamma_{22} OfficeSize_{it} + \gamma_{23} AUD\_WLC_{it} + \gamma_j Industry\ FE + \gamma_k Year\ FE + \varepsilon_{it}$$

Brigham Young University

Research Design

- To test *H2a* and *H2b*:

$$Pr(Misstate_{it} = 1) = \gamma_0 + \gamma_1 ARDlastweek_{it} + \gamma_2 ARDlastday_{it} + \gamma_3 ARDNTperiod_{it} + \gamma_4 POST_{it} + \gamma_5 POST_{it}*ARDlastweek_{it} + \gamma_6 POST_{it}*ARDlastday_{it} + \gamma_7 POST_{it}*ARDNTperiod_{it} + \gamma_8 BigN_{it} + \gamma_9 Specialist_{it} + \gamma_{10} ICMW_{it} + \gamma_{11} LnAssets_{it} + \gamma_{12} Leverage_{it} + \gamma_{13} MTB_{it} + \gamma_{14} FIN_{it} + \gamma_{15} FREEC_{it} + \gamma_{16} M\&A_{it} + \gamma_{17} ROA_{it} + \gamma_{18} Loss_{it} + \gamma_{19} ARINV_{it} + \gamma_{20} FSCORE_{it} + \gamma_{21} Busy_{it} + \gamma_{22} OfficeSize_{it} + \gamma_{23} AUD\_WLC_{it} + \gamma_j Industry\ FE + \gamma_k Year\ FE + \varepsilon_{it}$$

Brigham Young University

Research Design

- To test *H3a* through *H3d*

$$CAR3_{it} = \alpha_0 + \alpha_1 ARDlastweek_{it} + \alpha_2 ARDlastday_{it} + \alpha_3 POST_{it} + \alpha_4 POST_{it}*ARDlastweek_{it} + \alpha_5 POST_{it}*ARDlastday_{it} + \alpha_6 LnAssets_{it} + \alpha_7 Leverage_{it} + \alpha_8 MTB_{it} + \alpha_j Industry\ FE + \alpha_k Year\ FE + \varepsilon_{it}$$

Brigham Young Universitv

Research Design

- To test *H3a* through *H3d*

$$CAR3_{it} = \alpha_0 + \alpha_1 ARDlastweek_{it} + \alpha_2 ARDlastday_{it} + \alpha_3 POST_{it} + \alpha_4 POST_{it}*ARDlastweek_{it} + \alpha_5 POST_{it}*ARDlastday_{it} + \alpha_6 LnAssets_{it} + \alpha_7 Leverage_{it} + \alpha_8 MTB_{it} + \alpha_j Industry\ FE + \alpha_k Year\ FE + \varepsilon_{it}$$

Brigham Young Universitv

Results

Variable	Pred.	DV = Misstate Coefficient	Wald χ2	p-value
ARDlastweek (*H1a*)	+	0.096**	3.189	0.037
ARDlasday (*H1b*)	+	0.261***	9.290	0.001
ARDNTperiod	+	0.606***	88.871	<0.001
POST	?	-0.031	0.053	0.819
POST*ARDlastweek (*H2a*)	-	-0.126*	2.041	0.077
POST*ARDlastday (*H2b*)	?	0.019	0.026	0.871
POST*ARDNTperiod	?	-0.418***	12.510	<0.001
Intercept and controls		Included		
Industry and Year fixed effects		Included		
N		47,459		
Area under ROC curve		0.65		

Brigham Young University

Results

Variable	Pred.	DV = Misstate Coefficient	Wald χ2	p-value
ARDlastweek (*H1a*)	+	0.096**	3.189	0.037
ARDlasday (*H1b*)	+	0.261***	9.290	0.001
ARDNTperiod	+	0.606***	88.871	<0.001
POST	?	-0.031	0.053	0.819
POST*ARDlastweek (*H2a*)	-	-0.126*	2.041	0.077
POST*ARDlastday (*H2b*)	?	0.019	0.026	0.871
POST*ARDNTperiod	?	-0.418***	12.510	<0.001

Test:		Wald χ^2	p-value
ARDlastweek=ARDlastday		4.016**	0.045
ARDlastweek=ARDNTperiod		51.694***	<0.001
ARDlastday=ARDNTperiod		12.437***	<0.001
ARDlastweek+POST*ARDlastweek=0	(?)	0.165	0.684
ARDlastday+POST*ARDlastday=0	(+)	10.128***	0.001
ARDNTperiod+POST*ARDNTperiod=0	(+)	2.654*	0.052

Intercept and con

Industry and Yea

N

Area under ROC curve 0.65

Brigham Young University

Results

Variable	Pred.	DV = Misstate_LATEAREA Coefficient	p-value
ARDlastweek (*H1a*)	+	0.162**	0.016
ARDlasday (*H1b*)	+	0.304***	0.005
ARDNTperiod	+	0.665***	<0.001
POST	?	0.093	0.644
POST*ARDlastweek (*H2a*)	-	-0.202**	0.042
POST*ARDlastday (*H2b*)	?	0.032	0.839
POST*ARDNTperiod	?	-0.483***	0.005
Intercept and controls		Included	
Industry and Year fixed effects		Included	
N		47,459	
Area under ROC curve		0.657	

Brigham Young University

Results

Variable	Pred.	DV = Misstate_LATEAREA Coefficient	p-value
ARDlastweek (*H1a*)	+	0.162**	0.016
ARDlasday (*H1b*)	+	0.304***	0.005
ARDNTperiod	+	0.665***	<0.001
POST	?	0.093	0.644
POST*ARDlastweek (*H2a*)	-	-0.202**	0.042
POST*ARDlastday (*H2b*)	?	0.032	0.839
POST*ARDNTperiod	?	-0.483***	0.005

Test:	Wald χ^2	p-value
ARDlastweek=ARDlastday	1.611	0.204
ARDlastweek=ARDNTperiod	24.334***	<0.001
ARDlastday=ARDNTperiod	6.907***	0.009
ARDlastweek+POST*ARDlastweek=0	0.183	0.669
ARDlastday+POST*ARDlastday=0	8.770***	0.001
ARDNTperiod+POST*ARDNTperiod=0	1.181	0.138

Intercept and cor

Industry and Yea

N

Area under ROC curve 0.657

Brigham Young University

Results

Variable	Pred.	Coefficient	T-stat	p-value
		DV = CAR3		
ARDlastweek (*H3a*)	-	-0.0014	-1.070	0.143
ARDlasday (*H3b*)	-	-0.0023	-0.930	0.176
POST	?	-0.0028	-0.760	0.449
POST*ARDlastweek (*H3c*)	+	0.0015	0.400	0.345
POST*ARDlastday (*H3d*)	?	0.0024	0.540	0.588
Intercept and controls		Included		
Industry and Year fixed effects		Included		
N		22,885		
Adjusted R squared		0.002		

Brigham Young University

Additional Analyses

Variable	Pred.	Coefficient	T-stat	p-value
		DV = CAR90		
ARDlastweek (*H3a*)	-	-0.0474***	-7.250	<0.001
ARDlasday (*H3b*)	-	-0.0268**	-2.180	0.015
POST	?	-0.0249	-1.200	0.229
POST*ARDlastweek (*H3c*)	+	0.0636***	2.990	0.001
POST*ARDlastday (*H3d*)	?	0.0258	1.050	0.292
Intercept and controls		Included		
Industry and Year fixed effects		Included		
N		22,885		
Adjusted R squared		0.008		

Brigham Young University

Additional Analyses

How is the market capturing this information?

Variable	Pred.	DV = Resign Coefficient	DV = Resign p-value	DV = Dismiss Coefficient	DV = Dismiss p-value
ARDlastweek	+	0.407***	0.008	0.000	0.996
ARDlasday	+	0.203	0.471	0.328**	0.011
ARDNTperiod	+	0.921***	<0.001	0.375***	<0.001
POST	?	-0.314	0.505	-0.094	0.757
POST*ARDlastweek	-	-0.574*	0.077	0.083	0.582
POST*ARDlastday	?	0.079	0.851	0.052	0.790
POST*ARDNTperiod	?	-0.366	0.241	-0.236	0.221
Intercept and controls		Included		Included	
Industry and Year fixed effects		Included		Included	
N		47,459		47,459	
Area under ROC curve		0.798		0.660	

Brigham Young University

Conclusion

- Pre-SFAS 165, higher likelihood of misstatement when ARD is near or at the filing deadline
- This is especially pronounced for areas typically completed late in the audit
- Post-SFAS 165, no longer association between ARD near the filing deadline, suggesting diminished ability to identify auditors under heightened deadline pressure

Brigham Young University

Conclusion

- The market did not appear to understand this audit quality signal, but it was predictive of auditor resignations and slowly incorporated into price Pre-SFAS 165
- Post-SFAS 165, no longer associated with higher auditor resignation

Brigham Young Universitv

Implications and Contribution

- Suggests that deadline imposed time pressure does indeed negatively impact audit quality
- Suggests that a potentially observable indicator of audit quality could be the date the auditor completes fieldwork (perhaps dual-dating)
- Suggests that audit report lag as a measure of audit efficiency or audit quality may be less useful post-SFAS 165

Brigham Young Universitv

How Do Look-Back Analyses and Evidence Specificity Affect Auditors' Planning Judgments?

Ann Backof
University of Virginia

Roger Martin
University of Virginia

Jane Thayer
University of Virginia

University of Virginia
McIntire School of Commerce

Research Question

How does the **direction of a prior period estimation inaccuracy** in a forward-looking assumption underlying a complex estimate **and** the **specificity of the evidence provided by management to support that prior period assumption** affect auditors' planning decisions regarding the current period audit of complex estimates?

University of Virginia
McIntire School of Commerce

Motivation

- Complex estimates play an increasingly important role in financial reporting (e.g., Bratten et al. 2013; Lev et al. 2010).
- Audit planning is a crucial step in the completion of an effective audit (Mock and Wright 1993).
- Relatively little is known about the factors that affect auditors' planning for the audit of complex estimates.

University of Virginia
McIntire School of Commerce

Contributions

Characteristics of management-provided evidence

↓

Auditors' perceptions of management's credibility

↓

Auditors' reliance on management-provided evidence and explanations (e.g., Hirst 1994; Goodwin 1999).

University of Virginia
McIntire School of Commerce

Contributions

- Influence of auditors' *ex post* review of evidence obtained and evaluated as part of a prior period audit on the current period audit.

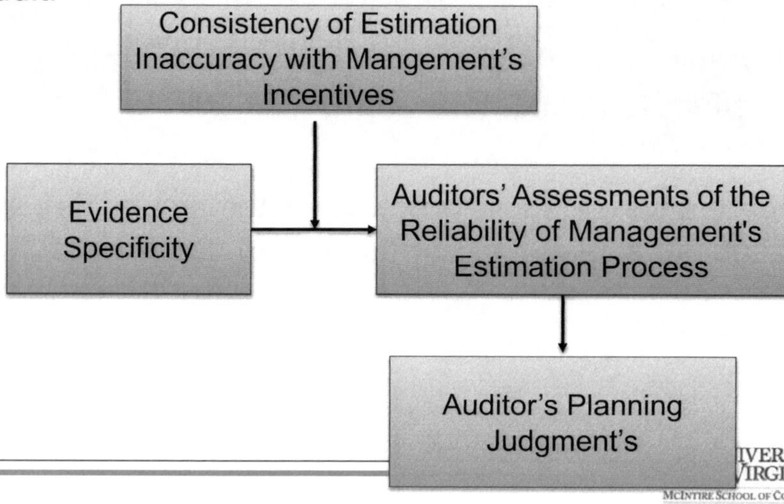

Contributions

- Extend the research examining the auditing of complex estimates (e.g., Cannon and Bedard 2014; Griffith et al. 2015a, 2015b) by identifying two factors that affect auditors' planning for the current period audit of complex estimates.
  - Complex estimates enhance the relevance of information provided to financial statement users (Lundholm 1999), but management has the ability to opportunistically manage those estimates (Hodder et al. 2006; Dechow et al. 2010).
  - The reliability of the information reported in the financial statements hinges on the effectiveness of the audit of these estimates (Griffith et al. 2015a).

Theoretical Model

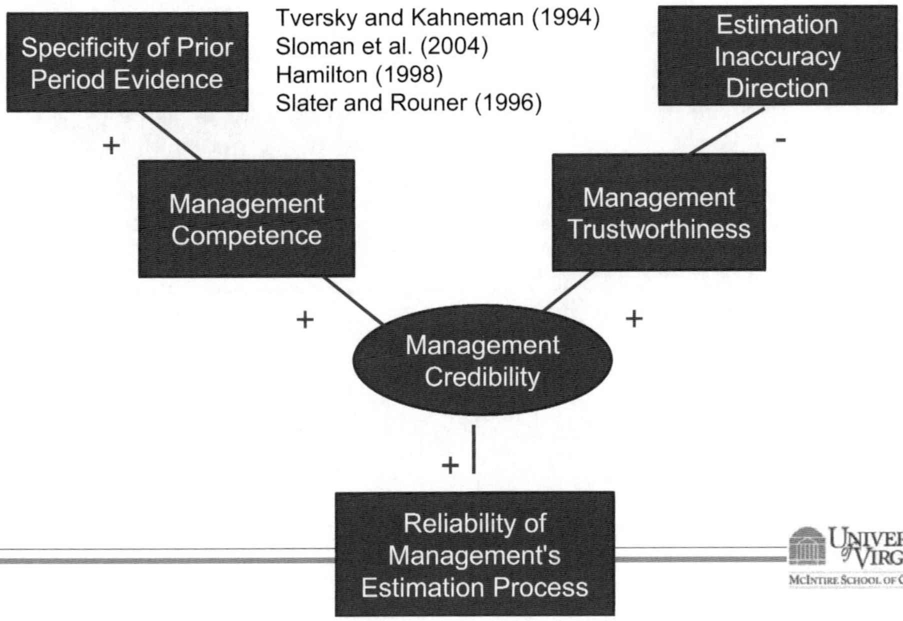

UNIVERSITY of VIRGINIA
McINTIRE SCHOOL OF COMMERCE

Hypothesis 1

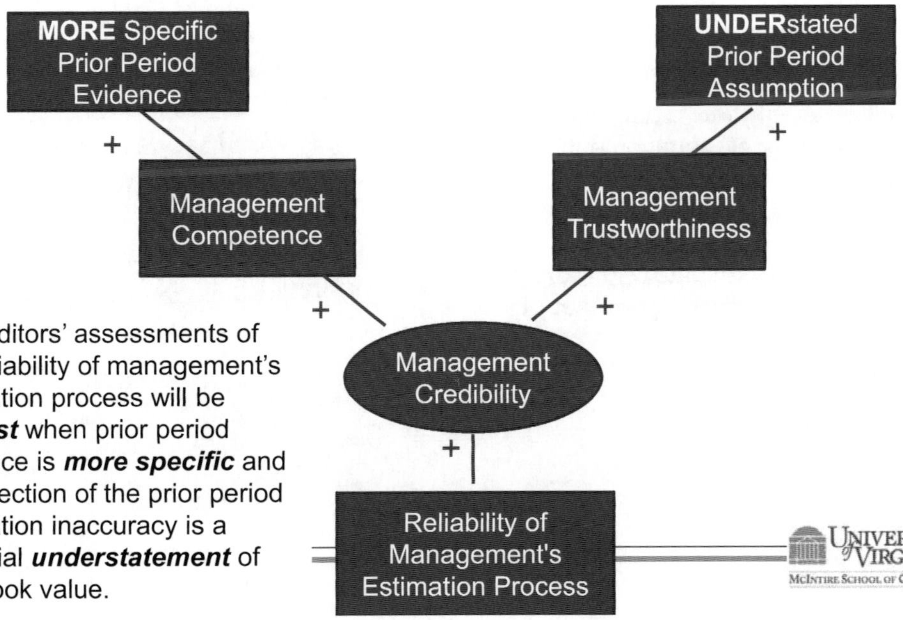

H1:Auditors' assessments of the reliability of management's estimation process will be ***highest*** when prior period evidence is ***more specific*** and the direction of the prior period estimation inaccuracy is a potential ***understatement*** of firm book value.

UNIVERSITY of VIRGINIA
McINTIRE SCHOOL OF COMMERCE

Hypothesis 2

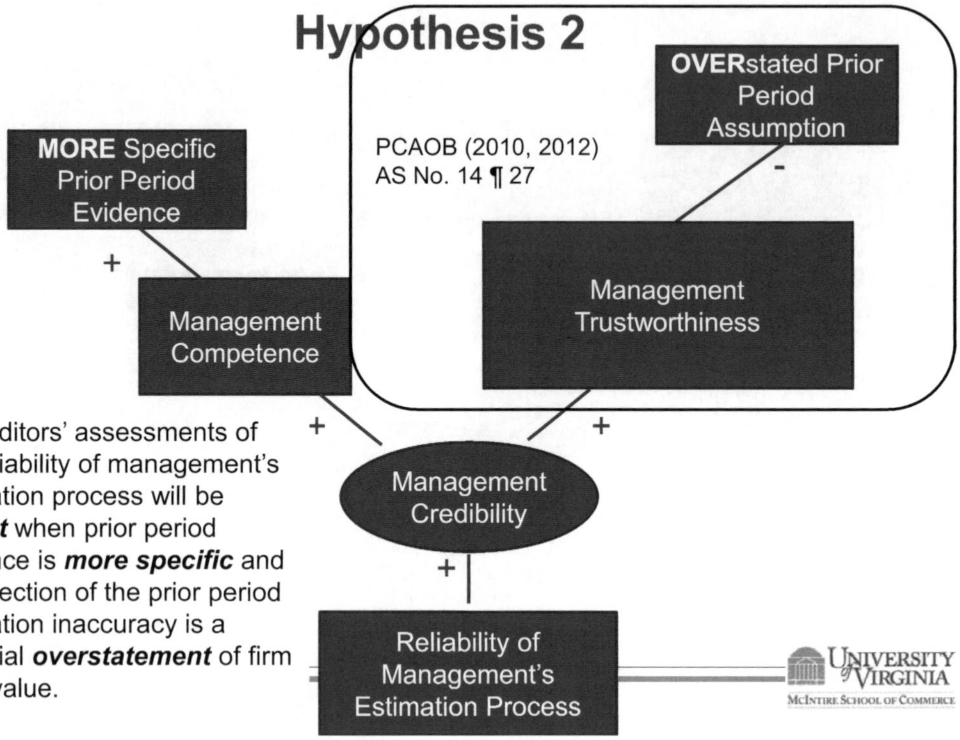

H2:Auditors' assessments of the reliability of management's estimation process will be ***lowest*** when prior period evidence is ***more specific*** and the direction of the prior period estimation inaccuracy is a potential ***overstatement*** of firm book value.

University of Virginia
McIntire School of Commerce

Hypothesis 3

H3: **Lower (higher) reliability assessments** of management's estimation process will lead to **higher (lower) risk assessments** of material misstatement in the current period estimate and **more (less) allocation of planned audit effort**.

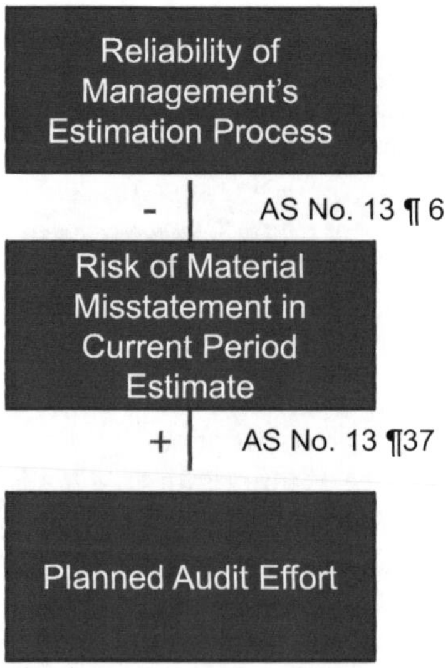

University of Virginia
McIntire School of Commerce

Research Method

- 117 audit seniors* from 8 accounting firms
- Planning audit of impairment analysis of trademark
  - Look-back analysis
  - Actual year-to-date results for current year
- 2 x 2 between-subjects design
  - Specificity of prior period evidence
  - Estimation inaccuracy direction
- Dependent Variables
  - Reliability of management's estimation process
  - ROMM in current period estimation
  - Likelihood of changing hours allocated for current prior audit

University of Virginia
McIntire School of Commerce

PRIOR YEAR WORKPAPER

KEY ASSUMPTION #2

Revenue Growth Rate

Management's Assumption: 8% annual growth in revenues by location through 2018, 3% thereafter.

Management-provided justification for this assumption:

When we acquired the Chatsworth Cheddar trademark in 2003, the average revenues (per store) from sales of Chatsworth Cheddar was $21,390. In 2013, the average revenues (per store) from sales of Chatsworth Cheddar was $42,074.

We expect **revenues (per store)** from sales of Chatsworth Cheddar to **grow annually at 8% through 2018 and 3% (average inflation rate) thereafter**. The 8% growth rate is consistent with the projected average industry growth rate which the company has historically met. We plan to achieve our expected growth by:

- Increasing sales prices – We intend to increase prices in the 3% to 5% range each year, which is consistent with historical pricing practices of the company and our competitors. Results of recent market research indicate that price increases can be maintained and marketing plans are in place to educate both our distributors and our consumers on the rationale for price increases.
- Increasing customer demand – Brand recognition of Chatsworth Cheddar as a consistent and high quality cheese has led to increased sales volume each year since 2003. Our new marketing campaigns, third party endorsements, and prime retail space are expected to increase awareness of the Chatsworth Cheddar brand in future periods.

University of Virginia
McIntire School of Commerce

CURRENT YEAR LOOK-BACK ANALYSIS

KEY ASSUMPTION #2

Revenue Growth Rate

In **planning for the audit of the year ending December 31, 2014**, you are asked to **perform a look-back analysis** of the assumptions used to derive the valuation of the trademark as part of the impairment analysis for the year ending December 31, 2013. The estimated fair value as of December 31, 2013 was calculated using a discounted cash flow model based on three key assumptions, including management's revenue growth rate assumption. Below is a chart showing management's **revenue growth rate assumption** used in the 2013 estimate, as well as the actual revenue growth since the prior year estimate was made.

Management's key assumption (as of 12/31/2013):	8% annual growth rate through 2018; 3% annual growth rate thereafter
Update since prior year estimate (as of 8/31/2014):	Revenues per store have grown ***9%*** compared to the same time period in the prior year.
Sensitivity analysis:	If a 9% (instead of 8%) growth rate had been used in the prior year estimate, the fair value estimate of the trademark increases to $3.343 million which is $278,000 above the book value. See the attached revised DCF calculation for this computation, as well as the results of the look-back analysis for the estimated fair value as of December 31, 2012 and December 31, 2011.
Additional information gathered as part of look-back analysis:	Conversations with management indicate that actual growth differed from predicted growth due to a few factors. In particular, the projected price increase and new branding of the cheese went into effect sooner than anticipated, positively impacting actual growth. However, management attributes the majority of the difference between expected and actual revenue growth in the current year to a new fermentation process that the company's main competitor implemented this year on a trial basis…

UNIVERSITY of VIRGINIA
McINTIRE SCHOOL OF COMMERCE

Current Year Sensitivity Analysis
Management-Prepared Impairment Analysis for Chatsworth Cheddar Trademark
(Amounts in 000s)

	12/31/2013 Updated	12/31/2013 Original	12/31/2012	12/31/2011
Fair value estimate	$ 3,343	$ 3,205	$ 3,284	$ 3,265
Book value	3,065	3,065	3,065	3,065
Fair value is in excess of book value	$ 278	$ 140	$ 219	$ 200

Projected Net Cash Flow ($ in 000s)

	2014	2015	2016	2017	2018	2019	2020	2021 into Pertuity
(1) No. of Stores Selling Chatsworth Cheddar during the year (**Assumption**: 7 new stores each year up to cap of 120 stores)	77	84	91	98	105	112	119	120
(2) Projected Average Sales per store (**Assumption**: Revenue growth of **9% per store** through 2018, 3% thereafter)	45.86	49.99	54.49	59.39	64.74	66.68	68.68	70.74
(3) Projected Royalties (**Contractual**: 4% of sales)	141.25	167.96	198.33	232.81	271.89	298.71	326.90	339.54
(4) Projected Net Cash Flow	141.25	167.96	198.33	232.81	271.89	298.71	326.90	(4b) Projected Royalties 2021 into Perpetuity: 4,850.59
(5) Present Value of Projected Net Cash Flows (**Assumption**: 10% Discount Rate)	128.41	138.81	149.01	159.01	168.82	168.62	167.75	2262.84
Summed Present value of net cash flows	$ 3,343							

(1) No. of Stores Selling Chatsworth Cheddar = No. of Stores in Prior Year + 7. Maximum number of stores = 120.
(2) Projected Average Sales per Store = Average Sales per Store in Prior Year * (1+.09) Years 2014-2018
= Average Sales per Store in Prior Year * (1+.03) Years after 2018
(3) Projected Royalties = [Projected Average Sales per Store for Current Year * 4%] * No. of Stores Selling Chatsworth Cheddar in Current Year
Note: Royalties paid are based on a contractual rate of 4% of per store sales of Chatsworth Cheddar.
(4a) Projected Net Cash Flow = Projected Royalties
(4b) Projected Royalties 2021 into Perpetuity {Gordon-Growth Model} = Projected Net Cash Flow in 2021 / (.10 - .03)
(5) PV of Projected Net Cash Flows = Projected Net Cash Flows / $(1+.10)^{\text{No. of years to discount}}$

Assumptions:
- **9% revenue growth through 2018**
- **3% steady growth rate after 2018**
- **4% royalty rate**
- **7 new stores opening each year up to a maximum of 120 stores**
- **10.0% discount rate (WACC)**

Auditors' Assessments of the Reliability of Management's Estimation Process

	Understated	Overstated	
Less Specific	7.37 (1.39) n=27 **A**	7.62 (1.18) n=29 **B**	7.50 (1.28) n=56
More specific	7.73 (1.19) n=26 **C**	7.17 (1.47) n=29 **D**	7.43 (1.36) n=55
	7.55 (1.29) n=53	7.40 (1.34) n=58	

H1 supported
($F_{1,106}$ = 2.28,
one-tailed p = 0.067)

H2 supported
($F_{1,106}$ = 2.68,
one-tailed p = 0.052)

	df	**MS**	**F**	**Two-tailed *p*-value**
Big 4	1	12.35	7.61	0.007
Specificity	1	0.01	0.01	0.956
Direction of Inaccuracy	1	1.11	0.68	0.410
Specificity * Direction	1	5.91	3.64	0.059

UNIVERSITY of VIRGINIA
McINTIRE SCHOOL OF COMMERCE

Auditors' Planning Judgments

- H3: Lower (higher) reliability assessments of management's estimation process will lead to higher (lower) risk assessments of material misstatement in the current period estimate and more (less) allocation of planned audit effort.

- H3: ROMM b = -0.26 one-tailed p = 0.036
  Effort b = -0.24 one-tailed p = 0.021

H3 supported

UNIVERSITY of VIRGINIA
McINTIRE SCHOOL OF COMMERCE

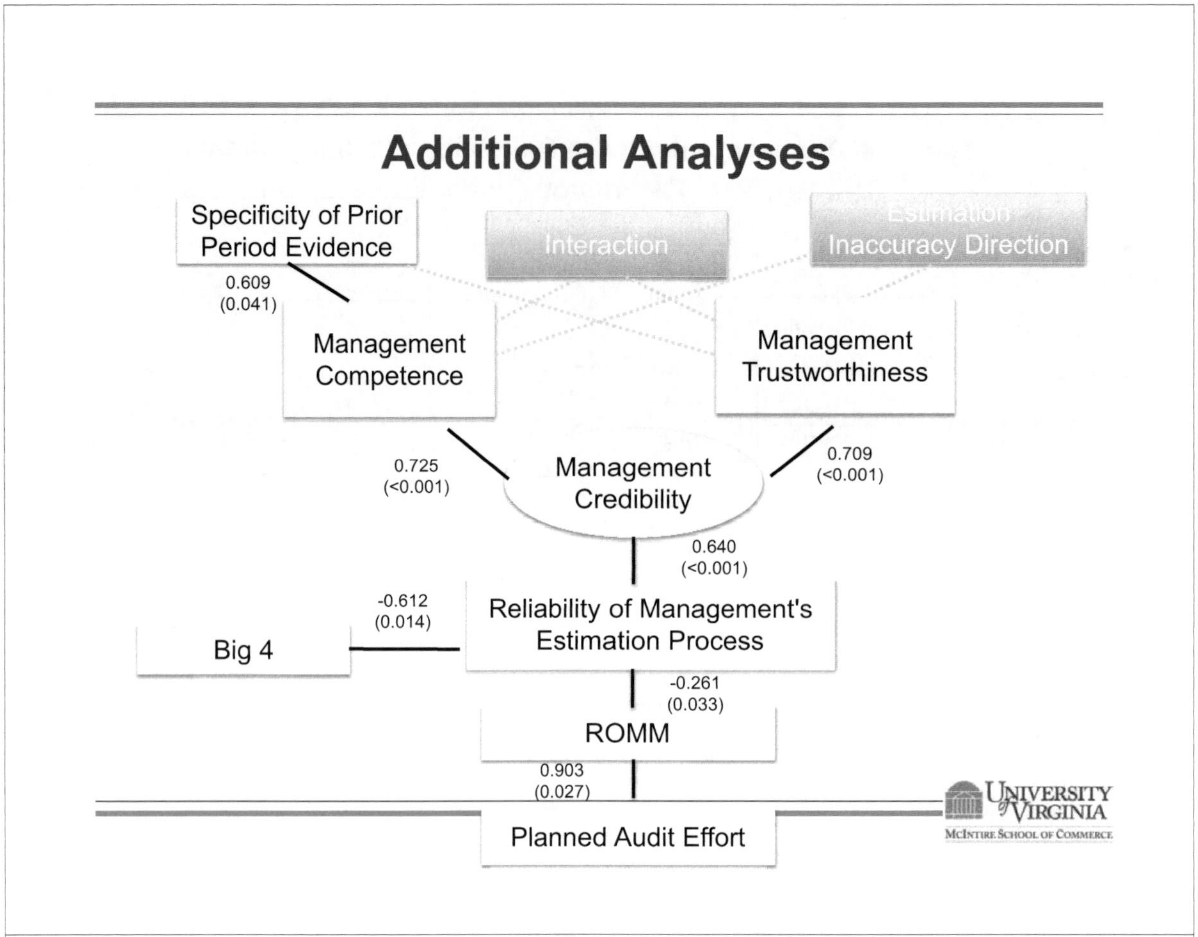
Additional Analyses
Specificity of Prior Period Evidence
Interaction
Estimation Inaccuracy Direction
0.609 (0.041)
Management Competence
Management Trustworthiness
0.725 (<0.001)
Management Credibility
0.709 (<0.001)
0.640 (<0.001)
-0.612 (0.014)
Big 4
Reliability of Management's Estimation Process
-0.261 (0.033)
ROMM
0.903 (0.027)
Planned Audit Effort
University of Virginia
McIntire School of Commerce

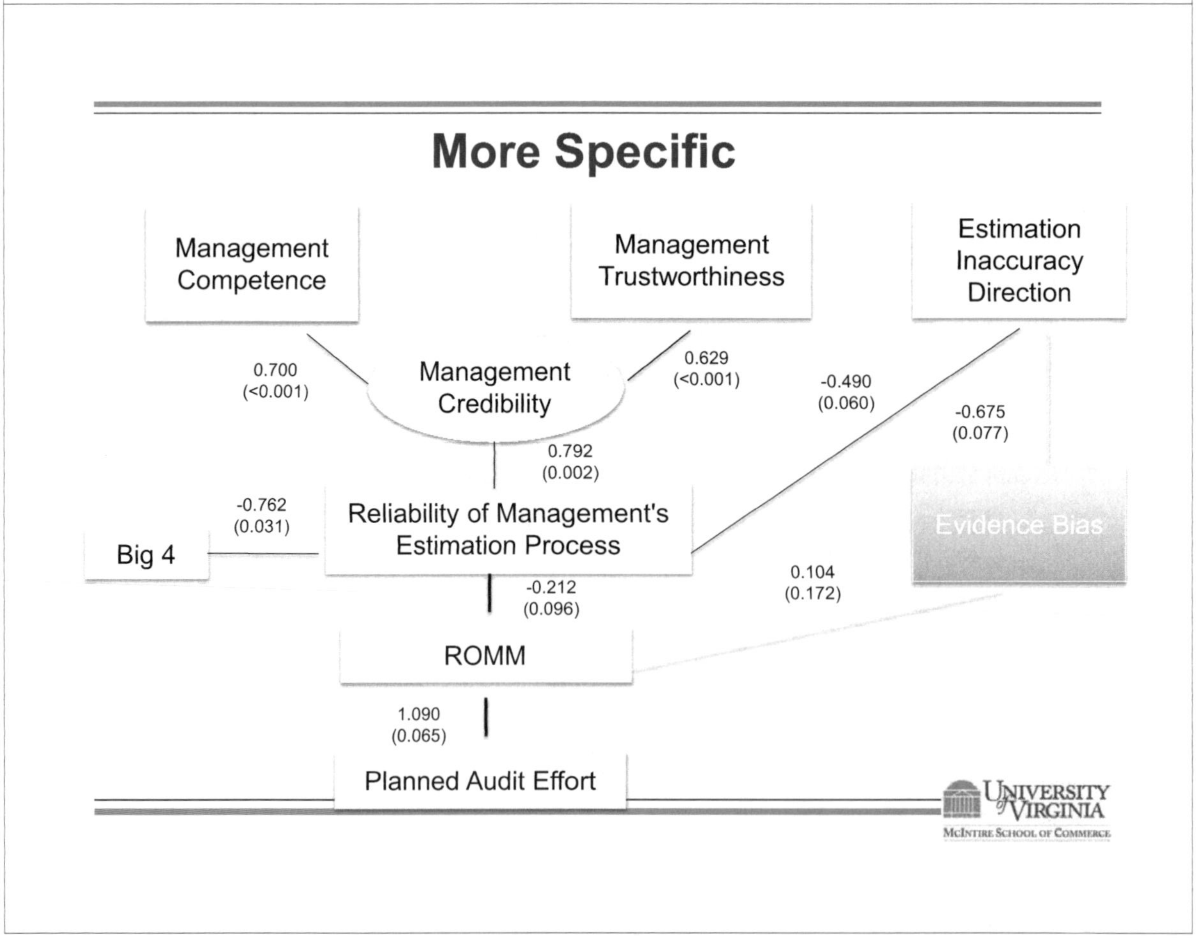
More Specific
Management Competence
Management Trustworthiness
Estimation Inaccuracy Direction
0.700 (<0.001)
Management Credibility
0.629 (<0.001)
-0.490 (0.060)
-0.675 (0.077)
0.792 (0.002)
-0.762 (0.031)
Big 4
Reliability of Management's Estimation Process
Evidence Bias
-0.212 (0.096)
0.104 (0.172)
ROMM
1.090 (0.065)
Planned Audit Effort
University of Virginia
McIntire School of Commerce

Less Specific

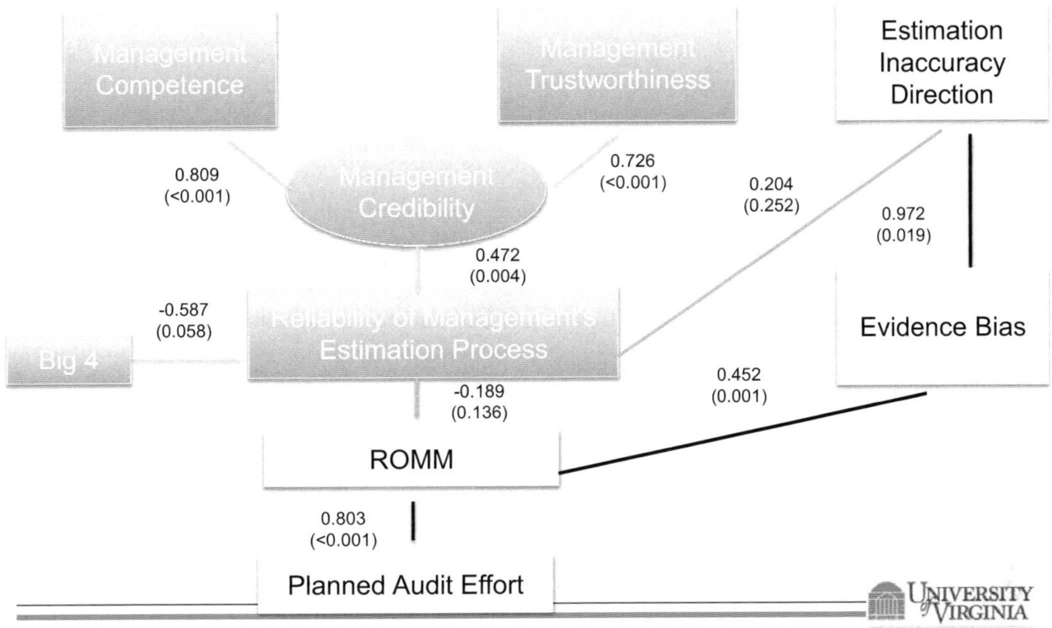

Conclusions

- Auditors reviewing more specific evidence when the prior period estimation inaccuracy is ***inconsistent (consistent)*** with management's incentives provide the ***highest (lowest)*** reliability assessments of management's estimation process.
- These effects then flow through to auditors' planning judgments, with higher (lower) reliability assessments leading to lower (higher) risk assessments and planned audit effort.
- The way in which the direction of the estimation inaccuracy impacts auditors' planning judgments (i.e., **perceptions of estimation process or evidence bias**) depends on the specificity of prior period evidence.

Thank you!

UNIVERSITY of VIRGINIA
MCINTIRE SCHOOL OF COMMERCE

Investor Reliance on PCAOB Inspection Reports

Jeffrey Cohen (Boston College)
Ganesh Krishnamoorthy (Northeastern)
Marietta Peytcheva (Lehigh)
Arnie Wright (Northeastern)

1

PCAOB Inspection of Audit Reports

Under the SOX (2002), the PCAOB is required to conduct inspections of a sample of conducted audits

- Significant deficiencies are reported to investors in public portion of report
- Engagements are selected using a risk-weighted approach
- Provides process-based information on audit quality
- However, more research is needed on;
  - How investors interpret the findings in these reports in making assessments about audit quality; and
  - The extent to which they affect investment decisions

2

PCAOB Inspection of Audit Reports - Concerns

- Only deficiencies in issuer audits are disclosed
  - Audits are complex and multifaceted
  - Not including significant audit strengths results in potentially less balanced assessments of audit quality

- Risk-weighted inspection selection method instead of random selection
  - Findings may not be representative of the audit quality of the audit firm's work
  - Potential to negatively bias investors' assessments of audit quality and thus impact efficiency of capital markets
  - Disclosed late in report - may not be noticeable to investors

3

Prior Relevant Research on the Impact of PCAOB Inspection Reports

- Although evidence is somewhat mixed, there is growing literature to support the assertion that the inspection process has helped improve audit quality
  - Lennox and Pittman (2010) find deficiencies in inspection reports were not associated with subsequent changes in clients' choices of audit firms.
  - Carcello et al. (2011) found a significant decrease in client's earnings management following findings in firms' inspection reports.
  - Gunny and Zhang (2013) find significant positive association between abnormal accruals of clients and deficiencies identified in inspection reports.

4

Research Question

- What is the effect of disclosure in the inspection report of both strengths and deficiencies, and the inspection selection method (risk-weighted vs. random), on investors' investment decisions?

5

Information Integration Theory

Anderson 1971; Anderson 1981

- Predicts that the inferential value of a piece of information is predicted on two basic parameters:
  - Direction - how a piece of information is evaluated
  - Weight - the importance of the information
- Posits that new pieces of information are integrated with existing information to arrive at beliefs and assessments

6

Hypotheses

H1: Investors' investment decisions will be progressively more favorable when the inspection report moves from deficiencies only, to more deficiencies than strengths, and then to more strengths than deficiencies.

We do not predict a significant main effect for inspection selection approach because:

- Risk-weighted approach could be viewed as more conservative and hence signal higher audit quality
- Random approach could be viewed as providing a more unbiased assessment and hence may be viewed as signaling higher audit quality.

7

Expectancy Violations Theory

Burgoon 1978; Burgoon and Hale 1988; Hastie 1984

- More favorable behavior or outcome than expected = positive violations
- Less favorable behavior or outcome than expected = negative violations

- When observations depart from expectations, the response is more pronounced than when observations conform to expectations.

8

Expectancy Violations Theory

- When inspection method is random, the expectation is for a more balanced report with both deficiencies and strengths. Hence, a negative violation will occur when only deficiencies are disclosed.
- Conversely, when inspection method is risk-weighted, the expectation is for a report with more deficiencies. Hence, a positive violation will occur when more strengths than deficiencies are disclosed.

9

Hypotheses

H2a: Investors' investment decisions will be the least favorable when the inspection report indicates deficiencies only and the inspection selection method is random.

H2b: Investors' investment decisions will be the most favorable when the inspection report indicates more strengths than deficiencies and the inspection selection method is risk-weighted.

10

Method

- Design: 3 x 2 Between-Participant Design
  Independent Variables
  - Inspection Report Findings
    - Deficiencies only (DO)
    - More deficiencies than strengths (D>S)
    - More strengths than deficiencies (S>D)
  - Inspection Selection Method
    - Risk-weighted selection
    - Random selection

11

Case

- Company in the retailing industry
- Company received unqualified audit opinions in prior years from audit firm
- Participants were provided with:
  - Background information about the company
  - Auditing and financial reporting environment
  - Summary of financial data from past two years
  - Information regarding PCAOB and its inspection process (including selection method)
  - Summary of most recent inspection report issued by PCAOB

12

Method

- Inspection Report Findings: Strength (Deficiency)
- Stow and Taunton appropriately followed (did not appropriately follow) adequate procedures to evaluate the reliability of management explanations for the valuation of inventory.
- Stow and Taunton appropriately performed (did not appropriately perform) cut-off tests to ensure inventory is matched to the appropriate reporting period.
- Stow and Taunton appropriately compared (did not appropriately compare) various inventory ratios at the business unit level to industry segment averages.

13

Method

- Inspection Selection Method: risk-weighted **[random]**
- ...areas of inspection focus are selected on a risk-weighted basis and not randomly **[random basis, and not on a risk-weighted basis]**. A risk-weighted basis implies that audit work is generally selected for inspection based on factors that, in the inspection team's view, heighten the possibility that auditing deficiencies are present, rather than identify a representative sample **[A random basis implies that audit work is generally selected for inspection based on a process that, in the inspection team's view, is intended to identify a representative sample, rather than heighten the possibility that auditing deficiencies are present]**.

14

Method

- Dependent variables
  - Investment Decision
    - (a) likelihood of investing in the company (0 = not at all likely; 10 = extremely likely)
    - (b) attractiveness of the company as an investment (0 = not at all attractive; 10 = extremely attractive)
    - In order to provide a more comprehensive measure they were combined into a single scale

15

Method

- Participants: Graduate business student from two universities in Northeastern U.S. (n=147)
  - Considered reasonably informed investors:
    - An average experience investing in stock for 11 months (SD = 25)
    - An average experience investing in mutual funds of eight months (SD = 23)
  - On average two years of work experience (SD = 3.57)
    - Involving finance or accounting for six moths (SD = 13)

16

TABLE 1. Investment Decision
PANEL A. Descriptive Statistic

INSPECTION REPORT FINDINGS

Mean, (Std. Deviation), *N*

		Deficiencies Only	**More Deficiencies Than Strengths**	**More Strengths Than Deficiencies**	**Totals**
INSPECTION SELECTION METHOD	**Random**	4.43 (1.96) *23*	4.98 (1.79) *26*	5.44 (2.03) *24*	4.96 (1.94) *73*
	Risk-Weighted	4.50 (2.22) *24*	5.60 (2.14) *26*	5.88 (1.78) *24*	5.33 (2.11) *74*
	Totals	4.47 (2.08) *47*	5.29 (1.98) *52*	5.66 (1.90) *48*	

18

TABLE 1. Investment Decision
PANEL B. ANOVA

Source	**df**	**MS**	**F**	***P-value***
Inspection Report Findings	2	17.59	4.43	*.014*
Inspection Selection Method	1	5.09	1.28	*.259*
Inspection Report Findings x Inspection Selection Method	2	0.96	0.24	*.785*
Error	141	3.97		

19

TABLE 1. Investment Decision
PANEL C. Planned Contrast

	Value of Contrast	*t*	*P-value (one-tailed)*
Deficiencies Only & Random Selection < All Other Conditions *DO & Random = -5; All Others = 1*	4.22	1.86	*.033*
More Strengths than Deficiencies & Risk-Weighted Selection > All Other Conditions *S>D & Risk-Weighted = 5; All Others = -1*	4.43	1.99	*.025*

20

Hypotheses

H1: Investors' investment decisions will be progressively more favorable when the inspection report moves from deficiencies only, to more deficiencies than strengths, and then to more strengths than deficiencies.

H2a: Investors' investment decisions will be the least favorable when the inspection report indicates deficiencies only and the inspection selection method is random.

H2b: Investors' investment decisions will be the most favorable when the inspection report indicates more strengths than deficiencies and the inspection selection method is risk-weighted.

21

Additional Analyses

- Path Analysis
  - To provide further evidence on the theoretical link between manipulated variables and the consequent investment decision.
- Mediating Effect of Audit Quality
  - To examine the extent to which the assessment of audit quality explains participants' investment decisions
- Incremental Effect of Audit Strength vs. Deficiencies
  - To examine whether investors consider both strengths and deficiencies as relevant information in assessing audit quality and making investment decisions
- Qualitative Responses
  - To obtain additional insights regarding investor reliance on the PCAOB inspection reports in the experiment

22

FIGURE 2. Path Model Results

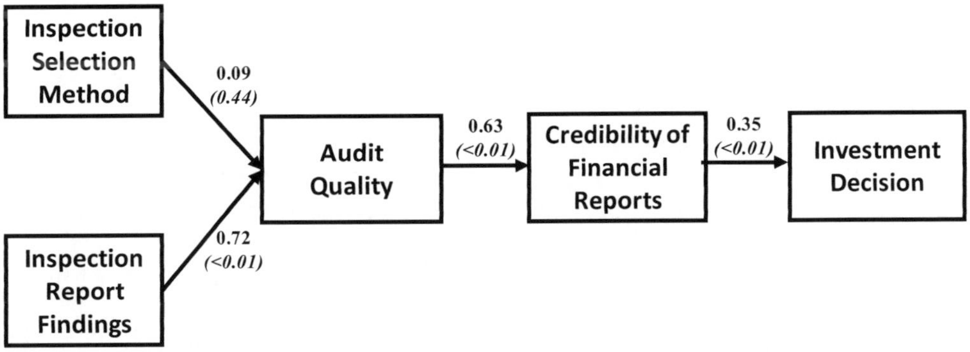

23

TABLE 2. Qualitative Responses. Reasons for Participants' Investing Decisions.

	Deficiencies Only DO			More Deficiencies than Strengths D>S			More Strengths than Deficiencies S>D		
	Random *N* = 23	Risk-Weighted *N* = 24	Total *N* = 47	Random *N* = 26	Risk-Weighted *N* = 26	Total *N* = 52	Random *N* = 24	Risk-Weighted *N* = 24	Total *N* = 48
Refer to PCAOB report	74%	58%	***66%***	46%	42%	***44%***	46%	38%	***42%***
Refer to Deficiencies	74%	58%	***66%***	46%	39%	***44%***	46%	38%	***42%***
Refer to Strengths	N/A	N/A	***N/A***	0%	0%	***0%***	0%	4%	***2%***

Inspection Report Findings was manipulated at three levels: deficiencies only (DO), more deficiencies than strengths (D>S), and more strengths than deficiencies (S>D). *Inspection Selection Method* was manipulated at two levels: risk-weighted versus random. All dependent variables were coded 1 if the statement was true for a participant's qualitative response, and zero otherwise.

24

Conclusions & Implications

- Results suggest that there is a significant interaction effect between report findings and the inspection selection method
  - Investment decisions are the least favorable when DO and random selection
  - Investment decisions are the most favorable when S>D and risk weighted selection
- Results also provide limited evidence on negativity bias in investors' judgments, since investors' decision processes appear to be more heavily influenced by negative findings in the PCAOB inspection report
- Should PCAOB consider adopting a more balanced approach to the disclosure of the inspection findings?
- Future research could examine if there is potential contagion effect for investors if for example, client industry is disclosed.

25

UNIVERSITY OF PITTSBURGH
PITTBUSINESS | Joseph M. Katz Graduate School of Business & College of Business Administration

Auditor Multinational Expertise and Audit Quality

Joshua L. Gunn
Joseph M. Katz Graduate School of Business
University of Pittsburgh

Paul N. Michas
Eller College of Management
University of Arizona

5/21/2016

UNIVERSITY OF PITTSBURGH
PITTBUSINESS | Joseph M. Katz Graduate School of Business & College of Business Administration

Multinational Group Audits

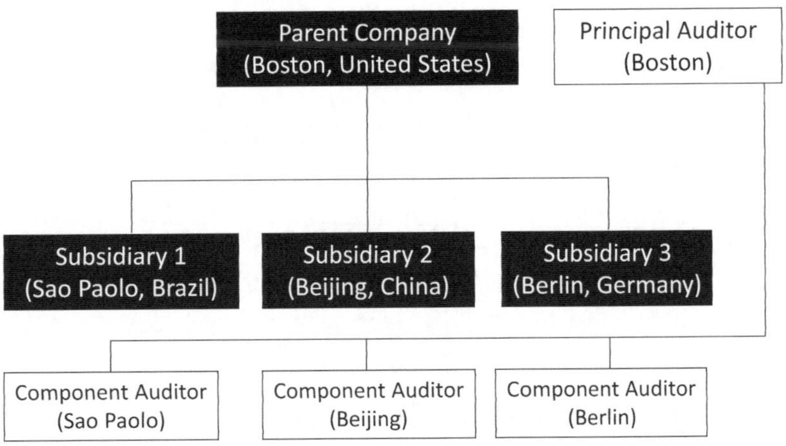

UNIVERSITY OF PITTSBURGH
PITT BUSINESS | Joseph M. Katz Graduate School of Business & College of Business Administration

Motivation

"Global audits.....involve the largest companies whose shares figure prominently in many investors' savings plans. For that reason, these audits need to be good."

James Doty, 2011
Chairman, PCAOB

UNIVERSITY OF PITTSBURGH
PITT BUSINESS | Joseph M. Katz Graduate School of Business & College of Business Administration

Motivation

- PCAOB has recently expressed concern about group audits.
  - Overseas inspections revealed problems (Doty 2011)
  - Recently required the disclosure of significant component auditor involvement.
- Existing research offers some support for these concerns (Dee et al. TAR 2015)

UNIVERSITY OF PITTSBURGH
PITT BUSINESS | Joseph M. Katz Graduate School of Business & College of Business Administration

Research Questions

- Does the concept of multinational expertise exist in the audit market?
- If so, can multinational expertise be leveraged to conduct higher quality audits?
- In which situations is such expertise particularly important?

UNIVERSITY OF PITTSBURGH
PITT BUSINESS | Joseph M. Katz Graduate School of Business & College of Business Administration

Challenges of a Multinational Audit

- Work across international boundaries can be challenging
  - Culture, language, regulations, preferences and management styles (Jensen and Szulanski 2004)
- Affiliates are separate legal entities, with potentially different incentives for quality
  - Uncertainty about where the "minimum audit quality bar" is (Aobdia 2015)

Challenges of a Multinational Audit (cont.)

- "Considerable management feat" (Barrett, Cooper and Jamal 2005)

- These challenges can be overcome
  - May require experience and learning
  - Especially at the principal auditor office-level

- The *Principal Auditor* retains ultimate responsibility for the conduct of the audit
  - Significant discretion over various audit planning and execution choices
  - E.g., which locations to audit, extent of procedures at those locations, setting component materiality, identifying global risks, developing and communicating the audit plan

UNIVERSITY OF PITTSBURGH
PITT BUSINESS | Joseph M. Katz Graduate School of Business & College of Business Administration

Prior Literature – Test Variables

- Auditor industry specialization literature – market leaders are the 'experts'
  - (Francis, Reichelt and Wang 2005; Reichelt and Wang 2010; Francis and Michas 2013)
- Market leadership measured at both the national and the office level (Francis and Yu 2009; Francis and Michas 2013; Francis, Michas and Yu(2013)
  - Office-level measures, as opposed to national-level, are more strongly associated with audit quality proxies

UNIVERSITY OF PITTSBURGH
PITT BUSINESS | Joseph M. Katz Graduate School of Business & College of Business Administration

Research Design

Audit Quality = f(Auditor City-level Multinational Expertise, National Expertise, Auditor and Client Controls

Audit Quality Proxies:

1) Likelihood a client receives a going concern modified audit opinion
2) Analyst Forecast Accuracy
3) Absolute Abnormal Accruals

Multinational Expertise

- City Level – auditor who audits the largest amount of total client foreign sales within an MSA-industry-year grouping (minimum 50%)
- National Level – within industry-year groups (minimum 30%)
- Also city-only, national-only and both city/national that are mutually exclusive to each other

UNIVERSITY OF PITTSBURGH
PITT BUSINESS | Joseph M. Katz Graduate School of Business & College of Business Administration

- When is multinational expertise most important?
  1. High percentage of foreign sales relative to total sales.
     - Largest opportunity for MN expertise to make an impact
  2. Higher portion of foreign sales generated in weak rule of law countries.
     - Earnings management is more likely when subsidiaries domiciled in weak rule of law countries (Dyreng, Hanlon and Maydew 2012)

UNIVERSITY OF PITTSBURGH
PITT BUSINESS | Joseph M. Katz Graduate School of Business & College of Business Administration

Sample – Table 1

	N
Firms headquartered in the United States on Compustat from 2001-2014 with positive assets and sales	147,963
Less:	
Regulated and financial firms	(42,689)
Firms that do not match to the Worldscope database based on CUSIP	(8,590)
Firms with missing data in the Audit Analytics database	(20,761)
Firms with no foreign sales	(49,756)
Firm that hire a non-Big "7" audit firm	(3,152)
Firms with missing data required for model variables	(13,615)
Final Base Sample of Firm-Year Observations	**9,400**
Number of Individual Firms	1,666
Less (subtracted from Base Sample):	
Firms with a going concern audit opinion in year t-1 (or missing data on this):	(1,121)
Non-distressed firms (with cash flow or net income less than zero in year t)	(5,509)
Final Going Concern Audit Opinion Sample	**2,770**
Number of Individual Firms	880
Less (subtracted from Base Sample):	
Firms with missing analyst forecast data	(1,850)
Final Analyst Forecast Accuracy Sample	**7,550**
Number of Individual Firms	1,354
Less (subtracted from Base Sample):	
Firms with missing data necessary to calculate abnormal accruals	(0)
Final Abnormal Accruals Sample	**9,400**
Number of Individual Firms	1,666

UNIVERSITY OF PITTSBURGH
PITT BUSINESS | Joseph M. Katz Graduate School of Business & College of Business Administration

Baseline Results: – Table 4

	Dependent Variable = Prob. (GC = 1)			
	Probit	OLS	Probit	OLS
Test Variables – Coefficient (p-value):				
CITY_MN_EXP	.210 (.134)	**.019 ** (.049)**		
NAT_MN_EXP	.176 (.209)	.012 (.196)		
CITY_ONLY_MN_EXP			.187 (.219)	**.019 * (.093)**
NAT_ONLY_MN_EXP			.110 (.597)	.010 (.395)
BOTH_MN_EXP			**.412 ** (.024)**	**.032 ** (.012)**
Year Fixed Effects	YES	YES	YES	YES
Industry Fixed Effects	YES	YES	YES	YES
N	2,190	2,770	2,190	2,770
Pseudo R^2 / R^2	29.6 %	13.2 %	29.6 %	13.3 %
Area under ROC Curve	.89	n/a	.89	n/a

UNIVERSITY OF PITTSBURGH
PITT BUSINESS | Joseph M. Katz Graduate School of Business & College of Business Administration

Results: – Foreign Sales % - Table 5

Test Variables – Coefficient (p-value):	Dependent Variable = Prob. (GC = 1) Probit	OLS	Probit	OLS
HIGH_FOR_SALES_PERC	-.302 (.147)	-.011 (.320)	-.320 (.142)	-.010 (.396)
(a) *CITY_MN_EXP*	-.001 (.991)	.001 (.946)		
(b) *HIGH_FOR_SALES_PERC * CITY_MN_EXP*	**.476 ** (.022)**	**.038 *** (.010)**		
a+b (Chi-Square / F-statistic p-value)	**.475 *** (.010)**	**.039 *** (.003)**		
(c) *NAT_MN_EXP*	.052 (.785)	.008 (.478)		
(d) *HIGH_FOR_SALES_PERC * NAT_MN_EXP*	.193 (.438)	.006 (.737)		
c+d (Chi-Square / F-statistic p-value)	.245 (.184)	.014 (.290)		
(e) *CITY_ONLY_MN_EXP*			-.043 (.816)	.002 (.898)
(f) *HIGH_FOR_SALES_PERC * CITY_ONLY_MN_EXP*			**.531 ** (.029)**	**.035 ** (.044)**
e+f (Chi-Square / F-statistic p-value)			**.488 ** (.017)**	**.037 ** (.013)**
(g) *NAT_ONLY_MN_EXP*			-.044 (.856)	.010 (.516)
(h) *HIGH_FOR_SALES_PERC * NAT_ONLY_MN_EXP*			.344 (.359)	-.002 (.905)
g+h (Chi-Square / F-statistic p-value)			.300 (.345)	.008 (.591)
(i) *BOTH_MN_EXP*			.101 (.691)	.009 (.579)
(j) *HIGH_FOR_SALES_PERC * BOTH_MN_EXP*			**.616 ** (.048)**	**.048 * (.052)**
i+j (Chi-Square / F-statistic p-value)			**.717 *** (.002)**	**.057 *** (.004)**
Control Variables / Year and Industry Fixed Effects	YES	YES	YES	YES
N	2,190	2,770	2,190	2,770
Pseudo R^2 / R^2	30.1 %	13.4 %	30.1 %	13.5 %
Area under ROC Curve	.89	n/a	.89	n/a

2.5 to 5.0 fold increase in likelihood

UNIVERSITY OF PITTSBURGH
PITT BUSINESS | Joseph M. Katz Graduate School of Business & College of Business Administration

Results: – Rule of Law - Table 6

Test Variables – Coefficient (p-value):	Dependent Variable = Prob. (GC = 1) Probit	OLS	Probit	OLS
WEAK_RULE_OF_LAW	-.257 * (.093)	-.016 (.106)	-.294 * (.073)	-.018 * (.073)
(a) *CITY_MN_EXP*	-.012 (.939)	.003 (.796)		
(b) *WEAK_RULE_OF_LAW * CITY_MN_EXP*	**.487 ** (.020)**	**.035 ** (.023)**		
a+b (Chi-Square / F-statistic p-value)	**.475 *** (.010)**	**.038 *** (.004)**		
(c) *NAT_MN_EXP*	.161 (.374)	.018 (.140)		
(d) *WEAK_RULE_OF_LAW * NAT_MN_EXP*	.007 (.973)	-.015 (.384)		
c+d (Chi-Square / F-statistic p-value)	.168 (.354)	.003 (.765)		
(e) *CITY_ONLY_MN_EXP*			-.079 (.677)	-.001 (.978)
(f) *WEAK_RULE_OF_LAW * CITY_ONLY_MN_EXP*			**.580 ** (.017)**	**.042 ** (.024)**
e+f (Chi-Square / F-statistic p-value)			**.501 ** (.014)**	**.041 *** (.009)**
(g) *NAT_ONLY_MN_EXP*			-.017 (.942)	.009 (.573)
(h) *WEAK_RULE_OF_LAW * NAT_ONLY_MN_EXP*			.283 (.457)	.002 (.918)
g+h (Chi-Square / F-statistic p-value)			.266 (.405)	.011 (.439)
(i) *BOTH_MN_EXP*			.216 (.329)	.025 (.123)
(j) *WEAK_RULE_OF_LAW * BOTH_MN_EXP*			**.418 * (.094)**	.014 (.517)
i+j (Chi-Square / F-statistic p-value)			**.634 *** (.005)**	**.039 ** (.028)**
Control Variables / Year and Industry Fixed Effects	YES	YES	YES	YES
N	2,190	2,770	2,190	2,770
Pseudo R^2 / R^2	30.0 %	13.4 %	30.1 %	13.4 %
Area under ROC Curve	.89	n/a	.89	n/a

3.0 to 4.0 fold increase in likelihood

UNIVERSITY OF PITTSBURGH
PITT BUSINESS | Joseph M. Katz Graduate School of Business & College of Business Administration

Results: – Analyst Forecast Accuracy - Table 7

Test Variables – Coefficient (p-value):		FOR_SALES_PERC	RULE_OF_LAW
HIGH_FOR_SALES_PERC or WEAK_RULE_OF_LAW		-.325 *** (.005)	-.268 *** (.005)
(a) CITY_ONLY_MN_EXP	.030 (.677)	**-.202 ** (.039)**	-.117 (.209)
(b) HIGH_FOR_SALES_PERC or WEAK_RULE_OF_LAW CITY_ONLY_MN_EXP*		**.470 *** (.000)**	**.324 *** (.008)**
a+b (Chi-Square / F-statistic p-value)		**.268 *** (.004)**	**.206 ** (.031)**
(c) NAT_ONLY_MN_EXP	.015 (.886)	-.102 (.531)	-.187 (.267)
*(d) HIGH_FOR_SALES_PERC or WEAK_RULE_OF_LAW * NAT_ONLY_MN_EXP*		.257 (.220)	**.393 * (.074)**
c+d (Chi-Square / F-statistic p-value)		.155 (.271)	.206 (.146)
(e) BOTH_MN_EXP	.003 (.971)	-.202 (.109)	-.104 (.303)
*(f) HIGH_FOR_SALES_PERC or WEAK_RULE_OF_LAW * BOTH_MN_EXP*		**.394 *** (.008)**	.197 (.137)
e+f (Chi-Square / F-statistic p-value)		**.192 * (.087)**	.093 (.461)
Control Variables / Year and Industry Fixed Effects	YES	YES	YES
N	7,550	7,550	7,550
R^2	7.2 %	7.5 %	6.6%

14.4% to 21.9% increase in accuracy

UNIVERSITY OF PITTSBURGH
PITT BUSINESS | Joseph M. Katz Graduate School of Business & College of Business Administration

Results: Absolute Abnormal Accruals - Table 8

Test Variables – Coefficient (p-value):		FOR_SALES_PERC	RULE_OF_LAW
HIGH_FOR_SALES_PERC or WEAK_RULE_OF_LAW		-.012 (.102)	-.003 (.473)
(a) CITY_ONLY_MN_EXP	**-.014 *** (.008)**	**-.015 ** (.040)**	-.012 (.103)
(b) HIGH_FOR_SALES_PERC or WEAK_RULE_OF_LAW CITY_ONLY_MN_EXP*		.001 (.855)	-.008 (.366)
a+b (Chi-Square / F-statistic p-value)		**-.014 ** (.047)**	**-.020 *** (.003)**
(c) NAT_ONLY_MN_EXP	-.001 (.854)	.010 (.249)	.001 (.866)
*(d) HIGH_FOR_SALES_PERC or WEAK_RULE_OF_LAW * NAT_ONLY_MN_EXP*		**-.020 * (.057)**	-.001 (.930)
c+d (Chi-Square / F-statistic p-value)		-.010 (.157)	.000 (.964)
(e) BOTH_MN_EXP	**-.010 * (.098)**	-.014 (.112)	-.012 (.174)
*(f) HIGH_FOR_SALES_PERC or WEAK_RULE_OF_LAW * BOTH_MN_EXP*		.007 (.482)	.011 (.235)
e+f (Chi-Square / F-statistic p-value)		-.007 (.358)	-.001 (.970)
Control Variables / Year and Industry Fixed Effects	YES	YES	YES
N	9,400	9,400	9,400
R^2	39.8 %	39.8 %	36.9 %

Abnormal accruals lower by 5.1% to 7.2%

UNIVERSITY OF PITTSBURGH
PITT BUSINESS | Joseph M. Katz Graduate School of Business & College of Business Administration

Sensitivity Tests

- Restatement as an additional measure of audit quality and find consistent results
- Propensity Score Matching
  - Clients audited by a MN expert or not, matched on log of foreign sales, % of foreign sales, and log of total assets
- Is it simply industry specialization?
  - Drop city-industry-expert control variable
  - Regress out industry expertise from multinational expertise and use the residual

UNIVERSITY OF PITTSBURGH
PITT BUSINESS | Joseph M. Katz Graduate School of Business & College of Business Administration

Sensitivity Tests

- # of countries where foreign sales generated instead of % of foreign sales
- Multinational expertise measured based on total client assets audited instead of sales
- Use percentage of foreign sales audited by the auditor instead of dichotomous expertise variables
- Mean instead of median forecast error

UNIVERSITY OF PITTSBURGH
PITT BUSINESS | Joseph M. Katz Graduate School of Business & College of Business Administration

Conclusion

- City-level multinational expertise is associated with:
  - a higher likelihood of issuing a going concern audit opinion
  - higher analyst forecast accuracy
  - lower absolute abnormal accruals
- Only for client firms:
  - With a relatively high percentage of foreign sales
  - Where foreign sales are generated in relatively weak rule of law countries

UNIVERSITY OF PITTSBURGH
PITT BUSINESS | Joseph M. Katz Graduate School of Business & College of Business Administration

Contribution

- The literature on group audits is relatively sparse despite increased globalization and regulatory attention
- No studies examine variation in the quality of multinational audits
- Quality concerns may not need to be universal – some auditors/offices better than others
- Deepens our understanding of auditor 'expertise'

UNIVERSITY OF PITTSBURGH
PITT BUSINESS | Joseph M. Katz Graduate School of Business & College of Business Administration

THANK YOU!

PCAOB Form 2 Disclosure: A Firm-Level Signal of Audit Quality?

Steve Buchheit
University of Alabama

William Buslepp
Louisiana State University

LSU
E. J. Ourso College of Business
Department of Accounting

Publicly Available Audit Inputs

- Publicly available audit input data has been scarce in the United States
  - Engagement-level audit hour information is publicly available in Greece and Korea.
  - Public identification of audit engagement partners is available in Australia, China, Finland and Sweden.
- In the U.S., the standard - yet problematic - proxy for expended audit effort has been audit fees or abnormal audit fees

Audit Fees

Audit Fees = rate x hours (effort)

Advantages:

- Audit Fees should be positively correlated with hours worked.

Disadvantages:

- Does not distinguish between the *increased effort* and *increased billings* (Bedard and Johnstone 2004).
- Price may be influenced by several factors include:
  - Litigation risk (positively)
  - Client market pressures (negatively)
  - Expertise on the audit committee (negatively).
  - Industry specialization (positively)
  - Ex-ante assessment of accounting quality (negatively)

PCAOB Form 2

- Background
  - Required by Section 102(d) of the Sarbanes-Oxley Act and PCAOB Rule 2200
  - Must be submitted annually each year on or before June 30.
  - Each report covers a 12-month period from April 1 of year t to March 31 of year t+1.
  - Available since the second quarter of 2010
  - Public information about non-public clients (the first ever?)
- Content

Part I	Identity of the Firm and Contact Persons	Part VII	Certain Relationships
Part II	General Information Concerning this Report	Part VIII	Acquisition of Another Public Accounting Firm or Substantial Portions of Another Public Accounting Firm's Personnel
Part III	General Information Concerning the Firms	Part IX	Affirmation of Consent
Part IV	Audit Clients and Audit Reports	Part X	Certification of the Firm
Part V	Offices and Affiliations	Part XI	Exhibits
Part VI	Personnel		

4

Human-Resource-Based Audit Input Ratio

Data from PCAOB Form 2:

- **Item 3.2.a.1** – Provides the percentage of total firm fees billed to issuer audit clients *for audit services* during the annual reporting period (***Audit Services %***).
- **Item 4.1** – Provides a listing for each issuer client for which the firm provides an audit report (***Audit Reports***).
- **Item 6.1.a** – Provides the total number of firm accountants (***Accountants***).

$$WORKLOAD = \frac{Audit\ Reports}{Accountants \times Audit\ Service\ \%}$$

Big Four Workload Metrics

PricewaterhouseCoopers Annual Report

Average annual hours worked in excess of 40 hours per week (2,088 annually)

	FY15	FY14	FY13[3]
Partner	461	475	495
Senior Manager/Manager	345	378	401
Senior Associate	305	347	356
Associate	268	311	312

Ernst & Young Annual Report

Average annual hours incurred by audit professionals

	Fiscal 2015	Fiscal 2014	Fiscal 2013
Partners	2,619	2,596	2,603
Executive directors	2,559	2,534	2,521
Senior managers and managers	2,483	2,472	2,467
Seniors and staff	2,399	2,400	2,385

Hypothesis

- The PCAOB is concerned about heavy partner and staff workloads potentially impacting audit quality.
- Lopez and Peters (2012) and Bills, Swanquist, and Whited (2015) suggest that limited human resource capacity in audit firms may manifest itself in the form of a less rigorous audit.
- Assuming our measure is:
  - Associated with audit quality and
  - Detects differences in output-based audit quality,

  We expect that *WORKLOAD* will be negatively associated with output-based audit quality.
- Formally, we predict:

  H1: *Ceteris paribus, a relatively high ratio of audit reports-to-auditors will be associated with relatively low ex-post audit quality.*

Audit Quality Proxies

- Test our measure using output-based audit quality proxies including:
  - Restatements
  - Abnormal Accruals/Changes in Abnormal Accruals
  - Propensity to issue a New Going Concern Opinion

Form 2 Descriptive Information - 2nd Quarter 2015

Firm Name	1. Audit Services %	2. Audit Reports	3. Accountants	2 ÷ (1 × 3) Workload Ratio	4. Non Public %	5. Total Personnel
Deloitte & Touche	17%	2,399	23,768	0.594	77%	72,104
PricewaterhouseCoopers	25%	1,991	26,726	0.298	65%	45,081
Ernst & Young	28%	2,128	22,607	0.336	64%	38,753
KPMG	26%	1,535	16,658	0.354	68%	27,891
McGladrey	12%	214	6,501	0.274	84%	8,519
Grant Thornton	18%	1,900	4,121	2.561	80%	6,859
BDO USA	20%	382	3,468	0.551	78%	5,172
CliftonLarsonAllen	0%	31	2,722	1.139	100%	3,867
Crowe Horwath	5%	169	1,888	1.790	95%	2,966
CohnReznick	2%	72	2,085	1.727	98%	2,815

Audit Quality Proxy #1: Restatements

- Restatements suggest that an auditor has failed to detect and prevent a material error during a prior audit engagement (Blankley, Hurtt and MacGregor 2012).
- Test our hypothesis using the following model:

$$RESTATE = \gamma_0 + \gamma_1 \mathbf{WORKLOAD\ or\ LnWORKLOAD} + \gamma_2 LnPERSONNEL + \gamma_3 \%NONPUBLICREV + \gamma_4 ABFEES + \gamma_5 BIG4 + \gamma_6 TIER2 + \gamma_7 SPECIALIST + \gamma_8 P\_SCORE + \gamma_9 LAGREST + \gamma_{10} SIZE + \gamma_{11} AGE + \gamma_{12} TENURE + \gamma_{13} NEG\_EQUITY + \gamma_{14} MERGER + \gamma_{15} FIN + \gamma_{16} LOSS + \gamma_{17} CURRENT\_ACCRUAL + \gamma_{18} LEV + \gamma_{19} INV\_INT\_COV + \gamma_{20} SALEGR + \gamma_{21} BTM + \gamma_{22} EXT\_FIN\_DEMAND + \gamma_{23} MW + \gamma_{24} CLIENT\_IMPORT + \gamma_{25} YEAR\_END + \Sigma YEAR + \Sigma OFFICE + \varepsilon$$

Audit Quality Proxy #1: Restatements

Variable	Predicted Sign	2000-2009	RESTATE (1)	(2)	(3)	(4)
Intercept	(-)	-3.029 (-22.78)***	-4.046 (-20.18)	-4.723 (-11.67)***	-5.010 (-11.65)***	-5.042 (-11.33)***
WORKLOAD	(+)				0.122 (1.91)**	
LnWORKLOAD	(+)					0.298 (1.72)**
LnPERSONNEL	(?)			0.171 (2.03)**	0.195 (2.30)**	0.190 (2.24)**
%NONPUBLICREV	(?)			-0.010 (-2.87)***	-0.011 (-3.07)***	-0.011 (-3.10)***
ABFEES	(-)	-0.119 (-2.52)***	0.065 (1.10)	0.013 (0.22)	0.018 (0.30)	0.018 (0.29)
Control Variables		Yes	Yes	Yes	Yes	Yes
RESTATE N		4,951	1,473	1,473	1,473	1,473
NO RESTATE N		30,279	16,092	16,092	16,092	16,092
N		35,230	17,565	17,565	17,565	17,565

Audit Quality Proxy #2: Abnormal Accruals

- Examine whether opportunistic managerial reporting discretion is constrained differentially based on auditor workload
- Estimate performance-adjusted abnormal accruals, based on the cross-sectional modified Jones (1991) model, adjusting for the prior year's operating performance (Kothari et al. 2005).
- Test our hypothesis using the following model:

$$|ACCRUALS| = b_0 + b_1 \mathbf{WORKLOAD\ or\ LnWORKLOAD} + b_2 LnPERSONNEL + b_3\%NONPUBLICREV + b_4 ABFEES + b_5 BIG4 + b_6 TIER2 + b_7 SIZE + b_8\sigma(CFO) + b_9 CFO + b_{10} LEV + b_{11} LOSS + b_{12} M/B + b_{13} LIT + b_{14} ALTMAN + b_{15} TENURE + b_{16}|ACCR\_1| + b_{17} MW + b_{18} CLIENT\_IMPORT + b_{19} YEAR\_END + \Sigma YEAR + \Sigma OFFICE + e$$

Audit Quality Proxy #2: Abnormal Accruals

Variable	Predicted Sign	|ACCRUALS|			
		(1)	(2)	(3)	(4)
Intercept	(?)	0.154 (1.78)*	0.070 (0.77)	0.062 (0.69)	0.052 (0.57)
WORKLOAD	(+)			0.006 (1.38)*	
LnWORKLOAD	(+)				0.021 (1.66)**
LnPERSONNEL	(?)		0.028 (3.13)***	0.030 (3.32)***	0.032 (3.47)***
%NONPUBLICREV	(?)		0.001 (0.06)	-0.013 (-0.66)	-0.019 (-0.91)
ABFEES	(-)	0.005 (3.08)***	0.004 (3.01)***	0.004 (3.02)***	0.004 (3.03)***
Control Variables		Yes	Yes	Yes	Yes
R^2		0.2451	0.2456	0.2457	0.2458
N		16,743	16,743	16,743	16,743

Audit Quality Proxy #2: Change in Abnormal Accruals

Variable	Predicted Sign	Δ|ACCRUALS|			
		(1)	(2)	(3)	(4)
Intercept	(?)	-0.037 (-0.37)	-0.036 (-0.37)	-0.043 (-0.44)	-0.042 (-0.43)
ΔWORKLOAD	(+)			0.009 (2.58)***	
ΔLnWORKLOAD	(+)				0.020 (2.16)**
ΔLnPERSONNEL	(?)		-0.001 (-0.38)	0.006 (1.52)	0.005 (1.24)
Δ%NONPUBLICREV	(?)		-0.005 (-0.20)	-0.075 (-2.09)**	-0.073 (-1.86)*
ΔABFEES	(-)	0.009 (4.09)***	0.009 (4.08)***	0.009 (4.15)***	0.009 (4.14)***
Control Variables		Yes	Yes	Yes	Yes
R^2		0.0735	0.0735	0.0741	0.0739
N		11,684	11,684	11,684	11,684

Audit Quality Proxy #3: Propensity to Issue a New Going Concern Opinion

- Examine whether workload constrained auditors issue fewer first-time going concern opinions to financially troubled clients relative to auditors with relatively low workloads.
- Test our hypothesis using the following model:

$$FIRST\_GC = \lambda_0 + \lambda_1 WORKLOAD \text{ or } LnWORKLOAD + \lambda_2 LnPERSONNEL + \lambda_3 \%NONPUBLICREV + \lambda_4 ABFEES + \lambda_5 BIG4 + \lambda_6 TIER2 + \lambda_7 NEW\_AUDITOR + \lambda_8 TENURE + \lambda_9 ALTMAN + \lambda_{10} SIZE + \lambda_{11} LnAGE + \lambda_{12} LEVERAGE + \lambda_{13} CLEVERAGE + \lambda_{14} CRATIO + \lambda_{15} ROA + \lambda_{16} LLOSS + \lambda_{17} RETURN + \lambda_{18} NEWDEBT + \lambda_{19} NEG\_EQUITY + \lambda_{20} CASHFLOW + \lambda_{21} DEFAULT + \lambda_{22} MW + \lambda_{23} CLIENT\_IMPORT + \lambda_{24} YEAR\_END + \Sigma YEAR + \Sigma OFFICE + \varepsilon$$

Audit Quality Proxy #3: Propensity to Issue a New Going Concern Opinion

		FIRST_GC			
Variable	Predicted Sign	(1)	(2)	(3)	(4)
Intercept	?	-3.418 (-4.69)***	-2.860 (-3.35)***	-2.436 (-2.70)***	-2.278 (-2.46)***
WORKLOAD	(-)			-0.155 (-1.49)*	
LnWORKLOAD	(-)				-0.464 (-1.62)*
LnPERSONNEL	(?)		-0.172 (-1.33)	-0.212 (-1.60)*	-0.217 (-1.64)*
%NONPUBLICREV	(?)		0.406 (0.69)	0.554 (0.93)	0.613 (1.02)
ABFEES	(+)	-0.205 (-1.67)	-0.172 (-1.36)	-0.187 (-1.49)	-0.187 (-1.49)
Control Variables		Yes	Yes	Yes	Yes
GOING CONCERN N		263	263	263	263
NO GOING CONCERN N		5,990	5,990	5,990	5,990
N		6,253	6,253	6,253	6,253

Conclusion

- We find that our firm-level workload metric is both:
  - significantly associated with audit quality and
  - incremental in explanatory value relative to the fee-based audit input metrics commonly used to proxy for audit effort.
- Our findings:
  - Support the development of audit quality indicators by the PCAOB (PCAOB 2015b).
  - Are similar to proposed audit quality indicators on 'audit professionals' that specifically consider partner workloads and manager and staff workloads (e.g., proposed audit quality indicators #2 and #3 in the recent PCAOB concept release)
  - Suggest that a significant element of "audit style" as described by (Francis, Pinnuck, and Watanabe (2014) might be inter-firm selection of human resource staffing levels.
- Overall, our findings suggest that regulatory and industry concern regarding human resource adequacy in the public audit environment (IOSCO 2009; PCAOB 2013; IAASB 2014) is well-founded because relatively high audit-firm-level workloads are associated with relatively low audit quality.

Improving Auditors' Consideration of Evidence Contradicting Management's Assumptions

Ashley A. Austin
Jacqueline S. Hammersley
Michael A. Ricci

Deloitte / KU Auditing Symposium
May 21, 2016

Terry | G

Motivation

Auditors verify management's estimate instead of critically evaluating its reasonableness (Griffith et al. 2015).

Auditors underweight or ignore contradicting evidence contained in their documentation (PCAOB 2010, 2012, 2014).

Auditors dismiss evidence contradicting management's assumptions.

Research Question

Can we reduce auditors' dismissiveness of evidence contradicting management's assumptions by:

1) Focusing auditors on documenting evidence inconsistent with their preferred conclusion

2) Strengthening auditors' goal of arriving at an accurate conclusion

Theory

Focusing auditors on documenting evidence inconsistent with their preferred conclusion will disrupt dismissive processing

- Auditors' *interpretation* of evidence will improve
- Auditors will make more *inferences* that contradict management's assumptions

Strengthening auditors' accuracy goals will make them less likely to initiate dismissive processing

- Auditors with weaker accuracy goals will benefit more from a focus on documenting preference-inconsistent evidence

Hypotheses

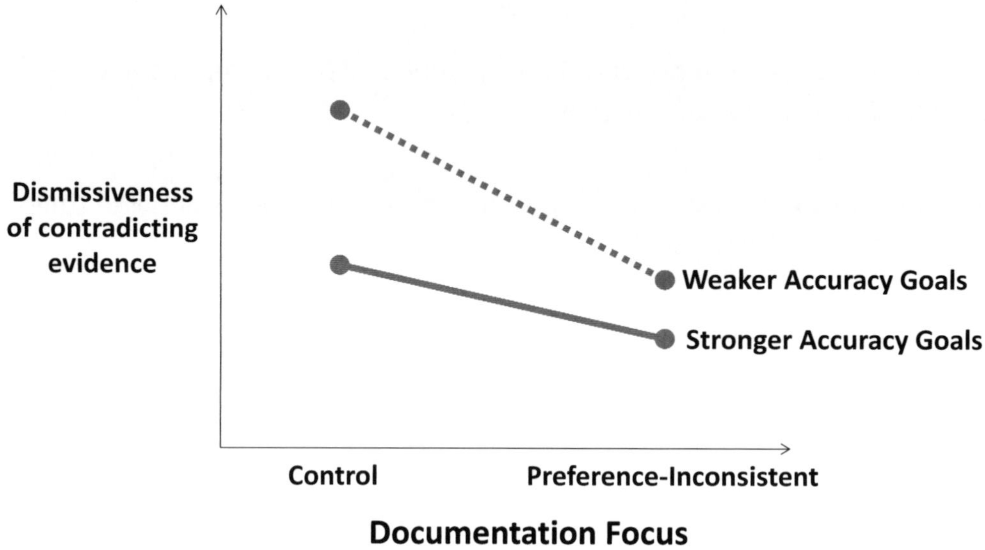

Experiment

Participants

- 114 senior auditors, average experience 48 months

Goodwill Impairment Task

- Listen to interviews suggesting the new product may release late
- Document interview evidence
- Assess the reasonableness of the estimate and decide next steps

2 x 2 Design

Independent Variables

- Documentation Focus
  - Document any issues identified that are inconsistent with your conclusion about the projections
- Accuracy Goal Strength
  - Arrive at an accurate conclusion, making sure the client's numbers are as accurate as possible

Dependent Variables

- Auditors' dismissiveness of contradicting evidence
- Auditors' evaluation of the biased estimate

Net Inquiry Inferences

	Documentation Focus:		
Accuracy Goal Strength:	Control	Preference-Inconsistent	
Weaker	-0.55 A	-2.07 C	-1.31
Stronger	-0.20 B	-1.80 D	-1.00
	-0.37	-1.94	

ANOVA Table:	**df**	**F**	**p-value**
Documentation Focus	1	9.83	0.002
Accuracy Goal Strength	1	0.39	0.535
Documentation Focus X Accuracy Goal Strength	1	0.01	0.939
Planned Contrasts:			
H1: Preference-Inconsistent < Control		9.83	0.001
H2: D – C < B – A		0.01	0.530

Structural Model

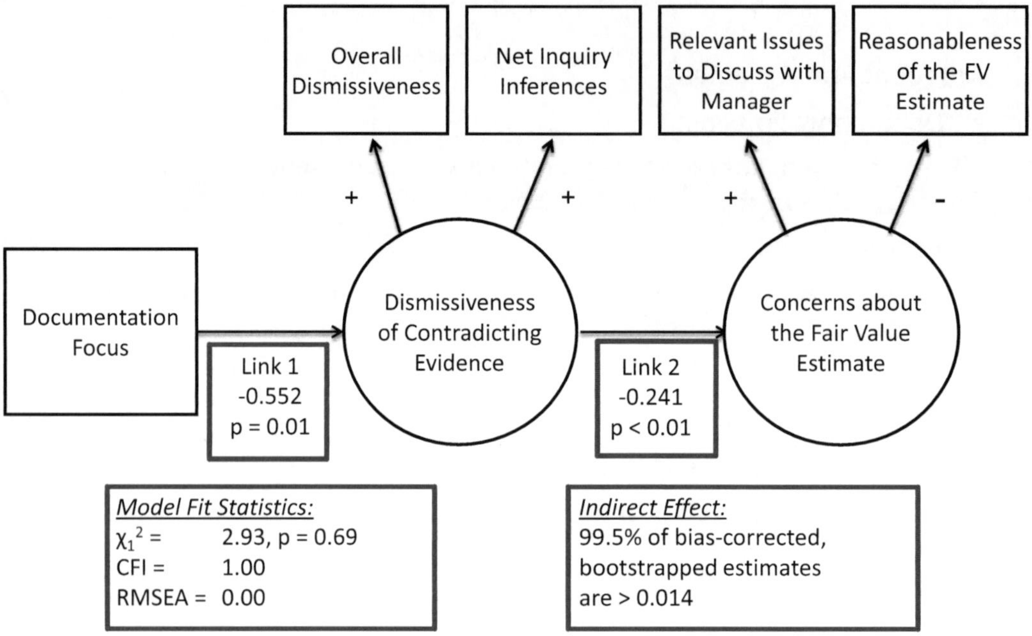

Supplemental Analyses

- A preference-inconsistent documentation focus affects auditors' *interpretation* of available evidence, but not their choice about which *facts* to document.
- Preference-inconsistent auditors do not just work harder.
- Auditors have strong accuracy goals, regardless of condition.

Conclusions

- A preference-inconsistent documentation focus interferes with dismissive processing and improves audit quality in a difficult area.
- Strong accuracy goals do not preclude dismissive processing.
- Documentation plays an important role in the formation of auditor judgments.

THANK YOU!

When Fraud Brainstorming Becomes Dysfunctional: Can The Generation of Many Fraud Risks Increase Anchoring on Client-Provided Explanations?

ANNA M. ROSE
Victoria University of Wellington

JACOB M. ROSE
Victoria University of Wellington

IKSEON SUH
Marquette University

JAY C. THIBODEAU
Bentley University

January 15, 2016

Acknowledgements: The authors would like to thank the participants from two Big 4 firms who took the time to complete the experimental materials. We also wish to thank Vicky Arnold, Steve Sutton, Greg Trompeter, John Sweeney and participants of a workshop at the University of Central Florida for their helpful suggestions.

When Fraud Brainstorming Becomes Dysfunctional: Can The Generation of Many Fraud Risks Increase Anchoring on Client-Provided Explanations?

Abstract

This study investigates the potential for fraud brainstorming during the financial statement audit to actually hinder professional skepticism by increasing auditors' tendencies to anchor on client-provided explanations. We conduct an experiment with 93 senior auditors from two Big 4 firms and find that the generation of more ideas while brainstorming about fraud increases anchoring on client explanations, which then leads to reduced assessments of fraud risk. Our findings call into question a key assumption from the fraud brainstorming literature – namely, that the generation of many ideas about potential frauds during brainstorming is beneficial and promotes professional skepticism. In addition, our findings imply that that it is critically important to consider the role of the anchoring effect in future studies that examine the effectiveness of alternative fraud brainstorming techniques.

Key Words: Anchoring; client explanations; counter-explanation; fraud brainstorming; fraud risk assessment

Audit Partner Characteristics, Audit Quality and Audit Pricing in the U.S.

Ally Zimmerman, Northern Illinois University, azimmerman5@niu.edu
Al Nagy, John Carroll University, alnagy@jcu.edu
2016 Deloitte/KU Audit Symposium, May 20

Introduction

- ***RQ: Do audit fees and audit quality vary among U.S. audit partners with partner experience and gender?***
  - Studies from other countries have found audit partner effects, but evidence is mixed
  - U.S. audit market different from other countries
    - Litigious environment, regulatory scrutiny/inspections
    - No Disclosure of audit partner identity to investors
  - No U.S. evidence yet - Partner identity disclosure will be required in the U.S. starting in 2017 on PCAOB Form AP
- ***Contribution***
  - Understanding the impact of individual auditors on audit outcomes over and above their audit firms/offices
  - What can data from the period 2004-2014 prior to disclosure of audit partner identity tell us about the impact of audit partner characteristics on audit pricing, quality?
  - Evidence pre- and post-disclosure can be compared in the future to isolate the impact of audit partner identity disclosure itself

Prior Research Outside of U.S.

- In Australia, Taylor (2011) finds that premium partners audit fewer clients than the discount partners, but on the contrary have shorter partner tenures.
- In Sweden, partner industry specialization is positively associated with audit fees (Zerni 2012).
- Ittonen and Peni (2012) find that firms with female audit engagement partners have significantly higher audit fees.
- Gul et al. (2013) identify significance of audit partner effects on audit outcomes in China.
- In Australia, Goodwin and Wu (2014) find that audit fee premiums are associated with partner-level industry expertise.
- Ye, Cheng, and Gao (2014) document that individual auditors with more auditing experience are less likely to be associated with audit failure.
- Hardies et al. (2015) also find a female audit fee premium among Belgian public companies.
- Cahan and Sun (2015) find that experience is positively associated with audit fees in China.
- Wang et al. (2015) find that, in some models of restatements, engagement and review partner experience is positively related to restatements (audit failures).

Does Partner Experience Matter in U.S.?

- Audit partner identity matters to management and audit committees in the auditor selection process
- Partners/their resumes are heavily vetted in the auditor selection process.
- Technical expertise as well as political capital within an audit firm arguably takes years to develop.
- Technical/industry expertise is associated with higher audit quality
- If partner political capital and expertise are valuable to clients, they would be willing to pay more for it through higher audit fees.

H1a/b: Audit partner experience is positively associated with audit fees and audit quality.

Does Partner Gender Matter?

- Females executives tend to be more diligent, more conservative, less overconfident and less tolerant of risk than males (e.g., Palvia et al. 2015; Huang and Kisgen 2013; Peni and Vahamaa 2010; Eagly and Carli 2003) -> Higher audit quality
- Female tolerance for less risk may affect the pricing decisions by increasing auditor effort.
- If females tolerate less risk, they may also charge a premium for taking on this risk.

H2a/b: Female audit partners have higher audit fees and higher audit quality than male audit partners.

NIU

8/16/2016 5

Data and Sample

- We identified through Audit Analytics SEC Comment Letter Database a total of 6,562 SEC comment letter correspondences from 2004 to Oct 2014 that copied 1,750 unique Big 4 audit partners
- Correspondences could copy more than one audit partner; if more than one partner copied, assumed the first person copied was the lead partner
- We assumed that the copied audit partner was an engagement partner on the audit of the firm in the year of the letter (alternatively the prior year based on CompuStat year)
- Partner background information hand-collected from LinkedIn
- Excluded financial firms, foreign-based, those missing model variable information and who partner information could not be located
- Final sample for analysis – 769 firm-year observations encompassing 479 unique firms and 471 unique partners
  - Some firms and partners but not all have multiple appearances

NIU

8/16/2016 6

Example SEC Correspondence Copying the Auditor

"In the accompanying consolidated statement of cash flows for the six months ended February 28, 2013, the Company corrected the classification of by operating activities to cash flows used by financing activities, which decreased cash flows used by operating activities and increased cash flows u documentary letters of credit a short-term financing activity and accordingly made this correction in order to properly present the changes in these ce of cash flows allowing users of its financial statements to better understand the level at which the Company uses documentary letters of credit. This c earnings per share, balance sheet or net cash flows used by investing activities in the consolidated statement of cash flows for the six months ended F

The Company acknowledges the following:

- the Company is responsible for the adequacy and accuracy of the disclosure in its filing; and
- staff comments or changes to disclosure in response to staff comments do not foreclose the Commission from taking any action with respect
- the Company may not assert staff comments as a defense in any proceeding initiated by the Commission or any person under the federal sec

Mr. John Cash
March 25, 2014
Page 2

Please contact the undersigned at (972) 308-5199 or Adam R. Hickey at (972) 308-4317 if you have any questions or would like additional information in res

Very truly yours,

cc: Joseph Alvarado, Chairman, President and Chief Executive Officer
Paul K. Kirkpatrick, Vice President, General Counsel and Corporate Secretary
Adam R. Hickey, Vice President and Controller
Audit Committee of Board of Directors
Paul L. Choi, Sidley Austin LLP
Gwen Mitchell, Deloitte & Touche LLP

Audit Pricing Model

$$AUFEE = \beta_0 + \beta_1 EXPER + \beta_2 GENDR + \beta_3 ASSETS + \beta_4 ROA + \beta_5 LEV + \beta_6 LOSS + \beta_7 NSUBS + \beta_8 REC + \beta_9 INV + \beta_{10} GC + \beta_{11} FORSA + \beta_{12} DECYE + \beta_{13} S404 + \beta_{14} SPEC + + \beta_{15} TEN + \beta_{16\text{-}23} IND + \beta_{24\text{-}33} YEAR,$$

EXPER = **number of years the partner is with the audit firm or the number of years the partner has been in practice (number of years elapsed since the bachelor's/master's degree).**

GENDR = **1 if partner is female, 0 if male.**

ASSETS = log of total assets.

ROA = ratio of net income to total assets.

LEV = ratio of long-term debt to total assets.

LOSS = 1 if company had a net loss in last 3 years, else 0.

NSUBS = log of the number of consolidated subsidiaries.

REC = ratio of receivables to total assets.

INV = ratio of inventory to total assets.

GC = 1 if going concern modification in the audit report, else 0.

FORSA = ratio of foreign sales to total sales.

DECYE = 1 if December fiscal year-end, else 0.

S404 = 1 if integrated SOX 404(b) and external audit is conducted, else 0.

SPEC = 1 if auditor is national specialist per SIC code (2-digit), else 0.

TEN = 1 if auditor tenure is less than 3yrs

Descriptive Statistics
Audit Fee Analysis

Variable[a]	*MEAN*	*MEDIAN*	*STD DEVIATION*
AUFEE	0.473	0.352	1.105
EXPER	19.17	19.00	8.195
GENDR	0.113	0.000	0.317
ASSETS	6.939	6.844	1.984
ROA	-0.864	3.450	14.616
LEV	0.203	0.146	0.244
LOSS	0.468	0.000	0.499
NSUBS	0.548	0.000	0.689
REC	0.126	0.104	0.103
INV	0.092	0.047	0.118
GC	0.417	0.000	0.493
FORSA	0.221	0.020	0.286
DECYE	0.620	1.000	0.486
S404	0.805	1.000	0.397
SPEC	0.247	0.000	0.432
TEN	0.108	0.000	0.310

8/16/2016 NIU 9

Audit Pricing OLS Regression Results

$$AUFEE = \beta_0 + \beta_1 EXPER + \beta_2 GENDR + \beta_3 ASSETS + \beta_4 ROA + \beta_5 LEV + \beta_6 LOSS + \beta_7 NSUBS + \beta_8 REC + \beta_9 INV + \beta_{10} GC + \beta_{11} FORSA + \beta_{12} DECYE + \beta_{13} S404 + \beta_{14} SPEC + \beta_{15} TEN + \beta_{16\text{-}23} IND + \beta_{24\text{-}33} YEAR$$

Variable	*Prediction*	*Coefficients*	*t- statistic*
EXPER	+	0.006	2.68***
GENDR	+	0.119	1.92**
ASSETS	+	0.485	34.17***

Number of Observations	769
Adjusted R2	77.28%
Model F-Value	82.66***

8/16/2016 NIU 10

Audit Quality Analysis

$$GC = \beta_0 + \beta_1 EXPER + \beta_2 GENDR + \beta_3 LSPEC + \beta_4 OFFSIZE + \beta_5 PBANK + \beta_6 ASSETS + \beta_7 AGE + \beta_8 LEV + \beta_9 CLEV + \beta_{10} LLOSS + \beta_{11} INVEST + \beta_{12} FEERATIO + \beta_{13} CFFO + \beta_{14} TENURE + \beta_{15\text{-}20} IND + \beta_{21\text{-}29} YEAR$$

LSPEC = 1 if auditor has highest local market share defined as two-digit SIC code within the metropolitan statistical area (MSA), else 0;

OFFSIZE = natural log of the total local office audit fees other than the observation;

PBANK = probability of bankruptcy measured by adjusted Zmijewski score;

ASSETS = natural log of total assets;

AGE = natural log of the number of years included in Research Insight;

LEV = ratio of total liabilities to total assets;

CLEV = change in LEV during the year;

LLOSS = 1 if company reported a loss for the previous year, else 0;

INVEST = short- and long-term investment securities (measured as current assets less receivables and inventory) divided by total assets;

FEERATIO = ratio of non-audit fees to total fees paid to the incumbent auditor;

CFFO = cash flow from operations divided by total assets; and

TENURE = natural log of years the audit firm on the engagement.

Descriptive Statistics (N=172)

Going Concern Analysis Sample

Variable[a]	*MEAN*	*MEDIAN*	*STD DEVIATION*
GC	0.401	0.000	0.492
EXPER	18.10	18.00	7.872
GENDR	0.105	0.000	0.307
LSPEC	0.424	0.000	0.496
OFFSIZE	17.94	17.98	0.916
PBANK	-3.198	-3.648	2.247
ASSETS	5.424	5.203	1.637
AGE	2.141	2.303	0.831
LEV	0.538	0.474	0.393
CLEV	-0.029	0.016	0.599
LLOSS	0.750	1.000	0.434
INVEST	0.453	0.404	0.289
FEERATIO	0.122	0.086	0.118
CFFO	-0.090	-0.004	0.264
TENURE	1.703	1.946	0.779

Going Concern Analysis Results

$GC = \beta_0 + \beta_1 EXPER + \beta_2 GENDR + \beta_3 LSPEC + \beta_4 OFFSIZE + \beta_5 PBANK + \beta_6 ASSETS + \beta_7 AGE + \beta_8 LEV + \beta_9 CLEV + \beta_{10} LLOSS + \beta_{11} INVEST + \beta_{12} FEERATIO + \beta_{13} CFFO + \beta_{14} TENURE + \beta_{15-20} IND + \beta_{21-29} YEAR$

Variable	*Prediction*	*Estimated Coefficients*	*Wald Chi-square*
EXPER	+	0.103	5.52***
GENDR	+	-0.428	0.19
LSPEC	+	1.317	3.67**

Number of Observations	172
Pseudo R^2	59.43%
Model Chi-square	135.57***

8/16/2016 13

Results Summary

- Strong Results for Audit Pricing
  - More experienced audit partners associated with higher audit fees
  - Female audit fee premium
- Mixed Results for Audit Quality
  - More experienced partners are more independent -> more likely to issue a going concern modified opinion for distressed companies
  - No difference in audit quality/ independence with respect to partner gender

8/16/2016 14

Conclusion, Contribution, Implications

- We provide initial evidence that audit pricing and audit quality do vary with audit partner characteristics in the U.S., indicating that partner identity could be valuable information to investors and supporting the PCAOB's initiative to have firms disclose audit partner identity.
- Following partner identity disclosure, partners will likely develop reputations separate from their audit firms
  - Whose reputation will matter more – partners or firms?
- Our results for audit pricing and audit quality are based on an environment pre-public disclosure of audit partner identity. Results using data post-public disclosure of audit partner identity can be compared to results of the paper to isolate the effect of disclosure on the audit market in the U.S.
- Future research to understand the underlying drivers of the experience and gender effects that we find.

NIU

8/16/2016 15

Future Analyses

- Checking for nonlinear relation (initial partner period vs. nearing retirement)
- Isolate partner experience from client experience with the partner's audit firm
- Additional audit quality analyses

NIU

8/16/2016 16

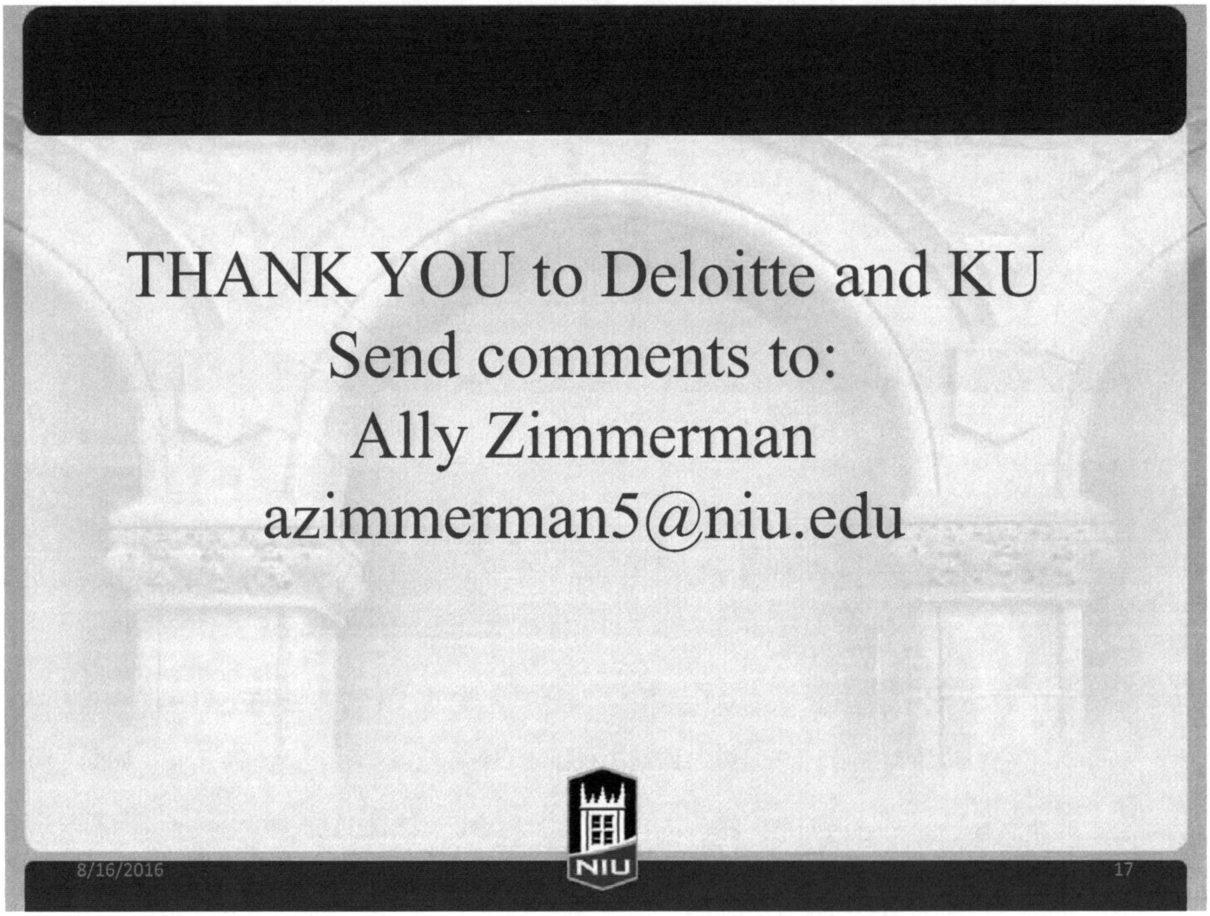
THANK YOU to Deloitte and KU
Send comments to:
Ally Zimmerman
azimmerman5@niu.edu
NIU
8/16/2016
17

Separating Auditor Provided Tax Compliance and Tax Planning Services: Audit Quality Implications

James Chyz
University of Tennessee

Ronen Gal-Or
Northeastern University

Vic Naiker
Monash University

2016 Deloitte/University of Kansas Symposium
May 21, 2016

1

Northeastern University D'Amore-McKim School of Business

Research Questions

RQ1: Does knowledge spillover between tax and audit functions depend on the nature of tax service provided (i.e. planning or compliance) to audit clients?

RQ2: Does knowledge spillover across tax and audit service lines arise between clients of the same office and does it depend on the nature of tax service provided?

RQ3: Do office-level tax compliance and tax planning NAS capture audit offices' allocation of resources and attention to the audit practice in ways that benefit or harm audit quality?

2

Findings

RQ1: Does knowledge spillover between tax and audit functions depend on the nature of tax service provided (i.e. planning or compliance) to audit clients?

- Yes... Audit quality enhancing knowledge spillovers at the engagement level derive from the provision of tax compliance, but NOT tax planning non-audit services.

RQ2: Does knowledge spillover across tax and audit service lines arise between clients of the same office and does it depend on the nature of tax service provided?

- Yes... High levels of office level tax compliance (but not planning) NAS is associated with improved audit quality.

RQ3: Do office-level tax compliance and tax planning NAS capture audit offices' allocation of resources and attention to the audit practice in ways that benefit or harm audit quality?

- High levels of office level tax planning NAS is associated with reduced audit quality.

3

The Tax NAS Debate

Continued regulatory/congressional/proxy advisor concerns surrounding tax NAS

- PCAOB Rule 3552 - prohibits audit firms from providing tax services that are related to the marketing, ***planning*** or opining in favour of transactions that would be considered aggressive tax position transactions
- Institutional Shareholder Services (ISS) - propose "withholding" auditor ratification and AC member vote if other non-audit fees (including fees paid for tax ***planning*** NAS) are excessive.
- Congressional (SEC) investigations regarding the tax ***planning*** services provided by PWC (EY) to Caterpillar (HP).

Practitioners contend that efficiencies and knowledge spillovers arise when both services are jointly provided.

- "We believe that a strong and leading-edge consulting practice makes us smarter — not only smarter as consultants, but also more knowledgeable as an overall firm regarding risks and challenges that affect our clients — audit and non-audit alike." – PWC 2014 Audit Quality Report

4

Northeastern University D'Amore-McKim School of Business

Engagement Level Tax NAS

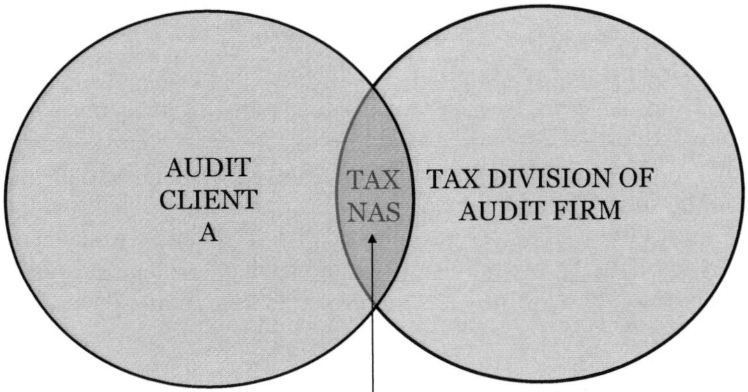

Kinney, Palmrose, and Scholz 2004; Paterson and Valencia 2011; Seetharaman, Sun, and Wang 2011; Gleason and Mills 2011; Krishnan, Visvanathan, and Yu 2013; Choudhary, Koester, and Pawlewicz 2014

Northeastern University D'Amore-McKim School of Business

Engagement Level Tax NAS

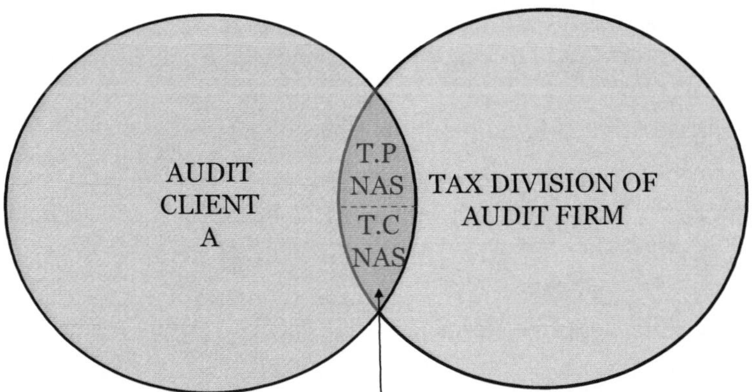

Paterson and Valencia (2011)
Recurring tax NAS (Tax Compliance NAS) ⇨ Lower likelihood of restatement
Non-recurring tax NAS (Tax Planning NAS)⇨ Higher likelihood of restatement

Northeastern University D'Amore-McKim School of Business

Hypothesis 1

Engagement Level Tax compliance NAS

More likely to yield knowledge spillovers

1. Provided by local audit office
2. Promotes continuous contact with client and audit team
3. Knowledge transfers are more likely to be unbiased, relevant, and high quality (cf. when knowledge is sourced from a third party)
4. Can better evaluate tax provisions, tax reserves, etc. but also...
5. Helps auditors to better understand corporate structure, state and federal NOLs, foreign divisions/subsidiaries, foreign tax credits, intercompany relationships, and information about specific accounts (i.e. capital expenditures and intangible assets)

H1: Engagement level tax compliance fees are positively associated with engagement level audit quality.

7

Northeastern University D'Amore-McKim School of Business

Hypothesis 2

Engagement Level Tax planning NAS

Could also lead to knowledge spillovers

Higher margin work could increase the cost of an audit failure (Gleason and Mills 2011)

Involved with less frequent interactions with clients

Deal with specific projects

Often outsourced from larger offices

Providers less likely to have accounting backgrounds (e.g. tax lawyers, transfer pricing economists)

Economic bonding concerns (if tax planning contracts more lucrative)

H2: Engagement level tax planning fees are not associated with engagement level audit quality.

8

Northeastern University D'Amore-McKim School of Business

Office Level Tax NAS

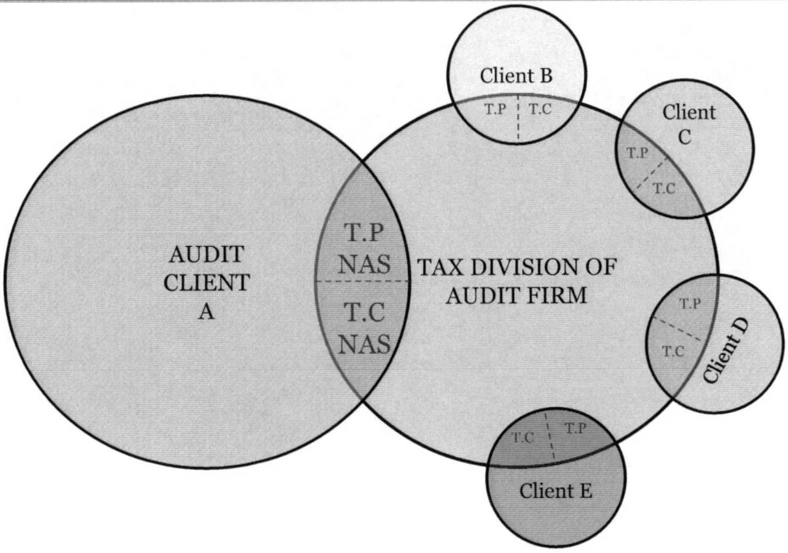

Northeastern University D'Amore-McKim School of Business

Office Level Tax NAS

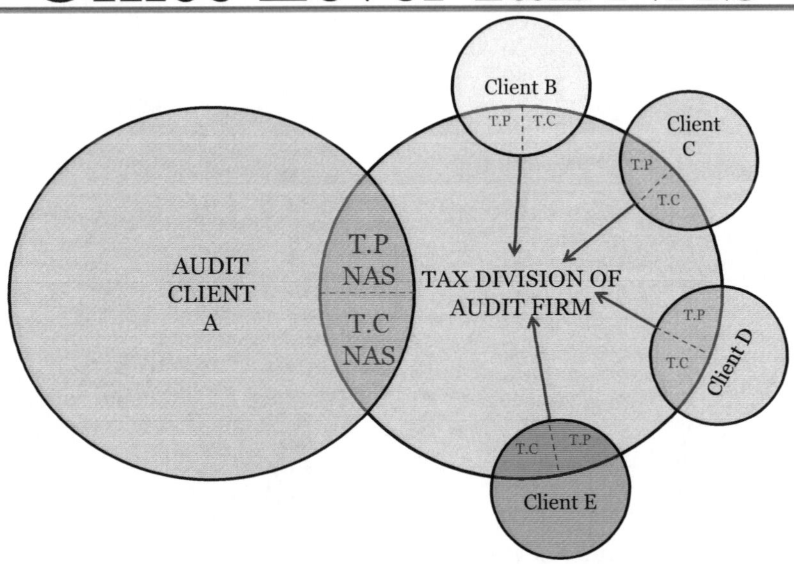

Northeastern University D'Amore-McKim School of Business

Office Level Tax NAS

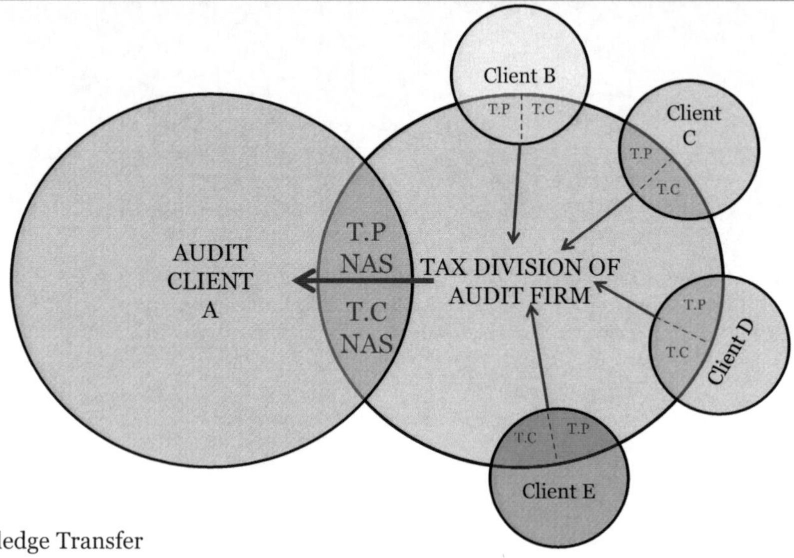

Knowledge Transfer

Northeastern University D'Amore-McKim School of Business

Office Level Tax NAS

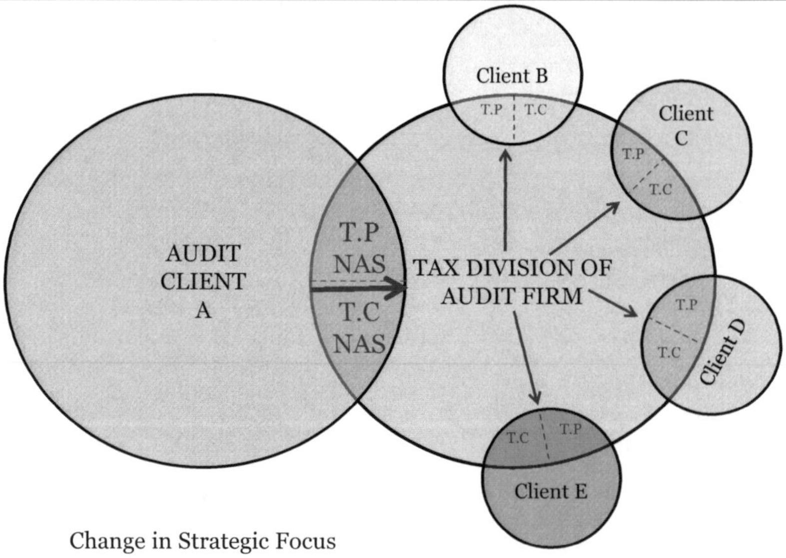

Change in Strategic Focus

Northeastern University D'Amore-McKim School of Business

Office Level Tax NAS

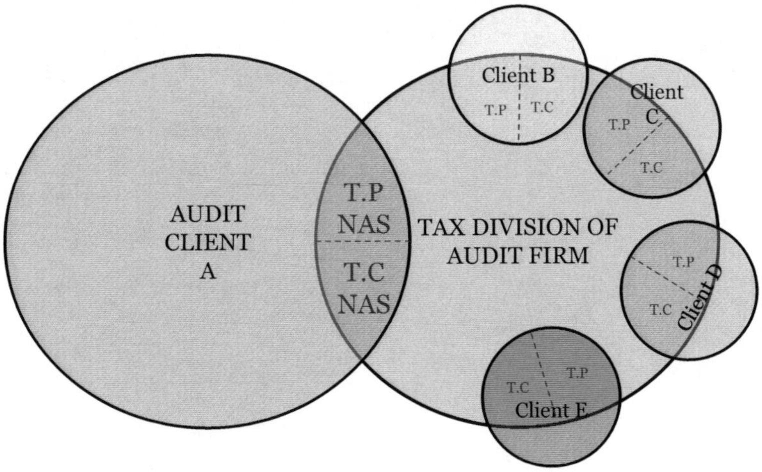

Audit Firm/Office
Culture Changes

Northeastern University D'Amore-McKim School of Business

Hypothesis 3 & 4

Office Knowledge sharing/spillover (O'Keefe et al. 1994, McGuire et al. 2012, Bianchi et al. 2014)

Shifts in strategic focus/culture Higher margin work (e.g., tax planning work) could lead to distractions from the audit and the audit firms "core values" – Former SEC Chief accountant (Paul Beswick), PCAOB Member (Steven Harris)
Beardsley et al. 2015 –Increased focus on NAS associated with an increased likelihood of misstatements (in the presence of fee pressure).

H3: Audit office level tax compliance NAS fees are positively associated with audit quality at the engagement level.

H4: Audit office level tax planning NAS fees are not associated with audit quality at the engagement level.

14

Northeastern University D'Amore-McKim School of Business

Sample Selection

Table 1 - Sample Selection

	Misstatement	Non-Misstatement[a]	Total
Initial firm-year observations from Audit Analytics and Compustat	2,058	24,332	26,390
Firm-year observations with missing variables	(410)	(6,642)	(7,052)
MSA requirement	(49)	(482)	(531)
Base Sample (2007-2011)	**1,599**	**17,208**	**18,807**

Firm-year observations with positive Tax NAS

1) No Disclosure of Tax Fee Breakdown	2) Disclose Tax Fee Breakdown	3) Firm-year observations with no Tax NAS
9,260	2,892	6,655

Final Sample

9,547

[a] - We require that non-misstatements firms do not restate their 2006-2012 financial statements

15

Northeastern University D'Amore-McKim School of Business

Research Design

$$RESTATE = \beta_0 + \beta_1 ENGAGE\_TAXCOMP\_RATIO + \beta_2 OFFICE\_TAXCOMP\_RATIO + \beta_3 ENGAGE\_TAXPLAN\_RATIO + \beta_4 OFFICE\_TAXPLAN\_RATIO + \beta_N Controls + \text{Industry F.E.} + \text{Year F.E.} + \varepsilon$$

H1 → β_1	(-)
H2 → β_2	(?)
H3 → β_3	(-)
H4 → β_4	(?)

16

Northeastern University | D'Amore-McKim School of Business

Table 3 – Primary Regressions

DV = *RESTATE*	Hypothesized Directional Expectation	(1)	(2)	(3)	(4)
ENG_TAXFEES	-	-0.789*	-1.182*		
		(-1.95)	(-1.71)		
ENG_TAXCOMP	-			-1.911**	-1.927**
				(-1.78)	(-1.80)
ENG_TAXPLAN	?			-0.089	-0.151
				(-0.07)	(-0.11)
OFF_TAXCOMP	-				-0.115**
					(-3.75)
OFF_TAXPLAN	?				0.108**
					(2.56)
ENG_LOG_AUDFEE	+	0.174**	0.052	0.053	0.059
		(2.39)	(0.56)	(0.57)	(0.62)
ENG_OTH_NAF	+	1.076***	1.327***	1.338***	1.372***
		(3.41)	(3.30)	(3.33)	(3.41)
OFF_LOG_AUDFEE	+				-0.017
					(-0.41)
OFF_OTH_NAF	+				-0.010
					(-1.03)
Other Controls		Yes	Yes	Yes	Yes
Industry and Year FE		Yes	Yes	Yes	Yes
Constant		-3.776***	-2.396**	-2.406**	-2.144*
		(-4.04)	(-2.09)	(-2.09)	(-1.78)
Observations		18807	9547	9547	9547
Pseudo R^2		0.023	0.023	0.023	0.028

A One Stddev increase in *ENG_TAXCOMP* is associated with an 8.73% reduction in misstatement likelihood

A One Stddev increase in *OFF_TAXCOMP* (*OFF_TAXPLAN*) is associated with an 16.78% reduction of (11.55% increase in) misstatement likelihood.

17

Northeastern University | D'Amore-McKim School of Business

Other Findings

1. The office-level results persist even for firms purchasing no tax NAS.
2. Results persist after controlling for the office-level propensity to disclose the tax fee breakdown.
3. Results persist after controlling for the decision to purchase tax NAS (Heckman two-stage analysis).
4. Changes in office-level tax compliance NAS immediately manifest in a lower likelihood of misstatement; Changes in office-level tax planning NAS gradually increase misstatement likelihood.
5. High levels of national-level tax planning NAS positively associated with misstatement likelihood.
6. The office level results are more prominent at the larger offices.
7. High office-level tax compliance is more strongly associated with errors rather than irregularities.

18

Northeastern University D'Amore-McKim School of Business

Conclusions

Insights into the Tax NAS debate

Compliance (not planning) drives the positive audit quality association

Office level effects matter

Beneficial knowledge sharing
Potential auditor distraction/culture

Regulator/legislator/proxy advisor concerns may be valid but...

Focus should be on the office, not engagement

19

Northeastern University D'Amore-McKim School of Business

Thank You

20

ENHANCING AUDIT QUALITY

A FOCUS ON PROFESSIONAL SKEPTICISM, QUALITY CONTROL AND GROUP AUDITS

IAASB International Auditing and Assurance Standards Board®

May 2016

IAASB International Auditing and Assurance Standards Board®

Beverley Bahlmann

IAASB Deputy Director

2

KEY PUBLIC INTEREST ISSUES TO ADDRESS

- The ISAs need to better address increasing complexity and new technologies in the business and audit environment, and deliver against the public's heightening expectations of audit quality
- The profile of tomorrow's auditor is to continue to be a critical challenger, supported by a regime focused on public interest and quality management, and well observable for stakeholders

3

WHY THE CONSULTATION?

IAASB ISA Implementation Monitoring Project

Ongoing Outreach

IAASB Strategy for 2015–2019 and Work Plan for 2015–2016

- Professional Skepticism
- Quality Control
- Group Audits

} ITC

- Financial Institutions / ISA 540 (accelerated timing)
- Audit Data Analytics (work commenced in 2015)
- ISA 315 (Revised) (work commenced in 2016)

IAASB International Auditing and Assurance Standards Board®

Professional Skepticism

IAASB International Auditing and Assurance Standards Board®

PROFESSIONAL SKEPTICISM: KEY QUESTIONS BEING CONSIDERED

- What is professional skepticism?
- What are the skills/competencies required to exercise PS?
- What are the impediments affecting the consistent application of PS?
- How can the concept of PS be emphasized in the context of the projects on quality control, group audits, and accounting estimates (ISA 540)?
- What other actions may be necessary by the IAASB / IAESB / IESBA ? Framework? Guidance? Training? .....

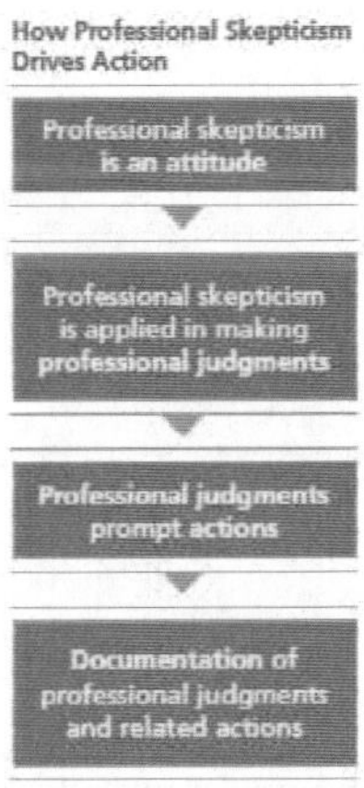

IAASB International Auditing and Assurance Standards Board®

PROFESSIONAL SKEPTICISM: QUESTIONS IN OVERVIEW

PS1. Is your interpretation of the concept of professional skepticism consistent with how it is defined and referred to in the ISAs? If not, how could the concept be better described?

PS2. What do you believe are the drivers for, and impediments to, the appropriate application of professional skepticism? What role should we take to enhance those drivers and address those impediments? How should we prioritize the areas discussed in paragraph 37?

PS3. What actions should others take to address the factors that inhibit the application of professional skepticism and the actions needed to mitigate them (e.g., the IAESB, the IESBA, other international or national standards setters, those charged with governance (including audit committee members), firms, or professional accountancy organizations)?

IAASB International Auditing and Assurance Standards Board®

Quality Control

IAASB International Auditing and Assurance Standards Board®

QUALITY CONTROL–QUALITY MANAGEMENT APPROACH

- Exploring a more proactive, scalable and robust response to managing quality:
  - More easily adaptable to rapidly changing business environment
  - Focus on monitoring and remediation – investigating root causes of identified deficiencies, reassessment of quality risks and implementing remedial actions
  - Emphasis on importance of firm governance, including leadership responsibilities for quality
  - Tone at the top – where is more emphasis needed?

IAASB International Auditing and Assurance Standards Board®

QUALITY CONTROL (cont.)

- Emphasis on importance of the role and responsibilities of the engagement partner
- Exploring transparency reporting trends, including feasibility of international requirements
- The impact on audit quality of evolving audit delivery models
- Involving other auditors that are not component auditors – is more guidance needed?
- Firms that operate as networks – are more requirements and guidance needed?
- Monitoring and remediation (including "root-cause" analysis)
- Engagement quality control reviews – reinforce importance and elevate prominence

IAASB International Auditing and Assurance Standards Board

QUALITY CONTROL – QUESTIONS IN OVERVIEW

QC1. We support a broader revision of ISQC 1 to include the use of a quality management approach (QMA) as described in paragraphs 51–66.

a) Would use of a QMA help to improve audit quality? If so why, and if not, why? What challenges might there be in restructuring ISQC 1 to facilitate this approach?

b) If ISQC 1 is restructured to require the firm's use of a QMA, in light of the objective of a QMA and the possible elements described in paragraph 65, are there other elements that should be included? If so, what are they?

c) In your view, how might a change to restructure ISQC 1 impact the ISAs, including those addressing quality control at the engagement level?

d) If ISQC 1 is not restructured to require the firm's use of a QMA, how can we address the call for improvements to the standard to deal with differences in the size and nature of a firm or the services it provides?

IAASB International Auditing and Assurance Standards Board

QUALITY CONTROL – QUESTIONS IN OVERVIEW

QC2. We are also thinking about revising our quality control standards to respond to specific issues about audit quality (see paragraphs 67–83).

a) Would the actions described in paragraphs 68–83 improve audit quality at the firm and engagement level? If not, why?

b) Should we take other actions in the public interest to address the issues in paragraphs 67–83?

c) Should we take action now to tackle other issues? If yes, please describe the actions, why they need priority attention, and the action we should take.

Group Audits

GROUP AUDITS – NEED FOR A FRESH LOOK?

- How to drive a "top-down" approach as groups become more complex and structures continue to evolve
- Focus on roles and responsibilities of the group engagement partner and group engagement team, including sufficient and appropriate involvement in component auditor's work
- Acceptance of a group audit (including access issues)
- Component materiality
- Work on components that are not significant
- Consolidation procedures
- Emphasis on importance of strong two-way communication between group engagement team and component auditors
- Requirements and guidance for component auditors?

IAASB International Auditing and Assurance Standards Board®

GROUP AUDITS – QUESTIONS IN OVERVIEW

GA1. We plan to revise ISA 600 (and other standards as appropriate) to respond to issues with group audits.

a) Should we increase the emphasis in ISA 600 on the need to apply all relevant ISAs in an audit of group financial statements? Will doing so help to achieve the flexibility that is needed to allow for ISA 600 to be more broadly applied and in a wide range of circumstances (see paragraphs 84–97)? If not, please explain why. What else could we do to address the issues set out in this consultation?

b) Would the actions we are exploring in relation to ISA 600 improve the quality of group audits? If not, why?

c) Should we further explore making reference to another auditor in an auditor's report? If yes, how does this impact the auditor's work effort?

d) What else could the IAASB do to address the issues highlighted or other issues of which you are aware? Why do these actions need priority attention?

IAASB International Auditing and Assurance Standards Board®

Wrap Up

IAASB International Auditing and Assurance Standards Board®

GENERAL QUESTIONS

G1. Table 1 describes what we believe are the most relevant public interest issues that should be addressed in the context of our projects on professional skepticism, quality control, and group audits. In that context:

a) Are these public interest issues relevant to our work on these topics?

b) Are there other public interest issues relevant to these topics? If so, please describe them and how, in your view, they relate to the specific issues identified.

c) Are there actions you think others need to take, in addition to those by the IAASB, to address the public interest issues identified in your previous answers? If so, what are they and please identify who you think should act.

G2. To assist with the development of future work plans, are there other issues and actions (not specific to the topics of professional skepticism, quality control, and group audits) that you believe should be taken into account? If yes, what are they and how should they be prioritized?

G3. Are you aware of any published, planned or ongoing academic research that may be relevant to the three topics discussed in this consultation? If so, please provide us with relevant details.

IAASB International Auditing and Assurance Standards Board®

WHERE TO NEXT?

- Jan–May 2016: Outreach (including events in Europe, Far East and USA)
- Comment period closed: **May 16, 2016**
- May–Dec 2016: Analysis of comments; IAASB and CAG discussions
- Dec 2016 IAASB meeting: Presentation of project proposals for Quality Control and Group Audits; discussion about way forward on Professional Skepticism
- 2017 onwards: Standard-setting activities – developing exposure drafts of changes to the ISAs and ISQC 1 for Quality Control and Group Audits

Other IAASB Projects

Auditor Reporting

- IAASB-supported efforts with objectives of
  - Promoting awareness of the standards
  - Informing and educating those who will use the auditor's reports
  - Opening a dialogue to learn about experiences of those responsible for adoption and implementation
  - Preparing for post-implementation review efforts
- www.iaasb.org/auditor-reporting
  - Auditor Reporting Fact Sheet and "At a Glance"
  - Basis for Conclusions
  - Publications on GC and KAM
  - Illustrative KAM examples

New and revised Auditor Reporting standards are effective for periods ending on or after December 15, 2016

IAASB International Auditing and Assurance Standards Board®

ISA 540 - Output to Date and Timeline

- Project proposal for holistic revision of ISA 540 approved in December 2015
- Published Project Update
  - Issued in early March 2016, includes material on audit issues regarding the move to Expected Credit Loss accounting
- Proposed project timeline
  - December 2016: Intended IAASB approval of exposure draft with 120-day comment period
  - 2017: IAASB deliberation of ED responses and IAASB CAG input
  - December 2017: Intended IAASB approval of ISA 540 (Revised)

IAASB International Auditing and Assurance Standards Board®

ISA 540 – Audit Challenges Identified

- Scope of the ISA
- Further emphasis needed on professional skepticism
- Risk assessment procedures and related activities
- Identification and assessment of risks of material misstatement
- Responses to assessed risks of material misstatement
- Other considerations
  - Disclosure considerations
  - Auditor reporting implications
  - Using the work of others (experts, third party data sources)

IAASB International Auditing and Assurance Standards Board

Other IAASB Projects

- NOCLAR
- ISA 315 (Revised)
- Agreed Upon Procedures
- Data Analytics
- Integrated Reporting

- Innovation – continuous monitoring of environment
- IASB Liaison – monitoring accounting standards

IAASB International Auditing and Assurance Standards Board

Looking Ahead: Our Work Plan for 2017–2018

- Most of our current projects and initiatives will continue beyond 2016 – assuming they all continue, no room for any new initiatives of substance
- Limited consultation to gather specific input, while laying out key milestones for current initiatives and capacity
- Survey
- To be issued in July 2016 with a 90-day comment period
- ITC also asked a specific question about whether other actions beyond those addressing professional skepticism, quality control and group audits are needed to enhanced audit quality
- Finalization of 2017–2018 Work Plan in December 2016

IAASB®

www.iaasb.org/focus-audit-quality

Integration of Internal Control and Financial Statement Audits: Are Two Audits Better than One?

Lori Bhaskar, Joe Schroeder, and Marcy Shepardson

Joe Schroeder
KU Audit Symposium
May 21, 2016

KELLEY SCHOOL OF BUSINESS
INDIANA UNIVERSITY

Research Question

Does having an audit of internal controls that is integrated with the financial statement audit affect financial statement audit quality?

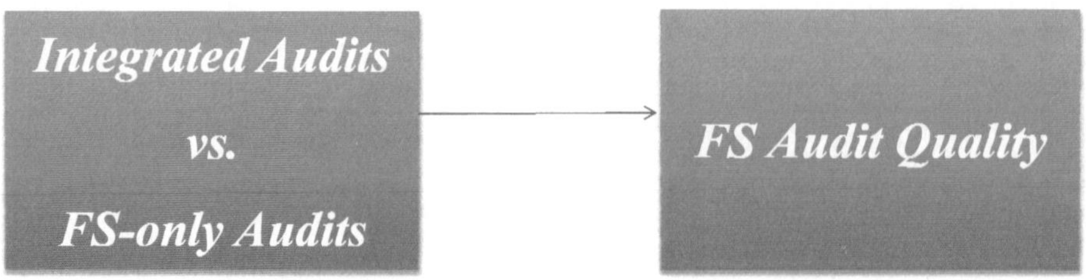

The Audit Risk Model (Rewritten)

$$DR = \frac{AR}{[IR * CR]}$$

- The ARM is a model, comprised of estimates, and therefore is assessed with error, such that frequently,

***Achieved Audit Risk** (**AAR**) ≠ **Planned Audit Risk** (**PAR**)*

- Audit quality concerns relate to potential that the auditor has not achieved the acceptably low level of AR that they planned

Achieved Audit Risk (AAR) > Planned audit risk (PAR)

Integration of ICFR and FS Audits: Theoretical Benefits

ICFR Audit ⟷ ***FS Audit***

- Increased precision of CR assessment
- More accurately integrate CR assessment into ARM
- Substantive procedures more effective reducing DR
- Achieved vs. planned Audit risk will be lower

Therefore, higher financial statement audit quality!

Integration of ICFR and FS Audits: Concerns

ICFR Audit ⟷ *FS Audit*

Over-reliance

- Insufficient ICFR testing to justify CR assessment
- Insufficient substantive procedures to achieve calculated DR

Low quality ICFR audits

- Inaccurately low CR assessment having adverse effects on ARM

Therefore, lower financial statement audit quality!

KELLEY SCHOOL OF BUSINESS

H1: There are no differences in FS Audit Quality between Integrated and FS-only Audits

INDIANA UNIVERSITY

KELLEY SCHOOL OF BUSINESS

ICFR Over-reliance and FS Audit Quality

- FS-Only Audits
  - ICFR testing is optional based on efficiency vs. effectiveness trade-offs
  - Prior to SOX many FS audits did not rely on ICFR (Graham 2015)
- ICFR and FS Integrated Audits
  - Required to test ICFR operating effectiveness (PCAOB 2007)
  - Incentives to rely on internal controls
- Control over-reliance more likely for clients subject to ICFR and FS audits

INDIANA UNIVERSITY

KELLEY SCHOOL OF BUSINESS

ICFR Over-reliance and FS Audit Quality

Top-down risk based approach under AS5 may lead to over-reliance

- Auditors likely to place greater reliance on entity level controls
- Less controls on more precise process level controls that likely prevent and detect misstatements
- Improper identification of the top-down ICFR approach identified by PCAOB as a root cause of audit deficiencies (PCAOB 2012)

INDIANA UNIVERSITY

KELLEY SCHOOL OF BUSINESS

ICFR Over-reliance and FS Audit Quality

1) Auditors may have difficulty assessing CR or performing sufficient control testing to support their CR assessment

Inappropriately rely on ICFR resulting in insufficient substantive testing

PCAOB 2015 Inspection Observations for Risk Assessment

"firms did not perform sufficient testing of the design and operating effectiveness of controls to support their planned level of control reliance"

INDIANA UNIVERSITY

KELLEY SCHOOL OF BUSINESS

ICFR Over-reliance and FS Audit Quality

2) Irrespective of CR assessment precision, auditors *may perform insufficient substantive procedures* to achieve calculated DR

Experimental Research on Risk Assessment

- Auditors fail to adequately adjust substantive procedures when RMM increases (Mock and Wright 1993; 1999; Glover et al. 2000; Johnstone and Bedard 2001)
- Substantive procedures are not appropriately risk adjusted (Allen et al. 2006; Asare et al. 2013)

INDIANA UNIVERSITY

KELLEY SCHOOL OF BUSINESS

ICFR Over-reliance and FS Audit Quality

Archival Research: MW => Lower FS Quality

- Suggests that auditors fail to adjust detection risk in response to known material weaknesses (Doyle et al. 2007; Ashbaugh-Skaife 2008)
- Hogan and Wilkins (2008) imply that auditors should increase substantive testing in response to control risk

PCAOB 2015 Inspection Observations for Risk Assessment

- Audit opinions not adequately supported due to deficiencies in auditor's risk assessments in 26 and 27 percent of 2013 and 2014 inspections, respectively

INDIANA UNIVERSITY

KELLEY SCHOOL OF BUSINESS

H2: There are no differences in FS Audit Quality between Integrated and FS-only Audits **due to over-reliance issues**

INDIANA UNIVERSITY

KELLEY SCHOOL OF BUSINESS

Low Quality ICFR Audits and FS Audit Quality

Low quality ICFR audits lead to inaccurate CR assessments resulting in inappropriate audit response.

PCAOB findings

- PCAOB Staff Audit Practice Alert No. 11 highlights auditors' failure to sufficiently test and evaluate ICFR (PCAOB 2013)
- Inspection findings for 2010 and 2011 suggest 15 and 22 percent of inspected ICFR audits failed, respectively (PCAOB 2012)

INDIANA UNIVERSITY

KELLEY SCHOOL OF BUSINESS

Low Quality ICFR Audits and FS Audit Quality

Recent Academic Studies

- 68 percent of restatement firms did not have ex ante MW disclosure (Rice and Webber 2012)
- Lower MW disclosure rate is due to underassessment (Ge et al. 2016)
- IC and FR quality is lower under AS5 vs. AS2 (Acito et al. 2016; Schroeder and Shepardson 2016)

INDIANA UNIVERSITY

H3: Integrated audits with **low quality ICFR audits** have *lower* FS audit quality compared to FS-only audits

– Incremental to over-reliance effect

Sample, DV and IV

- Firm years 2007 to 2012 (Compustat and Audit Analytics)
- Integrated audit measure
  - Accelerated filers: ICFR and FS audits
  - Non-accelerated filers: FS-only audits
- Financial Statement Audit Quality Measures
  - Material Misstatements (8-K Item 4.02 from AA)
  - Misstatements (from AA excluding non-technical, leases and option back dating
  - Absolute value of discretionary accruals (Kothari et al. 2005)
- Restrict to MVE < $150 million for comparability

ICFR Audit Quality Classifications

$$
\begin{aligned}
MW_{i,t} = {} & \beta_0 + \beta_1 LNMVE_{i,t} + \beta_2 LNAGE_{i,t} + \beta_3 LNBSEG_{i,t} + \\
& \beta_4 FOREIGN_{i,t} + \beta_5 M\&A_{i,t} + \beta_6 RESTRUCTURE_{i,t} + \\
& \beta_7 ARINV_{i,t} + \beta_8 AGROWTH_{i,t} + \beta_9 CFO_{i,t} + \\
& \beta_{10} LOSS_{i,t} + \beta_{11} MBR_{i,t} + \beta_{12} LIT_{i,t} + \beta_{13} BIGN_{i,t} + \\
& \beta_{14} AUD\_RESIGN_{i,t} + \beta_{15} ANC\_RST_{i,t} + \beta_{16} PY\_MW_{i,t} + \\
& \beta_{17} INTEGRATED_{i,t} + \text{Industry Fixed Effects} + \varepsilon_{i,t}
\end{aligned}
$$

Estimation process

- MW represents 302, 404(a) and 404(b) disclosures
- Estimated by year for a pooled sample of all filers
- Sensitivity vs. specificity cut-offs
- Classify based on predicted vs. actual MW disclosure

ICFR Audit Quality Classifications

FIGURE 1
Low vs. High-Quality ICFR Disclosures

Expected \ Reported	At least one Material Weakness Disclosed	No Material Weaknesses Disclosed
At Least One Material Weakness Expected	1. High-quality Adverse ICFR Disclosure	2. Low-quality Unqualified ICFR Disclosure "Type II ICFR Disclosure Error"
No Material Weaknesses Expected	3. Low-quality Adverse ICFR Disclosure "Type I ICFR Disclosure Error"	4. High-quality Unqualified ICFR Disclosure

Multivariate Models

Test of H1 and predicted vs. actual MW classification analyses

FS Audit Quality Measures = $\beta_0 + \beta_1 INTEGRATED + \beta$'s(Controls) + auditor indicators + year indicators + industry indicators + ε

Test of H2 and H3

FS Audit Quality Measures = $\beta_0 + \beta_1 INTEGRATED + \beta_2 INT*ICAQ\_L2 + \beta$'s(Controls) + auditor indicators + year indicators + industry indicators + ε

Univariate Statistics

	Integrated Audit Observations		FS-only Audit Observations	
	Mean	Median	Mean	Median
MAT_MISSTATE	0.046*	0.000*	0.035	0.000
MISSTATE	0.088*	0.000*	0.066	0.000
Sample Size	2,385		7,320	
ABSDCACC	0.172	0.087	0.238*	0.113*
Sample Size	2,203		5,442	

KELLEY SCHOOL OF BUSINESS

H1: Comparison of Integrated vs. FS-only Audits

	Pred. Sign	Material Misstatement Coef. (p-value)	Misstatement Coef. (p-value)	Discretionary Accruals Coef. (p-value)
INTEGRATED	**+**	**0.4134*** **	**0.5792*** **	**0.0291*** **
		(0.000)	**(0.002)**	**(0.000)**
Controls, Audit, Year and Industry Ind.		Yes	Yes	Yes
N/ROC /Adj. R^2		9,705/0.733	9,705/0.700	7,645/0.303

Integrated audits have lower FS audit quality
(99.3% higher likelihood of material misstatement)

INDIANA UNIVERSITY

KELLEY SCHOOL OF BUSINESS

H2 (over-reliance effect) and H3 (low quality ICFR effect)

	Pred. Sign	Material Misstatement Coef. (p-value)	Misstatement Coef. (p-value)	Discretionary Accruals Coef. (p-value)
INTEGRATED	**+**	**0.7248*** **	**0.4641*** **	**0.0306*** **
		(0.000)	**(0.001)**	**(0.000)**
INT * ICAQ_L2	**+**	**0.4782*** **	**0.3727*** **	**0.0224** **
		(0.007)	**(0.004)**	**(0.010)**
Controls, Aud, Year and Industy indicators		Yes	Yes	Yes
N/ROC/Adj. R2		9,705/0.735	9,705/0.700	7,645/0.304

Lower FS audit quality due to over-reliance main effect and incremental effect of low quality ICFR audits

Misstatement likelihood: 106.4% main effect and 61.3% incremental effect

INDIANA UNIVERSITY

KELLEY SCHOOL OF BUSINESS

Comparison Across Predicted vs. Actual MW Classifications (DV = Material Misstatements)

		High Quality ICFR Disclosures		Low Quality ICFR Disclosures	
	Pred. Sign	E(MW)=1 vs. MW=1	E(MW)=0 vs. MW=0	E(MW)=1 vs. MW=0	E(MW)=0 vs. MW=1
INTEGRATED	+	**0.5182***	**0.6602****	**0.9118****	**1.5743*****
		(0.070)	**(0.030)**	**(0.031)**	**(0.004)**
Controls, Audit Ind., Year Ind., and Industry Ind.		Yes	Yes	Yes	Yes
N		2,749	4,813	1,659	484
ROC		0.727	0.772	0.765	0.863

INDIANA UNIVERSITY

KELLEY SCHOOL OF BUSINESS

Comparison Across Predicted vs. Actual MW Classifications (DV = Misstatements)

		High Quality ICFR Disclosures		Low Quality ICFR Disclosures	
	Pred. Sign	E(MW)=1 vs. MW=1	E(MW)=0 vs. MW=0	E(MW)=1 vs. MW=0	E(MW)=0 vs. MW=1
INTEGRATED	+	**0.4134***	**0.1897**	**0.5792***	**1.0903****
		(0.073)	**(0.373)**	**(0.050)**	**(0.016)**
Controls, Audit Ind., Year Ind., and Industry Ind.		Yes	Yes	Yes	Yes
N		2,749	4,813	1,659	484
ROC		0.711	0.736	0.732	0.773

INDIANA UNIVERSITY

KELLEY SCHOOL OF BUSINESS

Comparison Across Predicted vs. Actual MW Classifications (DV = Absolute Value of Discretionary Accruals)

		High Quality ICFR Disclosures		Low Quality ICFR Disclosures	
	Pred. Sign	E(MW)=1 vs. MW=1	E(MW)=0 vs. MW=0	E(MW)=1 vs. MW=0	E(MW)=0 vs. MW=1
INTEGRATED	+	**0.0402***	**0.0268*****	**0.0557****	**-0.0115**
		(0.087)	**(0.001)**	**(0.012)**	**(0.765)**
Controls, Audit Ind., Year Ind., and Industry Ind.		Yes	Yes	Yes	Yes
N		1,745	4,303	1,206	391
Adj. R^2		0.279	0.230	0.321	0.302

INDIANA UNIVERSITY

KELLEY SCHOOL OF BUSINESS

Additional Analyses

- Match on MVE, Industry and Year
- Pre-integrated audit period (2001 to 2003)
- Announced restatements opposed to misstatements

Results are consistent with our primary analyses and predictions

INDIANA UNIVERSITY

KELLEY SCHOOL OF BUSINESS

In Summary

- FS audit quality is *lower* for Integrated vs. FS-Only audits
- Due to *over-reliance issues* resulting in poor integration and risk assessment
- Incremental effect of *low quality ICFR* audits
- Another potential cost of integrated ICFR and FS audits
- PCAOB and audit firms should continue to focus on ways to improve the integration of ICFR and FS audits to achieve a higher quality outcome

INDIANA UNIVERSITY

KELLEY SCHOOL OF BUSINESS

THANK YOU

INDIANA UNIVERSITY

THE GRESHAM'S LAW OF MEASUREMENT AND THE PCAOB AUDIT QUALITY INDICATORS PROJECT

Sri Ramamoorti

Associate Professor, School of Accountancy
Member, PCAOB Standing Advisory Group

University of Kansas/Deloitte Auditing Symposium
May 20-21, 2016

Kennesaw State University

Dedication: Arthur R. Wyatt

This presentation is dedicated to Dr. Arthur R. Wyatt, retired Arthur Andersen & Co. partner, former AAA President and Chairman, International Accounting Standards Committee, and member, Ohio State University Accounting Hall of Fame.

Art was my faculty mentor at the University of Illinois at Urbana-Champaign; this dedication is meant as an expression of my gratitude for his sagacious guidance over the years.

Kennesaw State University

DISCLAIMER

The views in this presentation are my own and should not be attributed to, nor assumed endorsed by, the PCAOB or the PCAOB Standing Advisory Group of which I am a current member.

Kennesaw State UNIVERSITY

Overview

- Significance of PCAOB's AQI project
- Philosophy of Science type critique
- Gresham's law of measurement
- Concepts: information integrity, feedback vs. measurement, static vs. dynamic, lookback/forward measures
- AQIs in PCAOB Concept Release (7/1/15) and some observations
- Audience Q&A

Kennesaw State UNIVERSITY

Significance of AQI Project

History: Goes back to recommendations of the Advisory Committee for the Auditing Profession (ACAP) of the U.S. Treasury Department

Addresses two gaps simultaneously:

The expectations gap: "difference between what users expect from the auditor and the financial statement audit, and the reality of what an audit is." (IAASB, 2012)

The information gap: "the existence of a gap between the information they [users] believe is needed to make informed investment and fiduciary decisions, and what is available to them through the entity's audited financial statements or other publicly available information." (ibid.)

Shakespeare on "bad news"

- ***Cleopatra:*** Horrible villain! or I'll spurn thine eyes
Like balls before me; I'll unhair thy head:
Thou shalt be whipp'd with wire, and stew'd in brine
Smarting in lingering pickle.

- ***Messenger:*** Gracious madam, I that do bring the news made not the match.

- ***Cleopatra:*** Though it be honest, ***it is never good to bring bad news.***

--from Antony and Cleopatra, Act 2, Scene v. (*emphasis* added)

Philosophical Critique

* It is the mark of maturity of a profession to have the ability to do soul searching...(Sigmund Koch, 1985)

* Because of the significance of the AQI project, it is appropriate to offer a well-reasoned critique, in the hope that this will stimulate further thought and result in better outcomes for all concerned

- Agree with "AQIs + context = Insight" characterization
- Goal: Replacement, modification, supplementing, and/or amplification of proposed AQIs in the PCAOB Concept Release dated July 1, 2015

Quantitative bias

U Chicago Richard Posner's question: "What do judges and justices maximize?" very different from the "profit maximization" criterion

"Its objectives are simply stated: **to identify a portfolio of quantitative measures** of public company auditing (called "indicators"), whose consistent use may enhance dialogue about and understanding of audits and ways to evaluate their quality..." (PCAOB, 2015, emphasis added)

Quantitative measures to evaluate quality? Sounds like "squaring the circle"...proven impossible in 1882.

Gresham's Law of Measurement

- **Gresham's law** – "Bad money drives good money out of circulation." Named for Sir Thomas Gresham (1519–1579) because he urged Queen Elizabeth I to restore the debased currency of England.

Gresham's Law of Measurement

"Easy-to-calculate quantitative metrics tend to crowd out more relevant but difficult-to-measure assessments."

Bias towards "portfolio of quantitative factors..."

Kennesaw State University

Principle of the Drunkard's Search

The Streetlight Effect--

"A policeman sees a drunk man searching for something under a streetlight and asks what the drunk has lost. He says he lost his keys and they both look under the streetlight together. After a few minutes the policeman asks if he is sure he lost them here, and the drunk replies, no, that he lost them in the park. The policeman asks why he is searching here, and the drunk replies, "this is where the light is."" (Freedman, 2010).

Kennesaw State University

Information integrity

"The accuracy, consistency, and reliability of information across content, process, system, and environment." (definition provided by the now defunct Information Integrity Coalition)

Three dimensions: Usability, Integrity, and Usefulness

But without integrity, the other two do not matter!

(GIGO: you can't make a good omelet out of bad eggs)

Kennesaw State University

Feedback versus Measurement

Feedback	**Measurement**
Context dependent	One size fits all, standardized
Self-determined; the system chooses what to notice	Imposed. Criteria are established externally.
Information accepted from anywhere	Information in fixed categories only
System creates own meaning	Meaning is pre-determined
Newness, surprise are essential	Prediction, routine are valued
Focus on adaptability and growth	Focus on stability and control
Meaning evolves	Meaning remains static
System co-adapts	System adapts to the measures

Kennesaw State University

Version of Gresham's Law

Where a tourist yells louder, hoping he'll be understood…(may be true, perhaps, if the local is slightly deaf)

"You cannot audit better than a client's environment will allow" (S. Marcello, KPMG)

INPUTS re process/oversight: Important to look at financial reporting supply chain and their contributions in RRT financial statements

Poor AC can have a pervasive impact on audit quality, but this is not factored in

Kennesaw State UNIVERSITY

Suggested Definition of Audit Quality

The quality of a specific audit (the primary focus of an audit committee and of investors) is best measured by the likelihood that it will detect and dispose of material errors in the financial statements (including disclosures).

This, in turn, is a function of the proper application of audit procedures (including assessment of findings) and the proper handling of the results of those assessments.

This is the best definition of "audit quality" and should be the ultimate objective.

(Comments by Phil Wedemeyer)

Kennesaw State UNIVERSITY

Suggested Definition of Audit Quality

An audit firm's processes and procedures and business model determine its capability and willingness to perform specific audits of an acceptable quality. I suppose you could call this the "quality of the firm's processes."

o Putting this together as an audit committee chair, my primary focus is on the specific engagement team assigned to my work and how they do their work.

(Comments by Phil Wedemeyer)

Describe the difference between "audit quality" (firm-level, macro-indicator) and a "quality audit" (engagement-level, micro-indicator)

Kennesaw State UNIVERSITY

Auditor Independence and Skepticism

Technical compliance with independence rules may not speak to challenging issues like:

- The auditor's willingness to act in the public interest (cf. Coffee, 2006)
- Exercising a high degree of professional skepticism when called for
- Process of audit being ill-understood, and what happens behind closed doors is critical
- Qualitative factors...

Kennesaw State UNIVERSITY

Staffing leverage, partner workload, etc.

Even if all competent resources are available, audit quality may still be elusive…

The "knowing-doing" gap, what anthropologists refer to as the distinction between "cultural competence" and "cultural performance"

You can take a horse to the water, but you cannot make it drink…

Performance is a function of expectations, and where there exists an "expectations gap"…?

Kennesaw State UNIVERSITY

Tone at the Top and Leadership

FRB NY William Dudley on Wall Street culture https://www.newyorkfed.org/newsevents/speeches/2014/dud141020a.html

Notoriously difficult to measure and evaluate

Perhaps PCAOB's "root cause analysis" and "firm quality control systems" projects will shed further light on questions related to firm culture and communication of core values.

Kennesaw State UNIVERSITY

Incentives: Quality ratings & compensation

Within the firm, incentives are important, but are the distribution of quality ratings among personnel indicative of the intrinsic quality of the personnel?

We are measuring one thing in hopes of learning about something entirely different…cf. Steve Kerr's (1985) classic paper,

"On the folly of rewarding A while hoping for B"

Kennesaw State University

Conclusion…1

Winnow down number of AQIs

Have both quantitative and qualitative factors

Provide safe harbors where appropriate

Track and monitor progress (static vs. dynamic measures), look-forward/lookback approach

Be vigilant about gaming behaviors, esp. in future periods when firms are familiar with potentially manipulable AQI metrics

Kennesaw State University

Conclusion…2

Engage with Audit Committees

Emergence of non-GAAP measures

Root-cause analysis and quality control projects undertaken by PCAOB must continue to inform AQI initiative

This is a continuing journey, but perhaps there are mileposts and markers that must be devised to measure progress

Overall, there is no question that:

AQIs + Context = Insight

Kennesaw State UNIVERSITY

Allies in the Break Room: The Effect of Accounting Alumni on Auditor Choice and the Hiring Agenda

Presented by Nam Ho
Joint with Andrew Bird and Thomas Ruchti

Tepper School of Business
Carnegie Mellon University

Research Question and Results

- Research Questions:
  - How do firms choose between similar auditors?
  - Do firms prefer auditors from whom they have more alumni? (Familiar auditors)
  - Do firms adjust their hiring practices based on their chosen auditor?
- Key Results:
  - Firms show a strong preference for auditors that they have more alumni from
  - Firms adjust their hiring agenda in favor of the incoming auditor after making a switch

Incentives

- Why might a firm choose to hire/hire from their external auditor based on their employees' alumni affiliations?
  - Pros: Trust (Lennox 2005), efficiency (Bird et al. 2016), reputation
  - Cons: Potential independence concerns, shareholder and public skepticism (Menon and Williams 2004; Naiker and Sharma 2009)

Data

- Sample consists of S&P 1500 companies audited by one of the Big 4 during the period of 2009-2013
- Sample contains biographical data on accounting employees working within these firms

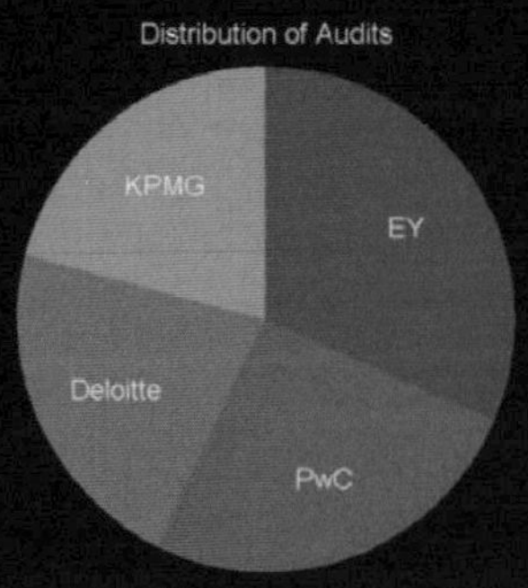

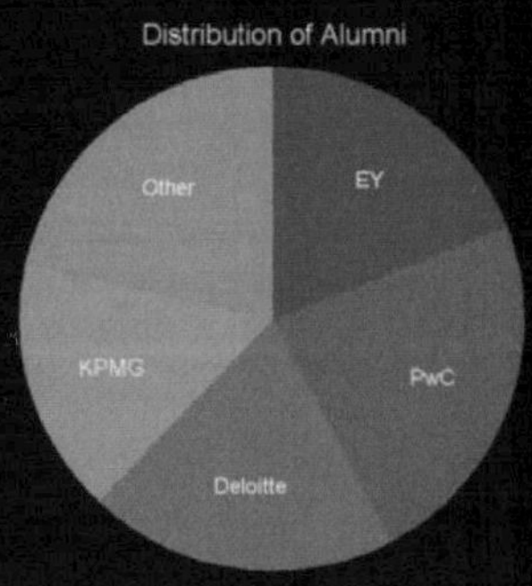

Hypotheses and Testing Methodology

- Hypothesis 1: *Firms prefer auditors from whom they have more alumni*

$$CHOICE = \beta_0 + \beta_1 xxRATE + CONTROLS\_xx + \varepsilon$$

  - Grouped, auditor specific, and multinomial logit
  - *CHOICE* is an indicator variable for if the *xx* auditor is chosen
  - *xxRATE* is the proportion of accounting employees at the firm that are alumni of auditor *xx*

- Controls include specialization indicators, affiliated CFO indicators, firm size, and leverage ratios

Mean Alumni Rates

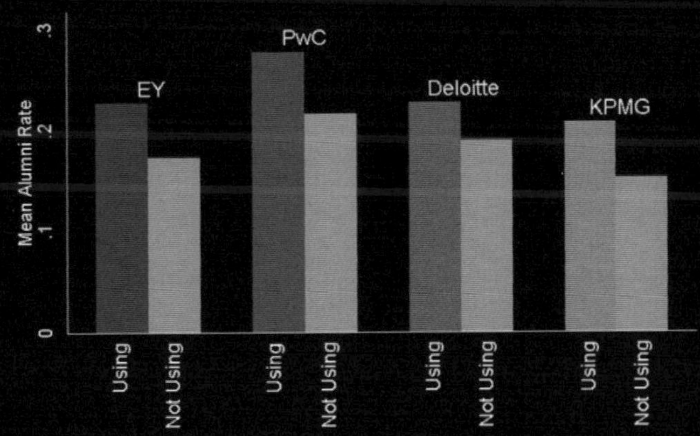

- Each of the Big 4 have a higher mean alumni rate at firms who employ them as their external auditor

Distribution of Alumni Rates

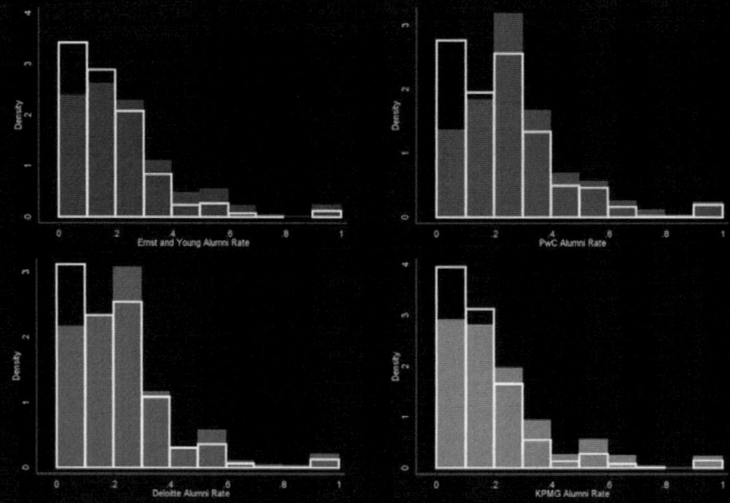

- Each of the Big 4 have a larger density of high alumni rate firms using their services (colored bars) than not (clear bars)

Auditor Choice: Grouped and Auditor Specific Logit

VARIABLES	Expected Sign	(1) *CHOICE*	(2) *EY*	(3) *PWC*	(4) *DELOITTE*	(5) *KPMG*
xxRATE	+	0.266***	0.333***	0.291***	0.178***	0.221***
		(8.655)	(5.384)	(5.658)	(3.360)	(4.278)
SPECIALIST_xx	+	0.160***	0.121***	0.144***	0.185***	0.190***
		(12.010)	(5.324)	(5.936)	(6.868)	(7.212)
CFO_xx	+	0.127***	0.140***	0.095	0.127***	0.124***
		(6.044)	(3.485)	(1.494)	(3.327)	(3.358)
LAT	?		-0.004	0.023***	-0.002	-0.016**
			(-0.457)	(2.986)	(-0.351)	(-2.240)
DEBTASSETS	?		-0.095	-0.099*	0.102**	0.038
			(-1.541)	(-1.684)	(2.071)	(0.735)
Constant		-0.306***	-0.226***	-0.434***	-0.319***	-0.181***
		(-43.083)	(-3.495)	(-7.534)	(-5.638)	(-3.523)
Observations		28,104	7,026	7,026	7,026	7,026

Clustered z-statistics in parentheses
*** $p<0.01$, ** $p<0.05$, * $p<0.1$

Auditor Choice: Partitioned

- Partitioned by median number of accounting employees

VARIABLES	Expected Sign	ABOVE MEDIAN (1) CHOICE	EQUAL TO OR BELOW MEDIAN (2) CHOICE
xxRATE	+	0.515***	0.222***
		(6.798)	(6.829)
Controls		Included	Included

Clustered z-statistics in parentheses
*** p<0.01, ** p<0.05, * p<0.1

- This result does not replicate when partitioning by firm size, organizational complexity, or corporate governance

Switches

VARIABLES	Expected Sign	ORIGINAL SAMPLE (1) SWITCH	EXTENDED SAMPLE (2) SWITCH
TOPRATE_xx	+	0.061	0.070***
		(1.417)	(2.661)
SPECIALIST_xx	+	0.072	0.071
		(1.298)	(1.309)
CFO_xx	+	0.280***	0.272***
		(2.743)	(2.692)
Constant		-0.275***	-0.296***
		(-11.059)	(-12.456)
Observations		410	1,418

Clustered z-statistics/chi-square in parentheses
*** p<0.01, ** p<0.05, * p<0.1

- Firms factor in their current employees when switching, this result replicates if alumni rate is used

The Hiring Agenda

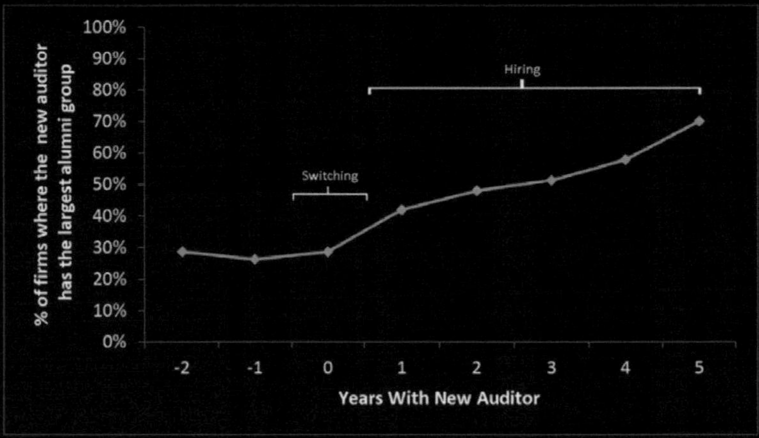

Conclusion

- Firms show a strong preference for auditors from which they have more alumni, both during switches and in the cross-section
- Firms adjust their hiring agenda in favor of the incoming auditor after a switch
- Implications:
    - Audit quality
    - Auditor growth
        - Firm culture

Audit Committee Influence on Audit Firm Selection and Retention

Brant Christensen – University of Missouri
Thomas Omer – University of Nebraska
Marjorie Shelley – University of Nebraska
Paul Wong – University of California, Davis

Background and Motivation

- Sarbanes-Oxley
  - Requires audit committees to be fully independent and have at least one financial expert.
  - Charges audit committee with hiring, oversight, and evaluation of external auditor.
- We know very little about how audit committees interact with the external auditor (Center for Audit Quality 2013; DeFond and Zhang 2014).
- Prior research focuses primarily on the role of management in the audit firm selection process (Beck and Mauldin 2014; Dhaliwal et al. 2015; Lennox and Park 2007).

Robert J. Trulaske, Sr.
College of Business
University of Missouri–Columbia

Research Questions

- Do affiliations between the audit committee and the audit firm affect:
  - Which audit firm is hired?
  - How long the firm is retained?
  - Audit timeliness and fees?

Robert J. Trulaske, Sr.
College of Business
University of Missouri–Columbia

Audit Firm Selection

- Attraction-Selection-Attrition theory
  - Employees are attracted to and are more frequently hired by companies perceived as a good "fit" (Schneider 1987; Schneider et al. 1995).
- Former partners may be inclined to benefit their former employer, albeit subconsciously (Iyer et al. 1997).
- *Management* with Big N experience more likely to hire their former firm (Lennox and Park 2007; Dhaliwal et al. 2015).
- H1: Companies with a former audit partner on the audit committee are more likely to hire that committee member's former firm as the external auditor.

Robert J. Trulaske, Sr.
College of Business
University of Missouri–Columbia

Audit Firm Evaluation

- Audit firms are evaluated negatively following restatements, overly conservative reporting, or high fees (Hennes et al. 2013, DeFond and Subramanyam 1998, Ettredge et al. 2007).
- Employer-employee "fit" reduces attrition.
- A committee member's former employment at the firm increases knowledge of the firm. Teams with similar backgrounds and work experience communicate more effectively (Pfeffer 1983).

- H2: Companies with a former audit partner on the audit committee are less likely to switch from that committee member's former firm as the external auditor.

Robert J. Trulaske, Sr.
College of Business
University of Missouri–Columbia

Audit Processes

- Having a former partner on the audit committee brings insights that may improve the efficiency of the audit.
  - H3: Affiliated audit committees are associated with shorter audit report lags.
- Affiliated partners may subconsciously seek to enrich former firm, but are also required to be independent and serve on behalf of shareholders.
  - H4: Affiliated audit committees are not associated with higher or lower audit fees.
- Affiliated partners are more familiar with the audit methodologies and can help improve overall audit quality.

Robert J. Trulaske, Sr.
College of Business
University of Missouri–Columbia

Sample

- Use BoardEx to identify audit committee members who were partners at a Big 4 firm.
  - More stringent than prior literature that allowed for any employment.
- Financial statement data from Compustat
- Audit data from Audit Analytics
- Final sample of 22,290 Big 4 client-year observations from 2004-2012.

Robert J. Trulaske, Sr.
College of Business
University of Missouri–Columbia

Methodology: Audit Firm Selection

$$CHG2BIGN_{t+1,t+5} = \beta_0 + \beta_1 AC\_BIGN_{it} + \beta_2 MGMT\_BIGN_{it} + Controls + Year\ Fixed\ Effects + \varepsilon$$

- Estimated for each firm individually (Lennox and Park 2007)
- Each subsample contains observations *not* audited by the firm in *t*, but that change firms in the next five years.
- Example
  - PwC subsample contains all non-PwC clients in year t that change firms in the next five years.
  - CHG2PWC equal to 1 if company changes to PwC in the next five years, 0 otherwise.
  - AC_BIGN equal to 1 if the AC has a former PwC partner, 0 otherwise.
- Positive coefficient on β_1 indicates more likely to switch to affiliated firm in next five years.

Robert J. Trulaske, Sr.
College of Business
University of Missouri–Columbia

Methodology: Audit Firm Evaluation

$$CHGFROMBIGN_{t+1,t+5} = \beta_0 + \beta_1 AC\_BIGN\_CONNECT_{it} + \beta_2 MGMT\_BIGN\_CONNECT_{it} + Controls + Year\ Fixed\ Effects + \varepsilon$$

- **Estimated for each firm individually (Lennox and Park 2007)**
- **Each subsample contains observations audited by the firm in *t*.**
- **Negative coefficient on β_1 indicates less likely to switch from affiliated firm in next five years.**

Robert J. Trulaske, Sr.
College of Business
University of Missouri–Columbia

Results: Audit Firm Selection (H1)

Variable	Sign	PwC	EY	Deloitte	KPMG
AC_PWC	+	0.969*** (0.000)			
MGMT_PWC	+	1.393*** (0.001)			
AC_EY	+		-0.128 (0.664)		
MGMT_EY	+		0.693* (0.064)		
AC_DT	+			0.498* (0.064)	
MGMT_DT	+			0.519 (0.173)	
AC_KPMG	+				0.944*** (0.000)
MGMT_KPMG	+				1.551** (0.011)

Robert J. Trulaske, Sr.
College of Business
University of Missouri–Columbia

Results: Audit Firm Evaluation (H2)

Variable	Sign	PwC	EY	Deloitte	KPMG
AC_PWC_CONNECT	-	-0.596*** (0.008)			
MGMT_PWC_CONNECT	?	-0.686 (0.129)			
AC_EY_CONNECT	-		-0.374** (0.049)		
MGMT_EY_CONNECT	?		0.451 (0.152)		
AC_DT_CONNECT	-			-0.651*** (0.003)	
MGMT_DT_CONNECT	?			-0.658 (0.150)	
AC_KPMG_CONNECT	-				-0.396** (0.026)
MGMT_KPMG_CONNECT	?				0.0125 (0.968)

Robert J. Trulaske, Sr.
College of Business
University of Missouri–Columbia

Results: Audit Efficiency (H3)

VARIABLES	Sign	PwC	EY	Deloitte	KPMG
AC_PWC_CONNECT	-	0.016 (0.853)			
AC_EY_CONNECT	-		0.011 (0.500)		
AC_DT_CONNECT	-			-0.010 (0.285)	
AC_KPMG_CONNECT	-				-0.046*** (0.001)

Robert J. Trulaske, Sr.
College of Business
University of Missouri–Columbia

Results: Audit Fees (H4)

VARIABLES	Sign	PwC	EY	Deloitte	KPMG
AC_PWC_CONNECT	?	0.003 (0.951)			
AC_EY_CONNECT	?		-0.060 (0.221)		
AC_DT_CONNECT	?			-0.083 (0.200)	
AC_KPMG_CONNECT	?				-0.017 (0.754)

Robert J. Trulaske, Sr.
College of Business
University of Missouri–Columbia

Results: Audit Quality

- **Menon and Williams (2004) find lower financial reporting/audit quality when a former partner is on the audit committee (sample from 1998-1999).**
- **We find *lower* rates of subsequent restatement when a former KPMG partner is on a KPMG client's audit committee (no effect for other firms).**

Robert J. Trulaske, Sr.
College of Business
University of Missouri–Columbia

Additional Analysis

- **Results robust to:**
  - **using a count of number of former partners on audit committee instead of indicator variable**
  - **Requiring affiliated member to sit on the AC in the year of the switch**
  - **Requiring affiliated member to be the AC chair**
  - **Using pooled multinomial logit instead of estimating for individual firms**
- **Pre-SOX results are much weaker, consistent with SOX strengthening the role of the audit committee**

Robert J. Trulaske, Sr.
College of Business
University of Missouri–Columbia

Next Steps

- **No evidence that actual audit quality is impaired in any way.**
- **Potential for *perceived* lack of independence between the audit committee and the audit firm**
  - **Likelihood of retaining after restatement announcement conditional on affiliation between AC and audit firm**
  - **Likelihood of company and affiliated audit firm being named in accounting-related lawsuit**

Robert J. Trulaske, Sr.
College of Business
University of Missouri–Columbia

Takeaways and Contribution

- After controlling for management's affiliations, audit committee affiliations with Big 4 firms influence the selection and evaluation of external auditor.
- Audit committee effect is in accordance with SOX's assignment of responsibility to the audit committee.
- Affiliations slightly increase efficiency of the audit, but at no cost to shareholders (fees), and result in higher quality audit.

Robert J. Trulaske, Sr.
College of Business
University of Missouri–Columbia

Promoting Flexible Idea Generation During Audit Planning

Elizabeth (E.B.) Altiero
University of Central Florida
altiero@ucf.edu

UNIVERSITY OF CENTRAL FLORIDA

UNIVERSITY OF CENTRAL FLORIDA

Research Question

- In the face of increased regulatory scrutiny, how can we help promote flexible thinking during audit procedure design?
  - Specifically: idea generation regarding available audit evidence
- Publicized failures lead to emphasis on error reduction
  - -Non-audit example: The Central Intelligence Agency

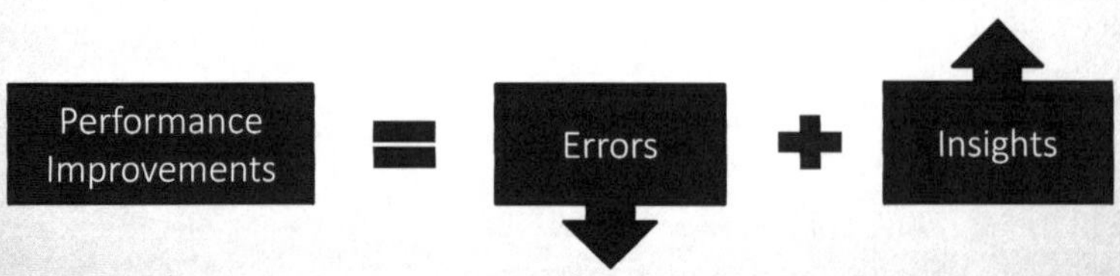

(Graphic adapted from Klein 2013)

UNIVERSITY OF CENTRAL FLORIDA

Motivation & Contribution

- Prior research focuses primarily on error reduction:

Performance Improvements = Errors (↓) + Insights (↑)

Errors:
- Expertise
- Effort
- Accountability
- Bias reduction
- Skepticism

Insights:
- Fraud brainstorming
- Pattern recognition

UNIVERSITY OF CENTRAL FLORIDA

Motivation & Contribution

- Why do we want flexible idea generation during audit planning? Error reduction is not enough!

Unfamiliar Tasks
- Keep up with the pace of business change (Chipman 2013; Arning 2013)
- Respond to unique situations encountered in the field (Altiero 2016)

Familiar Tasks
- Provide unpredictability in audit procedures (AICPA 2006; PCAOB 2007; IASB 2009; Bowlin 2011; Budescu et al. 2012)
- Improve audit effectiveness and efficiency of existing procedures (Altiero 2016)

UNIVERSITY OF CENTRAL FLORIDA

Rethinking Audit Evidence

- Auditors need to be able to consider new types of audit evidence to achieve these goals
- "New" might be:
  - New to an audit specifically
  - New to auditing in general

UNIVERSITY OF CENTRAL FLORIDA

Rethinking Audi

- Auditors nee
  evi

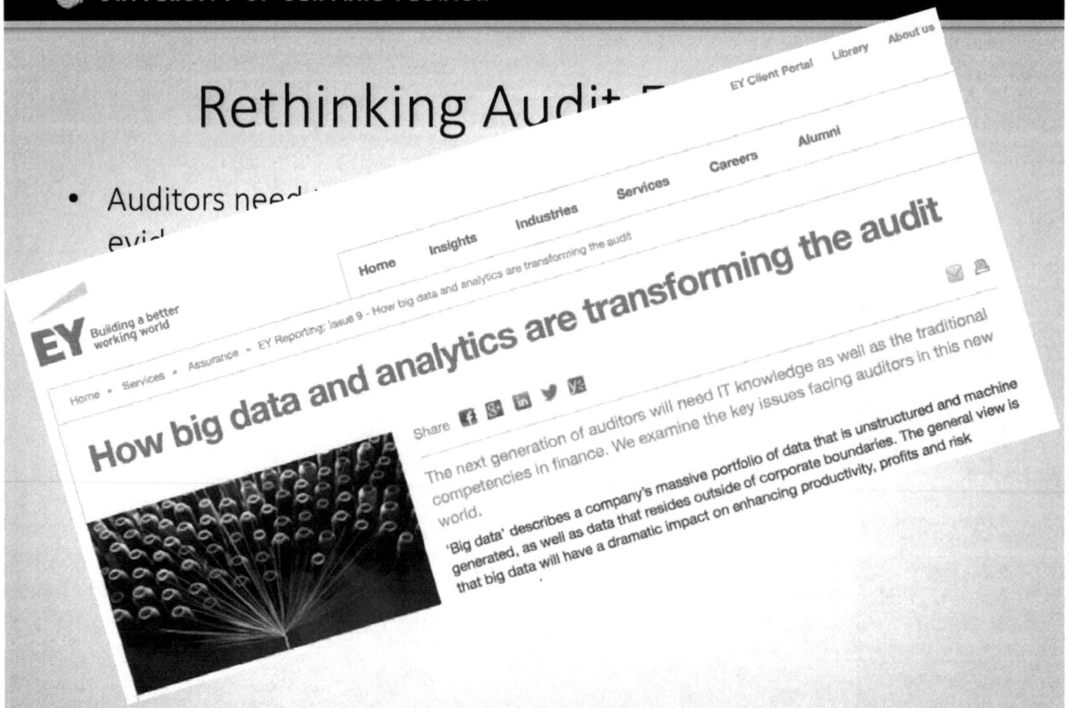
EY Client Portal Library About us

Home Insights Industries Services Careers Alumni

EY Building a better working world

Home • Services • Assurance • EY Reporting: Issue 9 - How big data and analytics are transforming the audit

How big data and analytics are transforming the audit

Share

The next generation of auditors will need IT knowledge as well as the traditional competencies in finance. We examine the key issues facing auditors in this new world.

'Big data' describes a company's massive portfolio of data that is unstructured and machine generated, as well as data that resides outside of corporate boundaries. The general view is that big data will have a dramatic impact on enhancing productivity, profits and risk

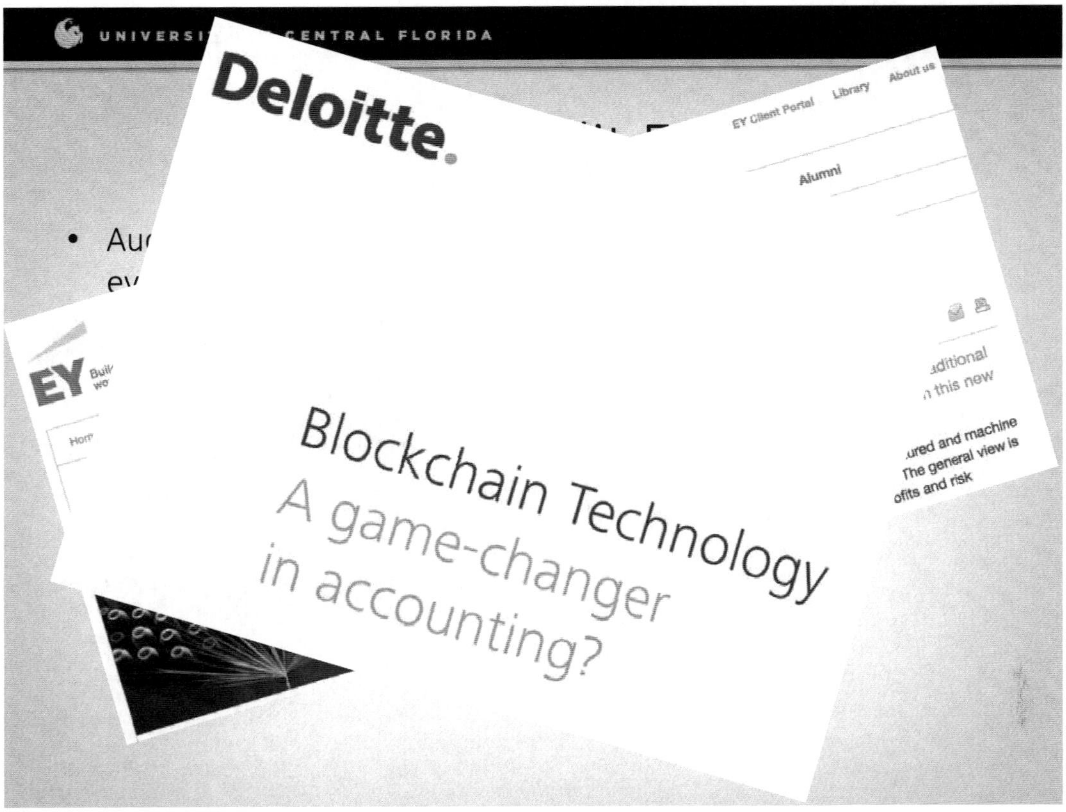

UNIVERSITY OF CENTRAL FLORIDA

Promoting Idea Generation

- Prior research shows auditors have difficulty modifying audit plans used in prior years (Wright 1988; Hammersley et al. 2011)
- How to improve idea generation depends on <u>why</u> auditors are having difficulty
  - Adherence to industry norms
  - Lack of incentives (Peecher et al. 2013)
  - Time pressure (see Bonner 2008 for a review)
  - Psychological barriers, such as anchoring and production blocking (Joyce and Biddle 1981; Wright 1988; Asare and Wright 2004; Brazel et al. 2004; Carpenter 2007)
  - Necessary changes are unclear due to changing business environment

UNIVERSITY OF CENTRAL FLORIDA

Search for Ideas in Associative Memory (SIAM)

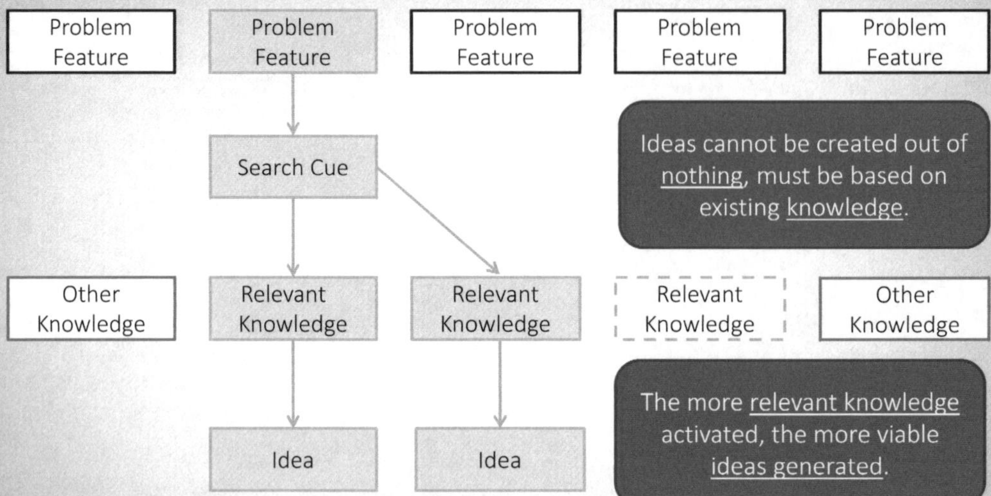

Ideas cannot be created out of nothing, must be based on existing knowledge.

The more relevant knowledge activated, the more viable ideas generated.

(Model adapted from Nijstad and Stoebe 2006)

UNIVERSITY OF CENTRAL FLORIDA

Counterfactual Mindset

- Potential to activate larger set of relevant knowledge
- Counterfactual *thinking* – consideration of what could have been
  - Increases consideration of disconfirmatory evidence (Kray and Galinsky 2003)
  - Increases information sharing in groups (Galinsky and Kray 2004)
  - Decreases effect of curse of knowledge (Kennedy 1995)
  - Increases skepticism of management's explanations (Koonce 1992)
- Counterfactual *mindset* – counterfactual thinking can carry over to subsequent, unrelated tasks (Galinsky et al. 2000; Galinsky and Moskowitz 2000)
  - Helps overcome functional fixedness (Galinsky and Moskowitz 2000)

Auditors are already trying to think of alternatives, so conscious prompt is not enough.

UNIVERSITY OF CENTRAL FLORIDA

Task Characteristics Matter

- Task characteristics impact the ability to process problem features into search cues
- *Familiarity* of task particularly important to idea generation
  - Ease with which task cues can be linked to relevant knowledge (input clarity in Bonner 1994 and Chen et al. 2014)
  - Degree to which contextual cues highlight or obscure audit content (Tversky 1977; Einhorn and Hogarth 1981)

UNIVERSITY OF CENTRAL FLORIDA

Search for Ideas: Familiar Task

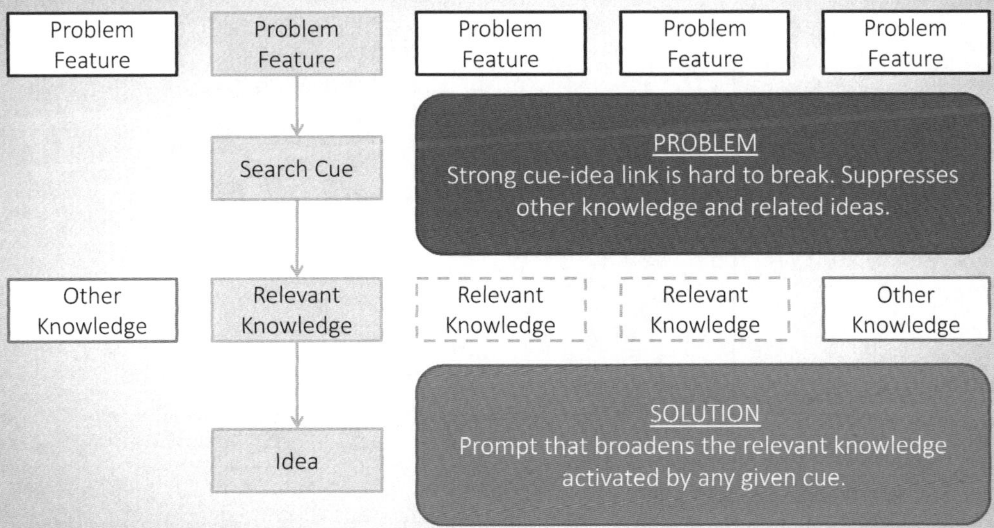

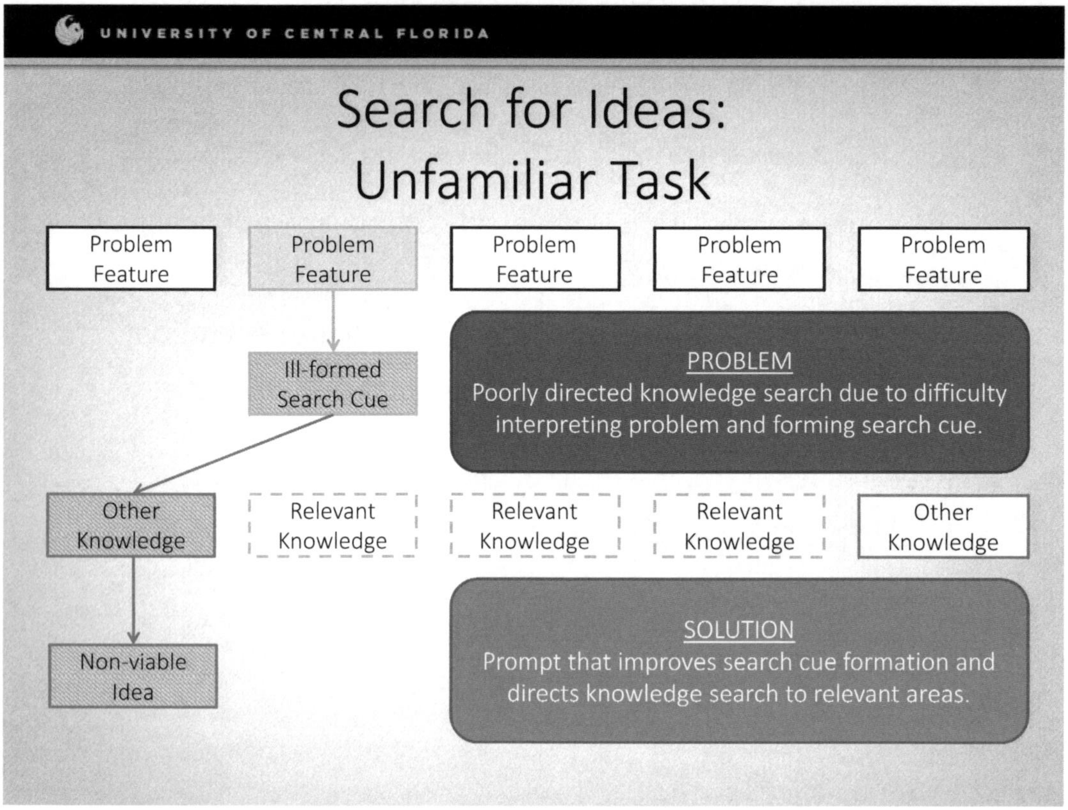
UNIVERSITY OF CENTRAL FLORIDA
Search for Ideas:
Unfamiliar Task
Problem Feature
Problem Feature
Problem Feature
Problem Feature
Problem Feature
Ill-formed Search Cue
PROBLEM
Poorly directed knowledge search due to difficulty interpreting problem and forming search cue.
Other Knowledge
Relevant Knowledge
Relevant Knowledge
Relevant Knowledge
Other Knowledge
Non-viable Idea
SOLUTION
Prompt that improves search cue formation and directs knowledge search to relevant areas.

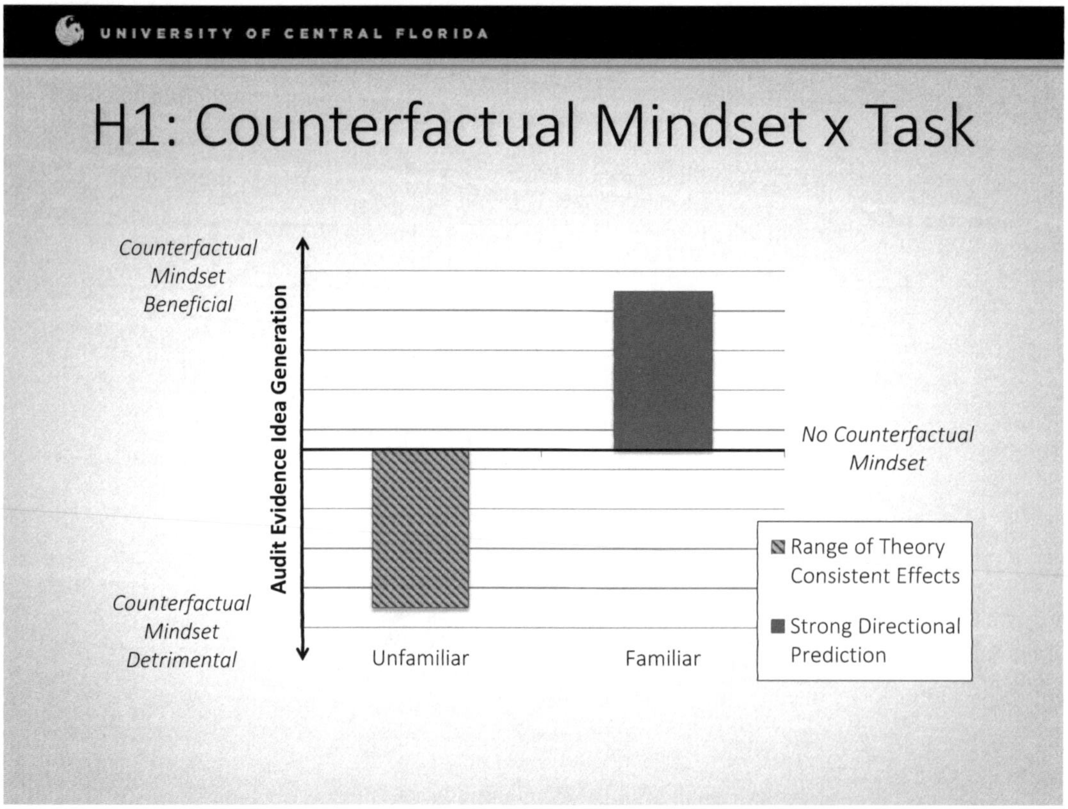
UNIVERSITY OF CENTRAL FLORIDA
H1: Counterfactual Mindset x Task
Counterfactual Mindset Beneficial
Counterfactual Mindset Detrimental
Audit Evidence Idea Generation
No Counterfactual Mindset
Unfamiliar
Familiar
Range of Theory Consistent Effects
Strong Directional Prediction

UNIVERSITY OF CENTRAL FLORIDA

Examples

- So how to better direct knowledge search (to help auditors with unfamiliar tasks)?
  - Improve search cue formation
  - Examples are well suited to task and highly present in audit setting
- From brainstorming and creativity literature
  - Ideas of others can act as cognitive stimulants (Carpenter 2007; Chen et al. 2012)
  - Cognitive stimulants act as, or add to, a search cue to stimulate relevant knowledge

But auditors have difficulty generating alternatives!
(Heiman 1990)
So maybe examples will decrease idea generation...

↓

Effectiveness depends on similarity to own ideas and timing of introduction
(Nijstad et al. 2003).

UNIVERSITY OF CENTRAL FLORIDA

Counterfactual Mindset and Examples

- Counterfactual mindset promotes relational processing style
  - Increased consideration of relationships between *task embedded* cues (Kray et al. 2006)
- Counterfactual mindset + Examples
  - Relational processing fixates cognition on relationship between the *problem features* and the *example as a solution*
  - Skips search cue formation → delays search for relevant knowledge (non-task embedded information)

UNIVERSITY OF CENTRAL FLORIDA

H2: Counterfactual x Example

Unfamiliar Task (H2a)

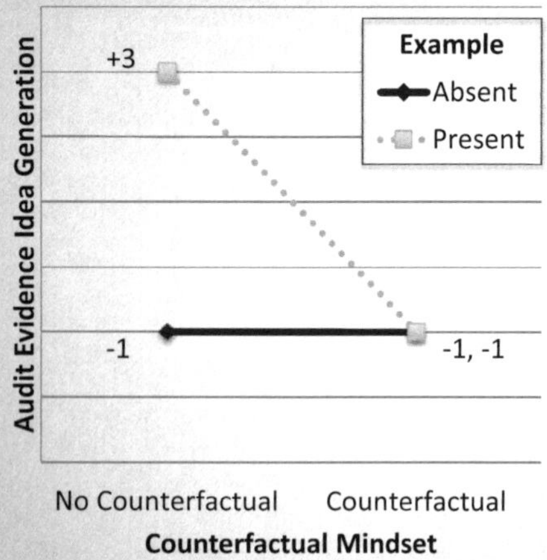

Familiar Task (H2b)

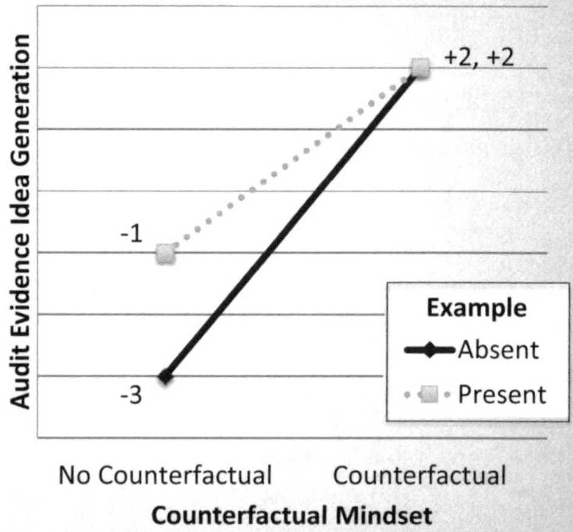

UNIVERSITY OF CENTRAL FLORIDA

Design

- 2 x 2 x 2 between subjects experiment
  - Counterfactual mindset (no counterfactual, counterfactual)
  - Example (absent, present)
  - Task (lower familiarity, higher familiarity)
- Task
  - List potential audit evidence items and audit procedures for hypothetical audit engagement
  - DV: Flexible idea generation
    - Coded for originality, fluency, flexibility and elaboration (Guilford 1967)
- 138 experienced audit professional participants

UNIVERSITY OF CENTRAL FLORIDA

Task

Lower Familiarity

- Identify audit evidence to gain assurance over number of golf balls that fit in a school bus
- High audit content – audit knowledge is relevant
- *Low audit context* – setting obscures relevance of audit knowledge

Higher Familiarity

- Identify audit evidence to gain assurance over the revenues from a toll booth's operations
- High audit content – audit knowledge is relevant
- *High audit context* – setting provides clear cues to relevance of audit knowledge

UNIVERSITY OF CENTRAL FLORIDA

Counterfactual Mindset

No Counterfactual

- Read story prior to primary task
- Jane wins a trip to Hawaii based on her seat at the concert
- Participants list thoughts Jane might be having

Counterfactual

- Read story prior to primary task
- Jane switches seats upon arriving at a concert
- Jane wins a trip to Hawaii based on her seat at the concert
- Participants list thoughts Jane might be having

UNIVERSITY OF CENTRAL FLORIDA

Example

Absent	Present
• Sentence of task that contains the example is omitted	• Example audit evidence that could be obtained

- *Both cases* – data for use in volume related analytical procedure
- *Lower familiarity*– school bus dimensions
- *Higher familiarity*– average daily traffic flow

UNIVERSITY OF CENTRAL FLORIDA

Flexible Idea Generation

- **Fluency** (number of ideas): 89.0% coder agreement
  - 1 point per evidence item listed
- **Breadth** (variety of ideas): 86.1% coder agreement
  - 1 point per category: inspection of documents, inspection of tangible items, observation, inquiry, etc. (AU 326)
- **Elaboration** (detail specification of ideas): 76.6% coder agreement
  - 1 point per modifier or additional detail
- **Originality** (uniqueness of ideas)
  - Point scale based on number of participants who gave each response (1 participant = 8 points; 2 participants = 7 points; etc.)
  - Final score equal to highest scoring response

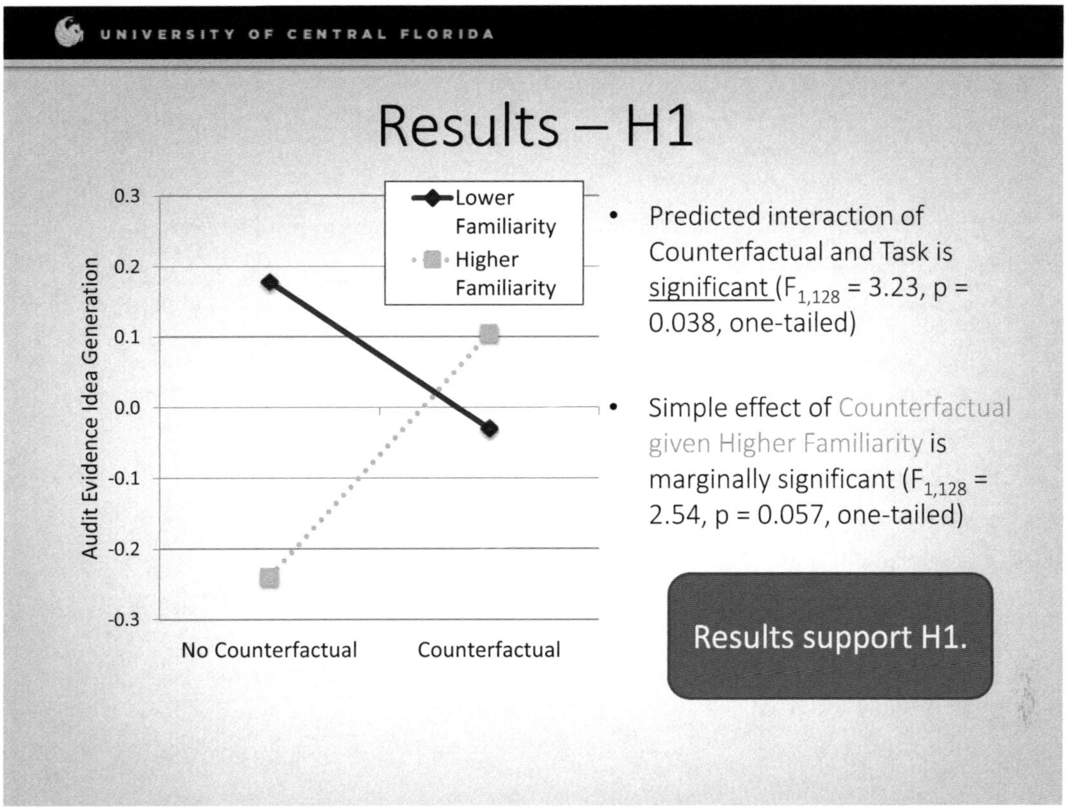
UNIVERSITY OF CENTRAL FLORIDA
Results – H1
Lower Familiarity
Higher Familiarity
Audit Evidence Idea Generation
0.3
0.2
0.1
0.0
-0.1
-0.2
-0.3
No Counterfactual
Counterfactual
Predicted interaction of Counterfactual and Task is significant ($F_{1,128}$ = 3.23, p = 0.038, one-tailed)
Simple effect of Counterfactual given Higher Familiarity is marginally significant ($F_{1,128}$ = 2.54, p = 0.057, one-tailed)
Results support H1.

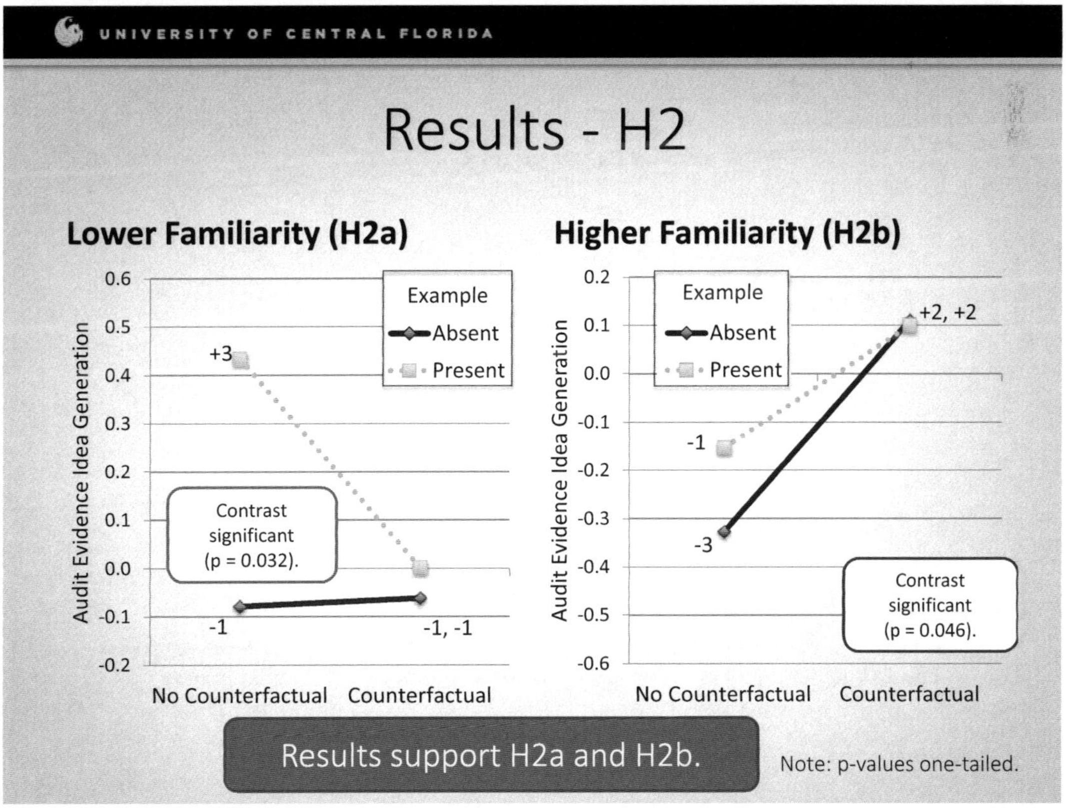
UNIVERSITY OF CENTRAL FLORIDA
Results - H2
Lower Familiarity (H2a)
Example
Absent
Present
Audit Evidence Idea Generation
0.6
0.5
0.4
0.3
0.2
0.1
0.0
-0.1
-0.2
+3
-1
-1, -1
Contrast significant (p = 0.032).
No Counterfactual
Counterfactual
Higher Familiarity (H2b)
Example
Absent
Present
Audit Evidence Idea Generation
0.2
0.1
0.0
-0.1
-0.2
-0.3
-0.4
-0.5
-0.6
+2, +2
-1
-3
Contrast significant (p = 0.046).
No Counterfactual
Counterfactual
Results support H2a and H2b.
Note: p-values one-tailed.

UNIVERSITY OF CENTRAL FLORIDA

Supplemental Analysis: Audit Efficiency

- Fewer estimated hours required in conditions with improved idea generation
- Promoting flexible idea generation has potential to improve audit efficiency

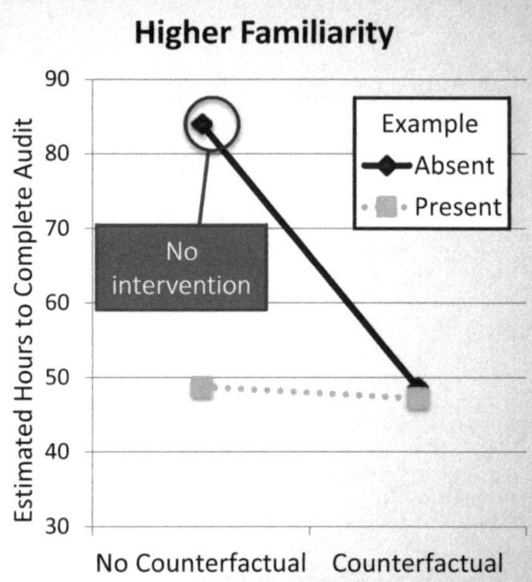

UNIVERSITY OF CENTRAL FLORIDA

Conclusions

- Flexible idea generation has potential to improve audit processes
  - Unfamiliar tasks:
    - Use examples
    - Avoid counterfactual mindset (How? Future research!)
  - Familiar tasks:
    - Prime a counterfactual mindset
- Recommendations to audit practice
  - Design audit planning system to follow above recommendations and aid auditors in overcoming subconscious psychological barriers
  - Use system as a control that can help generate insights rather than avoid errors

UNIVERSITY OF CENTRAL FLORIDA

Contributions

- Identify example presence and familiarity as new moderators of counterfactual thinking in idea generation tasks
  - Familiarity is closely linked to expertise (activation of relevant knowledge)
  - Highlights need for further research using professional subjects performing professional tasks
- Potential downstream benefit of improved audit planning on audit efficiency

UNIVERSITY OF CENTRAL FLORIDA

THANK YOU!

Elizabeth (E.B.) Altiero
University of Central Florida
altiero@ucf.edu

Note: The original slides could not be located, so this is a similar slide deck to the one used for the May 21, 2016 Presentation.

Archival Evidence on Bias in Auditors' Assessment of Client Risk and the Consequences for Audit Fees and Auditor Changes

by
Nicholas J. Hallman

Committee Members:
Jere Francis (Chair), John Howe, Inder Khurana, and Raynolde Pereira

Illustration of Contrast Effects

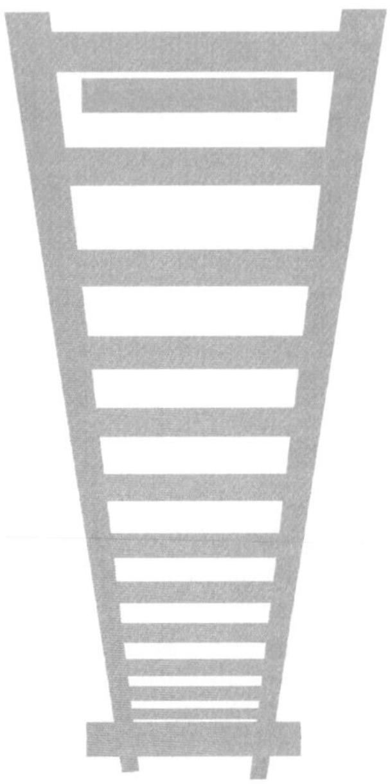

Robert J. Trulaske, Sr.
College of Business
University of Missouri–Columbia

Illustration of Contrast Effects

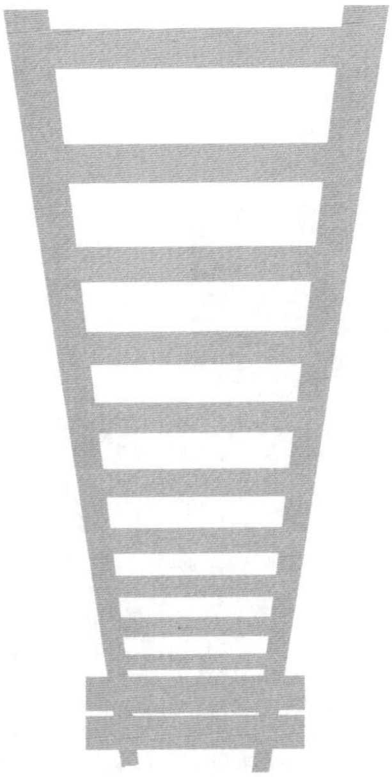

Robert J. Trulaske, Sr.
College of Business
University of Missouri-Columbia

Illustration of Contrast Effects

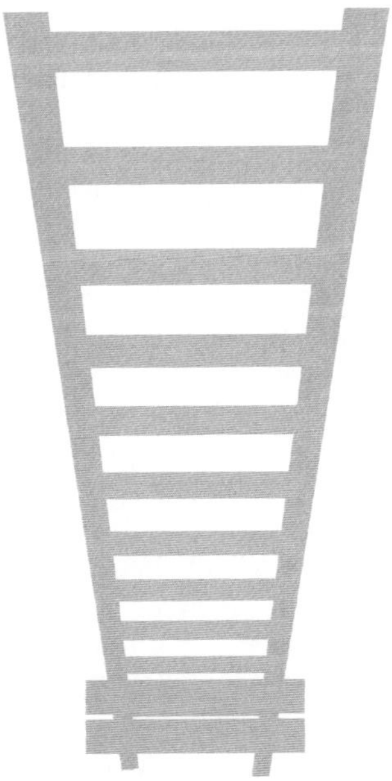

Robert J. Trulaske, Sr.
College of Business
University of Missouri-Columbia

Illustration of Contrast Effects

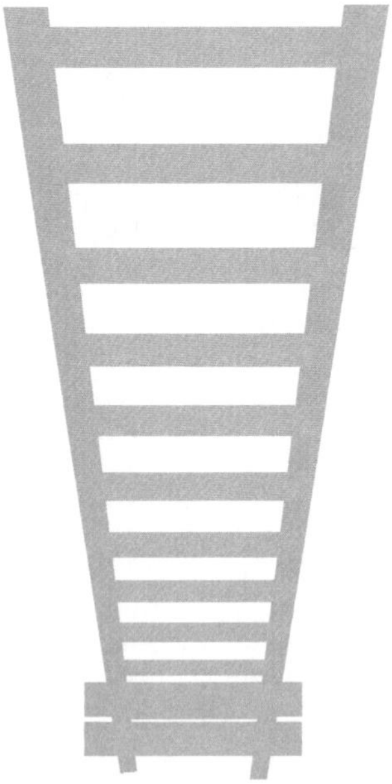

Robert J. Trulaske, Sr.
College of Business
University of Missouri–Columbia

Intuition of Contrast Effects in Auditing

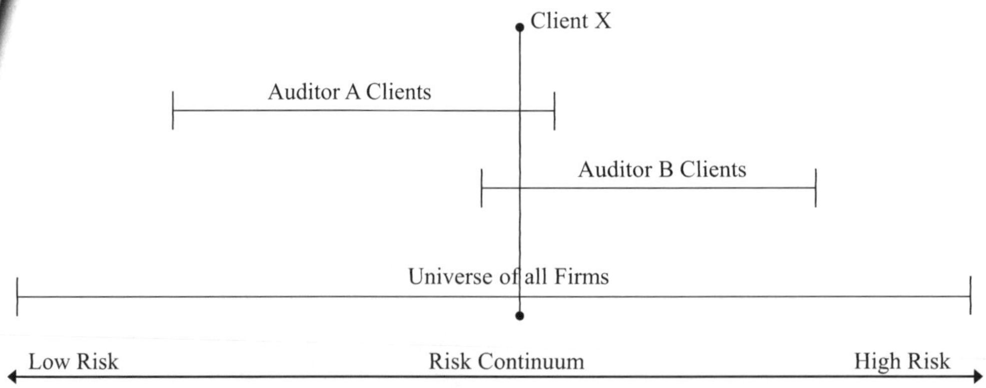

Robert J. Trulaske, Sr.
College of Business
University of Missouri–Columbia

Research Question:

Do auditors exhibit contrast-effects bias in their assessment of client risk and, if so, what are the consequences?

Robert J. Trulaske, Sr.
College of Business
University of Missouri–Columbia

Research Design

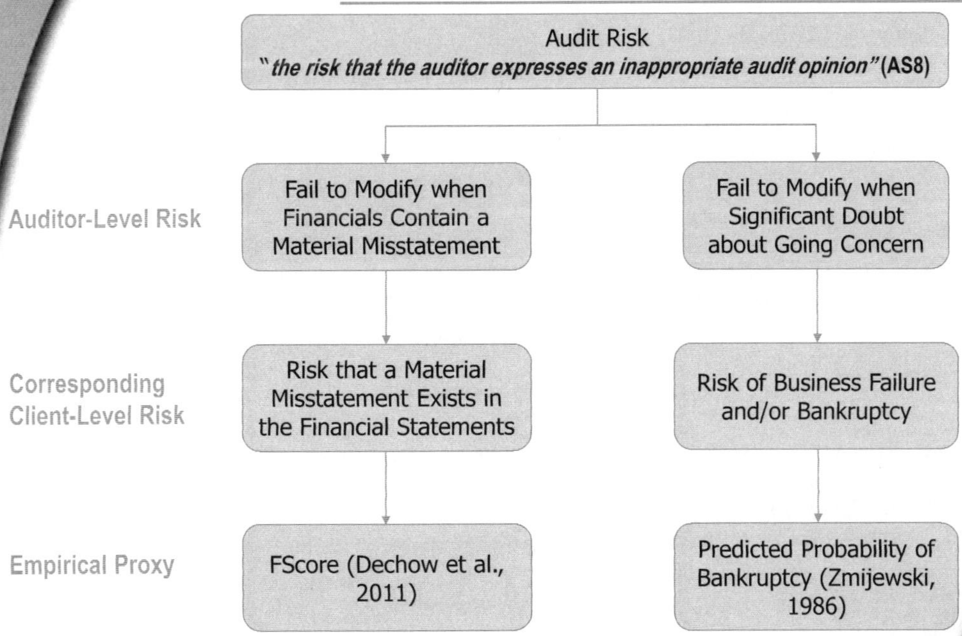

Robert J. Trulaske, Sr.
College of Business
University of Missouri–Columbia

Research Design

Figure 1:

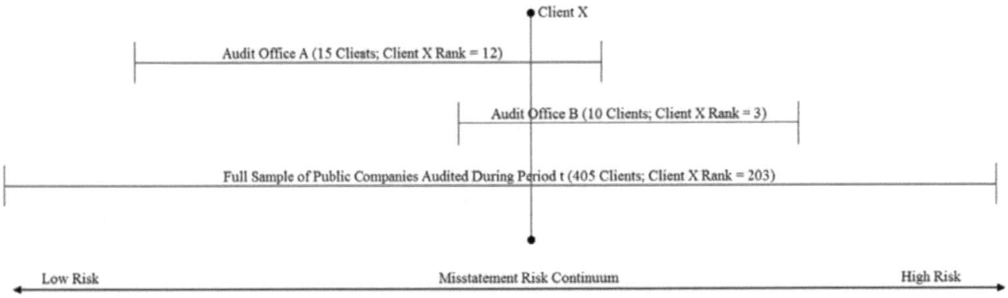

Misstatement Risk Bias (Measured Relative to Office A):

$$\frac{Rank\ of\ Misstatement\ Risk\ in\ Office\ A}{Number\ of\ Clients\ in\ Office\ A} - \frac{Rank\ of\ Misstatement\ Risk\ in\ Population}{Number\ of\ Clients\ in\ Population} = \frac{12}{15} - \frac{203}{405} = 0.30$$

Misstatement Risk Bias (Measured Relative to Office B):

$$\frac{Rank\ of\ Misstatement\ Risk\ in\ Office\ B}{Number\ of\ Clients\ in\ Office\ B} - \frac{Rank\ of\ Misstatement\ Risk\ in\ Population}{Number\ of\ Clients\ in\ Population} = \frac{3}{10} - \frac{203}{405} = -0.20$$

Robert J. Trulaske, Sr.
College of Business
University of Missouri–Columbia

Findings

- Do auditors exhibit bias?

Controlling for actual misstatement risk; higher measure of misstatement risk bias → lower abnormal accruals

Variables	Test 1 Abnormal Accruals
Variables of Interest	
Misstatement Risk Bias (Measured Relative to Office)	-0.109
	(-5.14)***
Bankruptcy Risk Bias (Measured Relative to Office)	
Risk-Related Controls	
Misstatement Risk	0.015
	(3.87)***
Median Office Misstatement Risk	-0.059
	(-3.05)***
Bankruptcy Risk	
Median Office Bankruptcy Risk	
Observations	41274
R-squared	0.289
Industry Fixed Effects	Yes
Year Fixed Effects	Yes
Standard Error Clustering	by firm

Robert J. Trulaske, Sr.
College of Business
University of Missouri–Columbia

Findings

- Do auditors exhibit bias?

Controlling for actual bankruptcy risk; higher measure of bankruptcy risk bias → higher likelihood of going concern opinion

Variables	Test 1 Abnormal Accruals	Test 2 Going Concern
Variables of Interest		
Misstatement Risk Bias (Measured Relative to Office)	-0.109	
	(-5.14)***	
Bankruptcy Risk Bias (Measured Relative to Office)		0.979
		(8.88)***
Risk-Related Controls		
Misstatement Risk	0.015	
	(3.87)***	
Median Office Misstatement Risk	-0.059	
	(-3.05)***	
Bankruptcy Risk		0.067
		(9.03)***
Median Office Bankruptcy Risk		0.054
		(5.30)***
Observations	41274	14193
R-squared	0.289	0.256
Industry Fixed Effects	Yes	Yes
Year Fixed Effects	Yes	Yes
Standard Error Clustering	by firm	by firm

Robert J. Trulaske, Sr.
College of Business
University of Missouri-Columbia

Findings

- What are the effects of the bias?

Controlling for actual risk; higher measures of risk bias proxies → higher audit fees

Variables	Test 1 Abnormal Accruals	Test 2 Going Concern	Test 3 Log of Audit Fees	Test 4 Log of Audit Fees
Variables of Interest				
Misstatement Risk Bias (Measured Relative to Office)	-0.109		0.136	
	(-5.14)***		(6.24)***	
Bankruptcy Risk Bias (Measured Relative to Office)		0.979		0.192
		(8.88)***		(8.02)***
Risk-Related Controls				
Misstatement Risk	0.015		0.005	
	(3.87)***		(3.64)***	
Median Office Misstatement Risk	-0.059			0.017
	(-3.05)***			(9.33)***
Bankruptcy Risk		0.067	0.005	
		(9.03)***	(0.27)	
Median Office Bankruptcy Risk		0.054		-0.009
		(5.30)***		(-3.51)***
Observations	41274	14193	41274	41274
R-squared	0.289	0.256	0.864	0.866
Industry Fixed Effects	Yes	Yes	Yes	Yes
Year Fixed Effects	Yes	Yes	Yes	Yes
Standard Error Clustering	by firm	by firm	by firm	by firm

Robert J. Trulaske, Sr.
College of Business
University of Missouri-Columbia

Findings

- What are the effects of the bias?

Controlling for actual risk; higher measures of risk bias proxies → likelihood of auditor change

Variables	Test 1 Abnormal Accruals	Test 2 Going Concern	Test 3 Log of Audit Fees	Test 4 Log of Audit Fees	Test 5 Auditor Change	Test 6 Auditor Change
Variables of Interest						
Misstatement Risk Bias (Measured Relative to Office)	-0.109		0.136		0.260	
	(-5.14)***		(6.24)***		(7.08)***	
Bankruptcy Risk Bias (Measured Relative to Office)		0.979		0.192		0.192
		(8.88)***		(8.02)***		(4.54)***
Risk-Related Controls						
Misstatement Risk	0.015		0.005		-0.006	
	(3.87)***		(3.64)***		(-1.70)*	
Median Office Misstatement Risk	-0.059			0.017		-0.016
	(-3.05)***			(9.33)***		(-4.86)***
Bankruptcy Risk		0.067	0.005		0.103	
		(9.03)***	(0.27)		(2.52)**	
Median Office Bankruptcy Risk		0.054		-0.009		0.053
		(5.30)***		(-3.51)***		(11.36)***
Observations	41274	14193	41274	41274	41468	41468
R-squared	0.289	0.256	0.864	0.866	0.178	0.181
Industry Fixed Effects	Yes	Yes	Yes	Yes	Yes	Yes
Year Fixed Effects	Yes	Yes	Yes	Yes	Yes	Yes
Standard Error Clustering	by firm	by firm	by firm	by firm	by firm	by firm

Robert J. Trulaske, Sr.
College of Business
University of Missouri-Columbia

Thanks!

Robert J. Trulaske, Sr.
College of Business
University of Missouri-Columbia

Primary Results: Hypothesis 1

Table 2: Absolute value of abnormal accruals as a function of relative restatement risk.

Variables	Model 2 Absolute Value of Abnormal Accruals	Model 3 Absolute Value of Abnormal Accruals	Model 4 Absolute Value of Abnormal Accruals	Model 5 Absolute Value of Abnormal Accruals	Model 6 Absolute Value of Abnormal Accruals
Variables of Interest					
Misstatement Risk Bias (Measured Relative to Office)	-0.109				-0.077
	(-5.14)***				(-2.83)***
Misstatement Risk Bias (Measured Relative to Office-Industry)		-0.039			-0.050
		(-1.79)*			(-2.40)**
Misstatement Risk Bias (Measured Relative to Firm-Industry)			-0.003		0.045
			(-0.05)		(0.63)
Misstatement Risk Bias (Measured Relative to Firm)				-0.006	0.033
				(-0.19)	(0.59)
Risk-Related Controls					
Misstatement Risk	0.015	0.012	0.009	0.012	0.013
	(3.87)***	(2.24)**	(1.66)*	(3.21)***	(1.86)*
Median Office Misstatement Risk	-0.059	0.005	-0.003	-0.028	-0.042
	(-3.05)***	(0.19)	(-0.21)	(-1.59)	(-1.80)*
Observations	41274	24130	31566	41274	22007
R-squared	0.289	0.314	0.233	0.288	0.250
Industry Fixed Effects	Yes	Yes	Yes	Yes	Yes
Year Fixed Effects	Yes	Yes	Yes	Yes	Yes
Standard Error Clustering	by firm	by firm	by firm	by firm	by firm

Robert J. Trulaske, Sr.
College of Business
University of Missouri–Columbia

Primary Results: Hypothesis 1

Table 3: Propensity to receive a going concern opinion as a function of relative bankruptcy risk.

Variables	Model 2 Going Concern Opinion	Model 3 Going Concern Opinion	Model 4 Going Concern Opinion	Model 5 Going Concern Opinion	Model 6 Going Concern Opinion
Variables of Interest					
Bankruptcy Risk Bias (Measured Relative to Office)	0.979				1.025
	(8.88)***				(3.28)***
Bankruptcy Risk Bias (Measured Relative to Office-Industry)		0.546			-0.214
		(4.46)***			(-0.73)
Bankruptcy Risk Bias (Measured Relative to Firm-Industry			0.767		0.553
			(7.70)***		(1.72)*
Bankruptcy Risk Bias (Measured Relative to Firm)				0.072	0.588
				(0.58)	(1.54)
Risk-Related Controls					
Bankruptcy Risk	0.067	0.106	0.110	0.096	0.093
	(9.03)***	(7.20)***	(8.31)***	(14.36)***	(5.28)***
Median Office Bankruptcy Risk	0.054	0.007	0.033	0.013	0.080
	(5.30)***	(0.24)	(1.26)	(1.42)	(2.09)**
Observations	14193	5915	10701	14193	5618
Pseudo R-squared	0.256	0.301	0.282	0.245	0.317
Industry Fixed Effects	Yes	Yes	Yes	Yes	Yes
Year Fixed Effects	Yes	Yes	Yes	Yes	Yes
Standard Error Clustering	by firm	by firm	by firm	by firm	by firm

Robert J. Trulaske, Sr.
College of Business
University of Missouri–Columbia

Primary Results: Hypothesis 2

Table 4: Audit fees as a function of relative restatement and bankruptcy risk.

Variables	Model 1 Log of Audit Fees	Model 2 Log of Audit Fees
Variables of Interest		
Misstatement Risk Bias (Measured Relative to Office)	0.136 (6.24)***	
Bankruptcy Risk Bias (Measured Relative to Office)		0.192 (8.02)***
Risk-Related Controls		
Misstatement Risk	0.005 (3.64)***	
Bankruptcy Risk		0.017 (9.33)***
Median Office Misstatement Risk	0.005 (0.27)	
Median Office Bankruptcy Risk		-0.009 (-3.51)***
Observations	41274	41274
R-squared	0.864	0.866
Industry Fixed Effects	Yes	Yes
Year Fixed Effects	Yes	Yes
Standard Error Clustering	by firm	by firm

Robert J. Trulaske, Sr.
College of Business
University of Missouri–Columbia

Primary Results: Hypothesis 3

Table 5:

Panel A: Propensity to switch auditors as a function of relative restatement and bankruptcy risk.

Variables	Model 1 Switch	Model 2 Switch	Model 3 Switch	Model 4 Switch
Variables of Interest				
Misstatement Risk Bias (Measured Relative to Office)	0.260 (7.08)***			
Bankruptcy Risk Bias (Measured Relative to Office)		0.192 (4.54)***		
Three Year Change in Misstatement Risk Bias			0.155 (4.68)***	
Three Year Change in Bankruptcy Risk Bias				0.096 (2.85)***
Risk-Related Controls				
Misstatement Risk	-0.006 (-1.70)*		-0.001 (-0.17)	
Bankruptcy Risk		-0.016 (-4.86)***		-0.013 (-3.89)***
Median Office Misstatement Risk	0.103 (2.52)**		0.083 (1.77)*	
Median Office Bankruptcy Risk		0.053 (11.36)***		0.051 (10.40)***
Observations	41468	41468	32856	36859
Pseudo R-squared	0.178	0.181	0.174	0.173
Industry Fixed Effects	Yes	Yes	Yes	Yes
Year Fixed Effects	Yes	Yes	Yes	Yes
Standard Error Clustering	by firm	by firm	by firm	by firm

Robert J. Trulaske, Sr.
College of Business
University of Missouri–Columbia

Primary Results: Hypothesis 3

Panel B: Change in relative risk after an change in auditors

Change in Relative Risk After Auditor Switch:	Mean	Median
Restatement Risk Relative to Office	-0.078***	-0.075***
Bankruptcy Risk Relative to Office	-0.092***	-0.079***

Robert J. Trulaske, Sr.
College of Business
University of Missouri–Columbia

Research Design

Figure 1:

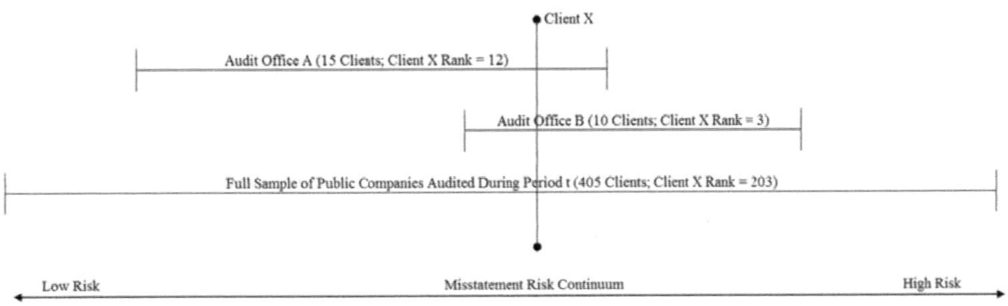

Misstatement Risk Bias (Measured Relative to Office A):

$$\frac{\textit{Rank of Misstatement Risk in Office A}}{\textit{Number of Clients in Office A}} - \frac{\textit{Rank of Misstatement Risk in Population}}{\textit{Number of Clients in Population}} = \frac{12}{15} - \frac{203}{405} = 0.30$$

Misstatement Risk Bias (Measured Relative to Office B):

$$\frac{\textit{Rank of Misstatement Risk in Office B}}{\textit{Number of Clients in Office B}} - \frac{\textit{Rank of Misstatement Risk in Population}}{\textit{Number of Clients in Population}} = \frac{3}{10} - \frac{203}{405} = -0.20$$

Robert J. Trulaske, Sr.
College of Business
University of Missouri–Columbia

Additional Analysis: Positive and Negative Bias

Table 6: Positive and negative bias modeled separately.

Variables	Model 1 Absolute Value of Abnormal Accruals	Model 2 Log of Audit Fees	Model 3 Switch	Model 4 Going Concern Opinion	Model 5 Log of Audit Fees	Model 6 Switch
Variables of Interest						
Misstatement Risk Bias (Positive)	-0.044	0.167	0.120			
	(-2.68)***	(5.87)***	(2.12)**			
Misstatement Risk Bias (Negative)	0.098	-0.110	-0.418			
	(5.76)***	(-4.09)***	(-6.94)***			
Bankruptcy Risk Bias (Positive)				1.044	0.257	0.141
				(7.93)***	(8.50)***	(2.47)**
Bankruptcy Risk Bias (Negative)				-0.837	-0.131	-0.261
				(-4.29)***	(-4.34)***	(-3.91)***
Difference [abs(Positive) - abs(Negative)]	-0.054***	0.057***	-0.298**	0.207	0.126**	-0.12*
Observations	41274	41274	41468	14193	41274	41468
R-squared	0.465	0.864			0.866	
Pseudo R-squared			0.178	0.256		0.181
Other Controls	Yes	Yes	Yes	Yes	Yes	Yes
Industry Fixed Effects	Yes	Yes	Yes	Yes	Yes	Yes
Year Fixed Effects	Yes	Yes	Yes	Yes	Yes	Yes
Standard Error Clustering	by firm	by firm	by firm	by firm	by firm	by firm

Robert J. Trulaske, Sr.
College of Business
University of Missouri–Columbia

Additional Analysis: Client Outcomes

Table 7: Client outcomes as a function of relative restatement and bankruptcy risk.

Variables	Model 1 Restatement	Model 2 Bankruptcy
Variables of Interest		
Misstatement Risk Bias (Measured Relative to Office)	-0.018	
	(-0.41)	
Bankruptcy Risk Bias (Measured Relative to Office)		0.494
		(1.60)
Risk-Related Controls		
Misstatement Risk	0.008	
	(2.28)**	
Bankruptcy Risk		0.145
		(4.74)***
Median Office Misstatement Risk	0.073	
	(1.79)*	
Median Office Bankruptcy Risk		-0.011
		(-0.40)
Observations	41202	13546
Pseudo R-squared	0.057	0.401
Industry Fixed Effects	Yes	Yes
Year Fixed Effects	Yes	Yes
Standard Error Clustering	by firm	by firm

Robert J. Trulaske, Sr.
College of Business
University of Missouri–Columbia

Additional Analysis: Propensity Score Matching

Panel A: Results of matching

	Before Match			
	Mean Treated	Mean Control	Difference	Bias
Restatement Risk Matching				
Restatement Risk	1.799	0.688	1.111***	36%
Median Office Restatement Risk	0.558	0.566	-0.008***	-3%
Client Size	18.516	19.097	-0.581***	-23%
Office Size	22.425	23.691	-1.266***	-37%
Big N	0.589	0.651	-0.062***	-13%
Bankruptcy Risk Matching				
Bankruptcy Risk	1.811	-0.728	2.539***	66%
Median Office Bankruptcy Risk	-0.853	-0.648	-0.205***	-10%
Client Size	18.200	18.394	-0.194***	-11%
Office Size	23.230	23.188	0.042	1%
Big N	0.671	0.549	0.122***	25%

Robert J. Trulaske, Sr.
College of Business
University of Missouri–Columbia

Additional Analysis: Propensity Score Matching

Panel A: Results of matching

	After Match			
	Mean Treated	Mean Control	Difference	Bias
Restatement Risk Matching				
Restatement Risk	1.799	1.728	0.071*	8%
Median Office Restatement Risk	0.558	0.553	0.005	2%
Client Size	18.516	18.494	0.022	1%
Office Size	22.425	22.351	0.074	2%
Big N	0.589	0.586	0.003	7%
Bankruptcy Risk Matching				
Bankruptcy Risk	1.811	1.691	0.12*	4%
Median Office Bankruptcy Risk	-0.853	-0.872	0.019	2%
Client Size	18.200	18.281	-0.081*	-6%
Office Size	23.230	23.200	0.03	1%
Big N	0.671	0.677	-0.006	-4%

Robert J. Trulaske, Sr.
College of Business
University of Missouri–Columbia

Additional Analysis: Propensity Score Matching

Panel B: Performance of tests in tables 3, 4, 5, and 6 using a matched sample.

Variables	Model 1 Absolute Value of Abnormal Accruals	Model 2 Log of Audit Fees	Model 3 Switch	Model 4 Going Concern Opinion	Model 5 Log of Audit Fees	Model 6 Switch
Misstatement Risk Bias (Measured Relative to Office)	-0.064	0.087	0.257			
	(-3.39)***	(2.92)***	(4.24)***			
Bankruptcy Risk Bias (Measured Relative to Office)				1.137	0.198	0.475
				(7.09)***	(4.01)***	(3.71)***
Observations	17153	17153	17221	7003	7049	7023
R-squared	0.517	0.858			0.812	
Pseudo R-squared			0.169	0.248		0.224
Other Controls	Yes	Yes	Yes	Yes	Yes	Yes
Industry Fixed Effects	Yes	Yes	Yes	Yes	Yes	Yes
Year Fixed Effects	Yes	Yes	Yes	Yes	Yes	Yes
Standard Error Clustering	by firm	by firm	by firm	by firm	by firm	by firm

Robert J. Trulaske, Sr.
College of Business
University of Missouri–Columbia

Additional Analysis: Cross-sectional Results

Table 9: Cross-sectional test

Panel A	**Small Audit Office (Stronger Predicted Effect)**		**Large Audit Office (Weaker Predicted Effect)**		**Difference**
Variables	Absolute Value of Abnormal Accruals	Going Concern	Absolute Value of Abnormal Accruals	Going Concern	
Misstatement Risk Bias (Measured Relative to Office)	-0.105		-0.056		-0.049**
	(-8.26)***		(-2.01)**		
Bankruptcy Risk Bias (Measured Relative to Office)		0.933		0.785	0.148
		(8.24)***		(1.50)	
Panel B	**Non-Big 4 Auditor (Stronger Predicted Effect)**		**Big 4 Auditor (Weaker Predicted Effect)**		**Difference**
Variables	Absolute Value of Abnormal Accruals	Going Concern	Absolute Value of Abnormal Accruals	Going Concern	
Misstatement Risk Bias (Measured Relative to Office)	-0.138		-0.078		-0.06**
	(-4.16)***		(-9.39)***		
Bankruptcy Risk Bias (Measured Relative to Office)		0.815		0.264	0.551***
		(5.49)***		(2.64)***	

Robert J. Trulaske, Sr.
College of Business
University of Missouri–Columbia

Additional Analysis: Cross-sectional Results

Panel C	Low Tenure (Stronger Predicted Effect)		High Tenure (Weaker Predicted Effect)		Difference
Variables	Absolute Value of Abnormal Accruals	Going Concern	Absolute Value of Abnormal Accruals	Going Concern	
Misstatement Risk Bias (Measured Relative to Office)	-0.101 (-3.22)***		-0.066 (-5.95)***		-0.035
Bankruptcy Risk Bias (Measured Relative to Office)		1.132 (5.81)***		0.923 (6.62)***	0.209

Panel D	Low Influence Client (Stronger Predicted Effect)		High Influence Client (Weaker Predicted Effect)		Difference
Variables	Absolute Value of Abnormal Accruals	Going Concern	Absolute Value of Abnormal Accruals	Going Concern	
Misstatement Risk Bias (Measured Relative to Office)	-0.092 (-7.74)***		-0.065 (-4.51)***		-0.027*
Bankruptcy Risk Bias (Measured Relative to Office)		1.601 (7.44)***		0.675 (4.88)***	0.926***

Robert J. Trulaske, Sr.
College of Business
University of Missouri–Columbia

Additional Analysis: Cross-sectional Results

Panel E	Non-Industry Leader Auditor (Stronger Predicted Effect)		Industry Leader Auditor (Weaker Predicted Effect)		Difference
Variables	Absolute Value of Abnormal	Going Concern	Absolute Value of Abnormal	Going Concern	
Misstatement Risk Bias (Measured Relative to Office)	-0.099 (-4.19)***		-0.062 (-5.45)***		-0.037*
Bankruptcy Risk Bias (Measured Relative to Office)		0.957 (7.13)***		0.217 (1.85)*	0.74***

Panel F	Pre-SOX (Stronger Predicted Effect)		Post-SOX (Weaker Predicted Effect)		Difference
Variables	Absolute Value of Abnormal Accruals	Going Concern	Absolute Value of Abnormal Accruals	Going Concern	
Misstatement Risk Bias (Measured Relative to Office)	-0.100 (-3.77)***		-0.065 (-5.48)***		-0.035*
Bankruptcy Risk Bias (Measured Relative to Office)		1.318 (6.94)***		0.759 (5.39)***	0.559***

Robert J. Trulaske, Sr.
College of Business
University of Missouri–Columbia

Additional Analysis: DDAR

Table 10: Test of DDAR's impact on bias at Deloitte

Variables	Model 1 Absolute Value of Abnormal Accruals	Model 2 Going Concern Opinion
Variables of Interest		
Misstatement Risk Bias (Measured Relative to Office)	-0.076	
	(-5.22)***	
*Misstatement Risk Bias * Deloitte * Post*	0.035	
	(2.18)**	
Bankruptcy Risk Bias (Measured Relative to Office)		1.247
		(4.15)***
*Bankruptcy Risk Bias * Deloitte * Post*		-0.842
		(-2.12)**
Other Variables		
*Misstatement Risk Bias * Post*	-0.010	
	(-0.83)	
*Misstatement Risk Bias * Deloitte*	-0.005	
	(-0.82)	
*Bankruptcy Risk Bias * Post*		-0.309
		(-0.92)
*Bankruptcy Risk Bias * Deloitte*		-0.039
		(-0.06)
Deloitte	0.006	-0.078
	(0.98)	(-0.20)
Post	0.058	0.810
	(1.59)	(3.41)***
*Deloitte * Post*	0.000	-0.029
	(0.07)	(-0.07)
Observations	26258	8257
R-squared	0.345	
Pseudo R-squared		0.304
Other Controls	Yes	Yes
Industry Fixed Effects	Yes	Yes
Year Fixed Effects	Yes	Yes
Standard Error Clustering	by firm	by firm

Robert J. Trulaske, Sr.
College of Business
University of Missouri–Columbia

AUTHOR INDEX

University of Kansas School of Business
1654 Naismith Drive
Lawrence, KS 66045
USA

ISBN 978-1-5108-4009-6

9 781510 840096

CURRAN ASSOCIATES INC.
proceedings.com

1st Joint Conference on Lexical and Computational Semantics 2012

(SEM 2012)

Montreal, Canada
7-8 June 2012

ISBN: 978-1-62276-502-7